THE MOST
EVIL
PIRATES
IN HISTORY

THE MOST
EVIL
PIRATES
IN HISTORY

SHELLEY KLEIN

BARNES & NOBLE

NEW YORK

© 2006 by Michael O'Mara Books Limited

This 2006 edition published by Barnes & Noble Inc.
by arrangement with Michael O'Mara Books Limited

Designed and typeset by Design 23

ISBN-13: 978-0-7607-8443-3
ISBN-10: 0-7607-8443-4

Printed and bound in Singapore

1   3   5   7   9   10   8   6   4   2

Every effort has been made to trace the copyright holders of each
illustration. These are acknowledged at the end of the book and the
publishers wish to apologize to those they were unable to trace.

CONTENTS

INTRODUCTION

In the mind of the mariner, there is a superstitious horror
connected with the name of pirate; and there are few subjects that
interest and excite the curiosity of mankind more than the
desperate exploits, foul doings and diabolical careers of these
monsters in human form.

Charles Ellms,
The Pirates Own Book

Charles Ellms was writing over 150 years ago, but the appeal of what he called 'Celebrated Sea Robbers' has by no means diminished. Numerous books, both fact and fiction, have been devoted to them, and today they can even inspire blockbuster movies. But what is it that has made this highwayman of the sea such an enduring figure? And why is it that despite being little more than thieves, pirates – at least in historical times – are thought of as such romantic, swashbuckling heroes?

Not that it was always possible to distinguish theft from legitimate pursuits. From the seventeenth to the nineteenth centuries, governments of all nations were commissioning privateers in time of war to plunder enemy ships. Many seafaring captains would be hailed as heroes when – if looked at from a different angle – it might be claimed they were no better than criminals. A good illustration of this is Sir Francis Drake, who was granted the authority to attack and loot enemy (that is, Spanish) vessels from none other than Queen Elizabeth I. Drake, after several successful raids in the West Indies, was hailed as a privateering hero in England, but in Spain he was seen as nothing more than a pirate who, if caught, would be swiftly executed.

Drake managed to die of natural causes; a little over a century later the infamous Captain Kidd was less fortunate. Beginning his career as a privateer with a commission from a powerful syndicate that included King William III, within six years he was swinging from the end of a rope, hanged as a pirate – a common criminal.

With the ever-present risk of capture and execution, why did so many seamen, who could otherwise have been employed in legitimate business, choose instead to turn to piracy?

The main reason, unsurprisingly, was money. Where Captain Kidd was concerned, his privateering commission did not get off to a good start. Those on board were paid only with a percentage of any booty captured so, when there was no booty, there was no pay. After months without sight of an enemy ship, Kidd was desperate to keep his crew from mutinying, so turned pirate and looted vessels that were not within his remit. But other sailors often actively chose to become pirates because pay on board a naval or merchant vessel was appallingly low – especially considering the hard labor and harsh discipline most recruits had to endure.

What's more, many of them may not have been on board through choice in the first place, forced into service against their will – 'These were the days of press-gangs, when men lay in ditches and bogs to escape the clutches of pig-tailed seamen led by cockaded officers, rounding up all whom they met.'[1] To make matters worse, many captains were sadists and enjoyed nothing better than inflicting bodily torments on those they employed. In his book *Life Among the Pirates*, David Cordingly sets the scene perfectly by listing all the implements on board a ship which a captain could use to torture his men: 'There were boathooks and brooms and iron bars to beat men with. There were axes and hammers and cutlasses to cause grievous wounds. There were ropes of all sizes which could be used to whip, strangle and stretch bodies and limbs.' Little wonder then that sailors might chose piracy over and above a job in the Royal Navy or merchant services – after all, on board a pirate ship if someone was to be flogged or marooned then it had to be done with the consent of all the pirates on board, not just the captain.

What's more, on a pirate ship violence was more likely to be directed toward captives, not crew – and what violence there was! The list is endless, with tales of prisoners being burnt alive, or hanged, or slashed to pieces by cutlasses and having their organs ripped out. In this respect, the pirates François L'Ollonais, Benito de Soto and Edward Low were masters of their art, true psychopaths who wholeheartedly embraced the image of the bloodthirsty buccaneer. Edward Low is said to have cut the ears off two of his prisoners and had them roasted, after which the prisoners were made to eat them – and Charles Johnson wrote that Low and his men 'often murdered a man from the excess of good humor as out of passion and resentment […] for danger lurked in their very smiles.'[2]

But Low, L'Ollonais and de Soto were far from the only vicious brutes sailing the high seas. Some of the worst, surprisingly in the male-dominated world of the eighteenth and nineteenth centuries, were women, such as Mary Read, Anne Bonny and the infamous Chinese pirate captain, Cheng I Sao. There are no first-hand accounts of Cheng participating in the torture and murder of captives, but there is no doubt that she instigated and was present during some very bloodcurdling episodes. For their part, Bonny and Read were both said to have enjoyed taking part in hand-to-hand combat, and when they were finally captured reportedly fought harder and more bravely than any of the men on board their ship.

Another infamous captain, who features strongly in the story of Calico Jack, was Charles Vane. In 1718 a report was handed in to Governor Bennett of Bermuda written by a sailor called Nathaniel Catling, who had been on board the *Diamond* when it was captured by Vane. Catling accused Vane and his companions of not only looting the vessel and beating and torturing all the ship's crew, including the captain, but also hanging him (Catling) up by the neck on the rigging until they believed he was dead. On cutting Catling down, the pirates realized he was still alive, whereupon they picked up their cutlasses and began hacking him to death. One blow struck his collarbone while another opened up a huge gash on his chest, and it was only by a miracle that at this point he didn't die – for some of the pirates persuaded Vane it would be too cruel to kill him, and Catling survived.

The treatment meted out by pirates to their victims wasn't always simply wanton cruelty – there could often be a reason behind the violence, such as 'persuading' captives to sign up to pirate articles and thereby joining the crew. In fact, pirate ships – much like those of the Royal Navy and merchant service – were always on the lookout for new recruits, particularly those who were skilled in some way (such as in medicine or carpentry). In 1725 a merchant ship, the *Fancy*, was stopped by a pirate called Captain Lyn. On board was a cooper (a man who makes tubs and casks) by the name of Ebenezer Mower, who as soon as the pirates boarded the vessel was taken aside and 'persuaded' to join them. 'One of the pirates struck Mower many blows on his head with the helve of an axe, whereby his head was much bruised and bloodied, after which the same pirate forced him said Mower to lay his head down on the coamings of the hatch, and lifting the axe over his head swore that if he did not sign their Articles immediately, he would chop his head off, the said Mower begging hard for his life.'³

But ultimately, the worst violence meted out by pirates was always toward captives, whose lives mattered little, if at all, to their murderers. Benito de Soto – the so-called 'last pirate of the Western Seas' – having captured a ship, thought nothing of locking all his prisoners in the hold and afterwards setting fire to the vessel so that everyone on board was burnt alive. Perhaps he took pleasure from it, he probably did, but there was also another reason why he perpetrated such a horrendous act – to advertise his ruthlessness so that when he came across another enemy vessel, no one on board would put up a fight. Nor was de Soto alone in this tactic, for one barbarous act could assure a pirate an evil reputation. It was the best advertising available in his line of work – even in those days, news could spread fast.

And some pirates would enhance their reputation by a fearsome appearance. The pirate Edward Teach decided to grow a big black beard, thus giving him his now famous cognomen. To add to the effect, he used to go into battle with lit fuses in and around his hat, so that it would appear as if smoke and flames were coming out of his head. Indeed, Teach probably did more for the image of pirates than any other individual in history (although Edward Low, who sported a scar down the side of his face, came a close second). Teach was the very image of a 'monster in human form', an almost superhuman creature who no doubt inspired many a fictional pirate.

In Mervyn Peake's 1950s novel *Gormenghast*, the young narrator daydreams of pirates as 'tall as towers':

their great brows beetling over their sunken eyes, like shelves of overhanging rocks. In their ears were hoops of red gold, and in their mouths scythe-edged cutlasses a-drip. Out of the red darkness they emerged…the water at their waists circling and bubbling with the hot light reflected from their bodies…And still they came on, until there was only room enough for the smouldering head of the central buccaneer, a great salt-water lord, every inch of whose face was scabbed and scarred like a boy's knee, whose teeth were carved into the shapes of skulls, whose throat was circled by the tattooing of a scaled snake.

No real-life pirate could ever be this extraordinary, of course, but in many ways

Peake's description illustrates the grip pirates had on the public's imagination. No other group of thieves has ever inspired this kind of fascination. Highwaymen come closest, but even they aren't thought of as either so evil or so romantic.

In this respect, writers such as Charles Johnson and Alexander Olivier Exquemelin (see Glossary) did a great deal to enhance the image of the pirate. Both authors, but in particular Exquemelin (who served with Henry Morgan during his raid on Panama City in 1671), concentrated on pirates' evildoings rather than any other aspect of their lives, calculating no doubt that sensational reports of this nature would increase sales of their books. Charles Johnson's description of Blackbeard has guaranteed the pirate's place in history – though as several authors have since pointed out, in comparison to pirates such as Bartholomew Roberts, who during his career captured in the region of 400 ships, Blackbeard's piracy pales into insignificance.

Much the same can be said of Captain Kidd for, as Philip Gosse wrote, 'if Kidd's reputation was in just proportion to his actual deeds, he would have been forgotten so soon as he had been "turned off" [i.e. hanged] at Wapping Old Stairs'.[4] Instead, Kidd's long-lasting appeal appears to rely on one fact alone – that he buried vast amounts of treasure (most of which was booty taken from a ship called the *Quedah Merchant*) on islands and other locations between India and Boston. This idea was then illustrated by Howard Pyle in his *Book of Pirates* (1921), where Kidd is seen standing over a treasure chest on Gardiners Island, while one of his fellow pirates digs a hole. But did he really bury untold fortunes in gold and jewelry? The reality is that no one has been able to find Captain Kidd's treasure (although many have tried), leading most historians to concur it was all part and parcel of the myth-making that surrounded pirates in the seventeenth to nineteenth centuries. Indeed, few, if any, pirates buried their treasure – rather, they divided their booty up and distributed it equally among themselves. It was normally spent on 'wine and women [who] drained [the pirates'] wealth to such a degree that, in a little time, some of them became reduced to beggary. They have been known to spend 2 or 3,000 pieces of eight in one night; and one gave a strumpet 500 to see her naked. They used to buy a pipe of wine, place it in the street, and oblige everyone that passed to drink.'[5]

Another pirate myth is the idea that they forced their prisoners to walk the plank. They certainly tortured their victims most cruelly but there are almost no references to 'walking the plank' in any pirate literature. The author David Cordingly points out one that appeared in *The Times* on 23 July 1829 (see the L'Ollonais chapter, pages 31-2) and a second reference, this time an illustration, that appeared in *Harper's Monthly Magazine* in 1887, drawn by Howard Pyle. In fact, Pyle, along with Charles Johnson and Exquemelin, seems responsible for most of the myth-making that surrounds pirates. Alternatively, if they weren't directly responsible, then they may have indirectly influenced other writers such as Lord Byron (*The Corsair*), Robert Louis Stevenson (*Treasure Island*) and J.M. Barrie (*Peter Pan*).

Much of the romantic image of piracy stems from our fascination with those people who live on the edge of society. Edward Teach, Jean Lafitte and Bartholomew Roberts were all in their own ways like Emily Brontë's Heathcliff – tough, brutal, untamable men, flawed characters all. It should never be forgotten, of course, that the romantic image that has delighted us in countless fictional pirate tales and swashbuckling movies from *The Sea Hawk*, starring Errol Flynn, to *Pirates of the Caribbean,* starring Johnny Depp, fifty years later, bears only a passing resemblance to that of the real pirates. We all like to believe in treasure maps and the loveable rogues who created them but there was very little about the real pirates that would commend them to our affections. They were cruel, barbarous, desperate men who killed and tortured for pleasure and profit. They were, without doubt, among the most evil and villainous characters in history.

1 Zacks, *The Pirate Hunter.*
2 Johnson, *A General History of the Robberies and Murders of the Most Notorious Pirates.*
3 *Boston Gazette,* 29 November 1725.
4 Gosse, *The History of Piracy.*
5 Leslie, *New History of Jamaica.*

THE PIRATES' CODE OF CONDUCT

Most people might assume that pirates, being nothing more than a group of thieves and brigands, were also a lawless, rebellious lot with few rules and even less inclination to follow any if they were presented to them – but, according to one of the most-quoted authors on pirates, Charles Johnson, this was far from the case. Twice in his book, *A General History of the Robberies and Murders of the Most Notorious Pirates* (1724), he illustrates the point by giving a list of regulations based on those that were initially employed by privateers, but subsequently taken up by pirates as a means of imposing some sort of discipline on their ships' crews. He cites the example of Captain Bartholomew Roberts (see page 90), who during one voyage laid down the following regulations in order that life on board his vessel would run smoothly and efficiently:

I

Every Man has a Vote in Affairs of Moment; has equal Title to the fresh Provisions, or strong Liquors, at any Time seized, & use them at pleasure, unless a Scarcity [no uncommon thing among them] make it necessary, for the good of all, to Vote a Retrenchment.

II

Every man to be called fairly in turn, by List, on Board of Prizes, because (over and above their proper Share) they there on these Occasions allow'd a Shift of Cloathes: But if they defrauded the Company to the Value of a Dollar, in Plate, Jewels, or Money, MAROONING was their Punishment. [Marooning was the barbarous custom of putting the offender on shore, on some desolate or uninhabited cape or island, with a gun, a few shot, a bottle of water and a bottle of powder, to subsist with, or starve. If the robbery was only between one crew member and another, they contented themselves with slitting the ears and nose of the guilty man, and setting him on shore – not in an uninhabited place, but somewhere he was sure to encounter hardships.]

III
No person to game at Cards or Dice for Money.

IV
The Lights & Candles to be put out at eight o'Clock at Night. If any of the Crew, after that Hour, still remained inclined for Drinking, they were to do it on the open Deck. [Which Roberts believed would give a check to their debauches, for he was a sober man himself, but found at length that all his endeavors to put an end to this debauch proved ineffectual.]

V
To Keep their Piece, Pistols, & Cutlass clean, & fit for Service. [In this they were extravagantly nice, endeavoring to outdo one another in the beauty and richness of their arms, giving sometimes at an auction (at the mast) thirty or forty pounds a pair, for pistols. These were slung in time of service, with different colored ribands over their shoulders, in a way peculiar to these fellows, in which they took great delight.]

VI
No Boy or Woman to be allow'd amongst them. If any Man were found seducing any of the latter Sex, and carried her to Sea, disguised, he was to suffer Death. [So that when any fell into their hands, as it chanced in the Onslow, they put a sentinel immediately over her to prevent ill consequences from so dangerous an instrument of division and quarrel; but then here lies the roguery; they contend who shall be sentinel, which happens generally to one of the greatest bullies, who, to secure the lady's virtue, will let none lie with her but himself.]

VII
To Desert the Ship, or their Quarters in Battle, was punished with Death, or Marooning.

VIII
No striking one another on Board, but every Man's Quarrels to be ended on Shore, at Sword & Pistol Thus: The Quarter-Master of the Ship, when the Parties will not come to any Reconciliation, accompanies them on Shore with what Assistance he thinks proper, & turns the Disputants Back to Back, at so many Paces Distance. At the Word of Command, they turn and fire

immediately (or else the Piece is knocked out of their Hands). If both miss, they come to their Cutlasses, and then he is declared Victor who draws the first Blood.

IX

No Man to talk of breaking up their Way of Living, till each had shared a 1000l [pounds]. If in order to this, any Man should lose a Limb, or become a Cripple in their Service, he was to have 800 Dollars, out of the publick Stock, and for lesser Hurts, proportionably.

X

The Captain and Quarter-Master to receive two Shares of a Prize; the Master, Boatswain, & gunner, one Share and a half and other Officers, one and a Quarter.

XI

The Musicians to have Rest on the Sabbath Day, but the other six Days & Nights, none without special Favor.

Charles Johnson also cites the example of Captain John Philips who, before setting sail on the *Revenge* to loot and plunder ships in the West Indies, had all his officers sit down to 'draw up articles, settle their little commonwealth, to prevent disputes and ranglings afterwards'.

THE ARTICLES ON BOARD THE REVENGE

1 Every Man shall obey civil Command; the Captain shall have one full Share and a half in all Prizes; the Master, Carpenter, Boatswain, & Gunner shall have one Share and quarter.

2 If any Man shall offer to run away, or keep any Secret from the Company, he shall be marooned, with Bottle of Powder, and Bottle of Water, one small Arm, and Shot.

3 If any Man shall steal any Thing in the Company, or Game, to the value of a Piece of Eight, he shall be marroon'd or shot.

4 If at any time we should meet another Marrooner [that is Pyrate] that Man that shall sign his Articles without the Consent of our Company, shall suffer such Punishment as the Captain and his Company shall think fit.

5 That Man that shall strike another whilst these Articles are in force, shall receive Moses' Law (that is, 40 Stripes lacking one) on the bare Back.

6 That Man that shall snap his Arms, or smoak Tobacco in the Hold, without a Capt to his Pipe, or carry a Candle lighted without a Lanthorn, shall suffer the same punishment as in the former Article.

7 That Man that shall not keep his Arms clean, fit for an Engagement, or neglect his Business, shall be cut off from his Share, & suffer such other punishment as the Captain & Company shall think fit.

8 If any Man shall lose a Joint in time of an Engagement, shall have 400 Pieces of Eight; if a Limb, 800.

9 If at any time you meet with a prudent Woman, that Man that offers to meddle with her, without her Consent, shall suffer present Death.

Captain William Kidd also had his men sign ship's articles – although, at the time, he was sailing on the *Adventure Galley* as a privateer rather than acting as a pirate, so his 'codes of conduct', quoted in *The Pirate Hunter* by Richard Zacks, were somewhat less harsh and restrictive than those of either Bartholomew Roberts or John Philips.

THE ARTICLES ON BOARD THE ADVENTURE GALLEY

1 The man who shall first see a Saile. If she be a Prize shall receive one hundred pieces of eight.

2 That if any man shall lose an Eye, Legg or Arme or the use thereof…shall receive…six hundred pieces of eight, or six able Slaves.

3 That whosoever shall disobey Command shall lose his share or receive such Corporall punishment as the Capt. and Major part of the Company shall deem fit.

4 That man is proved a Coward in time of Engagement shall lose his share.

5 That man shall be drunk in time of Engagement before the prisoners then taken be secured, shall lose his share.

6 That man shall defraude the Capt. Or Company of any Treasure, as Money, Goods, Ware, Merchandizes or any other thing whatsoever to the value of one piece of eight […] shall lose his Share and be put on shore upon the first inhabitted Island or other place that the said ship shall touch at.

7. That money or Treasure shall be taken by the said ship and Company shall be put on board of the Man of War and there be shared immediately, and all Wares and Merchandizes when legally condemned to be legally divided amongst the Ships Company according to Articles.

GRACE O'MALLEY
a most feminine sea captain

There came to me also a most feminine sea captain
called Granny Imallye and offered her services unto me,
wheresoever I would command her, with three galleys and two
hundred fighting men, either in Scotland or Ireland. She brought
with her her husband for she was as well by sea as by land well
more than Mrs Mate with him [...] This was a notorious woman
in all the coasts of Ireland.

Sir Henry Sidney,
Lord Deputy of Ireland, 1576

The names of only a handful of women pirates have become famous over the centuries, among them Cheng I Sao, Anne Bonny and Mary Read (who also feature in this book). Even so, their lives are not particularly well documented, and not a lot is actually known about them. One exception is a female pirate who would be fêted in poetry, folklore and fiction: Grace (Gráinne) O'Malley, or Granuaile as she is commonly known in Ireland – that country's pirate queen, a remarkable woman who not only provoked awe in her enemies, but also huge admiration among those who regarded her as a national heroine.

Born in Connaught, on the west coast of Ireland, around 1530, Grace O'Malley belonged to the clan Uí Mháille, a robust, resilient people more used to a life at sea than on land. Their family motto was 'Terra marique potens' – 'Powerful by land and sea' – and there were few clans in the west of Ireland who could outdo them in knowledge of that country's coastline.

Grace's father was a local chieftain who was said to have been descended from the eldest son of a High King of Ireland, a man by the name of Brian Orbsen who was killed during a battle in AD 388.[1] The O'Malleys owned many properties, including a castle at Belclare on Clare Island. They were also wealthy enough to maintain a whole fleet of ships, which were used not only to fish Irish waters, but also to trade with other passing vessels. More often than not, these selfsame ships also engaged in piratical activities, plundering and raiding neighboring territories. As a young girl it is almost certain Grace was privy to her family's methods of earning a living, and some commentators maintain that she earned her nickname Granuaile (which means 'bald') because she cut off all her hair when she was a child in order to fit in with the local boys who liked to take her sailing.[2] Other than this, very little is known about her childhood except that she probably received some type of formal education, as later in life she petitioned the English Court in writing and was also recorded as having conversed in Latin during her audience in 1593 with the English Queen, Elizabeth I.

The best part of O'Malley's childhood was probably spent watching her father on board his ships, learning about the world of trade and politics – and piracy. It is also fairly likely that she accompanied her father on fishing trips, particularly given her later aptitude at sea and her knowledge of tides, sea currents and trade winds.

More conventionally, in 1546 at the age of sixteen, Grace married a man called Dónal O'Flaherty who was the son of one Gilledubh O'Flaherty. After the wedding she moved home to Dónal's castle at Bunowen, about thirty miles south along the coastline. It might be expected that Grace felt a little strange, this being the first time she had lived away from her family. It might also be supposed that she felt more than a little claustrophobic, given that she was used to spending so much time at sea with her father and friends and now – as a married woman – she was to stay at home, concerning herself mainly with domestic duties. Grace bore Dónal two sons, Owen and Murrough, and a daughter called Margaret.

However, the O'Flaherty marriage was not destined to last long. In 1549 Dónal was accused of being party to the murder of one Walter Fada Bourke and, possibly in revenge, was subsequently murdered himself. Grace's reaction at being left a widow at so young an age is unknown, but after a short time she returned to her father's homelands where she set up base on Clare Island. Soon she had built up a fleet of three galleys together with a number of smaller vessels, which she used to plunder and loot other ships. Grace O'Malley had now started her career proper as a pirate and from this point until the end of her life she never looked back.

Gathering around her in the region of 200 men from different clans (among them O'Malley, MacCormack, O'Flaherty and Bourke), Grace is said to have made several plundering raids in both Ireland and Scotland – all of which were successful and all of which guaranteed the loyalty of her men. Indeed, she must have been a very charismatic woman to have commanded a position of such authority, a position that became all the more important when her father died, leaving most of his wealth, including his vast fleet of ships, to his only child. From this point on, her command of Irish waters was second to none. 'From Donegal to Waterford,' writes Anne Chambers in her excellent biography of O'Malley, 'all along the Irish coastline, her attacks by sea were numerous and widespread. Her fame grew. Stories of her exploits were peddled from port to port. On land she began to accumulate extensive cattle and horse herds, which later in 1593 numbered, by her own admission, over one thousand head, making her a very wealthy woman indeed.'

It is this period of her life that inspired hundreds of tales of Grace's legendary exploits. It was said that she blew up a section of Curradh Castle in Renvyle by firing a cannonball from her ship which was anchored below the castle in the bay. Other places to suffer her attacks included the castle of O'Loughlin in the Burren, the Aran Islands, Killybegs and Lough Swilly in Ireland and the castle of Doona on the coast of Erris.

In 1566, Grace married Richard Burke and moved to his family residence, Rockfleet

Rockfleet Castle in County Mayo became O'Malley's home when she married the owner, Richard Burke, in 1566. They agreed that the marriage could be terminated after a year if they so chose and Grace is said to have locked Burke out of the castle shortly after their first anniversary, although the couple ultimately did remain together for many years.

Clare Island guards the entrance to Clew Bay on the west coast of Ireland and the O'Malley family had owned a castle at Belclare on the island since Grace O'Malley was a child. It was on Clare Island that O'Malley established her base when she took to piracy.

(Carraigahowley) Castle in County Mayo. The castle, which still stands to this day, overlooks Clew Bay – a perfect safe haven for Grace's fleet of around twenty ships, which included several well-armed galleys. One of these galleys was so well equipped that it warranted a mention by a Captain Plessington of HMS *Tremontaney*: 'This galley comes out of Connaught, and belongs to Grany O'Malley.' He also observed that the vessel 'rowed with thirty oars, and had on board, ready to defend her, 100 good shot, which entertained skirmish with my boat at most an hour'.[3]

Legend has it that Grace, not wishing to be subservient to her new husband, married Richard Burke on her own terms – one of which stipulated a trial period: if she wasn't happy at the end of the first year, the couple would separate. Legend also has it that such an event did take place, with Grace locking Richard out of Rockfleet and shouting down from the ramparts that he was 'dismissed'. The truth of the matter, however, is that she and Richard remained married for many years, as various state papers attest.

Grace gave birth to their son Theobald some time in 1567, apparently on board one of her ships. At the time, it is said, the boat was being attacked by Algerian pirates and the captain, fearful that these foreigners were winning, went below deck where Grace was lying with her newborn child to persuade her to get up and rouse her men to action. Wrapping a blanket around herself, Grace gamely went up on deck and urged her men to take up arms, while at the same time picking up a musket and firing a round at the Algerians. Nor is this story as far-fetched as it might seem, for records show that several North African pirates were operating along both the south and west coasts of Ireland during this period, so it is highly likely that one of Grace's vessels should come under attack.

At this point in history, Ireland, while part of the British Isles ruled by Elizabeth I, was split into provinces that were generally governed by men appointed to the posts by the Queen. In Connaught, the province in which Grace lived, the regime was unhealthily repressive, a situation that led to frequent uprisings. Grace often led raids on other Irish chieftains, as well as looting passing merchant vessels, and was soon reported to the Governor of Connaught, Sir Edward Fitton. In 1574 Fitton sent a fleet of ships out to capture Grace, a mission led by Captain William Martin who sailed to Clew Bay with the sole purpose of laying siege to Rockfleet Castle and capturing Ireland's most wanted woman. However, Grace marshaled all the forces at her disposal and soon overcame Martin's fleet, making him flee the scene in fear for his life.

But, while she was successful in this campaign, her luck soon ran out: in 1577, while on a plundering mission against the Earl of Desmond in Munster, she was caught and imprisoned.

Confinement for any person, male or female, would have been horrific during this period, but for someone more used to the freedom of the high seas, for someone who had never been bound by the conventions of marriage, let alone any other conventions of the time, imprisonment would have been unbearable. Having been confined in Limerick jail for just over eighteen months, she was then moved, on the orders of Lord Justice William Drury, to Dublin Castle. The transfer took place on 7 November 1578, with Grace bound and chained. On meeting her, Drury described her thus: 'To that place was brought unto me Granie ny Maille, a woman of the province of Connaught, governing a Country of the Oflaherties, famous for her stoutenes of courage and person, and for some sundry exploits done at sea. She was taken by the Earle of Desmond a year and a half agoe and hath remained partly with him and partly in Her Matir'[Her Majesty's] gaole of Limerick, and was sent for now by me to come to Dublin.'[4]

Finally, in 1579, having paid her dues, Grace was released from captivity and she returned to Rockfleet Castle. But more storms lay ahead. On 18 July of that same year James FitzMaurice Fitzgerald decided to rally all of Ireland together in an attack against the 'heretic queen of England'[5] – Elizabeth I. In order to do this, Fitzgerald sought the support of the Earl of Desmond who, after pondering his options, decided to back the rebellion, as did Richard Burke and, more surprisingly given that Desmond had had her imprisoned, Grace O'Malley. What became known as the 'Desmond rebellion' wasn't the only battle that Grace and Richard had to face during this period, for toward the end of 1580, with the death of one MacWilliam of Mayo, Richard believed that he was entitled to take over MacWilliam's territory and position as clan chief. With Grace's help he mustered a huge army to support his claim and eventually, in no small part due to his wife's formidable powers of persuasion and her ability to lead men in battle, he got what he wanted, including 'territories pertaining to the title: Lough Mask Castle with 3,000 acres, Ballinrobe Castle with 1,000 acres and Kinlough near Shrule with 2,500 acres, together with the demesne lands scattered over the baronies of Kilmaine, Carra and Tirawley. In addition, he received all customary exactions and tributes due to the MacWilliam by his client chieftains in Mayo.'⁶

At this time Richard and, for a short while, Grace moved from their home at Rockfleet to Lough Mask Castle. Their son Theobald (Tibbot-ne-Long), now twelve years old, was fostered out to a neighboring family, the MacEvillys of Carra. However, having battled so long and hard for his newfound position, Richard did not live long to enjoy it. On 30 April 1583, just a few months after his accession, he died peacefully at home.

The loss to Grace cannot be measured. Often pitched against each other politically, as a couple they had been well suited. He was warlike; she enjoyed nothing better than looting and plundering. Nor had he felt threatened by her unconventional ways, her love of the sea or her penchant for piracy. After his death Grace claimed at least one-third of her husband's property, including one of his castles, after which she 'Gathered together all her own followers and with 1000 head of cows and mares departed and became a dweller in Carrikahowley in Boroswole.'⁷ But despite her riches, Grace was still in an awkward position. Vulnerable to attack, probably because her neighbors thought that as a woman alone she would make an easy target, Grace had to stamp her authority on those around her twice as hard as before. Launching several raids on the surrounding territories, she soon antagonized Sir Richard Bingham, who had succeeded Sir Edward Fitton as Governor of Connaught.

Bingham was an Englishman, born in Dorset. Introduced to the military at an early age, he saw active service at the Battle of Lepanto against the Turks as well as in France and the Netherlands. Given the governorship of Connaught at the age of fifty-six, he pronounced: 'The Irish were never tamed with words but with swords.'⁸ He soon acted on his own words, instigating a harsh regime that provoked a great deal of resentment in the province. Nowhere was this more in evidence than in his treatment of Grace O'Malley, whose son Theobald he now took hostage in order to halt Grace's opposition to him. Theobald was taken to Ballymote Castle where he stayed locked up for more than a year under the watchful eye of Bingham's brother, George Bingham, then Sheriff of Sligo. But it wasn't only Grace's youngest son who came under attack from Richard Bingham, for in July 1586 her oldest son by her first marriage, Owen O'Flaherty, was killed by Bingham who, according to Grace, had him bound with rope and stabbed twelve times with a knife.

Distraught at the murder of her beloved first-born, Grace O'Malley now gave her active support not only to her youngest son Theobald, but also to her late husband's friends and relations in their fight against Bingham.

Preparing to travel to Scotland to drum up support for the cause, she also entered into lengthy talks with the chief of the O'Donnell clan, but Bingham soon became wise to her plotting. Wary of the amazing influence she had over her followers, he had another brother, Captain John Bingham, place her under arrest. Apprehended, she was bound with rope and brought in front of Sir Richard, at which point she was accused of plotting 'to draw in Scots'. Nor was she alone in being charged with this offence, for several of her friends and relations were accused of the same crime, one that was considered treasonable and therefore punishable by death. Grace O'Malley's life was now on the line, and had it not been for her son-in-law offering himself as a hostage on condition that Grace would abandon any attempts at rebellion, she would have been executed. As it was, miraculously she was allowed to go free, but no sooner was her release secured then she ordered her fleet of ships made ready and straightaway headed for Ulster, where she intended to bring in the 'gallowglass' (an ancient term for a mercenary soldier).

On the way her ships were badly damaged in a storm, but this setback afforded Grace the opportunity of spending time with the O'Neill and O'Donnell chiefs while her fleet was under repair. These two men were among the most powerful in Ulster, and Grace stayed with them for a little over three months in 1587, pointing out, no doubt, that what Richard Bingham was doing in Connaught (curtailing the powers of the old Irish chieftains and destroying age-old customs) could soon happen in Ulster. While Grace was mustering support in the north, her arch-enemy was ordered by Elizabeth I to sail for active service in Flanders. As soon as Grace heard the news, she seized the opportunity to return south – this time to Dublin – where she sought out Sir John Perrot.

Perrot was Lord Deputy of Connaught and as such was supposed to work alongside Sir Richard Bingham to bring the province under control. However, while Bingham favored the sword, Perrot preferred a more conciliatory style of government and the two men frequently clashed. Grace O'Malley knew of this animosity and, on returning to Dublin, banked on the fact that Perrot, wanting nothing more than to snub his colleague, would grant her not only an audience but more than likely a pardon as well. Nor was Grace disappointed for, on arriving in Dublin and seeking out her target, she received 'her Majesty's pardon by Sir Perrot'[9] in addition to which she also secured a pardon for her sons and her daughter.

Having achieved so much and wiped the slate clean, it might be thought that Grace O'Malley would now settle down to a quieter life, but nothing could have been further from the truth. No sooner had she got what she wanted from Perot than she set about acquiring new galleys and renewing her piratical activities. Her timing could not have been more apposite, for on 29 July 1588 the Spanish Armada – an invasion fleet sent against Queen Elizabeth – was sighted off the Lizard in the south-west of England. The Spanish fleet was ultimately repulsed, but Ireland, particularly the west coast, saw many foreign ships sailing into its waters during this period. Sir Richard Bingham swiftly returned from Flanders with orders to make it a capital offence for anyone caught harboring Spanish soldiers. Obviously O'Malley was not a huge fan of Bingham, so it is possible she sided with the foreigners against both him and Elizabeth, but it is equally likely that – given her piratical history – she would have been tempted to plunder any Spanish vessel foundering along the Irish coastline.

Bingham put O'Malley under constant surveillance, but she was not his only problem – owing to his harsh treatment of the citizens of Connaught, he now faced an open rebellion. Accusations of his past misdemeanors, including charges of murder, torture and other cruelties, soon reached the ears of Queen Elizabeth, to her anger and dismay. She was counseled to put him on trial to determine once and for all whether he was guilty as charged.

Richard Bingham was brought to court in Dublin, but very quickly acquitted. In 1590 he returned to Connaught where he was given carte blanche to bring the rebellion to an end. Knowing only one way of doing this – by violence – he launched an all-out attack against his enemies, killing and plundering wherever he and his troops went. Naturally, this included land owned by Grace O'Malley and her relations. The estate she owned at Carraigahowley was devastated by Bingham, who not only stole her cattle but also burnt huge swathes of her crops.

Grace's only refuge was at sea and she sailed to the Aran Islands. But even there she found little respite, for news was brought to her that her second son by Dónal O'Flaherty, Murrough, had swapped sides and joined Bingham's forces. Infuriated by this disloyalty, she set out to attack her son – an action Bingham later reported to one of the Queen's representatives, William Cecil, as further evidence of O'Malley's unscrupulous character. 'His [Murrough's] aforesaid mother Grany (being out of charity with her sonne for serving her Matie.[Majesty]) manned out her Navy of Galleys and landed in Ballinehencie where he dwelleth, burned his towen and spoiled his people of their cattyle and goods and murdered 3 or 4 of his men which offered to make resistance…'[10]

But while one son acted in defense of Bingham, O'Malley's third son, Theobald, was doing the exact opposite. In the spring of 1592, along with several other conspirators, he mounted a spectacular attack on Bingham and his men. The assault failed, resulting in yet further animosity between Bingham and Theobald's mother.

Ever since the attack on her land at Carraigahowley, Grace's main source of income had been derived from the sea. She had painstakingly built up her fleet of galleys but, after Theobald's assault on him, Bingham retaliated by impounding her fleet – a blow from which Grace never fully recovered. Worse still, her son Theobald then decided to surrender to Bingham and, although he wasn't imprisoned or executed, he was stripped of his powers and forced to pay vast sums of money to Bingham as restitution for the acts he had committed.

By this point, Grace O'Malley was in her mid-sixties, an astonishing age for either a man or woman to reach in the sixteenth century, but even more so given her chosen lifestyle. Reduced to the status of widow – stripped of her lands, her cattle, her ships – with one son dead and one on the side of her mortal enemy, she was a broken woman and for this she blamed one man and one man alone: Sir Richard Bingham. It was he who had mercilessly pursued her, he who had killed her son and he who had brought her to her knees. Grace needed to do something spectacular if she was to survive.

In July 1593 Queen Elizabeth I received a letter from 'your loyal and faithful subject Grany Ne Mailly of Connaught in your Highness realm of Ireland.'[11] As Anne Chambers points out, the motivation behind this missive was first and foremost survival, but it was also a means of, if not ridding herself of Bingham completely, then at least tempering his influence over her life. Grace began by trying to refute Bingham's claims that she was a pirate and rebel by forwarding her version of events: 'of the continual discord stirs and dissention that heretofore long tyme remained amongh the Irishrye especially in west Conaght by the sea side everie cheeftaine for his safeguard and maintenance and for the defence of his people, followers and countrye took armes by strong hand to make head against his neybours which in like manner constrained your highness fond subject to take armes and by force to maintaine her selfe and her people by sea and land the space of fortye years past.'[12]

After this, she goes on to tell the Queen of her two marriages, of her children, of her present widowhood and her impoverished circumstances. She says she will willingly surrender her two remaining sons' properties and also the properties of her two nephews to Elizabeth, after which she brings up the main purpose of her letter: the return of her fleet in order that she may earn a living. She asks the Queen to 'grant unto your said subject under your most gracious hand of signet free libertye during her lyve to envade with sword and fire all your highness enemies wheresoever they are or shall be without any interruption of any person or persons whatsoever.'[13]

This last clause obviously refers to Sir Richard Bingham because, as Grace saw it, if she could gain Queen Elizabeth's favor then Bingham would be helpless to act against her.

Meanwhile, with this letter en route to England, things had taken a turn for the worse in Ireland. Another uprising had occurred, this time in Ulster. The northern Irish, fearing that the English were now going to try to expand their influence further north, had mounted a massive assault and Grace's son Theobald was implicated in the uprising. This was highly opportune for Bingham, who promptly charged Theobald with treason and had him thrown into prison at Athlone to await trial. Fearing for her son's life and knowing once again that she had to do something decisive in order to save him, Grace O'Malley now set off on the most dangerous voyage of her life.

Captaining the ship herself (or so legend has it), she sailed across the Irish Sea, past Land's End in Cornwall then up through the straits of Dover until finally she turned into the Thames Estuary and came to anchor next to London Bridge. At this time, given Grace's status as a pirate and rebel and given the tense political climate in England regarding foreign invasion (particularly the Spanish threat), this was a perilous, some might say foolhardy, journey. Nonetheless, having gained access to the city she now also gained access to the English court – most probably at Greenwich Palace, where it is said Elizabeth had fled in July 1593 owing to an outbreak of the plague in London itself.

At this point, Elizabeth was at the height of her power. She was the 'Goddesse Heavenly Bright' of Edmund Spencer's epic poem *The Faerie Queene* and what she lacked in beauty she certainly made up for with extravagant costumes and a razor-sharp wit. In contrast, Grace O'Malley, although around the same age as Elizabeth, had lived most of her life at sea and locked in battle on land, and looked a lot older than her years.

The two women are said to have met some time in late July and, as far as anyone can tell, their conversation took place in Latin – Queen Elizabeth being particularly fluent in this language. Legend has it that Grace was accompanied to this meeting by a group of her most loyal servants and that when she arrived at the English court, rather than dress up in whatever finery she could muster, she preferred to wear a traditional Irish costume and go barefoot. The meeting of the two women is further reported (in particular by the Irish) as being the meeting of two queens of equal standing. Elizabeth reportedly held out her hand to Grace, who was the taller of the two women – so 'the English queen was forced to raise her hand to the Irish queen.'[14]

During this meeting, Elizabeth is said to have lent a handkerchief to Grace who, after using it, threw it directly into a fire. Elizabeth is reported to have been shocked by this action, pointing out that in England handkerchiefs were usually kept in one's pocket, not disposed of in a fire. Equally shocking was Grace's apparent refusal to accept the title of countess from Queen Elizabeth, on the grounds that a title could not be bestowed upon someone of equal status. When Elizabeth made a comment regarding the difficulties of being a queen, with all the duties she had to perform, Grace is said to have retorted that women in Mayo had far greater problems . . . but how much of any of this is true is very hard to tell.

That the two women met is unquestionable (records show that Grace stayed at the English court from June until September 1593), but there is little doubt that over the course of time the two women's conversation has been greatly embellished, to the point where it is impossible to decide what was said and what was not.

What is in no doubt is that after their meeting Grace remained in London awaiting Elizabeth's decision as to her future. Meanwhile, Bingham, aware that Elizabeth was contemplating the reinstatement of Grace's fleet and the release of Theobald, wrote to the English court to the effect that 'for so long as Grany Ne Maly and he were of power to make any sturres the state was never troubled with their complaints but now that they are pulled dowen and forced in speight of their hartes to submit themselves to her Ma.ts [Majesty's] lawes they pretend many wronges and are not ashamed to ask recompence.'[15]

But Bingham's remonstrations were to little or no avail, for at the end of September Elizabeth wrote to him ordering the release

An educated woman, O'Malley sailed to London in 1593 to hold talks with Queen Elizabeth I, seeking her protection from persecution in Ireland and the release of her son from captivity.

of Theobald and furthermore that Grace was to be allowed to live in peace and enjoy her livelihood to the end of her days.

In the first instance Bingham begrudgingly complied, releasing Theobald from prison in Athlone some time late in September of the same year, 1593. But when it came to the Queen's second judgment – that Grace be allowed to live in peace and enjoy earning a living – he would not be so accommodating.

On her return to Ireland Grace immediately began to rebuild her fleet with the sole intention of re-establishing herself as a pirate or, as she put it, re-establishing her trade of 'maintenance by sea'. But the moment she set sail, Bingham sent a certain Captain Strittes together with a group of soldiers to harass her and detain her vessels. This situation continued until finally, in 1597, Sir Richard Bingham was replaced in Connaught by Sir Conyers Clifford – a man who took a far more conciliatory attitude toward Grace and her piratical activities.

By this time, however, Grace was nearly seventy years old so she wasn't best placed to return to her old trade. Instead, she sent her sons out in her place. They rebuilt her fleet and were soon reaping substantial rewards for their efforts.

The precise date of Grace O'Malley's death is unknown, but she is thought to have passed away at Carraigahowley Castle some time in 1603. Her grave is said to be in the ruins of a Cistercian abbey somewhere on Clare Island, overlooking the sea.

1 Chambers, *Granuaile – Ireland's Pirate Queen*.
2 Cordingly, *Life Among the Pirates*.
3 Ibid.
4 State Papers relating to Ireland, Public Record Office, London.
5 Chambers, op. cit.
6 Ibid.
7 State Papers, op. cit.
8 Calendar State Papers (Elizabeth I), vol. CLXX, p.128.
9 State Papers, op. cit.
10 Ibid.
11 Ibid.
12 Ibid.
13 Ibid.
14 Chambers, op. cit.
15 State Papers, op. cit.

FRANÇOIS L'OLLONAIS
Flail of the Spanish

When L'Olonnais [sic] had a victim on the rack, if the wretch did not instantly answer his questions he would hack the man to pieces with his cutlass and lick the blood from the blade with his tongue, wishing it might have been the last Spaniard in the world he had thus killed.

Alexander Olivier Exquemelin,
The Buccaneers of America

'The man from Olonne', sometimes known as Jean-David Nau but best remembered as François L'Ollonais, was, according to Alexander Olivier Exquemelin, one of the most notorious men ever to sail the high seas. And Exquemelin should know – he served under both L'Ollonais and Henry Morgan, writing up his experiences in his highly successful *Buccaneers of America*. L'Ollonais was cruel in the extreme, specializing in barbaric tortures – the very epitome of the type of bloodcurdling pirate of which nightmares are made.

Although the exact date of his birth is unknown, François L'Ollonais is thought to have been born in France around 1635, in the region of Sables d'Olonne. At an early age he was transported to the Caribbean where he was indentured as a servant for three years, after which he is said to have joined the cattle hunters of Hispaniola before finally settling on a career of piracy.

Early in the 1660s L'Ollonais moved to the island of Tortuga (see Glossary), where he was befriended by the Governor, a Monsieur de la Place, who bestowed upon him a ship. L'Ollonais was made captain of this vessel and instructed to go out and seek his fortune – which he did, by raiding mainly Spanish vessels. As Exquemelin says, 'his cruelties against the Spaniards were such that the very fame of them made him known through the whole Indies. For which the Spaniards, in his time, whensoever they were attacked by sea, would choose rather to die or sink fighting than surrender, knowing they should have no mercy nor quarter in his hands.' Indeed, his attacks on the Spanish were so atrocious that he earned the nickname 'Fléau des Espagnols' – or Flail of the Spaniards. Not that they didn't have their revenge; for after several successful attacks on Spanish vessels, L'Ollonais' ship was wrecked off the coast of Campeche during a particularly harsh storm. All on board managed to swim ashore, but on reaching dry land the Spanish settlers, realizing who they were, slaughtered most of them and even managed to wound L'Ollonais, who escaped death only by hiding among his comrades' corpses until the Spanish had left.

After this narrow escape, L'Ollonais fled to some woodland where he bound up his wounds and disguised himself as a Spanish peasant. He then set out for the city of Campeche where he befriended some slaves whom he persuaded to help steal a canoe. L'Ollonais then sailed out to sea, heading straight for Tortuga, 'the common place of refuge of all sorts of wickedness, and the seminary, as it were, of all manner of Pirates and thieves.'[1]

Once on the island, L'Ollonais then secured himself another ship and a crew of twenty-one men, after which he headed for Cuba and a little town called De los Cayos where he had been told rich pickings were to be had. Unbeknown to him, however, the citizens of De los Cayos – forewarned of his arrival – had sent word to the Governor of Havana that they were about to be raided. The Governor sent a ship armed with ten guns and fifty men to help repel the attack. Also on board, according to Exquemelin, was a Negro who was to serve as a hangman, for the Governor of Havana wanted to execute any pirates who were captured – any, that is, except L'Ollonais whom they were to drag to Havana to face justice.

But the Spanish were no match for L'Ollonais and soon the ship from Havana was captured along with her crew. L'Ollonais then ordered all the captured sailors one by one onto the deck where they were made to kneel down in front of him before having their heads cut off. Finally it was the turn of the Negro hangman. Throwing himself upon L'Ollonais' mercy, he begged not to be killed and promised to give him any information he wanted. This the Frenchman agreed, but no sooner had the hangman told him what he wanted than L'Ollonais had him murdered just like the others. Only one person was spared from death – a young boy who was sent back to Havana with a message from L'Ollonais to the Governor saying, 'I shall never henceforward give quarter to any Spaniard whatsoever; and I have great hopes I shall execute on your own person the very same punishment I have done upon them you sent against me. Thus I have retaliated the kindness you designed to me and my companions.'[2]

L'Ollonais, with a new ship in his possession, now set sail for Maracaibo where he captured a vessel laden with silver plate and other booty. Afterwards

Believed to have been born in France around 1635, François L'Ollonais harbored a bitter hatred of the Spanish and treated Spanish prisoners with appalling cruelty. The lucky ones were beheaded but others he hacked to pieces with his cutlass.

he returned to Tortuga where he gathered together a force of around 500 'picked scoundrels'[3] including a man by the name of Michael de Basco, whom L'Ollonais put in charge of overland attacks.

Having secured enough men with whom he could capture major ports and cities, in the spring of 1667 L'Ollonais and his fleet set sail for the north of Hispaniola, where they took on board supplies and afterwards headed for the eastern cape of the isle to Punta d'Espada. On the way they spied a Spanish cargo ship, which L'Ollonais determined to capture. The ensuing battle lasted about three hours, after which the cargo ship surrendered to the pirates. On board was a cargo of 120,000 weight (1,000 weight being 1,000lb) of cacao, 40,000 pieces of eight and innumerable jewels.

L'Ollonais selected several of his most trusty men and had them return to Tortuga with this vessel, under strict instructions to unload her then return to join the fleet at the island of Savona. Meanwhile, he sailed on, meeting yet another Spanish cargo vessel – this time loaded with military provisions that included 7,000 weight of gunpowder together with a great many muskets and 12,000 pieces of eight. L'Ollonais and his men took this ship too, and also sent her back to Tortuga.

Riding high on these two successes, L'Ollonais' pirate fleet now proceeded to sail toward Maracaibo in the Gulf of Venezuela. The town was defended from attack by sea by a sizeable fortification and sixteen guns. However, the pirates easily overcame Maracaibo's soldiers, after which they 'marched into the town, and what followed may be conceived. It was a holocaust of lust, of passion, and of blood such as even the Spanish West Indies had never seen before. Houses and churches were sacked until nothing was left but the bare walls; men and women were tortured to compel them to disclose where more treasure lay hidden.'[4]

Later that night the pirates went into the woods and returned bringing with them 20,000 pieces of eight and mules laden with household goods, as well as twenty prisoners. The male prisoners were put on the rack to make them confess where they had hidden the rest of their treasure, but very little information could be extracted from them. L'Ollonais picked up a cutlass and hacked one of them to pieces in full view of the others, and told the rest that unless they complied with his commands they would all suffer the same fate. The threat was enough to frighten at least one of the prisoners into showing the pirates where he thought the rest of the Spanish were hiding, but by the time L'Ollonais and company got there everyone had disappeared and the poor man who had acted as their guide was hacked to pieces just like his fellow countryman.

This was obviously the only way L'Ollonais knew how to act in the face of opposition. Violence was second nature to him – as it was to practically every pirate. Such acts were used not only as a means of frightening their prisoners into submission, but also as a way of building up their reputations. The more terrifying people believed you to be, the more likely it was that they would comply with your demands. There are countless tales of pirate atrocities – Bartholomew Roberts (see page 88) was known far and wide for his acts of violence. Barbadians and citizens from Martinique were a particular bugbear of his, mainly because the governments of both these islands were at pains to capture Roberts and bring him to justice. The violence he used against seamen from both these places was sickening, as witnessed by the following extract from a report sent to London in 1721 to the effect that, after capturing a ship off Martinique and placing her crew under arrest, 'Some [the pirates] almost whipped to death, others had their ears cut off, others they fixed to the yard arms and fired at them as a mark.'[5] Roberts was far from alone when it came to such evil acts. It is said that when the pirate Philip Lynne was caught in 1726, he confessed to having murdered in the region of thirty-seven sea captains.

Another pirate notorious for his violence was Edward Low (see page 110) who, as Charles Johnson points out in *A General History of the Robberies and Murders of the Most Notorious Pirates*, was born to a life of crime. Low's early violent behavior was carried into later life and is well illustrated by one particularly gruesome incident that was reported by the Governor of St Kitts to the Council of Trade and Plantations in 1724.[6] Captain Edward Low 'took a Portuguese ship bound home from Brazil; the master of which had hung eleven thousand moydores of gold in a bag out of the cabin window, and as soon as he was taken by the said Low, cut the rope and let them drop into the sea; for which Low cut off the said Master's lips and broiled them before his face and afterwards murdered the whole crew being thirty-two persons.'[7]

Captain George Lowther was another infamous pirate whose despicable reputation included the looting of a ship called the *Greyhound*. The pirates 'not only rifled the ship, but whipped, beat and cut the men in a cruel manner, turned them aboard their own ship, and then set fire to theirs'.[8] Ignoble acts such as this were hardly the exception, rather they were the rule. As Alexander Olivier Exquemelin explains in his book *Buccaneers of America*, pirates from all over the world engaged in these acts. 'Among other tortures then used, one was to stretch their limbs with cords, and at the same time beat them with sticks and other instruments. Others had burning matches placed betwixt their fingers, which were thus burnt alive. Others had slender cords or matches twisted about their heads, till their eyes burst out of the skull.' Another pirate 'pastime' – something they did to amuse themselves when they were bored or fancied causing misery – was to play a game called 'Sweating'. Candles were set in a circle on deck and then lit, after which a captive or captives would be made to run around these objects while being stabbed by the pirates with knives or bayonets until the prisoners were too exhausted to move and fell down on deck.

Yet, familiar as they were with torturing prisoners, the author David Cordingly is at pains to point out in his book *Life Among the Pirates* that the custom of 'walking the plank' barely rates a mention in documents from this period. Indeed, the only incidence of it having been reported appears to have been in *The Times* newspaper on 23 July 1829 when mention is made of a Dutch ship, the *Vhan Fredericka*, which was on its way to Jamaica when it was captured by pirates who proceeded to loot the ship. During the mayhem the ship's Dutch crew tried to stop the pirates but were 'laughed at by the ruffians, who proceeded deliberately to compel the wretched men to what is termed "walk the plank"'. Other references to this practice are less reliable and tend – more

The barbarity of L'Ollonais was not confined to those captured at sea. Hundreds of prisoners were taken when he and his men raided coastal towns and harbors. They were tortured to reveal the hiding places of any valuables, with those who would not, or could not, cooperate enduring a slow and painful death.

than likely – to be the fanciful idea of one writer or other. Howard Pyle, in his *Book of Pirates*, accuses Blackbeard of the practice 'for in him we have a real, ranting, raging, roaring pirate per se – one who really did bury treasure, who made more than one captain walk the plank, and who committed more private murders than he could number on the fingers of both hands.' Pyle also famously drew a picture for *Harper's Monthly Magazine* in 1887, illustrating the practice by drawing a group of fiendish-looking pirates goading a blindfolded captive to his death at the end of a plank.

Of course, in an age when all manner of people, including women and children, could be put to death by the State for crimes such as stealing a loaf of bread, it is little wonder that pirates thought next to nothing of torture. These were violent times, times when everyone was far more familiar with death than most of us are now, where executions were held in public and it was considered a pastime to go and watch someone being hanged or having their head chopped off. Also, any man joining a naval unit would have been well aware of the strict discipline on board ship. Little wonder, then, that growing up in these times pirates such as François L'Ollonais thought nothing of tormenting his victims in the cruelest ways imaginable.

After the attack on Maracaibo, L'Ollonais finally left the town, only to venture across Lake Maracaibo to another community – a town called Gibraltar. After a protracted battle, during which L'Ollonais lost about seventy men, the garrison was overthrown and the town plundered. The pirates stayed in this region for a little over a month, looting and extorting ransoms in return for not burning down premises. Huge numbers of citizens died, many from starvation as the pirates took all the food and livestock for themselves. 'Finally, after having been in possession of the town four entire weeks, they sent four of the prisoners, remaining alive, to the Spaniards that were fled into the woods, demanding of them a ransom for not burning the town. The sum hereof they constituted ten thousand pieces of eight, which, unless it were sent to them, they threatened to fire and reduce into ashes the whole village.'[9] The threat worked and several days later the ransom was paid, but L'Ollonais still seemed dissatisfied with the amount of money he had secured. He and his men returned to Maracaibo where, for a second time in as many months, they threatened to set the town alight if they didn't receive a ransom of 30,000 pieces of eight. Eventually terms were settled: the citizens of Maracaibo paid the pirates 20,000 pieces of eight and 500 cows. L'Ollonais and his fleet then sailed to the Iles des Vaches (otherwise known as Cow Island), which was also a favorite haunt of the pirate Henry Morgan (see page 38). Here they unloaded their cargo of booty (in the region of 'two hundred and threescore thousand pieces of eight' along with jewels, silk, linen and 'other commodities'), which was then divided up between the men. Those who had been wounded during the voyage, particularly those who had lost limbs, were substantially recompensed for their injuries, after which the fleet set sail back to Tortuga.

When L'Ollonais arrived on the island he received a hero's welcome, whereupon he and his pirates proceeded to celebrate so hard that soon they had spent all their money on drinking, gambling and womanizing.

In late 1667 L'Ollonais resolved to mount a new mission, this time to Cuba where he planned to loot and pillage as many towns and villages as he could. He gathered together about 700 men aboard a fleet of ships and set sail. On the way, however, the pirate fleet was blown off course into the Gulf of Honduras. Here L'Ollonais labored long and hard trying to maneuver his fleet back to their original course, but to no avail; with supplies running low, he decided to drop anchor as close to the coastline as possible. The pirates then took canoes and paddled up the Xagua river, along whose banks lay several Indian settlements. The pirates robbed these dwellings of food and livestock, afterwards deciding to stay in the area looting and pillaging as much as they could until eventually they came to Puerto Cavallo. This Spanish port was relatively large and it so happened that at the same time as the pirates entered it, a large Spanish ship mounted with twenty-four guns was docked in the harbor. The pirates immediately seized this ship along with most of the houses in the port. They also took several hundred prisoners upon whom they committed:

> the most insolent and inhuman cruelties that ever heathens invented, putting them to the cruelest tortures they could imagine or devise. It was the custom of L'Ollonais that, having tormented any persons and they not confessing, he would instantly cut them to pieces with his hangar [sword], and pull out their tongues; desiring to do the same, if possible, to every Spaniard in the world. Oftentimes it happened that some of these miserable prisoners, being forced thereunto by the rack, would promise to discover the places where the fugitive Spaniards lay hidden; which being not able afterwards to perform, they were put to more enormous and cruel deaths than they who were dead before.'[10]

Eventually, after all but two of the prisoners were dead, the pirates marched toward the town of San Pedro. On the way they were ambushed by a group of Spaniards who killed several of their number, but who were eventually defeated. L'Ollonais then tortured all those who had not died in the fight – asking them if there were further ambushes ahead and if so, could another way be found to enter San Pedro? All the prisoners answered that yes, there were further ambushes ahead, but no they couldn't think of another way into the town. L'Ollonais didn't believe them, however, and dragging one unfortunate individual in front of him he is said to have opened his chest with a knife and pulled out his heart, which he then proceeded to bite and gnaw 'like a ravenous wolf' while shouting out to the others that this was what lay in store for them if they didn't show him another way into San Pedro.

Fearing for their lives, the remaining prisoners promised to show L'Ollonais another route into the town, but they added it was a very difficult road to negotiate. Shortly afterwards the prisoners and their captors then set off for San Pedro, but just as they had said the path was too treacherous and eventually L'Ollonais had to turn back and follow the original road.

The following day L'Ollonais was ambushed for a second time, but he dispatched the Spanish within a couple of hours, killing most of them on the spot. Those he didn't kill he took with him as prisoners. L'Ollonais was then ambushed for a third time, but, unlike the first two attacks, this one was mounted by a much stronger force of Spaniards who managed to kill and wound many pirates before finally running up the white flag. Eventually, L'Ollonais reached San Pedro, which he ransacked (although there was not much treasure to be had there, for the inhabitants had been forewarned of the pirates' approach and had fled with all their valuables into the surrounding countryside).

L'Ollonais and his men then made for the coast. Tired and hungry, the pirates now

Howard Pyle, who wrote and illustrated Howard Pyle's Book of Pirates, *produced this image of an unfortunate prisoner being forced to 'walk the plank', although this was not a common form of punishment or torture among the pirate fraternity.*

set about making fishing nets so that they could feed themselves and regain their strength before returning to their ships. The pirates had now been in the gulf for about three months, during which time they had looted and pillaged many Spanish towns and villages. Now they heard tell of a large Spanish vessel mounted with forty-two guns that was in the area. L'Ollonais lost no time in making his attack and eventually the ship was captured, but there was a surprise in store – far from being laden with booty, most of her cargo had already been unloaded. The only 'treasure' left on board consisted of some jars of wine, fifty bars of iron and a small parcel of paper.

Infuriated by these meager pickings, L'Ollonais called a council of the whole fleet and announced that he was going to sail to Nicaragua. Some of his men liked the idea, but the majority did not and resolved to go back to Tortuga. Thus relieved of a large portion of his fleet, L'Ollonais headed for Nicaragua's Mosquito Coast, but misfortune was once again to strike him. Sailing too near to the islands of De Las Pertas, his ship struck a sandbank where it 'stuck so fast that no art could be found to get her off into deep water again'.[11] The only way L'Ollonais could see of releasing the ship from its position was to unload it of all its guns, iron and other weighty material but, even after doing this, the ship would still not budge. L'Ollonais then ordered his men to break the ship up and build a much smaller boat out of the old planks and nails.

Meanwhile, two of L'Ollonais' crew, a Frenchman and a Spaniard, were sent into the surrounding forest to see what food they could gather. It was dangerous territory, the islands of De Las Pertas being inhabited mainly by Indians whom Exquemelin describes as 'savages'. The two men wandered into the woods to see what they could find, but soon came face to face with a group of Indians who chased them. When the Indians finally caught up with their prey a fight broke out. The pirates defended themselves well, but eventually the Spaniard was captured. The Frenchman escaped and ran back to where L'Ollonais and the rest of the pirates were rebuilding their boat. Twelve of them gathered together and set off to find out what had happened to their companion.

When they came to the spot where the Frenchman had last seen the Spaniard alive, all he and the other pirates found was the remnants of a fire and some pieces of flesh and bone, 'and one hand, which had only two fingers remaining'.[12] Determined to catch the people responsible for this cannibalism, the pirates went in pursuit of the Indians and, on finding them, brought five of the men and four of the women on board their new boat. But strangely, given that L'Ollonais was hardly the kindest of individuals or the most forgiving, he and his men did not treat the Indians roughly. Rather, they were said to have given them food and water and little trinkets to gain their trust. To no avail, though – the Indians remained terrified of their captors and eventually the pirates released them.

The building of the new boat continued, but it was a long and laborious task and, in order that they could eat, some of the pirates began cultivating the land, trying to grow fruit and vegetables. It is thought that L'Ollonais and his men stayed in De Las Pertas for a period of five to six months, after which time the new boat was completed. A selected group of pirates decided to head for the river of Nicaragua to see if they could steal some canoes from the native Indians and return to De Las Pertas to pick up the remaining men.

L'Ollonais and the selected few set out with every intention of returning, but misfortune was to dog the French pirate for, instead of coming across a group of Indians whom he could easily attack and capture, he encountered the Indians of Darien – a group of natives who were so wild and savage that even their Spanish neighbors, with all the weaponry they possessed, would never dare attack them. L'Ollonais was blissfully unaware of this and, thinking he could treat them much as he had treated all his other foes, charged headlong into their midst. It was a fatal mistake. The Indians fought hard and captured L'Ollonais – they 'tore him in pieces alive, throwing his body limb by limb into the fire, and his ashes into the air; to the intent no trace nor memory might remain of such an infamous, inhuman creature.'[13]

It seemed a fitting end for someone who had tortured and murdered his own captives so horribly. Nor did anyone mourn his passing – particularly not his own men, many of whom met the same end as their captain, being torn limb from limb and afterwards roasted over a spit and consumed.

1 Exquemelin, *The Buccaneers of America*.
2 Ibid.
3 Pyle, *Howard Pyle's Book of Pirates*.
4 Ibid.
5 Calendar of State Papers: Colonial, America and West Indies, vol. 1720–21, no. 463 (iii).
6 Cordingly, *Life Among the Pirates*.
7 Calendar of State Papers, op. cit., no. 102.
8 Johnson, *A General History…*
9 Exquemelin, op. cit.
10 Ibid.
11 Ibid
12 Ibid.
13 Ibid.

HENRY MORGAN

the greatest buccaneer of them all

Morgan's curls are matted,
His lips are cracked and dry,
His tawny beard is tangled,
And his plumed hat hangs awry:

But his voice still booms like thunder
Through the foetid jungle glade
As he marches, bold as Lucifer,
Leading his gaunt brigade.

'Henry Morgan's March on Panama',
A.G. Prys-Jones, 1888–1987

When Henry Morgan died at home in Jamaica on 25 August 1688 the Duke of Albermarle was said to be overcome with sorrow. In fact, he was so grief-stricken that he immediately ordered a state funeral with a salute of twenty-two guns. Morgan's body was subsequently taken to the King's House in Port Royal, where it lay in state so that friends and relations could pay their last respects. Afterwards the coffin was placed on a horse-drawn gun-carriage that made its way through the streets of the town until it came to the church of St Peter. Captain Laurence Wright noted the events in his diary thus: 'Saturday 25. This day about 11 hours noon Sir Henry Morgan died, & the 26th was brought over from Passage-fort to the King's house at Port Royal, from thence to the Church, & after a sermon was carried to the Pallisadoes and there buried. All the forts fired an equal number of guns, we fired two & twenty and after we & the Drake had fired, all the merchant men fired.'[1]

It was an extraordinary send-off for any man, let alone a buccaneer, someone who had spent a large part of his life on the outer edges of respectability, a man who in his time had looted and plundered not only on the high seas, but in attacks on numerous Spanish settlements, encouraging his men to use brutal tortures to extract information from their victims. But then Henry Morgan was no run-of-the-mill pirate, no commonplace individual.

At the start of his career he quickly took over as leader of a group of privateers and pirates who were known as the Brethren of the Coast (see Glossary). Later he ransacked Puerto Principe in Cuba and afterwards raided Portobello. In 1671 he took the city of Panama, which at that time was said to be the richest settlement in the New World. Three years later Morgan was granted a knighthood and also made Lieutenant-Governor of Jamaica by no less an individual than King Charles II. What's more, he maintained a stable family life, happily married to Dame Mary Elizabeth Morgan for more than twenty years. Henry Morgan was also an astute entrepreneur, one who purchased several hundred acres of land on Jamaica, which he ran as a highly successful business.

Morgan was born in Glamorganshire in Wales around 1635. His father was Robert Morgan of Llanrhymni, a small village now located near the city of Cardiff. Little is known of Morgan's early life, except that he is thought to have had two uncles who were soldiers – Major General Sir Thomas Morgan, and Colonel Edward Morgan who later became Governor of Jersey. Determined to follow his uncles into the armed services, in 1654 Henry joined a military force led by Admiral Penn and General Venables whose main aim was to capture Hispaniola (see Glossary). The Spanish resisted fiercely, however, and eventually Penn and Venables had to withdraw.

Regrouping, Penn and Venables' next course of action was to attack Jamaica – with far more success than on their previous mission, probably because fewer Spanish soldiers were there to defend the island. Henceforth, Jamaica was proclaimed British and consequently become a safe haven for both the Royal Navy and numerous privateers. Henry Morgan then spent a couple of years engaged in attacks on Spanish settlements in Central America. In 1663 he led a raid that devastated Villahermosa and he also looted Gran Granada in Nicaragua.[2]

Returning to Jamaica in 1665, Morgan was now a man of some military importance. When Edward Mansfield (sometimes spelt Mansvelt), who was then leader of the Jamaican privateers and buccaneers, was executed by the Spanish in Havana, it seemed only fitting that Morgan should replace him. Duly elected to the post, Morgan became what was generally known at the time as the 'Admiral of the Brethren of the Coast' – a rowdy fraternity of privateers who were united by a love of adventure, a taste for gold and a loathing of Spain and the Spanish.

Morgan's first act as 'Admiral' was to plan an attack on Santa Maria de Puerto Principe (also known as Camaguey). He and his buccaneers sailed to mainland Cuba where they disembarked and began a thirty-mile trek overland toward the targeted town. News of Morgan's advance, however, soon reached Principe, where local officials hurriedly began burying all their treasures while also erecting defenses against the impending assault. When Morgan arrived he discovered the main routes into the town had been blocked and were impassable. He had to take his men the long way round, through a wooded area that opened out on to fields. Despite all the effort the locals put into defending their town, once Morgan's men reached the outskirts of Principe and engaged them in hand-to-hand combat, they were quickly vanquished. With the town at their mercy, Morgan's buccaneers rounded up as many men, women and children as they could and imprisoned them in various church buildings. They then set a ransom on each prisoner's head and told them they wouldn't be given food or water until the money was paid. Many people died during this so-called 'siege' – although some of the detainees did manage to come up with enough gold and jewelry to satisfy the buccaneers' greed and were subsequently released. Finally, after spending about two weeks looting and pillaging the town, Morgan and his men left to return to Jamaica, where shortly afterwards he plotted another daring attack, this time on the Spanish city of Portobello (Puerto Bello) in Panama.

Portobello was the third largest city in the New World (after Havana and Cartagena) and offered very rich pickings, as the buccaneer surgeon, Lionel Wafer, pointed out when he visited the place in 1680. According to him, Portobello was 'a very fair, large and commodious harbor, affording good anchoring and good shelter for ships, having a narrow mouth and spreading wider within. The galleons from Spain find good riding here during the time of their business in Portobel; for from hence they take in such of the treasures of Peru as are brought thither over land from Panama.'[3]

Setting his heart on capturing Portobello, Morgan made it his business to learn the port's weaknesses, which turned out to be that the two Spanish forts defending the city from the sea were inadequately manned. Calculating that a surprise attack from the land would be his best course of action, in July 1668 Morgan sailed his fleet of twelve ships into the Bay of Boca del Tora, which lay to the west of Portobello. There he ordered his 500-strong fighting force to climb into a series of specially constructed canoes in which, under cover of darkness, the men paddled along the coast until they were in sight of their target. At around midnight the buccaneers abandoned their canoes and continued overland, arriving outside Portobello just before dawn.

A great strategist, Morgan knew his first mission was to capture the town's lookout post, a mission he quickly accomplished, but not before one of the sentries fired a shot that alerted the soldiers who guarded the two Spanish forts. These soldiers quickly raised an alarm that woke the entire city, sending hundreds of citizens fleeing for their lives. His surprise attack foiled, Morgan sent his men charging toward the town where they expected to come under heavy fire from Santiago Castle, but in the event only one cannon was fired from the battlements . The shot was poorly aimed and did nothing to deter the attackers. Seeing their opportunity, the buccaneers now rushed into the town and rounded up as many men, women and children as they could, locking them up in a church. A second group of buccaneers then climbed up a small hill, from the top of which they could look out over the whole of Portobello. From there they began firing at the soldiers in Santiago Castle, dispatching them one by one.

Having taken the town, Morgan and his men set their sights on the two forts of San Geronimo and Santiago. San Geronimo was situated on an island near to the harbor quay and, although at first the soldiers (who numbered about 150) resisted Morgan's attack, when they saw how many buccaneers were wading out to toward them, they swiftly decided to surrender.

Santiago was a far more difficult prospect and, realizing this, Henry Morgan is believed to have employed treacherous tactics. Knowing that he couldn't safely lead his men up to the castle without them being attacked from the battlements, he had several hundred of his hostages (including women and children) dragged from the church where they had been locked up and used them as a human shield. The ploy worked, for although several shots were fired from the fort's battlements, only a few of Morgan's men died.

Meanwhile, not satisfied with attacking the fort by land only, Morgan also had a detachment of his buccaneers approach the building from the seaward position, from where they hoisted ladders and scaled the fort's walls. Breaking into the castle, these men then raised the red flag – the signal for the remaining buccaneers to storm the fort, which they did with some force. Forty-five of the garrison's eighty soldiers were killed in the subsequent battle, including the constable of artillery who, according to some accounts, was said to be so humiliated by the defeat of his soldiers that he begged to be shot – one of Morgan's men 'obligingly executed him with his pistol'.[4] Other reports have Morgan's men raping and pillaging round the town for the next fifteen days – but this is refuted by the buccaneer surgeon Richard Browne, who was present during the assault on Portobello and wrote in 1671, 'What was in fight and heat of blood in pursuit of a flying enemy I presume pardonable. As to their women, I know or never heard of any thing offered beyond their wills. Something I know as cruelly executed by Captain Collier in killing a friar in the field after quarter given, but for the Admiral [Morgan] he was noble enough to the vanquished enemy.'[5]

With Santiago Castle now his, the following morning Morgan sent two of his buccaneers across the harbor to the Castle of San Felipe (or San Phelipe), demanding that it now surrender to him. But despite having very few provisions, the garrison leader at first refused Morgan's orders. He determined to hold out until the very last moment, but, when Morgan sent over a few hundred of his most ferocious-looking buccaneers to stake out the fort, the garrison leader changed his mind. This 'about-turn' didn't go down well with San Felipe's other officers, who began questioning their commander's decision. While the enemy were busy arguing among themselves, Morgan sent a troop of buccaneers inside the garrison which was subsequently forced to surrender.

Having captured not only the town but also Portobello's principal forts, Henry Morgan now sent a letter to the President of Panama, Don Agustin de Bracamonte, demanding 100,000 pieces of eight otherwise the entire town would be destroyed along with all its citizens. Infuriated by Morgan's impertinence, Bracamonte gathered together 800 of his best soldiers and set off to drive the buccaneers out of Portobello. The going was tough, however, and soon the Panamanian soldiers were demoralized not only by having to struggle through swamps and other difficult terrain, but also by the lack of adequate provisions. Nevertheless they reached Portobello, where they set up camp. Negotiations then dragged on for three weeks, with Bracamonte's men growing more and more dissatisfied until finally he gave in and on 3 August, according to David Cordingly, sent Morgan a ransom of 4,000 pesos in gold coins, 40,000 pesos in silver coins and numerous chests packed with silver plate, along with silver bars worth in the region of 43,000 pesos.

The capture of Portobello and the ransom that was subsequently paid to Henry Morgan was one of the boldest campaigns ever pulled off by a buccaneer. Returning to Port Royal in Jamaica, Morgan was treated like a king. His exploits were even heard of as far away as London, where the Spanish Ambassador petitioned Charles II to have Morgan arrested for theft and the booty returned, but the King refused.

Back in Port Royal, meanwhile, although Morgan's buccaneers had acquired vast amounts of booty in Portobello, they proceeded to fritter most of it away in true pirate fashion on alcohol and women. At that time Port Royal was the equivalent of a pirate heaven, a playground full of grog shops, punch houses, brothels, taverns and gaming parlors. 'This town,' wrote one seventeenth-century clergyman, 'is the Sodom of the New World and since the majority of its population consists of pirates, cut-throats, whores and some of the vilest persons in the whole of the world, I felt my permanence there was of no use.'[6]

Little wonder then that Henry Morgan's men soon spent their ill-gotten gains and found themselves 'clamoring to their Captain to put to sea; for they were reduced to a starving condition'.[7]

In October 1668 Morgan sailed his fleet of vessels to the Iles des Vaches (otherwise known as Isla Vaca or Cow Island), one of his favorite rendezvous points. There he was joined by Captain Edward Collier, who was commander of the Royal Navy frigate the *Oxford* which boasted an armory of thirty-four guns. The British government had sent

A captured Spaniard kneels before the victorious Henry Morgan after the Welsh buccaneer had captured the city of Panama following an arduous march overland through fifty miles of jungle. The Spanish laid explosives in the city and burned it to the ground during their retreat.

the *Oxford* out to Jamaica and her environs expressly as a privateer to keep the Spanish at bay and also to reap as many riches as possible to swell their own coffers. By January 1669 Morgan's fleet consisted of a total of ten ships and over 700 men. But all was not smooth going for, having transferred his flag over to the *Oxford* (she being the best-equipped and largest of all the vessels) and having called a council of war at which it was decided to raid the Spanish city of Cartagena, Morgan and his men then set about drinking and carousing and firing guns to celebrate their decision. Suddenly one of the shots hit a gunpowder barrel, and before anyone could stop it from happening, the ship exploded. The *Oxford* sank immediately, killing 350 crew members. Morgan miraculously escaped, but he was among only ten men to do so.

The surgeon, Richard Browne, once again provides a good eyewitness account: 'I was eating my dinner with the rest when the mainmasts blew out and fell upon Aylett and Bigford and others and knocked them on the head. I saved myself by getting astride the mizzenmast.'[8]

The explosion put paid to any idea Morgan had of capturing Cartagena, so instead he sailed with his few remaining men to the lagoon of Maracaibo, off the coast of Venezuela, and once there set about looting and plundering various ports. Hearing of Morgan's presence, however, Don Alonso del Campo, who was Admiral of Spain's West Indian fleet, gathered three warships together and sailed them out to Maracaibo, intending to block off the lagoon so that Morgan couldn't escape.

Morgan had to act swiftly. He had recently captured an old Cuban merchant vessel, and now disguised her as a warship by cutting gun-holes in her sides and sticking logs through them to resemble cannons. On deck Morgan then lined up more logs that he draped with cloth so that to all intents and purposes they looked like seamen. He then packed the vessel with gunpowder and fuses. 'With Morgan's flag at her masthead the merchant ship led the attack, accompanied by two small frigates. They headed straight at the largest of the anchored Spanish ships, the *Magdalena* of 142 tons. The merchant ship was sailed alongside the *Magdalena* and secured to her with grappling irons. The fuses were lit and the twelve buccaneers on board escaped in the boats.'[9] After only a few seconds the merchant ship exploded and set fire to the *Magdalena*, which then sank without a trace. The other two Spanish vessels quickly set sail for harbor, but in their haste one ran aground on a sandbank, while the other was captured by Morgan.

A full victory, however, was still a little way off, for although Morgan had destroyed Don Alonso's three ships, he still had to negotiate his way past the harbor fort in order to sail back to Jamaica. He entered into negotiations with Don Alonso, but when these talks broke down he switched tactics and decided to deceive the Spanish instead. Morgan sent a whole fleet of small boats ashore filled with soldiers in order to make Don Alonso believe he was about to mount a land attack on the fort. But, under cover of darkness, these small vessels returned to Morgan's ship with all their men still inside them. The trick worked. The Spanish, believing Morgan was about to attack them by land, concentrated all their forces on the landward side of the fort. Meanwhile, Morgan upped anchor and silently slipped past the fort out to sea.

Sailing back to Jamaica, he was hailed a hero once again, but a month after his return Morgan received bad news. The Governor of Jamaica, Sir Thomas Modyford, had just received a letter from Lord Arlington in London to the effect that hostilities with Spain were to cease. Putting a brave face on the matter, Morgan decided his best course of action would be to rest up until the political situation settled. Accordingly, he turned his mind to business and ploughed some of his money into the purchase of 836 acres of land in the parish of Clarendon near Chapeltown village.

But his men were far from happy for, having spent all the proceeds from their Maracaibo raid, they once again began pressurizing Morgan to organize an expedition. It was his job as their leader to do this, they said. It was his duty to see that they were provided for. At the same time Sir Thomas Modyford received word that the Queen of Spain had – despite England ceasing hostilities with Spain – authorized her men to take up arms against the English in the Spanish West Indies. Consequently, a corsair by the name of Captain Rivero attacked the Cayman Islands and afterwards raided a Jamaican privateer vessel that at the time was sailing near Cuba. Not satisfied with these two victories, in June 1670 Rivero then landed at Montego Bay in Jamaica and proceeded to raid the town and burn some of its houses. Worse still, news then reached officials in Port Royal that Spain had declared war on Jamaica. Modyford, alongside other officials, gathered together to debate the issue, finally agreeing that Henry Morgan be given an official commission to assemble a fleet 'and to attack, seize and destroy all the enemy's vessels that shall come within reach'.[10]

Henry Morgan received his instructions on 1 August 1670 and subsequently sailed out of Port Royal in his new flagship, the 120-ton *Satisfaction*, which was armed with twenty-two big guns, six small guns and a number of supplementary small brass guns. The *Satisfaction* was also accompanied by thirty-six other ships (twenty-eight of which were English), which between them carried more than 2,000 men. Sailing toward his favorite rendezvous point on Iles des Vaches, 'Morgan gave all the captains commissions in writing, authorizing them to act against the Spanish nation and to take what ships they could, either at sea or in port, in the same way as if they were declared enemies of the King of England.'[11] On top of this, Morgan also held a council of war at which it was agreed that their main goal, the subject of their combined attack, should be the 'treasure city of Panama'.

Barely a week later, on 11 December 1670, the fleet set out from Iles des Vaches toward San Lorenzo at the mouth of the River Chagres. Once there they had to capture Santa Teresa Castle, which stood at the river's mouth. The castle and its soldiers mounted a fierce defense against Morgan's men, and many lives were lost on both sides, but eventually the building was captured and the English flag raised over the battlements. From there Morgan's fleet sailed upriver where at some point they stopped, and transferred themselves into smaller vessels and canoes which were then rowed even further upstream until finally all the men had to disembark and proceed through nearly fifty miles of jungle on foot. It was a hard journey and several of the buccaneers lost their lives during the trek, either from hostile Indians or from

This illustration shows Henry Morgan's fleet in action against the Spanish near Maracaibo, Venezuela. Morgan plundered towns and ports along the coast before destroying one Spanish warship and capturing two others.

malnutrition or diseases such as malaria and yellow fever. Nor were things much better when they emerged from the jungle onto the plain. The president of the city's council, Don Juan Perez de Guzman, had received advance warning of Morgan's attempt on Panama, and had assembled his troops – more than 2,000 men, including 400 on horseback – across Morgan's path.

On 21 January 1671 Morgan, having rested his men for as long as possible, decided to attack the Spanish.

> There was a vanguard of 300 under Captain John Morris and Colonel Lawrence Prince, a main body of 300 under Morgan on the right and 300 under Collier on the left, and a rearguard of 300 under Colonel Bledri Morgan [...] Morgan called this lozenge formation his 'tertia', with narrow gaps between the van, middle and rear sections. Aged 36 years old, Morgan was about to attack the only city that rivaled Lima for the richest city in the 17th century world.[12]

Knowing, however, that it would be foolish to mount a full-frontal attack on Don Juan's army, Morgan cleverly dispatched one of his units to go round the side of the Spanish and secure a hilltop to the right of the city. Meanwhile, Don Juan's men – both those on horseback and on foot – believing Morgan's troops were retreating, charged forward. The resulting mayhem meant that Morgan's men, who stoically stood their ground, could pick them off with accuracy. Suddenly the Spanish, who had had the advantage of being well fed, rested and ready for battle, found themselves in retreat. As they fled, Morgan's men followed them, hacking their enemies to pieces – tearing them limb from limb – severing heads and arms and legs until by midday the plain was littered with hundreds of dead or dying Spanish.

But although the Spanish were losing the battle, Don Juan still had a surprise up his sleeve. While Morgan and his men had been hacking their way through the jungle, Don Juan had been loading vessels with all Panama's treasure and shipping it out to sea. Not only that, but he had had several houses within the city itself packed full of gunpowder and had instructed his Captain of Artillery to blow up these ammunition dumps if Morgan's men reached the city.

With the Spanish army retreating, Morgan's men hastily followed them into Panama, at which point the Captain of Artillery lit the fuses on the barrels of gunpowder. The explosions, which sounded as if the heavens had opened, could be heard miles away. Soon houses were alight and whole streets burning. Don Juan had ordered more of his men to run around the city's environs with torches, setting light to any wooden structure in sight. Desperate to find treasure among the burning buildings, Morgan's buccaneers were running from one house to the next, hoping to discover stashes of gold and other precious items. But the longer they searched, the angrier they grew as it slowly dawned on them that the most valuable treasure had been removed. By nightfall the whole city was alight and by dawn only a few stone structures were left standing. 'Thus was consumed,' wrote Morgan to Thomas Modyford back in Port Royal, 'the famous and ancient city of Panama, the greatest mart for silver and gold in the whole world.'[13]

But if Don Juan thought he had got away with hiding Panama's treasures, then he was sorely mistaken. After the fires died down, Morgan's men set about torturing anyone they thought could give them information about the Spanish gold – and eventually this course of action paid off. After several weeks, Morgan's buccaneers accumulated considerable amounts of plunder that was carried back through the jungle to Morgan's ships. However, when it was time to share out the spoils, it is said that each man received only about £15 a head. The paltry amount was due no doubt to the fact that there were so many soldiers who had to receive a share of the spoils, although some people maintain it was all down to Morgan – that he had cheated his men out of their fair share. One of these people was Alexander Olivier Exquemelin, who was to write the celebrated *Buccaneers of America*. Almost half this work is devoted to Henry Morgan, whom he paints as a cruel, mendacious, unscrupulous pirate. Indeed, after the sack of Panama, Exquemelin accused Morgan of torturing several of the city's citizens for information about the hidden treasure. One poor man was subjected to more than his fair share:

> Not being able to extort any other confession out of him, they [Morgan's men] first put him upon the rack, wherewith they inhumanly disjointed his arms. After this, they twisted a cord about his forehead, which they wrung so hard, that his eyes appeared as big as eggs, and were ready to

fall out of his skull. [...] Whereupon they soon after hung him up, giving him infinite blows and stripes, while he was under that intolerable pain and posture of body.[14]

Nor did the torture stop there, for still not hearing what they wanted to hear, Exquemelin then claims Morgan's men cut off their victim's nose and ears before burning his face with straw. Finally, realizing the man wasn't going to divulge any useful information, they ordered a black slave to run the man through with a sword.

When Exquemelin's book was published in English, copies were sent to Morgan who, far from taking umbrage at the scenes of torture, instead objected to the author calling him a pirate rather than a privateer. Morgan subsequently sued the publishers for libel, but before the matter came before the judges the case was settled out of court with Morgan receiving £200 in damages. The book's later editions were then amended, but by that time the damage was already done and to this day many people still believe Exquemelin's version of events to the exclusion of all others.

After the assault on Panama, Morgan returned to Jamaica, leaving most of the buccaneers who had fought alongside him to disperse at their will. Many of the French contingent sailed to Hispaniola and the island of Tortuga, while others decided to go to Honduras and set up as logwood cutters. The assault on Panama was the last combined action of Morgan's Brethren of the Coast. Piracy, in all its many forms, did continue in these waters – in fact, it grew to such levels that at one point trade in the West Indies became almost impossible. But these were individual assaults by individual pirates, not a whole fleet fighting under one flag.

Morgan returned to Jamaica and a hero's welcome. On 10 June 1671 the Council of Jamaica thanked him personally for his attack on Panama. But if those in the Indies were grateful to him, those in London weren't best pleased for, despite the Queen of Spain's letter to the effect that Spanish corsairs were to attack the English in the Indies, London still insisted it was not at war with Spain. The Spanish maintained that they were shocked and horrified by Morgan's actions in Panama, and news of the assault was said to have put the Queen of Spain into such 'a distemper and excess of weeping and violent passion as those about her feared it might shorten her life'.[15]

London thereafter blamed the debacle firmly on the privateers who, they insisted, were not acting under official orders. As a consequence, Sir Thomas Modyford was removed from office and replaced as Governor of Jamaica by Sir Thomas Lynch. On his return to England, Modyford was thrown into the Tower of London (probably to appease the Spanish) where he remained for two years before being released. The Spanish, however, were not appeased and continued to create such a furor that eventually, on 2 April 1672, Henry Morgan was placed under arrest and returned to England on HMS *Welcome*.

For two years Morgan waited to hear his fate. He put his time to good use, petitioning Lord Arlington on how Jamaica's sea defenses could be improved, while also keeping in constant touch with Governor Lynch, who in turn kept Morgan informed regarding piratical activities in and around Jamaica. But if the Spanish hoped Morgan

When Henry Morgan attacked and captured Portobello in Panama, he sent a letter to the President of Panama demanding 100,000 pieces of eight, threatening that, if the ransom was not paid, he would destroy the town and all of its inhabitants. The ransom was eventually paid.

was going to be imprisoned for his part in the Panama expedition, their expectations were dashed, for there was no judge or jury in England who would dare to convict him. Indeed, far from punishing Morgan, on 22 January 1674 he was knighted by King Charles II, after which Morgan was said to be so much in favor with the King that the latter presented him with a snuff box decorated with his portrait and set with diamonds.

Shortly after, Governor Lynch was relieved of his post in Jamaica, to be replaced by a combination of Lord Vaughn as Governor and the recently knighted Sir Henry Morgan as Deputy Governor.

Morgan sailed back in triumph to the West Indies on a ship called the *Jamaica Merchant*. Even when he was shipwrecked on the Iles des Vaches – his vessel having sunk – he wasn't downhearted. Nor should he have been, for a couple of days after he and his crew were washed up on shore, they were rescued by a passing merchant vessel and duly delivered to Port Royal on 6 March 1676.

For the next few years Morgan concentrated on his role as Deputy Governor, while also administering to his sugar plantations and other business interests. Sadly, he did not find working with Lord Vaughn easy and the latter was said to have complained in writing to Sir Joseph Williamson of Morgan's 'imprudence and unfitness to have anything to do with civil government [...] Sir Henry has made himself and his authority so cheap at the Port, drinking and gaming at the taverns, that I intend to remove there speedily myself for the reputation of the island.'[16] This may have been sour grapes on Lord Vaughn's part – the fact was that in a landlocked role, Morgan did not function well. It was only when Lord Vaughn was relieved of his post and Morgan took over as acting Governor of Jamaica that he really came back into his own.

Fearing attacks from the French, Morgan ordered the building of two new forts to guard Port Royal harbor. He also sent a couple of sloops out to the Iles des Vaches, where the *Jamaica Merchant* had sunk, in order to retrieve that ship's guns. The mission was successful and twenty-two cannon were saved and brought back to Jamaica to help build up her defenses. Morgan also attempted – perhaps a little hypocritically – to rid Port Royal of the hundreds of pirates who now used it as their base. What success the clean-up operation had was due for the most part to Morgan threatening to have the pirates hanged at Gallows Point if they didn't leave the island.

Eventually, in 1682, Sir Henry Morgan resigned from his post as Governor of Jamaica. Having always enjoyed alcohol, he now took to the bottle in earnest and continued with his dissolute lifestyle right up to the end. Hans Sloane, who was his physician at this time, described Morgan in these later years as being 'lean, sallow with yellowish eyes and a prominent belly'.[17] But despite his obvious ill-health Morgan continued to abuse his body, indulging in week-long drinking binges with his friends and acquaintances till 'his body swelled so as not to be contained in his coat'.[18]

Sir Henry Morgan died on 25 August 1688, aged about fifty-three. Nearly four years later, on 7 June 1692, a combined earthquake and tidal wave hit Port Royal, Morgan's home for so many years, almost laying it flat. The death toll was estimated to be between 2,000 and 3,000, while barely 200 houses survived the assault.

Port Royal was not rebuilt. Kingston subsequently became the main harbor on the island, but visitors to the old town today will find a Jamaica National Heritage Trust plaque which reads:

> Once called 'the richest and wickedest city in the world', Port Royal was also the virtual capital of Jamaica. To it came men of all races, treasures of silks, doubloons and gold from Spanish ships, looted on the high seas by the notorious 'Brethren of the Coast' as the pirates were called. From here sailed the fleets of Henry Morgan, later lieutenant-Governor of Jamaica, for the sacking of Camaguey, Maracaibo, and Panama, who died here, despite the ministrations of his Jamaican folk-doctor [...].

Although seen by some as a hero and having achieved during his life a position of great importance and high social standing, Henry Morgan must surely be remembered as one of the most successful and ruthless pirates ever to have lived.

1 Pope, *Harry Morgan's Way.*

2 Cordingly, *Life Among the Pirates.*

3 Pope, op. cit.

4 Ibid.

5 Breverton, *Admiral Sir Henry Morgan.*

6 Ibid.

7 Ibid.

8 Ibid.

9 Cordingly, op. cit.

10 Pope, op. cit.

11 Course, *Pirates of the Western Seas.*

12 Breverton, op. cit.

13 Earle, *The Sack of Panama.*

14 Exquemelin, *The Buccaneers of America.*

15 Pope, op. cit.

16 Ibid.

17 Course, op. cit.

18 Pope, op. cit.

CAPTAIN KIDD

pirate or privateer?

I am now going to give an account of one whose name is better
known in England, than most of those whose histories we have
already related; the person we mean is Captain Kidd,
whose public trial and execution here, rendered him the subject
of all conversation, so that his actions have been chanted
about in ballads...

Captain Charles Johnson,
A General History of the Robberies and
Murders of the Most Notorious Pirates.

On 23 May 1701, at a little after two o'clock in the afternoon, a small group of convicted pirates were driven from Newgate prison by cart on a three-mile procession through the streets of London to face the gallows. The journey would take the men not only past the East India Company headquarters on Leadenhall, but also close by the Tower of London – that huge stone fortress that symbolized English power. Enormous crowds had gathered for the event, and the journey took over two hours to complete. All along the way the crowds shouted and tried to jostle the prisoners until eventually the cart reached its final destination, Execution Dock. There the gallows stood: 'one wooden beam held up by two vertical beams, and a raised platform, with some steps leading up to it. Short stout posts, that could be yanked, supported the platform, which had to be sturdy enough to hold the doomed men, the executioner and a couple of priests.'[1]

There were ten prisoners in total, six of whom, on getting out of the cart, were led to one side where they were granted pardons. The remaining four were not so lucky. The executioner led them to the gallows where ropes were placed around their necks, after which each man was allowed a few last words. Three out of the four – Darby Mullins, Jean DuBois and Pierre Mingueneau – were barely able to speak, so frightened were they of what was to come. The fourth man was different – Captain William Kidd, though drunk on rum, managed to shout out that far from being guilty, it was his mutinous crew that had done wrong. His words were futile and minutes later, after a short prayer had been said, the trap doors were released. Each man dropped six inches and began kicking, 'dancing the hempen jig', but then something extraordinary occurred.

Captain Kidd fell to the ground. Suddenly the crowd stopped baying; everyone turned to the executioner. Sometimes, when such an event occurred, the authorities, believing it to be an act of God, would allow the convicted criminal to walk away a free man, but in Kidd's case this wasn't to be. No sooner had he struggled to his feet than the executioner led him back up on to the scaffold, where once again a rope was placed around his neck. This time when the trap door was released Captain Kidd met his end. All four bodies were then cut down and tied to posts where three tides were allowed to wash over them – the traditional manner of execution by the Admiralty (see also the chapter on John Avery, pages 71-3). Later still, Kidd's body was untied from the post and taken by boat twenty-five miles downriver to Tilbury Point, where the corpse was hoisted up in an iron cage as a warning to all other seamen not to follow Kidd's example. It was a ignominious end to a life that had been full of adventure, a tawdry death for a man who was largely responsible for the legends of daring escapades and buried treasure that have come to epitomize pirate life.

William Kidd was born around 1645 in the Scottish port of Greenock on the Firth of Clyde. Apart from the fact that his father was a Presbyterian minister, not much else is known about the young Kidd's early years except that as a teenager he went to sea, soon becoming a privateer – not a pirate, but a type of nautical mercenary usually employed by the government of the day to attack ships of an enemy nation in exchange for a percentage of the spoils (see Glossary). In Elizabethan times both Sir Walter Raleigh and Sir Francis Drake had acted as privateers against the Spanish, making it a legitimate profession, one that could afford a successful practitioner a good living.

The first ship of which Kidd was captain in his own right was the *Blessed William*. Stationed in the Caribbean, he first raided the French territory of Marie Galante in the Windward group of islands off Guadeloupe, and afterwards fought against five French warships near the island of St Martins. However, no sooner had Kidd secured these victories than his men decided that rather than be privateers, they preferred the easier life of the pirate. In February 1690, in Falmouth Harbor, Antigua, they seized the *Blessed William* and, to all intents and purposes, abandoned Kidd. Shipless and penniless, this might have been the end of him, but, as luck would have it, the Governor of Nevis, grateful to Kidd for having seen off the evil French, presented him with a sixteen-gun French warship that Kidd renamed the *Antigua*.

In 1691 Captain William Kidd sailed for New York. There had been rumors that his old ship, the *Blessed William*, was harbored there, but by the time Kidd reached the city it had already departed. Nevertheless, Kidd stayed on in New York and on 16 May married a woman by the name of Sarah Oort, sixteen years her husband's junior and said to be one of the wealthiest women in the city, owning five prime pieces of real estate in Manhattan. The newlyweds were therefore spoilt for choice when it came to choosing a place to live, but eventually settled on a house in Pearl Street at the southernmost tip of Manhattan Island, near to the old harbor. For the next four years Kidd built up several successful businesses, as well as fathering two daughters, but as a man who had spent the best part of his life at sea, he soon yearned to be back on board ship. In 1695 he returned to England, where he hoped to pick up several new privateering commissions.

It was at this juncture that Kidd met up with Robert Livingstone, a merchant from Albany in America, who had recently arrived in London himself. Together the two men set about looking for sponsors for their privateering operations and eventually contacted Lord Bellomont, who was not only a member of Parliament, but also the recently

Scottish pirate William Kidd had spent most of his life at sea until he married and settled down in New York in 1691. He established a number of successful businesses and even started a family before the lure of the sea became too strong for him to resist.

nominated Governor of Massachusetts Bay – and in desperate need of money himself. The three men created a syndicate, whereby they would buy a ship and furnish it with a crew of sturdy men who would sail it out to the Indian Ocean, where Kidd would then capture as many pirate ships as he could.

It was Bellomont's job to raise the funds, which he duly did – persuading four Whig peers to donate large sums of money to the operation: Lords Shrewsbury, Somers, Romney and Orford. The syndicate then approached the Admiralty for a privateering commission which – because England was at war with France – was granted them insofar as French vessels were concerned. In order to hunt down pirate ships, the syndicate had to obtain a patent under the Great Seal signed by the Lord Keeper of the Great Seal (who, conveniently enough, was Lord Somers) to the effect that Kidd could track down 'Pirates, Free-booters, and Sea Rovers'.[2] But perhaps the best part of the whole operation was that the King himself was persuaded to become involved. William III gave his approval to Kidd's privateering commission and authorized that all the partners involved could keep the profits from any ships that Kidd captured as long as he received a 10 per cent share.

Once this was established, all that remained to be done was to buy a warship and eventually a vessel was chosen – a thirty-four-cannon, 287-ton merchant ship called the *Adventure Galley*. She had been built at Deptford, on the banks of the Thames, in 1695 and had oarports and sweeps (the extended oars that could be used when the ship entered calm waters). The *Adventure Galley* was also capable of carrying upward of 150 men – yet despite her size she was also capable of going as fast as, if not faster than, any of the Royal Navy's warships.

On 10 April 1696 Captain William Kidd set sail for America, arriving in New York in the summer of that year where he recruited a further ninety men to join his crew. From New York Kidd then sailed toward Africa, a journey of about 3,100 miles, and on 27 January 1697 dropped anchor at Funchal, off the west coast of Madagascar. For a month the ship's crew rested before setting sail once again, first to Johanna Island, then to Mohilla Island where unfortunately Kidd lost thirty of his men to disease. Although these deaths were unsettling, what the crew found more distressing was the fact that up until this point they hadn't so much as touched oars with an enemy vessel. As they were on a 'no purchase, no pay' contract this in effect meant they had earned nothing over the past few months. Times were getting desperate. Kidd had to do something quickly, otherwise his men would desert him, but it is interesting to note that even though he was in difficulties, at no point did he seem to be considering piracy. As Charles Johnson points out, 'It does not appear all this while that he had the least design of turning pirate; for near Mohilla and Johanna both, he met with several Indian ships richly laden, to which he did not offer the least violence, though he was strong enough to have done what he pleased with them.'[3]

Instead, he told his crew that they would sail to the Red Sea but, on arriving there, far from trying to locate legitimate targets, something appears to have pushed Kidd to consider capturing ships that could never be considered his legitimate targets. He was allowed to capture only French ships or those vessels that flew the pirate flag, but somewhere between Madagascar and the Red Sea he decided to break the law.

On 11 August 1697 the Red Sea fleet departed from Mocha under the heavy protection of three European vessels employed by the East India Company – the most prominent of which was the forty-gun *Sceptre* commanded by Edward Barlow, who had recently been promoted to this position after the sudden death of the previous captain. Noticing a strange ship tailing them, Barlow became even more suspicious when he observed that the vessel was flying a red flag – not, as some commentators have suggested, the no-mercy flag of piracy, but instead the thinner red flag sometimes employed by the Royal Navy to signify a ship claiming superiority. Barlow was confused, but, wary of pirate ships and determined not to become the victim of an ambush, decided to ready his ship for attack. He fired a warning shot and raised the flag of the East India Company but, undeterred, Kidd made for one of the other ships in Barlow's convoy. Barlow then ordered his men to lower a boat and have him rowed across to the *Adventure Galley*. As he approached, he ordered his guns to fire at Kidd who, fearing for his life, swiftly retreated from the scene and sailed away.

Humiliated by this debacle and with an increasingly mutinous crew on his hands, Kidd was now desperate. Approaching the Malabar coast and spying a small trading vessel, the *Mary*, which was heading from Aden to Bombay, he had his men fire a warning shot across her bows then drew alongside. The ship, which was flying the English flag, was not a legitimate target for Kidd; nonetheless, he detained her commander, a man by the name of Captain Thomas Parker, while also torturing the *Mary*'s crew to find out where they had stowed their valuables. Johnson writes, 'He also used the men very cruelly, causing them to be hoisted up by the arms, and drubbed with a naked cutlass, to force them to discover whether they had money on board, and where it lay, but as they had neither gold nor silver on board, he got nothing by his cruelty.'[4] Instead, Kidd decided to use Captain Parker's comprehensive knowledge of the Indian coastline for his own purposes, and forced him to pilot the *Adventure Galley* down the coast of India where he hoped to plunder richer ships and thus make both him and his crew wealthy men.

Meanwhile, the ransacked *Mary*, having been abandoned by Kidd, sailed on to the port of Bombay where her crew immediately reported to the Portuguese authorities that Kidd had committed an act of piracy against them.

By now the *Adventure Galley* was sailing into Carawar on the west coast of India. Morale on board was at an all-time low – not only had the crew received no pay since leaving England, they were almost out of water. Kidd arranged for water to be taken on board, then rowed ashore to meet representatives of the East India Company who had offices in Carawar. These two gentlemen, Thomas Pattle and John Harvey, subsequently reported on the meeting to Sir John Gayer at company headquarters in Bombay:

> He [Captain Kidd] has on board 140 well men and 36 guns. He sayeth he
> hath been at Mohilla, Madagascar, etc. other places to look for pyrates,
> but yet hath not met with any and now is come to this coast with ye same

purpose; we understand he hath been at Moco [Mocha]. He says he thought to meet with pyrates there, but we are inclined to believe had it not been for ye convoy ships he would have made no scruple of taking 2 or 3 Surratt men. He makes many protestations that he will not injure anyone but those he has a commission from King of England. But not withstanding his fair pretences we much doubt his designes are as honest as they should be.[5]

Despite their reservations, Pattle and Harvey decided not to antagonize Kidd by attempting to arrest him, but concluded that the best course of action was to watch and wait for further evidence. Nor did they have to wait long for, shortly after Kidd had returned to his ship, two of his crew members, Benjamin Franks and Jonathan Treadway, turned up at the East India Company offices seeking asylum. The reason for this request? That Kidd was attempting to turn them into pirates against their will. If this wasn't condemnatory enough, Franks and Treadway further accused Kidd of having looted an English ship off Bombay – the *Mary* – and of detaining her captain against his will. From this point forward Captain William Kidd was officially labeled a pirate, although it was another incident altogether that really made his reputation as a man who shouldn't be crossed.

On 30 October 1697 an argument broke out between Kidd and his gunner, William Moore. As usual, the crew of the *Adventure Galley* had been grumbling about the lack of riches they had come across in their travels, when all of a sudden Kidd, tired of listening to talk of this nature, rounded on Moore and called him a lousy dog. Moore was then said to have replied, 'If I am a lousy dog, you have made me so; you have brought me to ruin and many more.'[6] Infuriated by this remark, Kidd then picked up an iron-hooped wooden bucket and brought it down on the gunner's temple. Moore immediately fell to the deck and, despite the surgeon's best efforts, never regained consciousness. He died the following day, but, far from feeling sorry for what he had done, Kidd remained unrepentant – something that didn't best please the crew who now felt even more loath to serve under their captain.

Nevertheless, serve they did and a few months after Moore's death, on 30 January 1698, the *Adventure Galley* detained the *Quedah Merchant*, a 400-ton merchant ship carrying eighteen guns, off the Malabar coast. Under the command of an English captain, John Wright, the *Quedah Merchant* was carrying a cargo of opium, muslin, silk, brown sugar, iron and calico to Bengal. Kidd, seeing his opportunity to make a quick killing, brought the *Adventure Galley* alongside while flying a French flag. At this time on the high seas it was normal for merchant vessels to carry passes of several nationalities to avoid capture by privateers. As Captain Kidd was flying the French flag, Captain Wright produced a French pass. This was a fatal mistake. Kidd, knowing he could legally attack French vessels, did just that – although in fact the *Quedah Merchant* wasn't French at all, but rather Armenian in origin (her owner being one Coji Baba), with a cargo that belonged for the most part to the Grand Moghul of India.[7]

None of this mattered to Kidd, who was eager only to sell off as much of the *Quedah*

Merchant's goods as he could as quickly as possible. He sailed her into the port of Kalliquilon (sometimes spelt Caliquilon) where he sold some of her goods for £7,000 (although he kept back a private stash of jewels and gold) before setting sail once again in search of further treasure.

Over the next few months Kidd successfully captured another ship, the *Rouparelle* and a Portuguese ship, which he kept as an escort for the *Adventure Galley*, then returned to Madagascar and the port of St Mary's. Already docked in the harbor was the pirate ship *Resolution*, under the command of Robert Culliford. This was a true test of Kidd's intentions. Had he been an honest privateer, then he would have had no option but to arrest Culliford and confiscate the *Resolution* (formerly known as the *Mocha Frigate*). But this never happened. Instead, Kidd informed Culliford that he wasn't going to place him in custody and indeed he went on to share several drinks with the old seadog.

Kidd stayed on in Madagascar for four months so that he and his crew could rest up. During this time he decided to abandon the *Adventure Galley*, which Charles Johnson describes as now being 'so old and leaky' that it was a hindrance to Kidd rather than a help. Replacing her with the far superior *Quedah Merchant*, Kidd renamed his new vessel the *Adventure Prize*, but, on sailing out in her and reaching one of the Dutch spice islands, it must have come as quite a shock to him when he heard that the East India Company (prompted by the complaint of Edward Barlow of the *Sceptre*) had declared him a pirate and that he was to be hunted down and brought to justice as soon as possible.

Kidd chose the Danish West India Company island of St Thomas to settle on next, and as soon as he arrived begged the Governor to grant him sanctuary. But Governor Laurents wanted nothing to do with Kidd – a refusal that soon made its way into the London newspapers where it was reported that 'the famous pyrate Captain Kidd in a ship of 30 guns and 250 men offered the Governor of St Thomas 45,000 pieces of eight in gold and a great present of goods, if he would protect him for a month, which he refused.'[8]

Setting sail once again, Kidd headed for Mona Island where he came across a man called Henry Bolton who, after much dealing and double-dealing, finally agreed to sell his vessel to Kidd. Kidd bought Bolton's sloop, the *St Antonio*, for 3,000 pieces of eight – well over what it was worth, but he was in no position to argue, as Bolton knew only too well. Further to this, Kidd also made a deal with Bolton that he would guard the *Quedah Merchant/Adventure Prize* while he, Kidd, set sail for New York

Kidd wanted to go home to America not only to see his family, but also to petition Governor Bellomont (the man who back in England had helped him gain his privateering commission) for a pardon, for more than anything else Kidd wanted to clear his name and have wiped from the record any inference that he was a pirate. It was a risky strategy, but on 9 June 1699 the *St Antonio* reached Oyster Bay, twenty-five miles from New York City, where Kidd was duly reunited with his wife and two daughters whom he had not seen for three years. Immediately afterwards he made contact with Lord Bellomont to see whether his old ally could help him.

At this point Captain Kidd was unaware that the Lord Justices back in England had a year previously sent orders to all their foreign governors, including Bellomont, to seize

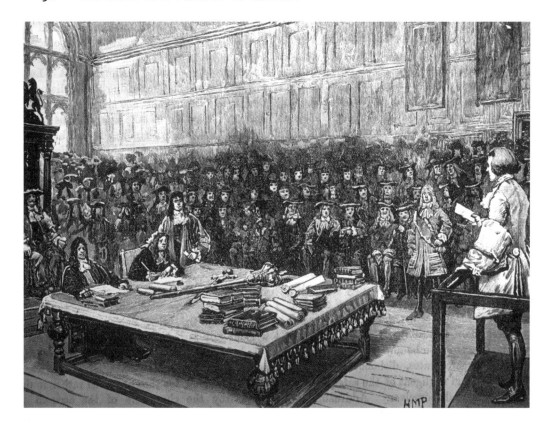

After his arrest for piracy, Kidd went to great lengths to prove his innocence, appearing before the House of Commons in London to try to prove that his deeds had been officially sanctioned. His influential friends had deserted him, however, and Kidd's pleas fell on deaf ears.

Kidd and return him to England where he was to stand trial for piracy. Bellomont, however, was a tricky fellow – although he had received this command, he hadn't relayed it to any of his council.

On the night of 13 June 1699 Bellomont met James Emott, Kidd's lawyer, who had already contacted Bellomont to the effect that:

> Kidd had brought 60 Pounds Weight of gold and 100 Weight of Silver and 17 Bales of East India Goods [...] That Kidd had left behind him a great Ship near the Coast of Hispaniola that nobody but himselfe could find out, on board whereof there were in bale goods, Saltpetre and other things to the value of £30,000: That if I would give him a pardon, he would bring in the Sloop and goods hither and would go and fetch the great Ship and goods afterwards.[9]

It was a difficult decision for Bellomont, one he didn't make lightly. After all, in many respects he was Kidd's business partner, but at the same time, by associating himself with Kidd, Bellomont also knew his political career might be in danger. Emott was sent away while Bellomont considered all his different options, only coming to a decision the next morning when he sent word to Kidd to the effect that he was welcome home; that he, Lord Bellomont, personally invited him to Boston and that a pardon was possible. Kidd duly arrived in Boston on 3 July 1699 for a meeting with his one-time sponsor, who had gathered together the entire Massachusetts Council for the occasion. In front of this august group Kidd was made to give an account of why he had seized the ships, together with an inventory of all the cargo he had accumulated. Kidd performed his task well, yet the council was not satisfied, requesting that Kidd return the following afternoon with documentation to back up his claims. This Kidd did, bringing with him five of his crew members: Samuel Arris (steward), Humphrey Clay (sailor), Abel Owen (cook), English Smith (sailor) and Hugh Parrot (gunner). All five men gave similar statements regarding the nature of their voyage and which ships they had captured, but the council was still not satisfied and asked Kidd to return that same afternoon.

Infuriated by their decision and annoyed that he had not been able to see Bellomont in private, Kidd decided to ambush his former ally while he was at lunch. Unbeknown to him, however, directly after he left the council chambers, Bellomont issued a warrant for Kidd's arrest. As soon as Kidd turned up at the building where Bellomont was dining, he was seized and thrown in jail. At the same time, the five crewmen who had accompanied him were also placed under arrest. The thing that eluded Lord Bellomont was the most prized possession of all: Captain Kidd's treasure – all the gold, silver and jewels that he had looted off the *Quedah Merchant/Adventure Prize*. For Bellomont (and for many treasure hunters down through the centuries) this was a huge blow, for everyone was convinced that Kidd had buried it somewhere between India and Boston – the most likely location being Gardiners Island near New York.

Back in London, meanwhile, news of Captain Kidd's arrest spread quickly – hardly surprising given that Kidd had initially had the backing not only of Whig peers, but the King himself. Public fascination was also rife, due to rumors about Kidd's 'buried' treasure (which was now estimated to be worth in the region of £400,000). The matter was even debated in Parliament, with a note of censure being handed out to the Whigs for their bad management of the affair.[10] Finally, the Admiralty ordered a ship be sent to Boston to bring Kidd back to England.

HMS *Advice* arrived in Boston in February 1700 during a particularly cold spell. So cold was it that the ship's commander, Captain Robert Wynn, said the entire Boston harbor was in danger of freezing over. Despite the icy conditions, Kidd, together with thirty-two other accused pirates, was escorted on board under heavily armed guard. The journey back to England was a long, arduous one with Kidd shackled in a cramped, windowless cabin. The room was unheated – a fact that soon began to affect Kidd's health. Nevertheless, he tried to make the best of his time and spent many long hours writing letters to both lawyers and friends. He also wrote a detailed journal of the voyage itself and began piecing together his defense.

On 10 April the *Advice* reached the Downs, a naval anchorage off the Kent coast.

The ship was met by the Admiralty Marshall, John Cheeke, flanked by two files of soldiers who removed Kidd from the ship, transferring him to the yacht called the *Katherine* which then set sail for London. A few days later, on 14 April, Kidd was delivered to the Admiralty office in Whitehall where he was interrogated by, among others, three Admiralty Lords: Sir George Rooke, Lord Haversham and the Earl of Bridgewater, who noted that, 'Captain Kidd was called in and particularly examined as to the severall pyracies layd to his charge, which Examination being read to him, he set his Name to it and then the Board signed it.'[11] Kidd defended himself by saying that he had captured only two ships and that these had both flown French flags and were therefore fair game under his privateering commission. Further to this, he also stated that his crew had forced him into acts of piracy and had not only robbed him of booty, but had also taken and destroyed all his records. The questioning took over seven hours to complete, after which Kidd was taken away to Newgate Prison where he remained for the next eleven months.

Newgate, even by the standards of eighteenth-century England, was a terrible place in which to be incarcerated. It was a dark, damp hellhole, a building that offered no comfort to its prisoners and one within which many died even before reaching trial. Kidd, already ill from his journey across the Atlantic, now suffered even more extensively. He spent ten long days negotiating his release from leg irons and would have had to barter for every scrap of food that he ate. The only reprieve from this continual degradation came in the form of a short trip to Whitehall on 27 March 1701 when he was to give evidence before the House of Commons.

Kidd was the first and only pirate ever to have done this, but after more than a year in Newgate he was hardly up to being dragged in front of the assembled Members of Parliament. A broken, wrecked man, he tried to accuse two of his former backers, Lord Somers and Lord Orford, of being complicit in the whole affair, but he failed dismally to convince anyone. Instead, on 31 March, Kidd was again called before Parliament, although the outcome of this hearing was much the same as before and he returned to Newgate in no better a position.

The Admiralty, meanwhile, had been busy gathering together evidence against their man. Henry Bolton, whom Kidd had left in charge of the *Quedah Merchant*, had been located and shipped to England, while Coji Baba – the merchant who had been on board that same ship when Kidd ransacked it – was brought over from India to give evidence to the effect that all his goods had been stolen. The Admiralty had also collated all of the documents relating to Kidd, including those kept by Lord Bellomont after he had had Kidd arrested in Boston.

In contrast, Kidd was given only two weeks in which to mount his defense (the trial date having been set for 8 May 1701), something he set about with as much energy as he could muster. Kidd asked for all the documentation concerning his privateering commissions be brought to him, along with the original orders he had received from the Admiralty as well as the French passes that were given to him by the captains of the *Quedah Merchant* and the *Rouparelle*. In fact, of all the documentation that Kidd asked

In Newgate Prison, where Kidd was held for over a year, the pirate's health deteriorated and he would have had to trade whatever was in his possession in order to acquire food. It was a poor way to prepare to defend himself when he was put on trial for his life.

for, the French passes were fundamental to his defense as they legalized his capture of both these vessels under his privateering commission. But luck was not on his side. The passes were nowhere to be found and Kidd was incandescent with rage. He accused the Admiralty of withholding vital evidence – an accusation which was probably correct, but he was hardly in a position to prove it. The Admiralty, on the other hand, wasn't unduly disturbed by Kidd's fury. Instead, so certain were they that he would be found guilty of piracy and put to death that even before his trial had started they began auctioning off his belongings.

Kidd, desperate to find any way out of his predicament, now began writing letters to as many influential people as he could, throwing himself on their mercy. He also wrote an impassioned speech, which he decided he would deliver in court, to the effect that it wasn't him that was guilty of piracy, but those men who had bought him his commission:

My Lord,

If the design I was sent upon, be illegal, or of ill consequences to the trade of the Nation, my Owners who knew the Laws, ought to suffer for It and not I, whom they made the Tool of their Covetousnesse. Some great men would have me die for Salving their Honour, and others to pacify the Mogull for injuryes done by other men, and not my selfe, and to secure their trade; but my Lord! Whatsoever my fate must be I shall not Contribute to my own destruction by pleading to this Indictment, till my passes are restored to me…Let me have my passes, I will plead presently, but without them I will not plead.

I am not afraid to dye, but will not be my own Murderer, and if an English

Court of Judicature will take my life for not pleading under my Circumstances, I will think my death will tend very little to the Credit of their Justice.

On Thursday 8 May 1701, Captain William Kidd, along with nine other men, was led from Newgate Prison to the Old Bailey. In front of them sat not only the five judges who were to hear the case (Sir Edward Ward, Baron Henry Hatsell, Justice Turton, Justice Gould and Justice John Powell), but also the Silver Oar of the Admiralty (a symbol of its authority), while all around curious onlookers gazed down from the public galleries. Kidd was accused of a long list of crimes, including the murder of William Moore (the man he had killed with the iron-hooped bucket) as well as the unlawful attack on the *Quedah Merchant* and four other vessels and the plundering of their cargo.

In his defense:

he insisted much upon his own innocence, and the villainy of his men; he said, he went out in a laudable employment, and had no occasion, being then in good circumstances, to go a-pirating; that the men often mutinied against him, and did as they pleased [...] As to the friendship shown to Culliford, a notorious pirate, Kid denied, and said, he intended to have taken him, but his men, being a parcel of rogues and villains refused to stand by him.[12]

In answer to the accusation that he had deliberately murdered William Moore, Kidd said that although he had never intended to kill him, he'd hoped that by striking Moore over the head it would put a stop to his villainous acts of defiance.

Unsurprisingly, however, the prosecution would have none of this. They had spent months amassing vast amounts of evidence against Kidd, not only paperwork, but also witnesses who now testified to his guilt. For instance, in the murder of William Moore the prosecution called to the witness stand ship's surgeon Robert Bradinham and crew member Joseph Palmer. Palmer was highly detailed in his account of what had happened. First he told the court that Kidd had walked up to Moore, who was busy grinding a chisel on deck, and immediately accused him of trying to turn the crew to piracy. Naturally Moore denied the charge after which Kidd (according to Palmer) had called Moore 'a lousy dog' and Palmer had replied, 'If I am a lousy dog, you have made me so; you have brought me to ruin and many more.' Kidd was then said to retort, 'Have I ruined you, you dog?' after which he picked up the bucket and brought it down hard on Moore's head.

Immediately Palmer had given this piece of evidence the prosecution asked him whether Kidd had given Moore the blow to the head *straight after* he had replied to Moore, or whether he had waited for awhile and then struck Moore. The answer was crucial in that the Crown wanted to prove Kidd guilty of murder, not manslaughter.

Palmer replied that Kidd had not struck Moore immediately, but had paced the deck several times, seemingly thinking about what to do next, before he delivered the fatal blow.

Kidd's fate was sealed. No amount of cross-questioning could get Palmer to give a less damning version of events. Worse even than this, had Kidd been given enough time by the court to access all the relevant documentation he might have been able to secure

Palmer's original deposition which he had made two years earlier back on Rhode Island and in which he stated that, 'I was not upon ye deck when ye blow was struck.'[13] As it was, Kidd was denied this opportunity and thus never stood a chance against the combined forces of the prosecution. When Bradinham came to give evidence he wasn't much more help to his former captain either, stating categorically that it was the blow to the head that killed Moore and, worse still, that Kidd had told him he didn't care that he had killed a man because he had influential friends back in England who would see him all right. Kidd was at a loss as to how to cross-examine this witness. He was a sailor, not a lawyer, but he pressed on to the best of his ability, cross-examining not just Bradinham but many other witnesses – though to little effect.

The jury withdrew to consider their verdict; meanwhile, the court pressed on with the second charge of the day: that of piracy against Kidd and nine other defendants. All ten delivered a plea of 'not guilty'.

Dr Newton, one of the chief prosecutors, then took to the floor. He accused Kidd not only of many piratical acts, but also of the torture of prisoners in order to elicit information as to the whereabouts of their valuables. As with the previous charge of murder, Kidd barely stood a chance. Dazed by the assault on his character (Newton called Kidd an 'Arch Pirate and Common Enemy of Mankind')[14], he hardly knew where to begin in his defense. One of the judges went on to accuse Kidd of bringing up the matter of the 'missing passes' too late and demanded to know why he hadn't complained about them before. Kidd was dumbfounded. He had done nothing but complain since being informed of their loss. There was nothing more to say and with that the jury retired.

Less than half an hour later they returned with their verdict: Kidd was guilty of all the charges laid against him. The court then adjourned until eight the next morning, at which point, after more legal argument, Kidd was sentenced to death. In reply to this pronouncement Kidd is said to have proclaimed, 'My Lord, it is a very hard Sentence. For my part, I am the innocentest Person of them all, only I have been sworn against by Perjured Persons.'[15] He was led from the dock, his thumbs bound by whipcord as was the tradition for men sentenced to death.

Having been hanged and his body then tied to a post on the waterfront where it was left for the tide to wash over it three times, Captain Kidd's remains were left dangling in an iron cage at Tilbury Point as a warning to other seamen not to turn to piracy.

A little under two weeks later Kidd was taken to Execution Dock. Pirate or privateer – in the end it mattered little, for he was hanged just the same.

Postscript

Although the bulk of Captain Kidd's treasure was never found, the Admiralty did confiscate certain items that were found either on or about his person, including some jewels and a small quantity of gold and silver. Eventually, on 13 November 1701, these were auctioned off by the Admiralty at the Marine Coffee House on Birchen Lane in London and fetched the grand total of £5,500. Some of the money was subsequently paid to Cogi Baba, the Armenian owner of the *Quedah Merchant*, while the rest was retained by the Admiralty.

1 Zacks, *The Pirate Hunter*.
2 Cordingly, *Life Among the Pirates*.
3 Johnson, *A General History…*
4 Ibid.
5 Zacks, op. cit.
6 Ritchie, *Captain Kidd and the War Against the Pirates*.
7 Cordingly, op. cit.
8 Brooks, *The Trial of Captain Kidd*.
9 Zacks, op. cit.
10 Cordingly, op. cit.
11 Ibid.
12 Johnson, op. cit.
13 Murphy, *Old Bailey*.
14 Zacks, op. cit.
15 Johnson, op. cit.

JOHN AVERY
King of Diamonds

[...]that he had built forts, erected magazines, and was master of
a stout squadron of ships, manned with able and desperate
fellows of all nations; that he gave commissions out in his own
name to the captains of his ships, and to the commanders of his
forts, and was acknowledged by them as their prince [...]. Yet all
these were no more than false rumors, improved by the credulity
of some, and the humor of others who love to tell strange things.

Captain Charles Johnson,
*A General History of the Robberies and
Murders of the Most Notorious Pirates*

Unusually, John Avery (also known as Henry Avery, Henry Every, Captain Benjamin Bridgeman, Henry Ivory and Long Ben) can probably put his longstanding notoriety down to a play that was written about him by the dramatist Charles Johnson (no relation to the Captain Charles Johnson who wrote the pirate history cited above), called *The Successful Pyrate*. The play, which was first performed in 1713, ran for several years at the Drury Lane Theatre in London, its success starting a long line of other, similar piratical melodramas, which culminated in 1879 with the Gilbert and Sullivan operetta *The Pirates of Penzance*. But it was Avery who set the ball rolling, who first inspired playwrights to put pen to paper and translate outlaws' lives to stage, becoming the prototype of many fictional pirates down through the centuries.

According to the historian Charles Grey, John Avery was born around 1653, near Plymouth at Cat Down in the south-west of England. Brought up first by his father, who was a 'landed proprietor', at the age of ten he was sent to live with an uncle when his father died. The uncle robbed the child of his inheritance (both money and property), after which he had the boy apprenticed to a 'brutal sea captain in the hope of his dying under the hardships of such a life'.[1] Despite this unfortunate start, Avery thrived at sea and eventually managed to find a position serving as a midshipman for the Royal Navy on board first HMS *Kent* and afterwards HMS *Rupert*. He saw active service at the bombardment of Algiers in 1671, and to all intents and purposes acquitted himself well there.

Never fully satisfied with his life in the Navy, he eventually furthered his career by joining a privateering operation, first on board the *Duke* and afterwards on the *Charles*. Both vessels had been hired to protect the trade of the Spanish West Indies from buccaneers and French smugglers. During this period, there was an alliance between Spain, England and Holland against France; however, according to Johnson, the French in Martinique began a smuggling trade with the Spanish in Peru – a trade that ran contrary to the laws of mainland Spain. Avery's ship was employed to put an end to this, but, evidently having an eye for the main chance, while the ship was in port in La Coruña he began persuading his fellow crewmen to seize it and set sail for the pirate haven of Madagascar in the Indian Ocean.

Madagascar (see also the chapter on Edward England, pages 99-109, and Glossary) was one of those islands that had over the years acquired a legendary status among pirates as being a safe haven, a place from which they could set sail and plunder merchant vessels before returning to its shores to enjoy their ill-gotten gains. First mapped by the Portuguese in 1506, it produced a seemingly never-ending source of food. 'It abounds with provisions of all sorts,' writes Johnson, 'oxen, goats, sheep, poultry, fish, citrons, oranges, tamarinds, dates, coconuts, bananas, wax, honey, rice; or in short, cotton, indigo, or any other thing they will take pains to plant and have understanding to manage.'[2] As a consequence, it was hardly surprising that the island in general and its main harbor at St Mary's Island (Isle Sainte Marie) in particular became a base for pirates from all over the world. Indeed, legend has it that the pirates on Madagascar lived like kings. 'They married the most beautiful of the Negro women, not one or two, but as many as they liked; so that every one of them had as great a

This depiction of John Avery shows him standing on dry land in a dramatic pose while his crew engages one of the ships of the Great Moghul. Avery plundered a fortune in gold, silver and jewels that were bound for the Moghul Empire in India.

seraglio as the Grand Seignior at Constantinople: their slaves they employed in planting rice, in fishing, hunting, &c, besides which, they had abundance of others, who lived, as it were, under their protection.'[3]

Among their number, Captain Kidd (see page 51) arrived at St Mary's Island in 1698 to set up home, while at the southern end of the island a pirate by the name of Abraham Samuel established himself at Fort Dauphin, where he was treated as a king by the natives. A third pirate called James Plantain set himself up as King of Ranter Bay where he kept a whole harem of women. But despite their successes, the idyll was not to last. Warfare broke out not just between the pirates, but also between rival groups of natives, added to which tropical diseases ran rife. Indeed, by the time Captain Woodes Rogers (see Glossary) arrived in Cape Town, South Africa, in 1711 and spoke to two former residents of Madagascar who had lived for several years with the pirates, things had gone from bad to worse. 'They told me that those miserable wretches, who had made such a noise in the world, were now dwindled to between 60 or 70, most of them very poor and despicable, even to the natives, among whom they had married.'[4]

But this was all long after Avery's decision to head for Madagascar. All he had to do was persuade enough of the *Charles'* crew to turn against their captain, after which he could take control of the ship and sail if not into the sunset then at least toward an equally golden destination. Nor was it too difficult for him to execute his plans for, as Charles Johnson describes:

> **It must be observed that the captain was one of those who are mightily addicted to punch, so that he passed most of his time on shore [drinking] . . . but this day he did not go on shore as usual. However, this did not spoil the design for he took his usual dose on board and so got to bed before the hour appointed for business: the men also who were not privy to the design turned into their hammocks, leaving none upon deck but the conspirators who, indeed, were the greatest part of the ship's crew.**

Avery, who had also persuaded the majority of the crew on board the *Charles'* sister ship, the *Duchess*, to join in the mutiny, waited for the second ship to join them before setting sail. It was only after the ships were at sea that Avery finally informed the captain he had been deposed and that he, Avery, was now in charge: 'I am captain of this ship now, and this is my cabin, therefore you must walk out. I am bound to Madagascar with a design of making my own fortune and that of all the brave fellows joined with me.'[5]

Naturally the captain was distressed, but Avery, far from wanting bloodshed at this early stage in his piratical career, gave the captain and the other crew members a choice. Either they could join him in his venture or they could go back to the mainland in a separate boat. The captain, together with a handful of men, chose the latter option and soon afterwards found themselves rowing toward the African coastline. In fact, between the years 1715 and 1737 (slightly later than the Avery mutiny, but none the less relevant to it) it was recorded that forty-eight mutinies occurred on the high seas – one of the most notorious of which was occasioned by a Scottish pirate called John Gow (sometimes known as John Smith) who, while sailing on board the *George Galley* from

Morocco to France in 1724, cruelly cut the throats of the ship's chief mate, her surgeon and her clerk and later did the same to the captain (Oliver Ferneau) whom he then shot in the head. Afterwards Gow threw the corpses into the ocean and forced the rest of the crew into piracy. Little wonder then that the seas were so unsafe or that captains feared their crew as much as, if not more than, attacks from other ships.

Having achieved his goal, Avery now changed the name of the ship – from the *Charles* to the *Fancy* – and hoisted his new flag, one that closely resembled the skull-and-crossbones-style Jolly Roger of piratical legend. During the sixteenth century, the skull-and-crossbones had often been used by pirates as a means of conveying to their victims that they should surrender without a struggle. What is not commonly known is that a plain red flag was in fact a more frightening symbol to mariners, because when this was hoisted on a pirate ship it signaled death to all who saw it. No one would be left alive if a red flag was flying – the pirates would give no quarter to their victims – whereas at least with the Jolly Roger mariners had a chance of surviving as long as they didn't put up a fight.

Avery now set sail southwards along the African coast. On arrival at the Cape Verde Islands the pirates plundered three British ships, while near São Tomé they destroyed two Danish vessels.

In the early part of 1695, Avery reached Johanna Island in the Comoros, where he and his men captured a French pirate ship that was loaded with booty. Most of the French pirates joined Avery's crew, bringing the total number of his men to about 170. The *Fancy* was now armed with forty-six guns and for a short while afterwards was joined by three other pirate ships: the *Pearl,* under the captaincy of William Maze (or May) and the *Portsmouth Adventure,* under the captaincy of Joseph Faro (or Ferro), both from Rhode Island, along with the *Amity* from New York which was captained by Thomas Tew. It was during this period, when Avery's resources were at their highest, that he enjoyed his most famous victory.

In May or June of 1695 the *Fancy* reached the Red Sea, where one of Avery's crew soon sighted a group of tall ships which at first he believed might be a group of Dutch East Indiamen making their way home. In the event, however, the ships turned out to be of far greater worth, for when the *Fancy* fired on them and signaled that they were to bring to, the first of the ships hoisted the Moghul's colors. Suddenly Avery realized what he had within his sights – the ships before him belonged to none other than the Emperor of the Moghul Empire in India. These ships would be loaded with riches: spices, gold, coffee, cloth and jewels.

After a protracted battle during which both sides suffered heavy losses, Avery's men eventually overthrew the first of the Great Moghul's vessels – the *Fath Mahmamadi* (or *Fateh Mahomed*) which was believed to have been carrying more than £50,000 in gold and silver. Buoyed up by their success, Avery's men then went after the jewel in the Great Moghul's crown – the *Ganj-i-Sawai* (sometimes known as the *Gunsway*) – which was the largest ship in the Indian fleet. At this point it is worth quoting a first-hand account that appears in Charles Grey's book, *Pirates of the Eastern Seas*, supposedly written by an approver called Philip Middleton (an approver being an accomplice in a crime who gives evidence against former partners):

After we had cruised for some time in the Red Sea without making prize, we had intelligence of two rich ships bound from Mocha to Surat, but missed them, they passing in the night. The next day we took a small junk bound inwards from which we heard of the ships being gone before, and so made haste after them. The next day we came up with the smaller (the Fateh Mahomed), which we took with little or no resistance. In the afternoon we came up with the large ship which fought us strongly for two hours killing many of our men. On this ship there were about 1,300 persons and on the smaller about 700. We kept both ships in our possession for two days, and all the men from the Fancy, saving Every himself, boarded them in turn.

We took out of the said ships provisions and all other necessaries, and all their treasure which was very great. But what we got was little in comparison to what was said to be aboard, of which none told, though we put them to the torture. Yet they would not confess. We took great quantities of gold, silver and jewels and a saddle set with rubies destined a present to the Great Mogul. The men lay with the women aboard, and there were several that, from their jewels and habits, seemed to be of better quality than the rest. The great ship was called the Gang-I-Sawai.

Avery had luck on his side when he attacked the Great Moghul's ship, the Gang-i-Sawai. *His prey was heavily armed with 400 riflemen and 40 cannon, but one of Avery's first cannon shots brought down his enemy's main mast.*

In fact, the *Gang-i-Sawai*'s captain, Muhammed Ibrahim, had forty guns at his disposal as well as 400 rifles ready to defend his ship against attack. But Avery had luck on his side – one of the very first shots fired from the *Fancy* brought down the *Gang-i-Sawai*'s mainmast. Shortly after this, one of the Indian ship's cannons exploded, causing a huge amount of confusion on board – all of which helped Avery's men to overcome their opponents and take the ship, which was laden with even more jewels, gold and silver than her sister vessel.

According to legend, however, there was an even bigger prize on board: one of the Great Moghul's daughters, together with several of her attendants and numerous slave girls. Some accounts have it that the ship's captain, Muhammed Ibrahim, persuaded these women to dress up as men and fight their attackers, but this is highly unlikely, as is the story by Charles Johnson which states that Avery subsequently 'married the Great Mogul's daughter [...] and that he had by her many children'.

What is less in doubt is that, with women on board, the pirates would hardly behave like gentlemen. Although Avery later stated that they weren't injured in any manner, one of his pirate crew, a man by the name of John Sparcks, later confessed before his death at Execution Dock on 25 October 1696 that they had committed 'the most horrid barbarities [...] which though upon the persons of heathens and infidels, such as the forementioned poor Indians, so inhumanely rifled and treated so unmercifully, declaring that he justly suffered death for such inhumanity.'[6] No doubt these acts included rape – a common enough practice among pirates who would have been at sea for weeks, if not months, without female company.

Afterwards the pirates, including John Sparcks, made their way back to the *Fancy* with their ill-gotten gains. Avery was all for setting sail then and there, but first the crews of all the different pirate ships persuaded him to divide the booty up between them, each member receiving about £1,000 apiece plus various items of jewelry – although Avery, as overall leader, was said to have taken double the share of any of his crew. The *Fancy* then set sail for Réunion Island.

However, according to Charles Johnson, Avery – not satisfied with having stolen from the Great Moghul – now decided he wanted to steal from his fellow pirates, in particular those Americans who had helped him ransack the *Gang-i-Sawai*.

Calling the captains of each of the American ships to come aboard the *Fancy* for a meeting, Avery suggested that until the ships docked on dry land their treasure was unsafe. For instance, if a storm occurred one of the ships might sink, or if they came across other pirate vessels one of their ships might be looted. Wouldn't it therefore be safer if they all gave him their treasure for safekeeping? After all, the *Fancy* was a far superior ship to either of theirs, sturdier in build and carrying more guns. Avery said he would take on board all their treasure and place it in crates which would then be sealed three times over. Surprisingly, the other captains agreed to this plan and duly brought their spoils aboard the *Fancy*, where they were placed in the crates and sealed up.

For the next two or three days, all the ships – the *Fancy*, the *Portsmouth Adventure*, the *Amity* and the *Pearl* – sailed closely together toward a common meeting point on dry land.

But during this time, Avery began persuading the *Fancy*'s crew that the best course of action would now be to give the other ships the slip and make off with all the treasure themselves. This agreed, Avery waited until nightfall and then, under cover of darkness, steered an opposite course to the other three ships until finally the *Fancy* slipped out of sight.

'I leave the reader to judge,' writes Johnson, 'what swearing and confusion there was among the sloop's men in the morning when they saw that Avery had given them the slip; for they knew by the fairness of the weather, and the course they had agreed to steer, that it must have been done on purpose.'

The *Fancy* headed first for Réunion Island, where most of the French pirates decided to stay. A handful of the English crew returned to England, while Avery and the rest of his men then set sail for America.

Meanwhile, the Great Moghul, having heard news of his fleet's fate and being informed it was English pirates who had looted his property, threatened to send a 'mighty army with fire and sword, to extirpate the English from all their settlements on the Indian coast'.[7] Consequently, the East India Company promised to bring Avery and his men to justice, but sending a whole fleet of ships to the Indian Ocean to wipe out the pirates would have been too expensive. Instead, Captain William Kidd, who at that time was acting as a privateer, was persuaded to pursue Avery, along with several other notorious pirates. This venture was supported by the King, but even with this royal seal of approval, the mission was doomed to failure, for no sooner had Kidd reached the Indian Ocean then he swapped allegiances and joined the pirates himself. Despite Kidd's betrayal, the East India Company did eventually capture six of Avery's crew, all of whom were put on trial at the Old Bailey in London in October 1696. All six were sentenced to hang at Execution Dock – a notorious place of public execution in London's East End.

Executions were public affairs, with the convicted pirates being taken from the Marshalsea Prison in London (or on occasion Newgate Prison) by cart, led by an officer carrying a silver oar – the symbol of the High Court of the Admiralty, whose job it was to patrol the high seas and ensure safe passage for all vessels. On arrival at Execution Dock, a few miles downstream from London Bridge, the prisoners would be led to the gallows, which were built on the foreshore of the River Thames at the low-tide mark. Standing on the wooden gallows with a rope placed round their necks, the pirates would be made to listen to a sermon from a chaplain before they were allowed their final speech. The pirates' last words were the subject of great speculation and were more often than not reprinted and handed out to the general public, whose appetite for such things was insatiable. After the execution the pirates' bodies would then be left until three tides had passed over them (a law first passed by the Admiralty), after which they would normally be cut down and either buried or hung in a gibbet cage. These contraptions were made of wood and were often made to fit, individual bodies – the victim would be measured before his execution so that the carpenter could get the exact proportions. After death, the body would be painted in tar to preserve the flesh for as long as possible, then placed in the cage and hung up as a grim reminder to others not to pursue a life of crime.

The treasure from the Great Moghul's ships was transferred to Avery's vessel, the Fancy, *at sea over a period of two days. Although the pirates did not believe that they had looted all of the ships' valuables, the passengers and crew denied under torture that there was any more hidden aboard.*

Executions and the practice of afterwards hanging corpses in chains were frequent in seventeenth- and eighteenth-century England, but, as the practice of piracy quickly spread far and wide, an Act of Parliament was passed authorizing the Vice-Admiralty Courts to be held in the colonies. Surprisingly perhaps, given the distance of these foreign hearings, the executions were remarkably similar to those held at Execution Dock back in England. In 1704 the pirate John Quelch and twenty-four of his comrades were put on trial in Boston. His crime was to have instigated a mutiny and taken over the ship on which he was serving, hoisting the pirate flag and looting nine Portuguese ships of their cargo, which included large amounts of gold and silver. The trial was a long affair, but eventually Quelch and seven of his men were convicted and sentenced to death. Taken from the jail, they were led to the Boston waterfront behind a man carrying a silver oar. They were then rowed across the harbor to an island on which was erected a wooden gallows. Judge Sewell, who was present at the time, noted: 'When I came to see how the river was cover'd with people, I was amazed. Some way there were 100 boats [...]When the scaffold was hoisted to a due height, the seven Malefactors went up. Mr Mather prayed for them standing upon the boat. Ropes were fastened to the gallows. When the scaffold was let to sink there was such a screech of the women that my wife heard it sitting in her entry next the orchard and was much surprised by it.'[8]

No doubt, this was almost exactly how Avery's six crew members were eventually executed yet, despite this one small success and much to their annoyance, the East India Company failed to capture Avery himself, a fact that only added to his growing reputation as an unassailable enemy, an outlaw who could never be tracked down nor brought to book. Indeed, it was this growing reputation that probably caused so much literature (including poetry) to be written about him, the culmination of which was Charles Johnson's play, where Avery appears as the character Arviragus, a successful pirate who eventually settles down on the island of Madagascar. At the beginning of the play we learn of the capture of an Indian ship by Arviragus who subsequently brings it into the port of Laurentia replete with gold, silver and jewels as well as the granddaughter of the Great Moghul, a beautiful young girl called Zaida.

The Great Moghul's granddaughter is in love with a boy called Aranes, but Arviragus is jealous – a conundrum which, much like in the plays of Shakespeare, is finally resolved when at the end of the play it transpires that Aranes is in fact Arviragus' long-lost son. The young couple marry with Arviragus' blessing while Arviragus himself retires to live off his ill-gotten gains.

Avery's real life, however, did not have such a happy ending. Sailing for America, he stopped off at the Bahamas where the Governor of Providence Island, Nicholas Trott, welcomed him and his men in return for a bribe. Once again, Philip Middleton provides a fascinating account of this time in his deposition:

At the Bahamas the Pyrates were hospitably received by Governor Nicholas Trott to whom they made a present of twenty dollars a man (about £900) and two gold sequins each. They were then permitted to come ashore and publicly entertained at his house. One of them accidentally broke a glass for which the Governor made him pay eight sequins (£3 16s). In the end they made a present of the ship and some elephant's teeth to the Governor which he shared with the Deputy Governor, Nicholas Taliaferro.'[9]

From the Bahamas, in a new sloop he had bought from Governor Trott (because he feared the *Fancy* would be recognized and he would be arrested), Avery then set sail for New England, calling in at various ports along the eastern coast where several of his men decided to chance their luck and disembark in order to set up home.

Eventually, Avery reached Boston, where he toyed with the idea of settling down himself. He'd had enough of piracy – he yearned for a simpler, less exacting life – but at the last minute changed his mind, due in the main to the fact that the major part of his wealth lay not in ready cash, but in diamonds, a far more difficult commodity to trade and one that was bound to draw attention to himself and his men. Avery decided, along with a small group of remaining pirates, to sail for Ireland instead.

On arrival, the pirates dispersed, some of them going to live in Dublin, while others went to Cork. Eighteen of their number then petitioned King William for a pardon, which, surprisingly, was granted them, but Avery was not among this lucky band. Instead he ran into the same problem he had had back in America – most of his wealth lay in diamonds and trading in these attracted too much attention. Avery then decided to sail for England where he knew a handful of men whom he trusted enough to trade the diamonds for money without turning him over to the authorities. Landing in the south-west, he sent word to Bristol for these individuals to meet him in the town of Bideford in Devon. Between them, they concluded that the safest way forward was for Avery's friends to arrange a meeting with some merchants who would take the diamonds, trade them and afterwards bring the cash back to Avery for a small commission. Avery seemed satisfied with this proposition and delivered his stash of jewels to the merchants then waited for them to return. In the meantime, he changed his name and continued to live on in Bideford, leading a quiet life, trying not to draw attention to himself.

Money was tight, however, and eventually he wrote to the merchants indicating that he needed funds. In turn, they sent him a small remuneration, but nothing like the amount that was owed him for the diamonds. Avery had run up huge debts that he could not pay off – he barely had enough money for bread – so eventually, in desperation, he traveled to Bristol to talk to the merchants face to face. But he was to be bitterly disappointed. As soon as he made contact with these men they left him in no doubt he would never see his money again. Indeed, they told him that if he continued to press them they would turn him over to the authorities who still wanted him in connection with the attack on the Great Moghul's ship. Frightened by this threat, Avery decided his best option was to sail back to Ireland, from where he continued to press the merchants for what was owed him. Naturally, they weren't forthcoming and Avery was reduced to begging on the streets. Eventually, he bought passage on a ship back to Plymouth and from there returned to Bideford where it is believed he lived on for a short time, a broken and bitter man, before falling sick and dying in penury.

Avery did not leave enough money even for a basic coffin and was therefore probably buried in a pauper's grave, although there is no record of this. In fact, there is no record of his death at all, but this might well be the result of his adopting so many different names.

Mr Hill mentions that a search through the Bideford registers of 1728 (when Every was supposed to have died) has revealed nothing [. . .]It may be noted that Captain Phillips [commander of the _Hannibal_ who, according to his own writings, came across Avery more than once], who probably knew Every personally, always speaks of him as 'Long Ben alias

Every' and it is quite possible that his true name was Benjamin Bridgeman.[10]

Whatever the case, fading away as he is believed to have done, rather than dying in battle or striding defiantly to the gallows, is a rather anti-climactic, drab end to the life of one of history's, and the theater's, most colorful pirates.

1 Grey, *Pirates of the Eastern Seas.*

2 Johnson, *A General History…*

3 Ibid.

4 Rogers, *A Cruising Voyage Round the World.*

5 Johnson, op. cit.

6. Hill, *Notes on Piracy in Eastern Waters.*

7 Johnson, op. cit.

8 Cordingly and Falconer, *Pirates: Fact and Fiction.*

9 Grey, op. cit.

10 Ibid.

EDWARD TEACH

Blackbeard

The beard was black, which he suffered to grow of an extravagant length; as to breadth it came up to his eyes. He was accustomed to twist it with ribbons, in small tails, after the manner of our ramilies wigs, and turn them about his ears.

Captain Charles Johnson,
*A General History of the Robberies and
Murders of the Most Notorious Pirates*

If a roll call was made of all the most notorious pirates in history, Edward Teach – better known as Blackbeard – would no doubt appear at the top. Mad, bad and dangerous to know, his terrifying appearance, daring raids and murderous exploits – not to mention the fact that he was said to have been married to no fewer than fourteen women – made him not only a legend in his own lifetime, but also one of the most terrifying pirates ever to have plagued the Atlantic Coast.

Most historians concur that at the time of his death Teach was thirty-five or forty years of age, which would put his birth at around 1680. Other than that, little is known of Teach's childhood except that he was from Bristol in the south-west of England. Given that this city is built where the rivers Avon and Frome meet and that the Bristol Channel is only about eight miles distant, it is little wonder Teach chose to follow a career at sea. There are no records, however, pointing to when this might have occurred; indeed the earliest mention of Teach comes in Captain Charles Johnson's *A General History of the Robberies and Murders of the Most Notorious Pirates* which states that Teach 'had sailed some time out of Jamaica in privateers, in the late French war; yet though he had often distinguished himself for his uncommon boldness and personal courage, he was never raised to any command, till he went a-pirating'.

That Teach ended up in the West Indies is not surprising, given that during the seventeenth and eighteenth centuries these islands were notorious for harboring rogues of all types. It was from here, after all, that the Brethren of the Coast (see the chapter on Henry Morgan, page 38, and the Glossary) operated, a group of buccaneers whose common love of adventure, gold and hatred of Spain made them a formidable fighting force.[1]

But Teach's story really begins only when he sailed to New Providence Island in the Bahamas – also a notorious rendezvous point for all manner of sea rovers – for it was here that he met up with a Captain Benjamin Hornigold. Hornigold was one of the fiercest pirates who ever operated out of New Providence. He commanded huge respect from other pirates and was held in very high esteem by the Brethren of the Coast. For a young, up-and-coming seadog, Teach could have apprenticed himself to no one better. From Nassau Harbor, Hornigold and his willing young apprentice made many a trip, during which they captured French and Spanish ships. 'As an eager young hand aboard Hornigold's pirate ship, Teach showed that he had a marksman's eye, an ability at dirty infighting and a thirst for blood unmatched by any pirate of his time. Hornigold recognized this early and made the young man his protégé.'[2]

Not only did he make Teach his protégé; some time during 1716, the two men having captured a large sloop, Hornigold gave its command over to his pupil. Equipping the ship with six cannons and appointing himself a crew of just over seventy men, Teach was in his element. He and Hornigold now set off together, each captaining his own vessel, and soon captured a sloop bound for Havana which was carrying a cargo of 120 barrels of flour. Next came two other vessels, one carrying gallons of wine and the other 'plunder to a considerable value'.[3]

Shortly after this, they spied a large vessel that was sailing from Madeira to South

Edward Teach became known as 'Blackbeard' after he grew his beard long, braiding it into separate strands and tying it with colored ribbons. He also tied lighted fuse cords under his hat so that he appeared to his victim amid a swirling cloud of smoke.

Carolina. Acting in tandem, Hornigold and Teach's vessels bore down upon their target so swiftly that it is said the captain barely realized what was happening. As a result, he put up no resistance to the pirates, who made off with a substantial amount of money.

Similarly, several months later, during the latter part of 1719, by which time Hornigold and Teach had sailed back to the West Indies, they spotted another large vessel, a French guineaman or slave ship, off the coast of the island of St Vincent. As with their previous attack, both pirates bore down on their prey with such speed that the merchantman's crew, commanded by one Captain D'Ocier, barely knew what was happening. 'Hornigold's sloop closed in on one quarter, Teach's sloop on the other. Before the merchantman's captain could decide what procedure to take, both pirate ships fired a broadside across his bulwarks that killed half his men and terrified the remainder into surrender.'[4]

The rewards were substantial. The guineaman, which was called the *Concord*, was carrying not only jewels and silver plate, but also a large amount of gold dust. It was around this time that Hornigold – perhaps realizing that he now had enough money to retire on – decided to stop pirating and turn his hand to more honest pursuits. He gave the *Concord* over to his pupil, bid him goodbye and returned to New Providence where he bought some land and set himself up in the plantation business. It was a sensible decision. Life for pirates in these waters was daily becoming less profitable and more dangerous. On 6 February 1718, for instance, Captain Rogers – who between the years 1708 and 1711 had commanded a privateering voyage around the world – arrived in the West Indies to take up the post as Governor of the Bahamas. His commission, which came directly from the British government, was to rid this area of its pirate community. Sailing into Nassau with three warships, Rogers had it within his powers to issue a King's Pardon to any pirate willing to abandon their trade. Those who didn't were to be treated just like any other common criminal – hunted down, brought to justice and afterwards executed.

Benjamin Hornigold, seeing an opportunity to settle down and begin a legitimate business, took full advantage of the King's Pardon. Teach did not. Instead, having been given the *Concord*, he renamed her the *Queen Anne's Revenge* and set about equipping her with forty new guns. Teach also employed the services of about 300 crewmen, then sailed southward toward the island of St Vincent, where he spotted a merchant ship called the *Great Allen*. It was commanded by Christopher Taylor and was bound to Jamaica from Barbados. After a lengthy battle Taylor surrendered to Teach who quickly transferred all the booty over to the *Queen Anne* and afterwards burned the *Great Allen*.

A few days later Teach encountered a British man-of-war called the *Scarborough* which was fitted with thirty guns and had been sent into those waters specifically to seek out and capture the *Queen Anne's Revenge*. Teach could probably have outrun his rival, but rather than flee he decided to stand and fight. A skirmish ensued, with the *Scarborough* opening fire first and Teach then firing a broadside that tore through the *Scarborough*'s sails. In fact, the skirmish continued for several hours, with the crews on both sides testing each other's nerves until eventually the commander of the

Scarborough, deciding that his ship had suffered enough damage, 'gave over the engagement and returned to Barbados'.[5] It was a blow to Teach, who never liked letting a quarry escape, but he decided not to give chase as it wasn't worth risking the lives of his crew in order to capture a vessel that was practically cargo-less. Instead, he allowed the *Scarborough* to escape while he sailed toward Spanish America.

According to Robert E. Lee in his book *Blackbeard the Pirate*, it was around this time that he decided to grow his eponymous beard. Teach already had a reputation for being a bold and fearless pirate, but, according to Lee, he now became convinced these attributes alone weren't sufficient 'if he was to become a successful pirate with the minimum of risk to his crew and ship. He needed an image. He was a student of psychological warfare far ahead of his time.'

Teach's beard was coarse and jet-black, and was said to extend across his whole face and to reach an extravagant length, almost down to his midriff. Not only that, but he then began separating out parts of it, braiding and tying them with different colored pieces of ribbon. The beard became his trademark, one that not only served to terrify his crew and his opponents alike, but which also guaranteed him lasting notoriety. Charles Johnson, for instance, noted that Teach 'assumed the cognomen of Blackbeard from that large quantity of hair which, like a frightful meteor, covered his whole face and frightened America more than any comet that has appeared there a long time'. Along with the beard, Teach was also prone to wearing (mostly in times of battle) a sling across his shoulder in which he kept two or three pistols, 'hanging in holsters like bandaliers [sic], and stuck lighted matches under his hat which appearing on each side of his face, his eyes naturally looking fierce and wild, made him altogether such a figure, that imagination cannot form an idea of a fury, from hell, to look more frightful'.[6] The 'matches', which were kept under his hat, were probably made out of hemp cord dipped in a mixture of saltpetre and lime water. They would have burnt slowly, but the smoke they caused to curl around his head must have made for the most extraordinary spectacle. Little wonder, then, that the sailors who were unfortunate enough to come across Blackbeard (particularly in battle) were said to think of him as the Devil.

But, as many commentators have pointed out, although his image was fearsome, although he struck the fear of death into his countless opponents, Blackbeard could also be a fair-minded man. When he detained a ship, if everyone on board did exactly as they were ordered then, apart from being relieved of their property, nothing worse would happen to them. If, on the other hand, they refused his orders then the consequences were severe. 'If a victim,' writes Addison Whipple in his book *Pirate Rascals of the Spanish Main*, 'did not voluntarily offer up a diamond ring, Blackbeard chopped it off, finger and all [for] while Blackbeard could be merciful to those who co-operated, woe to those who did not.'

Another example of the darker side to his nature involves a man by the name of Israel Hands, who one night was drinking with Teach and another pirate in Teach's cabin. Without provocation, or so the story goes, Teach drew out a pair of pistols and hid them under the table. The third man in the group, seeing him do this, quickly retired from the room, after which Teach is said to have blown out the candle, crossed his hands under the table and fired both guns. One of the bullets tore through Hands' knee, crippling him for life. When asked by his fellow pirates why he had done such an evil thing Teach was said to have replied that 'if he did not now and then kill one of them, they would forget who he was'.[7]

But if Blackbeard was the scourge of pirates and law-abiding citizens alike, there was one group of people who in particular flocked to his side and found him irresistibly charming. Women loved Blackbeard and Blackbeard loved women.[8] Whenever he entered a grog shop or tavern, girls would flock to him. It is said that Blackbeard was constantly taking women back to the *Queen Anne* where he would marry them, but whether this is true or not is almost impossible to establish. Certainly, Johnson describes Blackbeard at one time marrying a young girl who was barely more than sixteen years of age, 'and this I have been informed, made Teach's fourteenth wife, whereof about a dozen might be still living'. But there is no documentary evidence to back this claim up so although it could be true, it might also simply be part of the myth-making of which Blackbeard seemed so inordinately fond.

On 5 December 1717, spying a merchant ship – the *Margaret* – off the coast of Crab Island, Blackbeard ordered her commander, a Captain Henry Bostock, to join him on board the *Queen Anne's Revenge*. Blackbeard then proceeded to strip the *Margaret* of her cargo, which consisted mainly of livestock, after which he removed the *Margaret*'s guns and ammunition then returned the captain to his ship and allowed him and his crew (minus two men who joined up as pirates) to sail away without being harmed. Bostock subsequently docked at St Christopher's Island where he reported his encounter with Blackbeard to Governor Walter Hamilton, who asked Bostock to write out a deposition of the incident.

Meanwhile, Blackbeard, heading for the Bay of Honduras, came across a twenty-gun pirate sloop called the *Revenge*, commanded by Major Stede Bonnet. When they met, the two men got along famously. So well did they bond that for a while they decided to work alongside one another. However, the relationship was not to last long for Bonnet soon proved a fairly inadequate seaman, let alone pirate, and Teach grew tired of him, replacing him with his second-in-command – an old-time pirate called Lieutenant Richards.

The two pirate ships, the *Queen Anne's Revenge* and the *Revenge*, now sailed for Turneffe Island where they spotted a sloop called the *Adventure* from Jamaica and quickly caught up with her. Her commander, Captain David Harriot, was ordered aboard Blackbeard's vessel where he and his crew were 'invited' to join forces with the pirates. Wisely, he accepted this offer.

With a force of three well-armed ships and both Bonnet and Harriot's crews working for him, Teach was now in an extremely powerful position. On 9 April 1718 his fleet continued on toward the Bay of Honduras where they soon came across a large merchant vessel, the *Protestant Caesar* of Boston, along with four smaller sloops. No sooner were they spotted than Blackbeard and his cohorts descended upon them. In fear for their lives, all five crews surrendered. The *Protestant Caesar* was then 'relieved'

Blackbeard does battle with Lieutenant Robert Maynard. Maynard later testified that the pirate was shot in the chest five times and sustained at least twenty sword wounds to other parts of his body before a cut to the neck practically beheaded him.

of her cargo and set on fire, as was one of the smaller sloops. The other three were later released, but not before they had relinquished what little booty they carried on board.

From the Bay of Honduras the pirates now made their way to Grand Cayman, where once again they wrecked havoc, capturing several vessels, including a small turtler, a Spanish sloop and an English brigantine. Riding high on these successes, Blackbeard then began to steer his small squadron toward what would be their boldest exploit yet.

A letter dated 31 May 1718 from Governor Bennett of Bermuda to the Council of Trade and Plantations reported that among several pirate ships seen floating off their coastline was 'one Tatch [Teach] with whom is Major Bonnett of Barbados in a ship of 36 guns and 300 men, also in company with them a sloop of 12 guns and 115 men, and two other ships, in all of which, it is computed there are 700 men or thereabout.'[9]

What Teach was up to soon became clear. Some time near the end of May 1718 his small squadron of ships had arrived at the entrance to the harbor of Charleston, South Carolina, and proceeded to mount a blockade. At that time Charleston was one of the busiest ports in the southern colonies and therefore one of the most lucrative. Any ship wanting to pass either in or out was now stopped by Teach. In a little under a week he had plundered in the region of eight to nine vessels, including a ship called the *Crowley* which was bound for London. All the passengers on board were transferred to the *Queen Anne's Revenge,* after which they were questioned concerning the remaining ships left in port, what their cargoes might be, how heavily armed they were and so on. Afterwards the prisoners were returned to the *Crowley* and locked up in the cargo hold. Blackbeard had discovered that one of their number, a man by the name of Samuel Wragg, was a particularly wealthy individual and not only that, he was also a member of the Council of the Province of Carolina.[10] Wragg, as well as the *Crowley*'s captain and several other prominent passengers, all made perfect hostages. Blackbeard had one of his prisoners, a Mr Marks, go ashore accompanied by two pirates with a list of demands (the main one being for a chest of medicine), which if not met would result in the rest of the hostages being put to death.

Two days went by without a word from Marks, at which point it is said that Blackbeard, growing impatient at the delay, had Samuel Wragg dragged out of the cargo hold and brought before him. Wragg pleaded for the lives of the hostages and tried every possible means of pacifying Blackbeard, and for a time his pleas appeared to work. Later that same day a boat was spotted returning to the *Queen Anne's Revenge.* Everyone on board was convinced it was Marks and the two pirates returning with good news, but when the boat drew up alongside the *Queen Anne* it was not carrying any of those men. Instead, the fisherman on board informed Blackbeard that misfortune had struck Marks on his way into Charleston and that although everyone was safe, they needed more time to negotiate with the authorities.

Appeased, Blackbeard settled down to wait, but when after a few more days nothing was heard of Marks, he once again grew furious and decided upon a new plan of action. He had the captains of his various vessels sail into Charleston harbor alongside the *Queen Anne's Revenge* – all of them flying black flags. The maneuver worked. Charleston's citizens were terrified that the pirates were about to attack them and the government likewise, for 'though 'twas the greatest affront that could have been put upon them, yet for the saving of so many mens lives, (among them Mr. Samuel Wragg, one of the council) they complied with necessity and sent aboard a chest [of medicine] valued at between 300 and 400 pounds, and the pirates went back safe to their ships'.[11] The hostages were released and returned to shore, though the most richly dressed among them were stripped of their finery before they were allowed to return.

Much speculation has arisen as to why, when so much else could have been demanded of the Council of Charleston, medicine was first and foremost on the pirates' list of demands. Perhaps there had been an outbreak of some tropical disease among the crew, or perhaps, as the author Robert E. Lee has speculated, the medicine was to treat an outbreak of syphilis owing to the pirates' frequent use of brothels. One writer has even gone so far as to suggest that the mercurial preparations were for Blackbeard himself, 'because his most recent girl friend had not only married him but also left him with a venereal disease to remember her by'.[12] Whatever the case, having pulled off one of the greatest coups of his career without even firing one shot, and with eight or nine ships duly looted and the desired medicine chest delivered (not to mention that all the hostages had been returned safely ashore), Blackbeard now weighed anchor and headed up the Atlantic coast for North Carolina.

He was in a jubilant mood, though it was around this time (probably during the blockade of Charleston Harbor) that he heard news of Captain Rogers' mission to rid the West Indies of pirates. Realizing the boom days of piracy were near an end and feeling that he'd recently secured a sizeable enough booty on which to retire, Blackbeard decided to disband his fleet and sail northwards in search of a pardon from Governor Charles Eden of North Carolina.

In June 1718 Blackbeard passed through the Ocracoke Inlet and sailed onwards, eventually reaching Bath Town where he and about twenty of his crew sought out and received a royal pardon from Charles Eden. Afterwards Blackbeard is believed to have enjoyed several months of celebrity, often being invited into the homes of those who lived in the area where he was persuaded to regale them with tales of his exploits. It was also during this time that, according to Johnson, Blackbeard married his fourteenth wife – a sixteen-year-old girl who was the daughter of a Bath County planter. However, if all this points to Blackbeard wanting to settle down and live out the rest of his days as a law-abiding, virtuous citizen, nothing could have been further from the truth. Blackbeard had been brought up with the sea in his blood, he thrived on action and being in the thick of battle. Certainly, he'd accepted the King's Pardon, but this was only a temporary measure, probably entered into only so he could take a few months off to rest and recuperate.

Intent on returning to sea, Blackbeard now petitioned Governor Eden to reassign the *Adventure* over to him and give him a proper certificate of registration. Ostensibly, this was so that Blackbeard could begin trading legally at sea, but of course once the ship was back in use, legitimate business would be the last thing on Blackbeard's mind.

The first trip Edward Teach made on his newly commissioned vessel was to sail north for Philadelphia – at that time the largest city in America. But a surprise lay in store for him, for no sooner had he arrived than he was informed that Governor William Keith had, on 11 August 1718, issued a warrant for his arrest. Knowing that he was too easily recognized to continue living safely in Philadelphia, Blackbeard quickly left port and set sail instead for Bermuda. On the way he and his crew are said to have come across several ships, which they could have looted, but instead they only robbed them of provisions. Not that this state of affairs was to last long – soon they came across two

French vessels, one of which was carrying a cargo of sugar and cocoa, while the other was empty. It was too tempting an opportunity to miss, so Blackbeard devised a plan which would guarantee he could loot the ship first without fear of reprisal.

'The ship that had no lading he let go,' writes Charles Johnson, 'and putting all the men of the loaded ship aboard her he brought home the other with her cargo to North Carolina, where the Governor and the pirates shared the plunder.' In fact, what Teach did was to take the ship that was loaded with booty back to Governor Eden, whereupon he told him that he had found it floating at sea without a crew. The Governor then convened a meeting of the Vice Admiralty Court in Bath Town and they subsequently agreed that the ship was derelict and therefore the booty could legally be divided among them all. Blackbeard received his portion, for which he was duly grateful, and shortly afterwards set sail again, this time for Ocracoke Inlet where it is said he set up a pirate base from where he began looting and pillaging as many merchant vessels as he could.

Infuriated by the attack on their trade and desperate to have the pirates removed from the region, the sloop owners sent a deputation of men to Virginia to petition the then Governor of that region, Alexander Spotswood.

On 24 November 1718 Governor Spotswood issued a proclamation offering rewards for either the conviction or killing of the pirates: 'for Edward Teach, commonly called Captain Teach, or Black-beard, one hundred Pounds, for every other

The crew of Blackbeard's ship, the Queen Anne's Revenge, *and other vessels in his fleet, would meet up ashore on the coast of Carolina, resting and enjoying themselves. It was during one of these rest periods that Blackbeard accepted a pardon, although he soon broke his vow to give up piracy.*

Commander of a Pyrate Ship, Sloop, or Vessel, forty pounds; for every Lieutenant, Master, or Quarter-Master Boatswain, or Carpenter, twenty Pounds; for every other inferior Officer, fifteen pounds, and for every pirate Man taken on Board such Ship, Sloop, or Vessel, ten Pounds.'[13]

Two men-of-war were dispatched, HMS *Lyme,* commanded by Captain Brand, and HMS *Pearl,* commanded by Captain Gordon. In addition, two sloops, the *Ranger* and the *Jane,* were also commissioned, as was Lieutenant Robert Maynard ('an experienced officer and a gentleman of great bravery and resolution')[14] who was put in overall charge of the operation. Maynard took command of the *Jane* while a Mr Hyde took command of the *Ranger.*

On the evening of 21 November 1718 Maynard arrived at Ocracoke Inlet and, having discovered the exact location of Blackbeard's *Adventure,* decided to wait until the tides changed the next morning (the inlet otherwise being too shallow for his ship to sail up) before making his first attack. Always an astute tactician, he made sure that no other vessel entered the inlet to warn Blackbeard what was about to happen. Maynard also posted a lookout on both sloops so that Blackbeard could not escape across open water and out to sea without being spotted.

At dawn the sloops weighed anchor (the two men-of-war were too heavy to proceed through these waters) and set off toward the *Adventure.* Maynard ordered a smaller boat to go ahead but, as soon as it came across Blackbeard's vessel, it came under heavy fire and quickly had to retreat. Nevertheless, the odds were still in Maynard's favor as Blackbeard had a greatly reduced crew (some say as few as eighteen). Added to this, Blackbeard had apparently spent most of the previous night drinking with his shipmates so was not in the best state to repel an attack. (According to Howard Pyle it was also on this night that one of Blackbeard's shipmates asked the pirate if his young wife knew where his treasure trove was hidden, to which Blackbeard was said to have replied, 'No, nobody but the devil and I knows where it is, and the longest liver shall have all.')[15]

Yet despite being below par physically, one thing Blackbeard did have to his advantage was his intricate knowledge of the narrow channels and numerous sandbanks that made up the inlet. With Maynard's initial approach to the *Adventure* successfully repelled, Blackbeard now weighed anchor and headed for one of those narrow channels, with Maynard in hot pursuit. Soon, however, the latter got into difficulties, his two sloops running aground on a sandbank. A verbal exchange now took place between the two men, of which the most popular, and certainly the most dramatic, version is that recorded by Johnson in his *General History* (apparently basing his account on newspaper reports):

> **Black-beard hail'd him in this rude Manner: Damn you for Villains, who are you? And from whence came you? The Lieutenant made him Answer, You may see by our Colours we are no Pyrates. Black-beard bid him send his Boat on Board, that he might see who he was but Mr Maynard reply'd thus; I cannot spare my Boat, but I will come aboard of you as soon as I can, with my Sloop. Upon this Black-beard took a Glass of Liquor, &**

drank to him with these Words: Damnation seize my Soul if I give you Quarters, or take any from you. In Answer to which, Mr Maynard told him, That he expected no Quarters from him, nor should he give him any.

Maynard then ordered his men to do their best to release the sloops from the sandbanks, a task eventually achieved once the tides changed. They then set sail once again after Blackbeard, who fired a broadside against the first of the sloops, the *Ranger*, which was packed with nails and other bits of iron and lead and swan shot. Mayhem ensued – Mr Hyde, alongside five other men, was killed outright while several more of Maynard's men were severely injured. With the *Ranger* temporarily out of action, Maynard sailed on alone in the *Jane* and after several unsuccessful attempts managed finally to shoot away the *Adventure*'s jib and fore-halliards, which effectively forced Blackbeard ashore. Maynard then ordered all of his crew (save two) to hide with their weapons below deck in the cargo hold while he sailed as close to the *Adventure* as he could without hitting her.[16]

Blackbeard, on seeing the *Jane* virtually crewless, assumed that he'd killed most of them in his previous assault. Feeling safe in the knowledge that he wouldn't come to any harm, he and his pirates climbed aboard the *Jane* only to be met by Maynard's men pouring out of their hiding places, weapons drawn. A newspaper, the *Boston News Letter* (of 23 February–2 March 1719), reports the fight thus: 'Maynard and Teach themselves began the fight with their swords, Maynard making a thrust, the point of his sword went against Teach's cartridge box, and bended it to the hilt. Teach broke the guard of it, and wounded Maynard's fingers but did not disable him, whereupon he jumped back and threw away his sword and fired his pistol which wounded Teach.'

In total, or so Maynard later testified, Blackbeard took five shots to the chest, along with twenty cuts to other parts of his body, but the fatal blow was the one he received to his neck, which, as the *Boston News Letter* reported, 'cut off his head, laying it flat on his shoulder'.

Although Blackbeard was slain, it by no means meant the end of the battle, for the remaining pirates mounted a serious defense. In fact, by the time the *Ranger* caught up with the *Jane* it is said that the latter's decks were crimson with blood, the corpses of sailors and pirates alike lying in every part of the ship. How many casualties there actually were on either side is unknown. Captain Brand reported that a total of eleven sailors were killed and more than twenty wounded, while the number of pirates slaughtered was anywhere between nine and twelve, the final count not being known as several of their number jumped overboard to their deaths.

As for Blackbeard, local legend has it that when his headless torso was thrown overboard into the water, the corpse swam around the sloop several times before finally sinking beneath the waves. Lieutenant Maynard picked up Teach's head and had it suspended from the bowsprit of his sloop as a trophy. It was a fitting end to Blackbeard's career – a fitting death for a pirate who had wreaked so much havoc over the course of his lifetime. And naturally, the press, once apprised of the details, had a field day writing the battle up. In propaganda terms even the British government looked upon it as a great coup – even better than the capture and execution of Captain Kidd back in 1701.

Perhaps Charles Johnson best summed up Blackbeard's life, when he wrote, 'Here was the end of that courageous brute, who might have passed in the world for a hero had be been employed in a good cause.'

1 Lee, *Blackbeard the Pirate.*
2 Whipple, *Pirate Rascals of the Spanish Main.*
3 Ellms, *The Pirates Own Book.*
4 Lee, op. cit.
5 Johnson, *A General History…*
6 Ibid.
7 Ibid.
8 Lee, op. cit.
9 Calendar of State Papers, Colonial Series, America and the West Indies,
Public Record Office, London; ed. Cecil Headlam, London, Cassell, 1930–3.
10 Lee, op. cit.
11 Johnson, op. cit.
12 Whipple, op. cit.
13 Johnson, op. cit.
14 Ibid.
15 Pyle, *Book of Pirates.*
16 Johnson, op. cit.

BARTHOLOMEW ROBERTS
Black Barty

Roberts himself made a gallant figure, [...] being dressed in a
rich crimson damask waistcoat and breeches, a red feather in his
hat, a gold chain round his neck, with a diamond cross hanging
from it, a sword in his hand, and two pairs of pistols hanging at
the end of a silk sling slung over his shoulders (according to the
fashion of the pirates) and is said to have given his orders
with boldness, and spirit.

Captain Charles Johnson,
*A General History of the Robberies and
Murders of the Most Notorious Pirates*

L ittle is known of Bartholomew Roberts' early life other than that he was born
(as John Roberts) around 1682 in Haverfordwest in Pembrokeshire, Wales, to
an impoverished family. But from humble beginnings great men may arise and,
according to Captain A.G. Course in his book *Pirates of the Western Seas*, Bartholomew
Roberts (or Black Barty as he was commonly known) was such an individual, quickly
establishing himself as one of the most successful pirates of his day.

To begin with, Roberts' life at sea was in the honest employ of a Captain Plumb on
board his ship the *Princess*. Roberts was Plumb's second mate on a voyage from
England to the west coast of Africa in November 1719. On the outward journey the
cargo was a general one, but once in Africa the *Princess* was to load up with slaves and
take them to the West Indies, after which she was to return to England with a cargo of
sugar and rum. Misfortune, however, was to strike the *Princess* almost immediately she
docked in the port of Anaboe (also spelt Anamaboe) in Guinea, for there she was
attacked by a pirate ship – the *Royal Rover* – under the command of Captain Howell
Davis. Roberts did not want to join Davis in his unlawful pursuits so at first he was an
unwilling 'guest' on board the pirate vessel, but was said to change his mind on seeing
how easy it was for Davis to make vast amounts of money from piracy.

Six weeks passed, during which time the *Princess* made one successful attack after
another, but then disaster struck. Davis had come up with a plan to rob the Governor
of a large Portuguese settlement of £40,000. He was to invite the Governor and his
principal officers on board the *Princess* for a dinner, after which he planned to 'detain'
his guests until a ransom was paid. But the plot was discovered and, when Davis and
his men went ashore to pick up their guests, they were ambushed and killed. Suddenly,
there was a vacancy on board the *Princess*. Her crew needed a new pirate commander

and although Roberts had only been on board a brief six weeks, it was him they turned to, because during that time he had shown great leadership skills. For his part, Roberts is said to have been pleased by the promotion, saying, 'that since he had dipped his hands in muddy water, and must be a pirate, it was better being a commander than a common man'.[1]

According to Course, Roberts' first action as captain was to avenge the death of Davis and the other pirates. He and a handful of his men attacked the Portuguese port, set it and alight and threw all the town's guns into the sea.

Roberts and his crew now sailed southwards down the Brazilian coast where, nearing the Bay of Los Todos Santos, they spied a fleet of forty-two Portuguese vessels loaded and bound for Lisbon. Kidnapping the captain of one of the vessels, Roberts demanded to know which ship among the fleet was loaded with the most booty. The Portuguese captain divulged all the information Roberts needed, after which he 'sailed to her and insisted that her captain came over to the pirate ship to receive an important message. He replied that he would come immediately; but it was seen his ship was preparing for action, so

This Dutch portrait of Black Barty emphasizes the fact that he was known to dress well and makes him look like a rather debonair gentleman, but he was actually a ruthless killer. Two of his crew who tried to desert were tied to the mast and shot in the head.

without delay, Roberts ordered a broadside to be fired into her which he followed up by sailing the *Royal Rover* alongside, grappling her gunwales, and boarding with his men.'[2] The ensuing battle was short-lived, with Roberts easily capturing the Portuguese vessel, which he had his men sail away while he returned to the *Royal Rover* and set sail himself. The captured vessel sailed alongside Roberts' ship to an island off the Guinea Coast, which was known to most pirates as Devil's Island. Here the pirates unloaded their booty, which included sugar, tobacco, animal skins, a gold cross encrusted with diamonds that was said to be a gift for the King of Portugal and – most valuable of all – 4,000 gold moidores (a Portuguese coin).

Buoyed up by his success and having been informed by some locals of a brigantine from Rhode Island loaded with provisions sailing nearby, Roberts chose a small sloop then went after this vessel, but luck was not on his side. After eight days at sea he lost sight of his prey due to bad weather. Disorientated by fog, lacking adequate food and water, Roberts built a raft and had everyone row to shore. Eventually, a long boat from the *Royal Rover* came to their rescue, but there was bad news to relay. Roberts had left the *Royal Rover* in the hands of a pirate called Kennedy. During Roberts' absence, the rest of the pirates had voted Kennedy their new captain and, except for the few crew members who had come to Roberts' rescue, the rest had sailed on to Barbados with Kennedy as their new leader. From Barbados Kennedy sailed to Jamaica where he captured a sloop bound for Boston. Later, along with several other pirates, he took the sloop back to Britain where under different circumstances most of the pirates were arrested and hanged. Kennedy himself tried to escape the death penalty by turning King's Evidence, but to no avail, and on 19 July 1721 he was hanged at Execution Dock.

Meanwhile, Roberts had formed a new company of pirates, with whom he sailed to the West Indies. It was here that he wrote up a list of rules and regulations that he demanded all his crew adhered to (see pages 12-14 for the full list).

With these rules in place, Roberts now set about capturing two sloops, a Rhode Island brigantine and a Bristol ship with ten guns, both of which were loaded with provisions and booty. The latter vessel was detained for three days by Black Barty, but was then released and subsequently sailed back to Barbados where her captain informed the authorities what had occurred. Two ships were then dispatched to chase the pirates – one commanded by Captain Rogers of Bristol and the other by Captain Graves of Barbados. It took these men only a couple of days to catch up with the pirates – the ensuing battle was so intense that Black Barty thought it best to try to escape. To this end, he unloaded his ship of all guns and heavy goods so that it would move more swiftly and, evading the clutches of both Rogers and Graves, headed straight for Dominica. Here he not only stocked up with food and fresh water, but also took on board thirteen extra men who all wanted to sign up with the pirates. Barty then sailed on to the Grenadines, but stayed there only a matter of days, having been tipped off that the Governor of Martinique had sent two sloops out to capture him.

In June 1720 Black Barty arrived off the coast of Newfoundland. Heading straight for the harbor of Trepassy, 'with their black pirate colors flying', their arrival caused much consternation among the locals. In addition to this, the crews of twenty-two other vessels harbored at Trepassy all ran ashore to escape being taken prisoner by Barty, who consequently ransacked the empty ships and afterwards set them on fire. From Trepassy the pirates made their way up the Newfoundland coast where it is said they destroyed nine French vessels and captured a large French ship which they decided to keep. Renaming this ship the *Fortune*, Black Barty then captured another four ships: the *Richard* which hailed from Bideford in England, under the command of Captain Jonathan Whitfield, the *Samuel* from London, under the command of Captain Cary, the *Willing Maid* from Poole and the *Expectation* from Topsham. 'The *Samuel*,' writes Johnson, 'was a rich ship, and had several passengers on board, who were used very roughly, in order to make them discover their money, threatening them every moment with death, if they did not resign everything up to them. They tore up the hatches and entered the hold like a parcel of furies, and with axes and cutlasses, cut and broke open all the bales, cases, and boxes, they could lay their hands on[...].'[3]

Captain Cary watched the pirates loot his ship, and told them that they could apply for a Royal Pardon if they wanted to give up their criminal activities, but Roberts and his men only laughed in Cary's face and then looted and sank several more ships to show him how little they cared for his suggestion. Afterwards they returned to the West Indies in order to loot some more vessels – particularly those carrying supplies of food because they were running short. In this instance, however, they were unlucky – there were no suitable vessels to attack so instead they sailed to St Bartholomew, where the Governor there welcomed them on shore and gave them all the supplies that they required.

Having restocked, Black Barty now made for the coast of West Africa, stopping only once in order to attack a large French ship from Martinique which he thought would make a more suitable vessel for him and his pirates to live aboard. Having swapped ships, Barty renamed his new vessel the *Royal Fortune* then headed for the Cape Verde Islands, but misfortune in the shape of strong north-easterly trade winds knocked him off course and, concerned that water supplies on board ship were running low, he turned the ship round and headed toward Surinam in Guiana. By the time he reached his destination the *Royal Fortune* had run out of fresh water. It was crucial for the men to bring several hundred barrels back on board – an operation that took several days to complete because everyone was so weak. Nevertheless, with the mission accomplished the *Royal Fortune* set sail once again and made toward Barbados, on the way looting a ship called the *Greyhound*.

It was at this point that Black Barty, recalling how the Governor of Martinique had sent two sloops out to track him down and capture him, decided to return to that island and take revenge. Knowing that trade was brisk between the merchants of Martinique and the Dutch, Black Barty sailed into the harbor of Fort de France under a Dutch flag. It was a good trick – one that had merchants from the island flocking to the *Royal Fortune* to do business. Taking their money, Barty then burnt all of their ships save one on which the merchants were allowed to return to shore. But Roberts was still angry at the Governors of both Martinique and Barbados and, according to Captain A.G.

These two flags were flown by Black Barty. The one on the left shows a pirate that can be taken to be Black Barty and a skeleton that symbolizes death. Between them they hold an hour glass, the intention being to signal to another ship that 'Between Black Barty and Death time is running out'. The flag on the right shows Black Barty balanced on two skulls, the letters standing for 'A Barbadian's Head' and 'A Martinician's Head'.

Course in his *Pirates of the Western Seas*, this prompted him to have a new pirate flag made which 'consisted of himself standing upon two skulls brandishing a sword and under each skull the letters A/B/H (A Barbadian's Head) and A/M/H (A Martinician's Head). He had another flag with death depicted as a skeleton holding an hour glass in one hand and a spear in the other.'

From Martinique, Black Barty headed toward the island of Dominica, where he promptly captured a Dutch ship and yet another Rhode Island brigantine. Both vessels were taken to Bennet's Key in Samana Bay, off the north coast of Hispaniola. Pirates favored this location, mainly because the locals always welcomed them there. Black Barty and his crew were no exception. They stayed at Bennet's Key for several weeks, indulging in the two things pirates are always said to like best – drinking rum and sexual debauchery. But not everything went Roberts' way for while most of the crew were enjoying themselves with the local women, a man by the name of Harry Glasby who was master on board the *Royal Fortune*, together with two other crew members, decided to jump ship and desert.

Black Barty, angered by what he saw as disloyalty, had the men hunted down and brought back to the ship to face trial. According to Charles Johnson, this trial took place in the steerage of the ship. Provisions were laid on in the shape of a large bowl of rum punch and pipes and tobacco, after which the prisoners were brought in and the articles of indictment read out against them. The accused had little to say in their defense and all those sitting in judgment soon came to the conclusion that no mercy should be shown and that all three men should be executed. Indeed, only one judge, a pirate by the name of Valentine Ashplant, spoke up in Glasby's favor, but even then his pleas fell on deaf ears so he made another request. 'G—d—n ye gentlemen, I am as good a man as the best of you; d—m my S—l if ever I turned my back to any man in my life, or ever will by G—; Glasby is an honest fellow, notwithstanding this misfortune, and I love him, D—l d—n me if I don't: I hope he'll live and repent of what he has done; but d—n me if he must die, I will die along with him.'[4] Ashplant then withdrew two pistols from his coat pocket, whereupon the other judges decided he'd made a good case for Glasby to be reprieved, but as for the other two prisoners – the only concession made to them was that they could choose 'four of the whole company to be their executioners.'[5] This done, the prisoners were tied to a mainmast and shot in the head.

Black Barty now took to sea again, but this time in two ships, the *Royal Fortune* and one of the captured brigantines that he renamed the *Good Fortune*. But after long weeks on dry land drinking and enjoying the company of women, discipline among the pirates was at an all-time low so Roberts decided to start exercising more control over them, severely punishing them for every misdemeanor. Having been insulted by one of the crew who had drunk too much rum, Roberts killed the man and afterwards, hearing one of the victim's friends (Jones) criticizing his actions, ran him through with a sword. Yet despite being wounded Jones did not die, but instead rounded on Black Barty, swung him over the barrel of a gun, and beat him severely. Suddenly the crew was divided; half of the men sided with their captain while the other half sided with Jones – and no doubt all hell would have broken loose had it not been for the *Royal Fortune*'s quartermaster who sentenced Jones to two whips of the lash from every crew member as punishment for attacking his captain.

Eventually, having received his punishment, Jones was dispatched to the other pirate ship, the *Good Fortune*, where it is said he persuaded the crew to break ranks with Black Barty, hijack the ship and escape.

Black Barty took this brazen challenge to his authority in his stride and, determined to keep the rest of his men satisfied, now set sail across the North Atlantic to the mouth of the Senegal River. Here he captured a sixteen-gun French man-of-war which he renamed the *Ranger*. Afterwards the *Good Fortune* and the *Ranger* sailed up the Sierra Leone River where they hid out for some time in order to take on provisions, which were supplied to them by an old pirate named Crackers. There were also many traders living in this area, most of them former pirates, who made Black Barty and his crew welcome. For several weeks Roberts and his men rested, after which they sailed south plundering more ships as they went. One of these was a vessel owned by the Royal African Company – the *Onslow*, commanded by a Captain Gee. At the time of her hijack most of the crew were ashore and therefore her capture was easy. Roberts swapped the *Royal Fortune* for this vessel as she was more commodious. Afterwards the newly named *Royal Fortune*, together with the *Range,* set sail for Calabar in Nigeria and once there captured two Bristol ships that were anchored in the port. Roberts also tried to trade with the natives of that area, but soon discovered they were hostile. But something more interesting was to happen to Roberts and his crew while in Calabar –

a company of British warships was on the hunt for them.

Moving swiftly, Roberts sailed to Annobon Island in the Gulf of Guinea where he took on fresh water, then sailed for the Ivory Coast where he came across a ship called the *King Solomon*, which was commanded by a Captain Trahern. The pirates rowed alongside the *King Solomon*, but when Trahern asked them which ship they came on, they tried to trick him by answering the *Defiance*. Trahern didn't believe a word of what they said so rather than invite them on board, he fired a musket at them. The pirates retaliated in kind, then boarded the ship, overcame her crew, cut the anchor cables and finally sailed her back to the *Royal Fortune* where they stripped her of all her cargo.

The following few weeks saw Black Barty capture and pillage several more vessels. He sailed the *Royal Fortune* into the harbor at Ouidah (also spelt Whydah) where he made several vessels each pay a ransom of 8 pounds of gold in order that their ships weren't destroyed – even giving some of the captains (according to Johnson) a receipt for their gold:

> **THIS is to certify whom it may or doth concern, that we GENTLEMEN OF FORTUNE, have received eight Pounds of Gold-Dust, for the Ransom of the Hardey, Captain Dittwitt Commander, so that we discharge the said Ship,**
>
> | **Witness our Hands, this** | **Batt. Roberts,** |
> | **13th of Jan. 1721–2.** | **Harry Glasby.** |

But one ship, a slave vessel called the *Porcupine*, wasn't prepared to pay out any money whatsoever. Her commander, a Captain Fletcher, told Roberts that the ship's owners hadn't given him the authority to pay out for ransoms and therefore none would be forthcoming. This answer infuriated the pirates, who subsequently waited till Fletcher and most of his crew had rowed into the harbor to do business, after which they set fire to the *Porcupine*. But in their haste the pirates hadn't made time to release the African slaves who were still on board, manacled to one another. Suddenly these 'poor unfortunates' had a terrible choice to make. Either they could stay on the *Porcupine* and burn to death or they could jump overboard where they would be 'seized by sharks, a voracious fish in this road, and, in their [the pirates'] sight, tore limb from limb alive'.[6] Everyone on shore was horrified at the sight, but not as horrified as Black Barty when he heard that two British warships, the *Swallow* and the *Weymouth*, had arrived in the Gulf of Guinea with the express purpose of capturing him and putting an end to his reign of terror.

For the next few weeks a cat-and-mouse game was played out on the high seas, until finally the *Swallow* caught up with the *Royal Fortune*'s sister ship, the *Ranger*, and fighting broke out. At first the pirates fared well, but soon several of their number were killed. No life had been lost on the *Swallow*, which prompted her captain to send out boats to capture the remaining pirates. 'Skyrne [acting captain of the *Ranger*] had lost a leg in the action but insisted in fighting on his stump. While the *Swallow*'s boats were going to the *Ranger* an explosion was heard to come from the Great Cabin. Six of the pirates had put powder there and fired a pistol in it. It did not blow them and the cabin up, but burnt them badly, one dying on the next day.'[7] The rest of the pirates were placed in pinions and shackles, after which the crew of the *Swallow*, having repaired the damage to the *Ranger*, sailed her and the prisoners back to Principle Island. Leaving them in the safekeeping of the authorities, they resumed their hunt for Black Barty.

On 9 February 1722 the *Swallow* sighted the *Royal Fortune* near Cape Lopez. She was anchored next to a ship called the *Neptune*, which was commanded by a Captain Hill. In fact, Roberts was having breakfast with Hill when one of his men came below deck to inform him of the *Swallow*'s presence close by. Roberts was none too perturbed, believing it to be either a Portuguese vessel or perhaps a French slave ship. He certainly didn't suspect it was a British man-of-war. It wasn't until the *Swallow* was well upon the *Royal Fortune* that Barty was made fully aware of her purpose. Realizing he was under attack, he quickly set sail, hoping to outwit the *Swallow* by allowing her to attack him then swiftly moving in the opposite direction. His only worry was whether or not his men were sober enough to acquit themselves properly, but there was only one way to find out – he sailed the *Royal Fortune* as close as he could to the *Swallow*, which, as expected, delivered a broadside.

At the subsequent trial of the pirates, one of the officers said:

About eleven a clock, she being within pistol shot abreast of us, and a black flag, or pendant hoisted at their main topmast head, we struck the French Ensign that had continued hoisted at our staff till now, and displayed the Kings Colors, giving her at the same time our broadside which was immediately returned by them again but without equal damage, their mizzen top-mast falling and some of their rigging being disabled.

The pirate sailing better than us, shot ahead above half gun shot, while we continued firing (without intermission) such guns as we could bring to bear...till by favour of the wind we came alongside again, and after exchanging a few more shot, about half past one, his main-mast came down, being shot away a little below the parrel.

At two she struck, and called for quarters, proving to be the Royal Fortune of 40 guns, formerly the Onslow...[8]

The engagement proved to be Black Barty's undoing. Standing alone on the poop aft, he received a fatal volley of grapeshot in the throat. He'd always said that if he was killed in action he wanted his body to be dispatched at sea – the crew respected his wishes and threw his corpse overboard, after which they surrendered to the British man-of-war.

With all the pirates safely captured, the *Swallow* (which hadn't suffered one casualty) now made its way back to Lopez Bay where they had already deposited the crew of the *Ranger*. Both sets of captives were then dispatched to Cape Coast Bay for trial, but on the way the prisoners on both the *Royal Fortune* and the *Ranger* began plotting a revolt against the small naval crew who were manning the operation. The plan, however, was discovered and the plotters – pirates Moody, Ashplant, Magnes and Mare – were subsequently placed in even closer confinement until the ships reached

Cape Coast Bay where all the pirates were imprisoned in Cape Coast Castle.

Before the trials began on 28 March 1722, one of the pirates, Joe Dennis, offered to turn King's Evidence and was subsequently granted a pardon. The other pirates didn't fare so well. The judges who tried them included Captain Mungo Heardman (President), James Phips Esq., (General of the Coast), Mr Edward Hyde (Secretary to the Royal Africa Company), Mr H. Davidson and Mr F. Boye (Merchants) and Lieutenants Barnsley and Fanshaw.

First, sixty-nine of the *Ranger*'s crew members were tried with the charge of being: **wickedly united, and articled together, for the Annoyance & Disturbance of his Majesty's trading Subjects by Sea. And have in Conformity to the most evil and mischievous Intentions, been twice down the Coast of Africa, with two Ships; once in the Beginning of August, and a second Time, in January last, sinking, burning, or robbing such Ships, and Vessels, as then happened in your Way. Particularly, ye stand charg'd at the Instance, & Information of Captain Chaloner Ogle, as Traytors & Pirates, for unlawful Opposition ye made to his Majesty's Ship, the Swallow, under his Command.**[9]

All the accused pleaded not guilty, after which the crew of the *Swallow* were asked to identify each and every one of the pirates and give an account of how they had been attacked by them. For their part, the pirates were asked how they came to be sailing with Roberts and why they had chosen to fight the *Swallow*, to which they replied that they willingly signed pirates' articles and shared in the plunder. Only a few men who had been with the *Ranger* a short while pleaded they had entered into piracy unwillingly, indeed that they were forced into the looting and sinking of ships.

The court then decided it would hear each case separately so as everyone could decide which of the pirates took part willingly and which had been coerced into doing so. Similar charges were also brought against the eighty-six members of the *Royal Fortune*, although sixteen of their number were further charged with piracy of the *King Solomon*. Where this later charge was concerned, Captain Joseph Trahern and his first mate, George Fenn, gave evidence against the pirates to the effect that in January 1722, while at anchor, they were approached by a boat full of men whom they presumed to be pirates. At first Trahern thought the best course of action was to attack the pirates, but, when it came to it, instead he surrendered. Subsequently, the pirates boarded the *King Solomon* and afterwards looted her. Among those men identified by Trahern was the quartermaster of the *Royal Fortune*, a man called Magnus; the bosun, who was called Main; the sailmaker called Petty; the cooper called Harbour, the carpenter called Griffen; and lastly the pilot, who was called Oughterlaney.

The court then asked why these six men, if they weren't willing participants in Black Barty's scheming, had been elected to these positions on board the *Royal Fortune*. The men had no answer to this and, along with ten others, were found guilty as charged. In fact, the only exception made by the court was toward four musicians who proved they had never taken part in any piracies whatsoever, eleven Englishmen who had been on board the *Royal Fortune* only a few days before she was captured and eighteen

*At Cape Coast Castle, Black Barty's men were held prisoner before facing trial after which
more than fifty of them were executed. Barty himself had died in battle but the cannons at
Cape Coast Castle point out to sea still, almost as if expecting his return.*

Frenchmen who had been taken prisoner by Black Barty. All these men were acquitted,
but the remainder were proved guilty and were addressed by the court to the effect that
piracy was an evil offence, one that forced honest, decent men into committing heinous
crimes thus destroying entire families. In addition to this, piracy also destroyed trading
nations and made commerce impossible. Given the seriousness of the crime therefore,
it was only proper that all those who were found guilty should receive 'exemplary
punishment'.[10]

The only pirate to receive special treatment was Black Barty's former master of the
Royal Fortune, Harry Glasby – who had witnesses to testify to his humanity. Not only
this, they also said that Glasby went out of his way to avoid cruelty and furthermore that
Black Barty had tried him for attempting to escape from the *Royal Fortune* and that on
being caught he had been whipped to within an inch of his life. Other witnesses stepped
forward, including a woman who had been a prisoner on board the *Royal Fortune* and
who testified that Glasby treated her kindly. One of the musicians (who had by then
been acquitted) also swore that Glasby had taken no part in any piratical activities.

In his own defense, Glasby said that he had been forced to work aboard the *Royal*

Fortune by Black Barty on pain of death, but even so he had refused to sign their articles and that he had escaped from the pirates only to be recaptured at a later date. The Court adjourned to decide their verdict. Much debate followed but essentially everyone was agreed that Glasby had been kept aboard the *Royal Fortune* against his will and that he hadn't, to the best of their knowledge, engaged in any robberies, therefore they would acquit him.

Nor was he alone in being set free. In total seventy-four of Black Barty's men were released, while fifty-two men were found guilty and executed. On top of this, twenty others were sentenced to seven years' servitude in West Africa for the Royal African Company of England, while seventeen others were sent to the Marshalsea prison in London for an indefinite term.

Of those who were executed it is said of one – Peter Scudamore, the ship's surgeon – that he asked for two days' reprieve during which time he spent praying and reading the Bible. Once on the scaffold with the noose round his neck Scudamore sang Psalm 31. Another pirate, David Symson from North Berwick in Scotland, took a different approach to death. On seeing a young woman in the crowd that had gathered around the scaffold, he proclaimed that he'd slept with her three times and here she was now, come to see him hanged.

Last was Charles Bruce, who hailed from Exeter in the south of England. At first he protested against his sentence and attributed his sins to a liveliness of temperament he couldn't control. Then he begged God's forgiveness for the harm he had caused his victims. He concluded, 'I stand here as a beacon upon a rock to warn erring mariners of danger.'[11]

1 Johnson, *A General History…*
2 Course, *Pirates of the Western Seas.*
3 Johnson, op.cit.
4 Ibid.
5 Ibid.
6 Ibid.
7 Course, op. cit.
8 High Court of Admiralty Records, 1/99.3, Public Record Office; reproduced in Cordingly, *Life Among the Pirates.*
9 Johnson, op. cit.
10 Course, op. cit.
11 Ibid.

EDWARD ENGLAND

the mild-mannered captain

England was one of these men, who seemed to have a great deal
of good nature, and did not want for courage; he was not
avaricious and always averse to the ill usage prisoners received.

Captain Charles Johnson,
*A General History of the Robberies and
Murders of the Most Notorious Pyrates*

Typically, the career of Captain Edward England was not a long-lived affair, lasting only two years – after which time (and much like Captain John Avery) he died alone and in poverty. During the two years that he was actively involved in piracy it is believed that he was a well-liked, but ultimately weak leader whose tendency toward clemency when dealing with captives ultimately saw his crew turn against him. Not as swashbuckling as Blackbeard, nor as cruel as Benito de Soto, Captain Edward England was nonetheless a fascinating individual, someone who combined wickedness with a certain intelligence and occasional moral sensibility.

Generally believed to have been born in Ireland, Edward England, according to some historians, originally went by the name of Jasper Seagar – although there is little, if any, evidence to support this claim. There is also little information on England's childhood or early career at sea; in fact, he first warrants a mention only when, as second-mate on a pirate sloop bound for Providence Island around 1718, his vessel was captured by another pirate, Captain Winter.

Edward England did not have the kind of bad reputation for the treatment of his prisoners that was enjoyed by some other pirates and that ultimately led to him being marooned. Unlike many who faced that cruel punishment, England survived and found his way to safety.

What occurred between the two men is unknown but shortly after this event, having dropped anchor at Providence Island, both pirates came across Captain Rogers who had recently been made Governor of the Bahamas on the understanding that he would rid the islands (and in particular Providence Island) of its growing colony of pirates. Rogers had been granted powers to pardon any pirate who was willing to give up his unlawful practices and settle down to an honest life (see Glossary).

The offer was open up until September 1718, and it is believed that England was approached by Rogers who was more than willing to grant him this Act of Grace. However, England turned him down. Given that Charles Johnson was later to describe England as a good-natured man who hated ill-treating his prisoners, this may be an unexpected choice, but, as Johnson writes in his *General History*: 'It is surprising that men of good understanding should engage in a course of life that so much debases humane nature, and set them upon a level with the wild beasts of the forest, who live and prey upon their weaker fellow creatures: a crime so enormous! that it includes almost all others, as murder, rapine, theft, ingratitude, etc.' For all his good-naturedness, England's positive rejection of a pardon is very indicative of the darker side of his character, a side that evidently set him hell-bent on piracy.

Turning his back on Providence Island, Edward England set sail for Africa where he was said to have captured several vessels, including one called the *Cadogan Snow* near Sierra Leone. The *Cadogan Snow* was commanded by Captain Skinner, who had seemingly already met several of Edward England's crew – some of the men having been previously employed by him. Unfortunately for Skinner, however, those pirates who had once sailed alongside him didn't have good memories of their time on board his vessel. In fact, the two factions had fallen out – with Skinner refusing to pay these men. When Captain England captured the *Cadogan Snow* and ordered Skinner to step on board his ship, 'the person he [Skinner] first cast his eye upon, proved to be his old boatswain, who stared him in the face like his evil genius, and accosted him in this manner. "Ah, Captain Skinner! Is it you? The only man I wish to see; I am much in your debt, and now I shall pay you all in your own coin."'[1]

Trembling at what fate was to befall him, Skinner begged his ex-employees for mercy, but his pleas fell on deaf ears. The pirates tied him to the windlass and began throwing broken glass bottles at him, cutting his skin to shreds. Skinner was then untied and whipped around the deck before, finally, one of the pirates picked up a pistol and shot him through the head. Afterwards two pirates threw Skinner's body into the sea while the rest of the crew looted a few select items from the *Cadogan Snow* – eventually leaving the vessel and the rest of her cargo under the command of the ship's first mate, Howel Davis.

A few days later Captain Edward England and his crew captured the *Pearl*, which was commanded by a Captain Tyzard. The *Pearl* was a much larger sloop than the one England was sailing in so the pirates swapped vessels and renamed Tyzard's ship the *Royal James*. England had the *James* fitted out for piratical purposes and afterwards, while sailing around the Azores and the Cape Verde Islands, was said to have captured several more vessels – some from Spain, some from England.

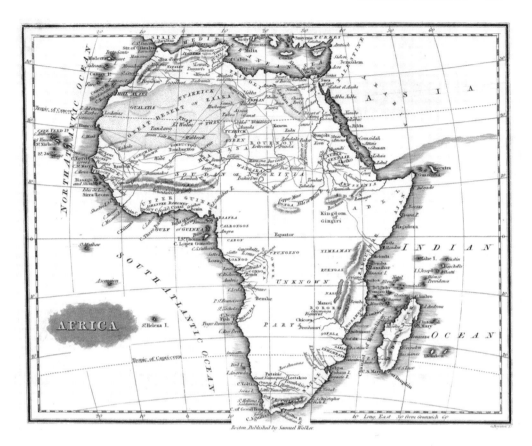

Many of Edward England's prizes were captured as he voyaged round the coast of Africa before he stopped off at the pirate haven of Madagascar to rest and for essential maintenance to his ship. He then headed for the East Indies.

Later, in the spring of 1719, he decided to set sail back to Africa where, starting out at the mouth of the River Gambia, he sailed down the coast, capturing an estimated ten or eleven vessels – including the following:

The Eagle pink [see Glossary], Captain Rickets commander belonging to Cork, taken the 25th of March, having six guns and seventeen men on board, seven of which turned pirates.

The Charlotte, Captain Oldson, of London, taken May the 26th, having eight guns, and eighteen men on board, thirteen of which turned pirates.

The Sarah, Captain Stunt, of London, taken the 27th of May, having four guns and eighteen men on board, three of which turned pirates.

The Bentworth, Captain Gardener, of Bristol, taken the 27th of May, having twelve guns and thirty men on board, twelve of which turned pirates.

The *Mercury*, Captain Maggot, of London, taken the 29th of May, having four guns and eighteen men on board, five of which turned pirates.

The *Elizabeth and Katherine*, Captain Bridge of Barbados, taken June 27th, having six guns and fourteen men on board, four of which turned pirates.[2]

The pirates burned some of the ships to a cinder, including the *Bentworth* and the *Charlotte*, while fitting out others for their own use, including the *Mercury*, renamed the *Queen Ann's Revenge* (under the command of Captain Lane), and the *Elizabeth and Katherine*, renamed the *Flying King* (under the command of Captain Robert Sample). Both these vessels, along with their new pirate crews, then left Captain England to make their way to Brazil where they subsequently captured a large number of Portuguese vessels. Their spell of good fortune was not to last long, however, for the *Flying King* was one day run ashore by a Portuguese ship who took all the pirates captive and afterwards hanged thirty-eight of them.

Meanwhile, Captain England, who was still cruising down the coast of Africa, captured a galley, the *Peterborough*, commanded by Captain Owen, and the *Victory*, commanded by Captain Rideout. The former captain had his ship taken from him, while the latter had his ship plundered and afterwards sunk. England then came across another two vessels along Cape Coast Road, the *Whydah* and the *John*. Determined to capture both ships, the pirates set fire to a small vessel that they had only recently captured and sailed her between the *Whydah* and the *John* in the hope that both their

When England captured the Cadogan Snow, *some of his crew recognized the captain, having served under him previously. These were clearly not fond memories as they beat him almost to death with broken bottles before putting a bullet in his head.*

crews would abandon ship. But the *Whydah* opened fire on Captain England, forcing him to sail in the opposite direction.

Putting into harbor, England now had the *Royal James* cleaned and restocked, while he had the recently captured *Peterborough* fitted out for piratical use. He also changed the *Peterborough*'s name to the *Fancy*, after which he and his men decided to settle in the area – living 'wantonly for several weeks, making free with the Negro women, and committing such outrageous acts, that they came to an open rupture with the natives, several of whom they killed, and one of their towns they set on fire'.[3]

Setting sail once again, Captain England asked his men to vote where they wanted to head for next. Madagascar being decided upon, they duly arrived on the island toward the beginning of 1720.

Madagascar and its adjacent islands was a pirate haven (see also the chapter on John Avery, page 66, and Glossary). Located just off the coast of Africa, it was perfectly positioned as a stop-off point for any sea captain wanting to careen his ship (that is, tilting it over and cleaning the hull) and refit it, as well as restock with fresh water and food. Oranges and limes, which in those days were like medicine to sailors who needed to stave off scurvy, were in plentiful supply – not to mention fresh meat and fish. And as Madagascar's popularity grew, so too did her trading depots and merchant stores, the first of which was opened by an ex-pirate called Adam Baldridge, who:

> **Having murdered, or otherwise fatally disposed of a comrade, in a fatal tavern brawl at Jamaica, he thought to take shelter at St. Mary's and there combine safety with profit [...] He built a fort and warehouses at the entrance, mounting a number of guns in the former, and enclosing the latter in a strong stockade wherein the pirates could find shelter whilst their ships were being treated, or they were having a spell ashore.[3]**

England now restocked his ship with provisions and then headed for the coast of Malabar in the East Indies. Here he and his men captured several Indian ships together with two European vessels that they exchanged for one of their own. Afterwards they returned to Madagascar, where several of their number were sent ashore to hunt wild boar and deer for fresh meat. The pirates then set sail for Johanna Island (not far from Madagascar), where they came across two large English ships and one large Dutch ship which were in the process of trading with the East Indies. Two of the ships managed to escape from the pirates, but the last ship – the *Cassandra*, commanded by Captain James Macrae – wasn't so fortunate.

Having fought off the pirates for many hours, during which time Macrae lost several men, both the *Cassandra* and the *Fancy* ran aground, after which the two sides began pounding each other with gunfire. In his book *A General History of the Robberies and Murders of the Most Notorious Pirates*, Charles Johnson includes what he purports to be a letter written by Macrae recording the events that now took place. Dated 16 November 1720, it says, among other things:

> **we endeavour'd to run ashoar; and tho' we drew four Foot Water more than the Pyrate, it pleased God that he stuck fast on a higher Ground**

than we happily fell in with; so was disappoint'd a second time from boarding us. Here we had a more violent Engagement than before. All my Officers, and most of my Men, behav'd with unexpected Courage; & as we had a considerable Advantage by having a Broadside to his Bow, we did him great Damage.

But this advantage soon evaporated, and in desperation Macrae left the ship in a long boat and rowed to shore – but not before seeing the pirates board his ship, where he witnessed them cutting 'three of our wounded Men to Pieces'. This was a terrible blow to Macrae, who had himself been badly injured. When he reached dry land he immediately set off for the nearest town (which was twenty-five miles away) in order to get help. By the time he reached King's Town, however, the pirates had already sent out word that they were willing to pay the sum of 1000 dollars to anyone willing to hand Macrae over. Fearing for his life once again, Macrae sent out word that he was dead and afterwards lay low for about ten days, by which time he hoped the 'Malice of our Enemies was nigh over'.

Macrae then petitioned the pirates to go aboard their ship to negotiate a deal with them – for he and his surviving men had no way of getting off Johanna Island without the pirates' help. It was, however, a very risky strategy. Although the pirates gave their word that no harm would come to him if he boarded the *Fancy*, the second he did set foot on the vessel some of their number threatened to kill him. Captain England, being a fairer, more peaceful-minded individual, treated his captive with respect and advised him to make a favorable impression upon a pirate by the name of John Taylor, whom the ship's crew respected, mainly 'because he was a greater brute than the rest.'[5]

Soon Macrae was plying Taylor with drink and desperately trying to find favor with him – with little success, until a drunken pirate with a wooden leg staggered up on deck and made his way over to where Macrae stood. Macrae thought he was about to be executed, but it turned out the pirate was one of his old employees who, putting his arm around his former boss, informed the rest of the crew that no one was to touch Macrae for he was as honest a man as had ever lived and had always treated his sailors fairly. (An interesting footnote to this exchange is that the wooden-legged pirate who was described by Johnson as 'a fellow with a terrible pair of whiskers, and a wooden leg, being stuck round with pistols, like the man in the almanack with darts…' was said to have been the inspiration for Robert Louis Stevenson's infamous character Long John Silver in *Treasure Island*.)

Suddenly John Taylor began to feel more warmly toward Captain Macrae, and ordered the rest of the pirates to leave Macrae alone (after which he fell into a drunken stupor). Captain England then told Macrae to leave the *Fancy* as quickly as possible for as soon as Taylor woke up chances were he'd change his mind. England also made certain that Macrae had an old vessel that the pirates no longer required, after which Macrae set sail 'together with 43 of my Ship's Crew, including 2 Passengers and 12 Soldiers, having but 5 Tons of Water aboard; & after a Passage of 48 Days, I arriv'd here [Bombay] October 26, almost naked and starv'd, having been reduc'd to a Pint of Water

In 1720, the East India Company ships Cassandra *and* Greenwich *reported that England flew the Jolly Roger – a black flag with a white skull and crossed bones beneath it. The Jolly Roger is thought to take its name from the French* joli rouge, *meaning 'pretty red'. Pirates flew a red flag to let their victims know that they would be shown no mercy and the Jolly Roger was intended to communicate the same message.*

a Day, & almost in despair of ever seeing Land, by Reason of the Calms we met with between the Coast of Arabia & Malabar'.[6]

Captain England, having aided Macrae so effectively, was left in an awkward position regarding his own crew who now viewed him as a weak and ineffectual. They believed that he should have allowed them to kill Macrae as they originally intended, or at least have kept him captive. The pirates further opined that Macrae was at that very moment probably fitting out a ship in order to come after them and place them under arrest. So angry were England's men – particularly John Taylor – at what they saw as their leader's feeble command, that, early in 1721, they mutinied and marooned him and three other men on the island of Mauritius.

As can be seen from the list of pirate articles drawn up by Bartholomew Roberts and which appear in Charles Johnson's *General History* (see pages 12-14), marooning was not an uncommon practice for all manner of offences, including that of theft. In Captain England's case, he was given no weapons with which to defend himself from wild animals or with which he could kill animals for food. Nor was he given fresh drinking water or any other supplies. Not that this was unusual either – given the severity of England's so-called crime, his crew probably saw his marooning as an almost symbolic gesture: they were casting him out of the group because he had placed their pirate community in jeopardy. As Howard Pyle writes in his *Book of Pirates*:

> **If a pirate broke one of the many rules which governed the particular band to which he belonged, he was marooned; did a captain defend his ship to such a degree as to be unpleasant to the pirates attacking it, he was marooned; even the pirate captain himself, if he displeased his followers by the severity of his rule, was in danger of having the same punishment visited upon him which he had perhaps more than once visited upon another. The process of marooning was as simple as it was terrible. A suitable place was chosen (generally some desert isle as far removed as possible from the pathway of commerce), and the condemned man was rowed from the ship to the beach.**

Nor was it a 'soft' punishment for, if given the choice between being marooned and being executed, pirates would often choose the latter as being a swifter, far less painful option. After all, when a pirate was marooned they were often stripped of all their belongings, including their clothes, and left with no food or water nor any weapons with which to shoot wild animals. Death was therefore often a long, painful affair, especially if the victim couldn't feed himself or find adequate shelter, for then he would almost certainly die of exposure or starvation.

Despite the grisly details of such a fate, however, in the eighteenth and nineteenth centuries being marooned was thought of as almost romantic. Of course, Shakespeare had covered the subject in his play *The Tempest* and Jonathan Swift had written about Gulliver being stranded on the island of Lilliput in *Gulliver's Travels* – but neither of these stories came close to capturing the public's imagination in quite the same way as a story published in 1719 whose title page bears the following inscription:

The Life and Strange Surprising Adventures of Robinson Crusoe, of York, Mariner: Who lived Eight and Twenty Years all alone in an un-inhabited Island on the Coast of America, near the Mouth of the Great River of Oroonoque; Having been cast on shore by Shipwreck, where-in all the Men perished but himself. With An Account how he was at last strangely deliver'd by Pyrates. Written by Himself.

Of all the stories ever written and all the factual accounts of people being marooned on desert islands, Robinson Crusoe's – as told by Daniel Defoe – is the best known and the most loved. Against the usual odds in real life, Crusoe managed to survive, and for many years – he didn't starve to death, succumb to a fatal illness, go mad or get eaten alive. Of course, Crusoe wasn't a pirate and hadn't been abandoned on the island as a punishment, unlike Captain England or the long list of other unfortunates who suffered similar ends, such as a pirate by the name of Andrew Barker who was marooned by mutineers in 1577. There was also the case of Thomas Cavendish who, in 1587, captured a Manila galleon and afterwards stripped her crew naked and dumped them in the California wastelands. In 1688 the pirate William Dampier was stranded on the Nicobar Islands without any supplies, while in 1718 Roger Stevens of Bristol – along with his boatswain – was abandoned on the island of Rattan by pirates who captured his ship and made off with her cargo.[7] Several of these men didn't survive the ordeal – indeed the majority of people who were marooned were never heard of again. 'A boat's crew from some vessel, sailing by chance that way, might perhaps find a few chalky bones bleaching upon the white sand in the garish glare of the sunlight, but that was all.'[8]

In Captain England's case, his pirate crew – now captained by the infamous John Taylor – took off without a second thought to their old captain's fate. Soon they were heading for India where they captured several European and Moorish vessels and afterwards were said to have spent the Christmas of 1720 at sea 'in carousing and forgetfulness, and kept it for three days in a wanton and riotous way, not only eating, but wasting their fresh provisions...'[9] They then repaired to the West Indies where they refitted their boat (the *Victory*), sailing out on 5 April 1721 toward Mascarine Island.

England was marooned along with three others on the island of Mauritius where he was expected to die of thirst or starvation in its hostile environment. Ironically, Mauritius is now an up-market holiday destination where visitors to the island can relax in luxury.

Here they were fortunate enough to capture a large Portuguese carrack (a cargo ship also fitted out for fighting) called the *Nostra Senhora de Cabo*, which had suffered terrible damage during a storm and therefore made easy pickings. The ship was loaded with food and other provisions, but her greatest treasure was the Viceroy of Goa who was carrying diamonds with him to the value of several million dollars. Taylor and his men took the jewels and afterwards detained the viceroy whom they then ransomed for a further 2000 dollars. The pirates then marooned everyone on board the *Cabo* on a small island and left them to their fate while they themselves sailed on to Madagascar with the *Cabo* in tow.

Once they arrived at the island Taylor then – according to Johnson – divided the booty up among the men, with each pirate receiving forty-two diamonds or the equivalent according to size. Some of the pirates subsequently took their riches and set up home on Madagascar, while the rest set about planning a new voyage. They decided that one of their ships, the *Victory*, had seen better days so they had her burned and replaced her with the *Cabo*, which they renamed the *Victory* in honor of their old vessel. Taylor and about half his original crew set sail again – only just as they were leaving Madagascar they had word that four British men-of-war had been sent out to the Indies to capture them, so they headed for Africa. Arriving at the small port of Delagoa, Taylor lay low for a few days, but, on spotting a small fortification along the coast, couldn't resist sending his men to capture it. This they did – afterwards discovering that the fort had been built by the Dutch East India Company, which had abandoned some of its employees there, all of whom begged the pirates not only for mercy, but that they be allowed to join them.

With a fresh influx of recruits, Taylor then set sail for the Spanish West Indies and on arriving in Cuba decided to sell his ship to the Governor of Porto Bello. After this, little if anything is known of his life or what he did subsequently, although it might be conjectured that with all the money he had made from the diamond haul, he settled down to enjoy the rest of his days in peace.

The same cannot be said for Captain England who, having been stranded on Mauritius, spent several days in despair as to what to do next. He and his three companions couldn't stay on the island, not if they wanted to survive, so eventually, pooling their skills, they built a small boat and took the great risk of sailing to Madagascar. Their provisions were barely adequate for such a journey – only a small amount of fresh water and little, if any, food – so that if they were to be at sea for more than a few days they would undoubtedly perish. For once luck was on Captain England's side and after several setbacks he and the other three men arrived at their destination, tired, hungry and hugely relieved.

Thereafter, little is known of Captain England's life. He is thought, much like the pirate John Avery, to have spent the remainder of his days begging on the streets for a living, scraping together barely enough to stay alive. It was a huge contrast to the bold, audacious career he had enjoyed while sailing as a pirate, but in many respects it was typical of the destitution many pirates endured at the end of their lives. 'Wine and women,' wrote Charles Leslie in his *History of Jamaica*, 'drained their [the pirates'] wealth to such a degree that, in a little time, some of them became reduced to beggary. They have been known to spend 2 or 3,000 pieces of eight in one night.' Captain Kidd, Benito de Soto, John Rackham and Edward Low all went out at the end of a rope, while Blackbeard and François L'Ollonais endured far bloodier deaths, but they were the exceptions to the rule. In reality, far more pirates ended up as drunken, disease-riddled down-and-outs, paupers who had spent their ill-gotten gains on women and alcohol. Indeed, the romantic view of most pirates' lives (and deaths) couldn't be further from the truth. Often their careers would only span four or five years, if that. John Avery barely lasted three years as a pirate, while Edward Teach only managed fifteen months in his chosen profession before he was killed. Nor were pirates' lives always action-packed or richly rewarded. They could spend months on end at sea without so much as spotting a suitable ship to attack and when they did finally capture one, more often than not her cargo wouldn't be worth half as much as they at first thought.

Edward England's life and death were, therefore, both fairly typical for a pirate. None mourned his passing; there is no gravestone to mark his death – in fact the only record of his ever having existed is Charles Johnson's account of his brief, if occasionally exciting, life.

1 Johnson, *A General History…*
2 Ibid.
3 Ibid.
4 Grey, *Pirates of the Eastern Seas.*
5 Ibid.
6 Johnson, op. cit.
7 Cordingly, *Life Among the Pirates.*
8 Pyle, *Howard Pyle's Book of Pirates.*
9 Johnson, op. cit.

CAPTAIN EDWARD LOW

evil personified

Some fight, 'tis for riches – some fight, 'tis for fame:
I fight, 'tis for vengeance! I love to see flow,
At the stroke of my saber, the life of my foe...

From *Pirate's Song*, Anon

In the introduction to his life of Edward Low, Charles Ellms pronounces that of any pirate living or dead he was born to his profession. 'This ferocious villain,' he says, '[...] received an education similar to that of the common people of England. He was by nature a pirate; for even when very young he raised contributions among the boys of Westminster, and if they declined compliance, a battle was the result.'[1]

Low was born in London in the early part of the eighteenth century. Apart from his education in the borough of Westminster, little is known of his early life – though one of his brothers also seemed destined for a life of crime. At a very young age, he persuaded an adult friend of the family to carry him round in a basket upon his back, and when the couple came across a crowd the young boy would steal hats and wigs. Whether Edward took part in these activities is uncertain. What is better known is that, together with an older brother, he went to sea for three or four years before parting company with this brother in America, where Edward found employment at a rigging house in Boston, New England. On 12 August 1714 Low is said to have married a woman called Eliza Marble. Eliza gave birth first to a son and later a daughter, but in the winter of 1719 she died, followed a few weeks later by her firstborn. Devastated by his loss, and never one to make life easy for himself, Low then fell out with his employer – at which point, feeling as if he had nothing to lose and leaving his daughter with his in-laws, he took a ship bound for the Bay of Honduras.

Shortly after the vessel arrived, Low found employment on a boat bringing logwood out to the ship. The boat was well armed to protect it from the Spaniards who were prone to stealing logwood whenever they could. One evening, having delivered a load of wood to the ship just before dinner time, Low wanted to stay on board and eat with the captain. The captain, however, had other ideas and instead of agreeing to dine with his men, he gave them a bottle of rum then ordered them to bring in another load of wood before sitting down to eat. The boat's crew were infuriated, but particularly Low who picked up a gun and fired at the captain. The bullet missed its target, but killed the man standing next to him. Low and the rest of his crew ran off, but the next day they returned to the ship, threw the captain overboard then raised the black flag and 'declared war with the whole world.'[2]

Low and his crew set sail for Grand Cayman Island where they may have had some intention to fit out their vessel for honest employment, but it was at this point that Low met George Lowther, a pirate. Lowther paid Low many compliments and eventually suggested Low join him as an ally. It was an offer Low could not afford to turn down and subsequently the two pirates worked side by side for some time, until May 1722, when they took a brigantine bound from Boston. At this point they decided to part company, with Low taking on the recently-captured vessel as his own. With forty-four trusted men to act as his crew, Low was now captain of his own ship, which he named the *Rebecca*.

His first adventure as captain occurred shortly afterwards when he captured a sloop

Low and the captain of one of the ships in his fleet attempted to persuade the master of a captured ship to join them in piracy, first by offering a bowl of punch and then by threatening him with a pistol. Their prisoner, Captain George Roberts, refused all their persuasions and counted himself lucky that his life was spared.

captained by one John Hance whom he stripped of all his possessions. Low stole all the provisions on board and took them back to the *Rebecca*. Later that same day he met another sloop, captained by a James Calquhoon. Low plundered this vessel too and afterwards 'cut away his [Calquhoon's] bowsprit and all his rigging, also his sails from the yards, and wounded the master, to prevent his getting in to give intelligence, and then stood away to the south-eastward, with all the sail he could make, there being then but little wind'.[3]

Calquhoon did not take kindly to being hijacked and as soon as Low had sailed away he set about rigging spars and sails, then made for Block Island from where he dispatched a whale boat back to the mainland to raise the alarm. By the following morning two of the fastest sloops available were fitted out and embarked to search for Edward Low. Captain John Headland commanded the first sloop, which was armed with ten guns, while the second vessel was commanded by Captain John Brown and had six guns on board. Frustratingly for both ships, although Low was spotted off the coast of Block Island, by the time they reached there, he had already escaped.[4]

The next sighting of Low occurred several days later when he sailed into Buzzard's Bay to fetch supplies of fresh water and other provisions. Some of his crew attacked a couple of whaling boats and plundered them for food, while others went ashore to steal sheep. Fully stocked up, Low sailed northwards to Nova Scotia where he put into Rosemary Harbor. There he found thirteen fishing vessels from Massachusetts Bay which were resting up for a couple of days before resuming their business. Hoisting the black flag, Low lost no time in dispatching his pirates to plunder the fishing boats and kidnap every able-bodied seaman they could lay their hands on, in order to force them into piracy. Low also decided that the largest of the fishing vessels – the *Mary* (eighty tons) – was more suitable as a pirate ship than the *Rebecca* and therefore swapped ships. He renamed the *Mary*, calling her the *Fancy*, then placed all those fishermen he didn't want as pirates in the *Rebecca*, which afterwards sailed back to Boston where they reported the incident to the authorities. Low headed for St John's in Newfoundland, arriving there midsummer. At first he was tempted to capture a ship anchored in the harbor, but at the last moment discovered she was a warship (the *Solebay*) and therefore made for the port of Carboneau, some forty-five miles northward.

At Carboneau, Low and his pirates ransacked the town, setting light to the houses before sailing for the Newfoundland fishing banks where they captured a French banker (a fishing vessel) lightly armed with just two guns aboard. At this point Low had a lucky escape from two sloops that were sailing up to the garrison fort at Annapolis-Royal in Nova Scotia. Both vessels were armed and had soldiers aboard and, as soon as the *Fancy* opened fire on them, they fired back. The only thing that saved Low and his men from being captured was an all-encompassing fog that enabled the *Fancy* to sail away undetected.[5]

Low now set a course for the Caribbean, but during the voyage encountered a terrible hurricane, which damaged the *Fancy* to such an extent that she had to take shelter in the Leeward Islands. Here Low had his ship repaired and took on new provisions, but, much to his annoyance, he also gleaned from the locals that several warships were hunting him in the West Indies, so it was decided to set sail across the North Atlantic toward the Azores.

'The good fortune of Low was now singular,' wrote Charles Ellms in his *Pirates Own Book*, for, 'in his way thither he captured a French ship of 34 guns, and carried her along with. Then entering St Michael's roads, he captured seven sail [the *Notre Dame*, the *Mere de Dieu*, the *Dove*, the *Rose Pink* and three other vessels], threatening with instant death all who dared to oppose him. Thus, by inspiring terror, without firing a single gun, he became master of all that property.'

But Ellms forgot to mention one bloodcurdling act that Low appears to have committed during this attack. In his book *Pirates of the Western Seas*, Captain A. G. Course accuses him not only of ransacking then burning several of the French vessels but afterwards – having said all the crew could go free – changing his mind and singling out a cook whom Low said was 'a greasy looking fellow' who 'should fry well'. This poor man was subsequently tied to the mainmast of one of the French vessels, after which the boat was set alight.

Low now sent word ashore to the Governor of St Michael's that in exchange for fresh water and provisions he would release the remaining ships, which hadn't been burnt. The Governor agreed, after which Low returned all the vessels save one, the *Rose Pink*, which he took as his own while giving control of the *Fancy* to his second-in-command, a man by the name of Harris.

The *Fancy* and the *Rose Pink* now set sail from St Michael's toward St Mary's Island, but on the way spotted the *Wright* – a galley under the command of a Captain Carter. Harris opened fire on the ship and Carter retaliated. In fact, so fierce was his resistance to the pirates that when eventually the *Wright* was overcome by them, Harris and his men attacked everyone on board with cutlasses, cutting and hacking them to pieces. Two Portuguese passengers suffered an even worse fate than this. They were hoisted up and hanged from each fore yardarm till they were part-asphyxiated, after which they were lowered onto the deck only to be hoisted up again seconds later – and this time both men's necks snapped. It was all part of the pirates' entertainment, something that amused them almost as much as slashing their victims to pieces.

Low watched the spectacle, having joined Harris on board the *Wright* directly after it was captured. Not that he had escaped without injury himself, for at one point he received a blow to the jaw. The ship's doctor had to stitch up the wound, but Low, having decided he'd not made a good enough job of it, found fault with the doctor, who in turn hit Low. The second blow to the jaw opened up the wound once more, but this time the doctor refused to help, telling Low he could stitch it up himself. Naturally, Low was incensed, and several writers have since commented that this was probably why Low replaced Harris as captain of the *Fancy* with a man called Spriggs – Harris was obviously unable to keep his men under control.

The *Wright* having been plundered and her sails destroyed, the *Fancy* and the *Rose Pink* now set sail to Madeira for fresh water, after which they continued southwards toward the Cape Verde Islands. Here they captured the *Liverpool Merchant*, which was under the command of Captain Goulding. According to Charles Johnson, their haul was '300 gallons of brandy, two guns and carriages, a mast, yard and hawsers, besides six of his men'. It was also while sailing among the Cape Verde Islands that Low captured and looted two Portuguese sloops headed for Brazil, an English sloop bound for Santa Cruz and three sloops from St Thomas that were on their way to Curaçao. Low also detained a trading sloop from England which he decided to keep for himself.

With his fleet now numbering three vessels, Low put in at Boavista in order to clean and restock each vessel, but no fresh water was available so the pirates had to sail onwards to the island of St Nicholas. Here, on 20 October 1722, at Carrisal Roads, they captured a vessel called the *Margaret*, which was commanded by Captain George Roberts.

At dawn on the morning of the 20th October 1722, Captain Roberts

Low narrowly escaped capture when the gunship Greyhound *engaged Low's ship, the* Fancy, *and another of his ships, the* Ranger, *off Rhode Island. The* Fancy *sustained a number of casualties in the action and a great deal of damage but slipped away in failing daylight. The* Ranger's *crew were jailed in Newport, with twenty-five of them subsequently hanged.*

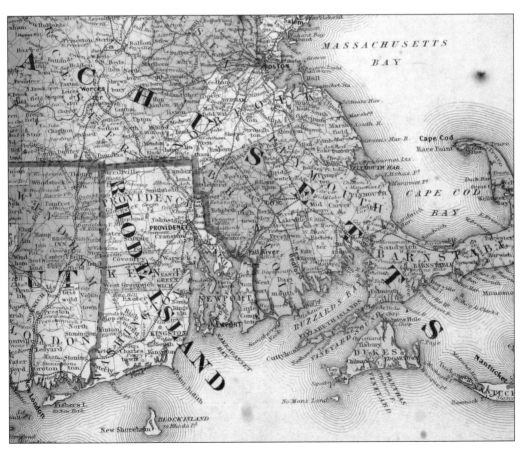

espied three ships cruising off the Bay of Carrisal, which on seeing him, backed their sails to await his coming up. When within about a mile, the nearest vessel stood toward the Margaret under the English flag and passing across his bows hailed him in a peremptory manner to come aboard with his boat. Accordingly the boat was sent, but Roberts not coming with it, the pirate captain hailed him, calling out 'You Dog, You Son of a Bitch. Why have you not come aboard us?' Upon hearing this rude greeting Roberts deemed it best to comply and accordingly, when the boat returned, got into it and ran alongside the Pirate ship.[6]

With Roberts on board, Low is said to have apologized for the initial unfriendliness, after which a meeting was held on the *Rose Pink* in order to decide what should be done with the prisoner. In fact, Roberts was detained overnight by the pirates, but the following morning was met by three of their number who recognized him as being their captain when they had all sailed on board a ship called the *Susannah* in 1718. The three pirates all warned Roberts that he was to be kept on board as a prisoner in order that he could navigate the *Rose Pink* down the coast of Brazil. These three pirates also had words with Captain Low to the effect that Roberts was a family man with a wife and four children, and they also said he had always treated his crew extremely well. Uncertain what to do, the following morning Low had his men hoist a green silk flag depicting a yellow man blowing a trumpet. This was known as a Consultation Flag and when hoisted was supposed to bring representatives over from the other pirate ships for a discussion.

At the gathering, Low asked Roberts about his family and if they were adequately maintained. Roberts replied that no, his wife and children were practically penniless, owing to him having poured all his money into refitting the *Margaret* and buying her cargo, but if the pirates let him go and allowed him to carry on trading, he could provide for his family properly.

Low is now said to have turned to a man called Russell, who was captain of the third of Low's ships, and said that Roberts should be released, but Russell disagreed. He wanted Roberts' cargo for himself. With matters at a deadlock, a vote was cast among the pirates, but while this was taking place Russell tried to persuade Roberts to join his merry band and become a pirate himself. To no avail – Roberts wanted nothing to do with either Low or Russell and said as much, after which he was detained once again overnight. The following morning Roberts was informed that his mate and crew had all joined the pirates, but still he himself could not be persuaded to do the same. Even when Russell suggested he stay on the *Rose Pink* and navigate them down the coast of Brazil, after which they would give him a better ship in exchange for the *Margaret*, Roberts declined the offer. He wanted his own sloop returned, but Russell wouldn't take no for an answer and instead invited him on to his own vessel to share a bowl of punch.

While on board, Russell twice attempted to persuade Roberts to change his mind. At one point he brandished a pistol in Roberts' face to try to get his point across, and it was only by the narrowest of margins that Roberts wasn't killed. Instead, Russell's gunner wrestled the pistol out of his master's hands and afterwards reminded him that he was infringing pirate laws by acting in this fashion. 'Thereupon a quarrel arose between the Gunner and Russell, the former requiring the Quartermaster [Russell] to be imprisoned, as he had attempted to kill a prisoner whose life had been guaranteed by the Majority. The Quartermaster [Russell] was then deprived of his arms and told that any further disobedience to the will of the majority would cause his certain death.'[7]

By morning tempers had died down and Russell was released, but he was still not happy that Roberts was to be given his ship back. Nevertheless, he deferred to Captain Low, but insisted that he and his crew should strip the *Margaret* of all her provisions before she was returned to Roberts. Low then pointed out that if they set the *Margaret* adrift without any food or water on board, Roberts and his men would die. Russell in turn replied that it was what the majority of the pirates wanted to happen. It was the gunner who had already intervened to help Roberts who saved him for a second time. According to Charles Grey in his book *Pirates of the Eastern Seas*, it was he who made an impassioned speech to the effect that he had joined the pirates to make money, not to commit acts of wanton violence, and that if Russell set Roberts adrift in the *Margaret* without provisions then he would leave the pirates forthwith.

Finally Russell relented, ordering that four pounds of biscuit together with a musket and ammunition, a bottle of water and some tobacco be left upon the *Margaret*. On 29 October 1722, Roberts and the remainder of his crew – that is to say all those who wanted to stay loyal to their captain – were released.

For the next fourteen days, Roberts struggled to steer his ship toward land. Eventually, his efforts paid off as he first reached one of the Leeward Islands and afterwards managed to get to Jamaica. But perhaps the most extraordinary part of this whole story was the leniency shown by Edward Low to his captive. Why this was, no one has been able to say – but one thing is certain: it wasn't characteristic of Low to act in this manner for, as Grey points out, only a few weeks later Low was said to have had the ears of a couple of prisoners sliced off, seasoned with salt and pepper and then roasted for supper!

With the *Margaret* episode behind them, Low's three vessels – the *Rose Pink* captained by himself, the *Fancy* captained by Spriggs and the schooner captained by Russell – all sailed for Brazil. For days they navigated their way down the coastline, but saw only one ship worth chasing and this vessel was too nimble to be caught. Dispirited, Low turned his fleet around and sailed instead to the Caribbean – the three islands off French Guiana known as The Triangles. Here Low had his ships careened (turned over for cleaning and repair). First it was the *Rose Pink*'s turn. Low ordered his men to stand aloft both on the yard arms and in the rigging on one side of the boat so that their weight tipped her over. But the whole operation happened too quickly and the *Rose Pink* quickly began taking in water through portholes that hadn't been closed properly. Suddenly the whole ship capsized and two men were drowned, although Captain Low managed to rescue one of the ship's surgeons by dragging him through a porthole.

After this disaster, the *Rose Pink* had to be abandoned, so Low took over the captaincy of the *Fancy* and set sail for Tobago. But even then luck wasn't on his side for light winds and a strong current meant that they missed the island and instead landed in Grand Grenada, about fifty-five miles north-west.

At this point the French authorities, who were stationed in Grand Grenada, boarded the *Fancy*, forcing Low to hide most of his crew in the hold so that they didn't raise suspicion. Afterwards, having passed the inspection, Low captured the French vessel and gave the command of her over to Spriggs.

The *Fancy* and Sprigg's new vessel (no more is heard of Russell at this point so it must be assumed he left Low's fleet and took off by himself) now went pirating in the Caribbean. In a very short space of time they captured seven locally owned vessels and afterwards a Portuguese sloop called the *Signoria de Vietbria*. Low had to torture several of the crew on this last ship in order to make them tell him where their money was hidden. Eventually, one of their number confessed that the captain had dropped approximately 11,000 moidores (Portuguese gold coins) out of his cabin window into the sea. Low was said to be incensed by what he had lost and consequently dragged the captain up on deck, after which he had him lashed to the mast, had his lips cut off with a cutlass then fried them and forced the Portuguese chief mate to eat them. Afterwards the chief mate together with the captain and thirty-two of his crew were murdered.

In January 1723 Low captured a brig called the *Unity* off Santa Cruz, which he then added to his pirate fleet. The pirates sailed to Curaçao and along the mainland coastline where they sighted two large vessels, a warship called the *Mermaid* and a merchant ship from the West Coast of Africa. At this point, according to Captain A.G. Course in his book *Pirates of the Western Seas*, 'The two pirate vessels chased the ships until they discovered the identity of the *Mermaid*; then they tried to escape. When the warship caught up with them they parted and sailed in opposite directions.'

The two ships met up again five weeks later, and took shelter in Roatan Harbor in the Gulf of Honduras, where Low decided he would have both vessels cleaned and overhauled. The pirates set up tents on dry land and, while the ships were being repaired, relaxed in the only way pirates are said to know how – drinking and carousing and debauching the local women.

After this Low and Spriggs both seem to have lain low for a couple of months – in fact it isn't until 27 May 1723 that much more is really known about Low's activities, for on that day he was spotted off the coast of Carolina in the *Fancy*. He was, according to certain reports, accompanied by a Captain Charles Harris who was in command of a sloop called the *Ranger*. Together Low and Harris chased and captured three ships: the *Crown*, the *King William* and the *Carteret*. Only a few days previously Low and Harris had also captured the *Amsterdam Merchant* from New England, which was under the command of Captain John Welland (or variously Williard). Low detested men from New England; as Charles Johnson puts it, 'as Low let none of that country depart without some marks of his rage, he cut off this gentleman's [Welland's] ears, slit up his nose, and cut him in several places of his body, and, after plundering his ship, let him pursue his voyage.'

Nor was Welland the last of Low's victims. A few days later he captured a sloop called the *Hopeful Betty* off Delaware, which was commanded by Captain Greenman, whose face he is said to have slashed with a cutlass. Greenman afterwards fled to Philadelphia where he reported what had happened and told the authorities that Low had boasted of recently capturing fifteen ships and looting about £80,000 in gold and silver from these vessels.

In response, the American authorities sent out a man-of-war called the *Greyhound* under the command of Captain Peter Solgard. The *Greyhound* was manned with '20 guns, and 120 men, rather inferior in force to the two pirate vessels'[8] but was still a formidable fighting force.

On the morning of 10 June 1723 Captain Solgard first sighted the pirate fleet. In turn, Low and Spriggs sighted Captain Solgard and, unaware that his vessel was a man-of-war, gave chase to the *Greyhound*. Meanwhile, Captain Solgard, not wanting to arouse Low's suspicions, pretended to escape, but at the same time he began clearing his decks for action. Soon the pirate vessels caught up with the *Greyhound*, at which point Solgard tacked ship and stood toward them. All the ships began firing – the action lasted two hours, after which the pirates took out their oars in order to pull away. But the *Greyhound* responded in kind and by about 2.30 in the afternoon is said to have caught up with the pirates. Fighting resumed, with the *Greyhound* maneuvering itself between the *Fancy* and the *Ranger* until finally, with one particular shot, she brought down the latter's mainsail. Low now fled the scene, leaving Harris to fare for himself, which he did by surrendering to Solgard along with all of his men. The following is an account of the action which was published in a local newspaper dated Rhode Island, 14 June 1723:

> **H.M. Ship Greyhound arrived here June 11th, Peter Solgard, Commander, and brought in pirate sloop of eight guns, Bermuda built, forty-two white men and six black of which number eight were wounded and four killed; the sloop was one commanded by Harris, very well fitted and loaded with all sorts of provisions [...] At 5 p.m., having got the prisoners on board, we continued [said Solgard] to chase the other sloop [captained by Low], and at 8 p.m. he bore from us N.W. by W., two miles, when we lost sight of him near Block Island. One pirate was for blowing up the Ranger rather than surrendering, and being prevented, went forward and blew out his brains with his pistol.**[9]

In fact, Solgard was certain that if there had been more daylight left, he would have captured Low and the *Fancy*, which he believed had been badly damaged in the action, with a number of Low's men either killed or wounded.

Meanwhile, thirty of the *Ranger*'s pirates along with Harris were now taken to Newport where they were jailed until their trial on 10 July 1723, held at the Court of the Admiralty, also in Newport. For the main part of the trial, the capture of the *Amsterdam Merchant* was used in evidence against the accused, mainly because there were several available witnesses who could testify that Captain Welland had suffered

When he learned that several warships were cruising the Caribbean searching for him, Low escaped by heading across the Atlantic to the Azores. Sao Miguel harbor in the Azores is now more used to accommodating luxury yachts than it is ruthless buccaneers.

grievous bodily harm at the hands of Low and company. In addition, Solgard also testified against the pirates, giving evidence regarding the fight between the *Greyhound* and Low and Harris' vessels. All the pirates pleaded not guilty, but few escaped with their lives: on 19 July 1723 twenty-five of their number, including Charles Harris, were executed near Newport, Rhode Island. Two others, John Brown and Patrick Cunningham, were found guilty, but given a respite and recommended for a King's pardon, while eight lucky men were found not guilty and subsequently set free.

Meanwhile, Low, having deserted his fellows, now began plotting new, more dastardly, crimes. His first victim was a whaling sloop from Nantucket that was working the New England coastline, commanded by Nathan Skiff. Skiff was an innocuous enough young man, but, on capturing the whaling sloop, Low took an immediate dislike to him and had him strip off his clothing so that the pirates could whip him. Low then had Skiff's ears cut off and finally ordered that he be shot through the head. The other whalers on board were then thrown into a small fishing vessel, given the barest of provisions and set adrift.

Two days later Low captured a second whaling vessel – only this time he had the captain's head lopped off with a cutlass. Later that same day he is said to have captured two further whaling sloops off Rhode Island. On the first vessel he ripped open one of the ship's masters and while he was still alive cut out his heart, had it roasted then force-fed it to the mate on the other whaler. Low was then all for murdering more of the whaling sloop's crew, but by this time his own men were becoming sickened by his actions and demanded that Low stop.

Tired of the east coast of America, Low set sail for Newfoundland, and near Cape Breton is said to have captured twenty-three fishing vessels – one of which was armed with twenty-two guns. Low had this one re-equipped for piratical duties and afterwards sailed his fleet out to the 'Banks' where he subsequently captured and plundered eighteen more boats.

Captain Solgard hadn't given up hope of tracking Low down, and began searching all the harbors up and down the coast of Newfoundland. On 16 June 1723 he met a Captain Durrell who was in command of HMS *Seahorse*. Subsequently, the two men joined forces. At the same time Low captured a ship called the *Merry Christmas*, but rather than looting and sinking it he decided to make her his flagship and give himself the title of Admiral. Low designed a new pirate flag for his new sailing vessel: a red skeleton against a black background.

Early in September 1723 Low sailed back to the Azores where he attacked an English brigantine owned by a Portuguese nobleman. Half the crew were also from Portugal – a fact that didn't escape Low, who had these 'foreigners' hanged from the yardarm while the English crew were allowed to go free.

From the Azores Low then sailed to the Canary Islands and the Cape Verdes, where he captured a schooner called the *Delight* which, much like the *Merry Christmas*, he had refitted for piratical service. But hereafter the story of Captain Edward Low begins to peter out. It is known that he captured a ship called the *Squirrel* in January 1724, and on 17 May it was reported that he looted a ship in Barbados. Curiously, not a lot else is known. Captain A.G. Course repeats the best-known story that, in the late spring/early summer of 1724 Low began having trouble with his crew and, after one particular dispute in which the quartermaster sided with the men rather than with Low, Low murdered the quartermaster in his sleep. The next day the crew, having discovered the body, mutinied and put Low into a boat with only a few provisions on board. Low was then said to have been picked up by a French vessel that took him back to Martinique, but while there he was recognized and subsequently put on trial for piracy, found guilty and hanged.

However, Charles Johnson is not so certain of Low's final days. In his account of this most disreputable villain he sums up by saying, 'we have had no news concerning him come to England, since this I have now mentioned; but I have heard that he talked of going to Brazil; and if so, it is likely we may too soon hear of some exploit or other; though the best information we could receive, would be, that he and all his crew were at the bottom of the sea.'[10]

1 Ellms, *The Pirates Own Book*.
2 Ibid.
3 Johnson, *A General History...*
4 Course, *Pirates of the Western Seas*.
5 Ibid.
6 Grey, *Pirates of the Eastern Seas*.
7 Ibid.
8 Johnson, op. cit.
9 Course, op. cit.
10 Johnson, op. cit.

JOHN RACKHAM
Calico Jack

He was handsome and well-built with black, wavy hair and
flashing dark eyes and undoubtedly attractive to women.
Unlike Blackbeard he sprinkled scent on himself. His love affairs,
according to him, were mostly with women of high social position
[...] though Anne Bonny found that many of his stories of
illicit love were lies.

Captain A.G. Course,
Pirates of the Western Seas

Known as Calico Jack for his habit of wearing colorful cotton clothing, Captain John Rackham was one of the most vibrant characters ever to have sailed the high seas. His flamboyance, however, was tempered by his dark side, the ruthlessness that characterized all of those who chose to terrorize the crews and plunder the cargoes of innocent merchant vessels. A ladies' man, it is said he kept several mistresses in Cuba, while on a one-to-one basis he met the already married Anne Bonny and persuaded her to run away to sea with him. Never one to do things by halves, he also employed another female pirate on board his ship, Mary Read, and the exploits of all three are inevitably closely linked. Rackham's colorful dress sense and lively way with the ladies may have marked him out as being distinctly different to other pirates, but he was not blessed with either a long or a fruitful career. Instead, he ended his days much like so many of his contemporaries, 'dancing the hempen gig' – dangling at the end of a rope.

Nothing is known of John Rackham's early life; indeed, he really only comes into his own when, around 1718, he is mentioned as being a quartermaster on board a pirate ship captained by Charles Vane. Vane was a demanding man who treated both his crew and his captives harshly, which might go some way to explaining why Rackham ended up challenging his captain over a decision he'd made concerning a French man-of-war.

According to Charles Johnson in his book *A General History of the Robberies and Murders of the Most Notorious Pirates*, Rackham confronted Vane over his reluctance to attack the French ship while it was sailing across the Windward Passage. 'Vane, the captain, was for making off as fast as he could, alleging the man-of-war was too strong to cope with; but one John Rackam [sic], who was an officer that had a kind of a check upon the captain, rose up in defence of a contrary opinion, saying that though she had more guns, and a greater weight of metal, they might board her, and then the best boys would carry the day.'

After Rackham's challenge, the crew labeled Vane a coward and decided almost to a man to elect Rackham as their new captain. This occurred (according to Johnson) on 24 November 1718, after which Vane was placed in a small sloop, along with the other

Calico Jack was known for his flamboyant dress sense, wearing colorful clothing and priding himself on his appearance. He was also known as a ladies' man, marrying Anne Bonny but maintaining several mistresses in Cuba.

pirates who had taken his side in the argument, and set adrift.

Rackham now took command of Vane's ship, the *Kingston*, and proceeded to mount a series of successful raids on a number of vessels sailing off Jamaica. Again, according to Johnson, there is little evidence to suggest that Rackham was anything but fair in his treatment of prisoners – there is no suggestion that he ever tortured or murdered anyone in cold blood. Indeed, quite the opposite, for after one raid on a Madeiraman, he returned the ship to her captain and afterwards arranged for a tavern-keeper called Hosea Tisdell, who was on board at that time, to be taken back to Jamaica so that he could carry on with his business. After this escapade Rackham then sailed to a small island retreat in order to spend 'Christmas ashore, drinking and carouzing [sic] as long as they had any liquor left'.[1]

Rackham then sailed toward Bermuda where he captured two vessels, one a ship bound for England from Carolina and the other a 'pink' (see Glossary) from New England. Rackham took both boats back to the Bahamas where he set about stripping them of their assets while at the same time cleaning and re-tarring his own vessel. While he was there, Captain Rogers, who was then Governor of the Bahamas, heard of his presence and sent out a well-armed sloop which retook the two stolen vessels, though Rackham managed to escape from the scene before being captured.

At this point, Rackham is believed to have sailed to Cuba where he kept 'a little kind of family'[2], which is a polite way of describing his harem of prostitutes. Rackham and his men remained in Cuba for several months, enjoying the women and no doubt plenty of alcohol, but eventually – their provisions running dangerously low – they decided it was time to put to sea again. At the same time a Spanish guard-ship arrived in port, bringing with it a small English sloop. On sighting Rackham's vessel, the guard-ship immediately attacked it, but Rackham quickly maneuvered his boat behind a small island in order that the Spanish couldn't get at him until the following day. When night fell Rackham then took his men across to the English sloop which he boarded quietly, threatening the Spaniards on board that they would be slaughtered if they raised an alarm. Rackham then sailed the sloop out to sea as quickly as he could. The next morning the Spanish attacked Rackham's old vessel, but of course by then it was empty. The Spanish had been fooled and Rackham had sailed away with a new ship.

By August 1720 Rackham was scouring the harbors and inlets around the north and most western parts of Jamaica, but rather than attack large vessels he preferred to loot smaller boats with smaller crews that were easier to overcome. In September Rackham captured eight fishing vessels off the coast of Harbor Island and afterwards sailed for the French part of Hispaniola, where he spent some days rustling cattle and hunting wild hogs. Having restocked his ship with fresh meat, he then captured two sloops which he plundered, before returning to Jamaica where, on 19 October, he took a schooner near Porto Maria Bay (on the north coast of the island) that was captained by Thomas Spenlow. The following morning Rackham spotted another sloop, this one anchored in Dry Harbor Bay, which he fired on, causing all the men on board to abandon ship, jumping into canoes to row ashore. When these sailors realized they had been attacked by pirates, rather than staying hidden they made it known that they would like nothing better than to join Rackham and his crew. Rackham agreed to their request and welcomed them on board. Everyone gathered on deck and drank to the health of the new recruits, who were said to be more than pleasantly surprised at the welcome.

Captain Rackham's regime was hardly a tough or harsh one. Rackham wasn't a Blackbeard or a Benito de Soto or even a Henry Morgan. Instead, he was the equivalent of a petty thief – he was a minor crook, a man who preferred to restrict his raids to fishing boats and other small vessels. Without doubt, he struck terror into the hearts of his victims, but perhaps found the threat of violence to be as effective as actually perpetrating atrocities on those whose ships he looted. This may also go some way to explaining his undoubted success as a ladies' man – far from endeavoring to capture as many ships as he could, far from attempting to slaughter and torture every other sailor in sight, he appeared to prefer a gentler way of life, a life that included women. This is what ultimately made him so famous – his relationship with Anne Bonny and, to a lesser extent, Mary Read.

Captain John Rackham first met Anne Bonny in May 1719 on Providence Island. Bonny was introduced to Calico Jack by Captain Jennings who at that time ran the pirate community on the island. 'There he [Jennings] introduced her to the pirate captains then in port; they were John Martel, Thomas Burgess, John Carter, Peter Courant, Thomas Cocklyn, Charles Bellamy, Benjamin Hornigold, John Auger and Edward Teach (Blackbeard). Anne and her husband stayed in Captain Jenning's house overlooking the harbour.'[3] It was after her husband went to sea that Bonny first met John Rackham and almost immediately fell in love with him.

Rackham had ostensibly gone to Providence Island to take advantage of the amnesty that Captain Rogers was offering to all pirates who were willing to renounce their old ways and give up piracy (see Glossary). But, having accepted the royal pardon, Rackham met Anne Bonny and persuaded her to leave her husband, taking her on board his ship. The lure of the high seas, combined with Anne's powers of persuasion, soon saw to it that he turned his back on Rogers' offer and returned to a life of piracy. Anne soon became pregnant, at which point Rackham sailed to Cuba where he left his lover with friends until after the baby was born. Cruelly perhaps for the child, it was subsequently handed over to these friends on a permanent basis while Anne returned to Rackham on board his ship. Dressing up as a man, Anne kept Rackham company, and, as Johnson says in his *General History*, 'when any business was to be done in their way, nobody was more forward or courageous than she […]'.

Around this time Mary Read also joined Rackham's crew. She had been sailing on a merchant ship (disguised as a man and calling herself Mark Read) which had been captured by Rackham, after which she was brought aboard his ship. Bonny (not realizing that the new crew member was a woman) found herself strangely attracted to Read – so much so that eventually Read had to be honest and reveal herself for what she was. The two women then told Rackham about Mary's true identity.

In the circumstances, it would have been only a matter of time before Mary Read's true identity was discovered. She was allowed to remain on John Rackham's ship – even falling in love with a young officer who was on board one of the ships that Calico Jack subsequently captured. The officer's name was Tom Deane. He was from Somerset and had been employed as a navigator on board a merchant vessel. But once Deane had been taken prisoner by John Rackham and was made to work as a pirate, a romance quickly sprang up between him and Mary. He even asked her to marry him. Mary too was said to be smitten, to the extent that when an argument broke out between Deane and another pirate, Mary deliberately picked an argument with that man so that she could fight the subsequent duel. All the parties involved were then rowed ashore, after which pistols were handed to Mary and her opponent, but when they were fired, both parties missed. Cutlasses were handed out, at which point Mary, who was a fearless swordswoman, killed her opponent – thus saving her lover, who had no experience of fighting either with cutlasses or with guns.

By the summer of 1720, Calico Jack, Anne Bonny and Mary Read had returned to Providence Island. There is no doubt that Captain Rogers was aware of their presence – in fact, it was a constant thorn in his side, and became even more so in August that year. On 22 August, the three pirates, together with the rest of Rackham's crew, quietly rowed out to a single-masted, twelve-ton sailing ship – the *William* – which was anchored in the middle of Nassau Harbour. The *William* was owned by a local man called Captain John Ham and was a beautiful vessel, with four guns mounted on her decks and two swivel guns on her rails; she was also well stocked with ammunition – an irresistible prize, duly captured by Rackham and company who sailed her swiftly out to sea.

Back on shore, Captain Rogers – certain that he knew who had stolen John Ham's vessel – issued a proclamation in *The Boston Gazette* that not only gave a full description of the *William*, but also named Rackham and his cohorts as the culprits. The proclamation went on to say that 'the said John Rackum [sic] and his said Company are hereby proclaimed Pirates and Enemies to the Crown of Great Britain, and are to be so treated and Deem'd by all his Majesty's subjects.'

In his fury, Rogers also sent a sloop out after the pirates – and then, on 2 September, a second one, armed with twelve guns and fifty-four men. But news of this mission soon reached Rackham who, having just looted a fleet of small fishing vessels, now headed south for Hispaniola. On 1 October Calico Jack captured a schooner off the north coast of Jamaica, and for the next three or four weeks sailed westwards along the island, not far distant from the sandy beaches of Ocho Rios, Falmouth and Montego Bay. Finally he came to Jamaica's most westerly point at Negril Bay. But, as Charles Johnson so aptly says, 'Rackham's coasting the island in this manner, proved fatal to him,' for word of his location soon got back to Rogers, who immediately sent a sloop out under the command of Captain Jonathan Barnet.

Meanwhile, Rackham, sailing off Negril Bay, had spotted a small vessel and hailed her crew, inviting them to join him on board the *William* for a bowl of punch. At first, the men refused the offer, but presently they changed their minds and boarded Rackham's vessel, only to be met by fifty or so pirates brandishing muskets and cutlasses. Fearing for

Mary Read was as vicious a fighter as any of her male counterparts, proficient in the use of the sword and the pistol. In this illustration, she taunts her opponent with a final insult, letting him know that he has been defeated by a woman before putting him to death.

their lives, the men were about to jump overboard when suddenly Captain Barnet's sloop sailed in to view. Now it was the pirates' turn to feel frightened – they weighed anchor and tried to escape as best they could. But Barnet set off in hot pursuit 'and having the advantage of little breezes of wind, which blew off the land, came up with her […]'.[4] Barnet then hailed the *William* and, asking for the captain's identification, received the reply, 'John Rackham from Cuba.' Barnet ordered Calico Jack and his crew to surrender, but Rackham was having none of it and is said to have fired a swivel gun at Barnet's vessel. The shot missed, but despite the fact it was now dark and almost impossible to see his opponent, Barnet returned fire with a broadside and a volley of small shot, bringing down 'the pirate's boom, effectively disabling their vessel'.[5]

Barnet and his men then swiftly boarded the *William* with every intention of engaging in hand-to-hand combat. Curiously, however, only two pirates on board seemed willing to take up arms against them: Mary Read and Anne Bonny. The rest of the crew appear to have been either too tired, perhaps too drunk or just too frightened to put up any defense. Eventually, all the pirates, including Bonny, Read and Calico Jack, were rounded up, placed in a boat and taken ashore by Barnet's men to Davis' Cove near Negril Point. The pirates were escorted across the island by Major Richard James and his troops where they were deposited in a jail in Spanish Town (the administrative capital of Jamaica in the eighteenth century).

The trial of Calico Jack and ten of his fellow pirates (excluding Anne Bonny and Mary Read who were tried separately) began on 16 November at the Admiralty Court. Sir Nicholas Lawes presided over the hearing alongside twelve commissioners, while the eleven accused were named as John Rackham, George Fetherston, Richard Corner, John Davis, John Howell, Patrick Carty, Thomas Earl, James Dobbin, Thomas Bourn, John Fenwick and Noah Harwood. Tom Deane was not put on trial for, according to Captain A.G. Course, Mary Read gave evidence at her trial to the effect that Deane had been employed on a merchant ship when he had been captured by John Rackham and afterwards forced into piracy against his will.

Four charges, however, were brought against the rest of the pirates: That Rackham and his crew 'did piratically, feloniously, and in an hostile manner, attack, engage and take, seven certain fishing boats'. That Rackham and his crew did 'upon the high sea, in a certain place, distance about three leagues from the island of Hispaniola [...] set upon, shoot at, and take two certain merchant sloops'. That Rackham and his crew did attack a schooner under the command of Captain Thomas Spenlow, after which they placed Spenlow and his men 'in corporeal fear of their lives'. That, not far out of Dry Harbour Bay in Jamaica, Rackham and his crew boarded and looted a ship by the name of the *Mary* and afterwards stole her tackle.

Two witnesses were called to testify for the prosecution. The first was Captain Thomas Spenlow of the aforementioned schooner who gave a full account to the court regarding how his vessel had been shot at by John Rackham's sloop and how 'they boarded him, and took him; and took out of the said schooner, fifty rolls of tobacco, and nine bags of pieminto [sic] and kept him in their custody about forty-eight hours, and then let him and his schooner depart.' The second witness was a sailor by the name of James Spatchears who had been aboard Jonathan Barnett's ship when it gave chase to the pirates. Spatchears gave a full and frank account of the action that occurred between Barnett and Rackham's vessels and how initially Rackham had refused to surrender. But having heard all of the evidence against them, the pirates still pleaded not guilty.

To no effect. Sir Nicholas Lawes and his twelve commissioners were unmoved by what they heard and the very next day five out of the eleven pirates were hanged at Gallows Point – a narrow piece of land that sticks out from Port Royal. Ironically, only a few months earlier, on 22 March 1720, Captain Vane, with whom John Rackham had begun his pirate career, had also been hanged here. Having been set adrift by Rackham back in 1718, Vane had eventually reached the Bay of Honduras, after which he'd regrouped and set sail once again, resuming his piratical activities with a vengeance. Unfortunately for him, however, after several successful raids on different nationality ships, in February 1719 his sloop was overwhelmed by a huge tornado that swept it onto an uninhabited island in the Bay of Honduras. The ship was smashed to pieces and most of her crew was drowned, but miraculously Vane survived. Helped by local fishermen, who visited the island to capture turtles, he was eventually rescued – but at this point his luck ran out completely for the man who had come to his aid, a Captain Holford, took him straight back to Jamaica where he handed Vane over to the authorities. A few days later Vane was hanged at Gallows Point.

Port Royal, where the gallows were erected, had become notorious not, as one might have supposed, for the piratical haven it had become, but for the number of pirates who ended their days there, swinging on the end of a rope. Vane was one such, the pirates who had sailed with Calico Jack were five others, but theirs weren't the only executions to take place on this dreary promontory. In May 1722 forty-one pirates were hanged there[7], whilst almost a century later Gallows Point was still a place of execution, as the following account by Captain Boteler of HMS *Gloucester* illustrates. Boteler had the dubious pleasure of being present when twenty Spanish pirates were hanged in 1823.

> **Early in the morning the Gloucester's boats, manned and armed with a guard of marine rums and fifes, went up to Kingston, returning in procession towing the launch with the captain and nine pirates, the drums and fifes giving out the 'Dead March in Saul', 'Adeste Fideles', etc. The following morning the other ten were also executed – a fearful sight. No men could go to their death with less apparent concern. Before the captain first went up the ladder he called upon his men to remember they were before foreigners and to die like Spaniards.[8]**

Captain John Rackham, having seen five of his men executed, knew he didn't have long to live. According to Johnson, he therefore made a last plea to be allowed to see Anne Bonny before he died. This was arranged and he was taken to see her in her cell, 'but all the comfort she gave him, was, that she was sorry to see him there, but if he had fought like a man, he need not have been hanged like a dog'.[9] It was hardly a glowing testimony to his manhood, nor perhaps was it the kind of loving response that might have been expected, but then Anne Bonny wasn't the type of woman to suffer fools gladly. Dismissed from her presence, Rackham was taken back to his cell. The next day he and the remaining five pirates were then taken to Kingston where they were all hanged. Afterwards the bodies of John Rackham, George Fetherston and Richard Corner were taken down from the gibbet and hung in gibbet cages, one at Bush Key, one at Gun Key and one at Plumb Point – all as a warning to other pirates.

The execution of known pirates, that being the punishment for their crime at the time, can never be regarded as a tragedy, but the executions of the sailors whom Rackham had captured off Negril, enticing them aboard to share a glass of punch, were surely a tragic travesty of justice. That John Eaton, Edward Warner, Thomas Baker, Thomas Quick, John Cole, Benjamin Palmer, Walter Rouse, John Hanson and John Howard had come on board Rackham's ship on the day that she was captured by Captain Barnet was to be their undoing for, having been found in the company of pirates, they were now branded with the same iron.

Their trial was postponed until 24 January 1721, probably so that enough evidence could be gathered against them to prove that they had 'piratical intention' when they boarded a known pirate vessel. Some of the charges against them were as follows: 'That they brought guns and cutlasses on board with them. That when Captain Barnet chased them, some were drinking, and others walking the deck [...] That during the time Captain Barnet chased them, some of the prisoners at the bar (but which of 'em he could not tell) helped to row the sloop, in order to escape from Barnet. That they all seemed to be consorted together.'[10]

In their defense the men said that they had bought their small ship in order to go turtling and being at Negril Point they had just got on shore when they saw the *William* whose men shouted over for them to join them on board. The nine men maintained that they had refused the offer, but after much persuasion they had given in. Shortly thereafter Captain Barnet then 'heaved in sight' at which point John Rackham had ordered them to weigh anchor. The men said that they had refused to go with him, but that Rackham then employed violent means in order to force them to remain. When finally Barnett boarded the *William* they had readily surrendered themselves and indeed were relieved to have been rescued.

Having given their evidence, the prisoners were removed from the bar, after which the court considered its verdict. According to Johnson, the commissioners present all believed the men to be guilty of piracy and therefore one by one they were condemned to death.

On 17 February 1721 John Eaton, Thomas Quick and Thomas Baker were all executed at Gallows Point, while the following day John Cole, John Howard and Benjamin Palmer were hanged at Kingston, but what happened to the final three men is unknown. In all probability they were hanged as well, 'which everybody must allow proved somewhat unlucky to the poor fellows', as Captain Johnson so aptly noted.

1 Johnson, *A General History...*

2 Ibid.

3 Course, *Pirates of the Western Seas.*

4 Johnson, op. cit.

5 A description of the fight between Barnet and Rackham appears in the printed transcript of Rackham's trial, *The Tryals of Captain John Rackham and other pirates*, Robert Baldwin, 1721 Colonial Office Records 137/14, Public Record Office. Extracts used here also appear in Cordingly, *Life Among the Pirates.*

6 Stockton, *Buccaneers and Pirates of Our Coasts.*

7 Pawson and Buisseret, *Port Royal, Jamaica.*

8 Ibid.

9 Johnson, op. cit.

10 Ibid.

ANNE BONNY

a most peculiar man

She was of a fierce and courageous temper, wherefore, when she
lay under condemnation, several stories were reported of her,
much to her disadvantage...

Captain Charles Johnson,
A General History of the Robberies and
Murders of the Most Notorious Pirates

O f all the famous pirate trials that occurred during the eighteenth century, including that of Captain Kidd, perhaps the most astonishing – the one that most captured the public's imagination – was a trial that took place in Spanish Town (then known as St Jago de la Vega), Jamaica, on 28 November 1720. Shortly before this, Captain John Rackham, who was better known by the soubriquet Calico Jack, had been apprehended by Jonathan Barnet, who had a privateering commission to intercept pirate ships. During the short battle that took place between Barnet's men and the pirates, it was discovered that two of Rackham's fiercest crew members were women dressed up as men – Anne Bonny and Mary Read.

Although not as famous as Blackbeard or Henry Morgan, because of their sex both women achieved almost legendary status and their memories live on to this day.

Anne Bonny, according to Charles Johnson, was born on 8 March 1700 near Cork in Ireland, the bastard child of William Cormac, a lawyer, and a servant-maid, Mary Brennan. Despite these inauspicious beginnings, Bonny's father was said to have been so fond of his child that he had her come live with him and his wife, but to avoid idle rumor had young Anne dressed up as a boy so that he could pretend to his wife that he was training the child up as a lawyer's clerk. Meanwhile, the wife, on discovering her husband's deception, stopped his allowance (for it was she who had been born wealthy) and this in turn caused such a scandal among the local dignitaries that eventually William Cormac decided to up sticks and leave the country for a new life abroad. Accompanied by Mary Brennan and Anne, he sailed to South Carolina in America, where he managed to scrape enough money together trading as a merchant to buy a small plantation near Charleston.

In his book *Pirates of the Western Seas*, Captain A.G. Course describes Anne at this age as being a very attractive young woman: 'She was a beautiful girl, tall with a full figure, had reddish-gold hair and greenish-brown eyes, all the signs of voluptuousness.' But as well as being a beautiful young woman, Anne was also said to have a fiery temper. At the age of thirteen, she allegedly stabbed a young servant girl in the belly with a carving knife. Perhaps this was an early indication of what was to come for, far from feeling content with her life on the plantation, Anne soon grew bored with her parents'

Anne Bonny is described as having been 'a beautiful girl, tall with a full figure, had reddish-gold hair and greenish-brown eyes'. Calico Jack was immediately attracted to her and Bonny clearly felt the same about him for, as soon as the opportunity presented itself, she deserted her husband to run off with Rackham.

agricultural idyll and when she was in her mid teens hooked up with a young renegade, 'a sailor without a shilling'[1] by the name of James Bonny. 'The avaricious father was so enraged, that, deaf to the feelings of a parent, he turned his own child out of doors. Upon this cruel usage, and the disappointment of her fortune, Anne and her husband sailed for the island of Providence, in the hope of gaining employment.'[2]

Providence at this time, around 1719, was a haven for pirates, mainly because the then Governor of the Bahamas had granted them an amnesty – a gesture that had seen Captain John Rackham accept a royal pardon and endeavor to lead a life on the straight and narrow. This attempt, however, was shortlived. Rackham was no more used to earning an honest living than the next pirate. Instead, he began to frequent the taverns around the waterfront area in Nassau, searching out new crew. It was here that he first came across Anne Bonny. Good-looking and well built, Rackham cut a fine figure and is said to have immediately caught Anne's eye. Rackham was also desperately attracted to Anne to whom, or so legend has it, he then laid siege, much as he might have done a ship he wanted to loot – 'no time wasted, straight up alongside, every gun brought to play, and the prize boarded'.[3]

No sooner had James Bonny joined the crew of a pirate vessel and left Providence, than Calico Jack persuaded Anne to leave her husband and join him as a pirate. Soon Anne was pregnant with their first child, but immediately after she had given birth, in Cuba, she abandoned the baby and joined Calico Jack as one of his crew – though dressed in men's clothing. Normally, women weren't allowed on board pirate ships unless, of course, they were prisoners – but in her disguise Anne fitted in well. Besides, she fought as adeptly as any of the men.

So how common was it for women to become pirates? Did they always have to disguise themselves in male attire? And, most curious of all, how did they keep their sex a secret on board ship, where living conditions were less than commodious? The answer to the latter question appears to be that they could not keep their gender a secret indefinitely and when Anne was joined on board Rackham's ship by a second female pirate, Mary Read, who had also disguised herself as a man (using the name Mark Read) the situation could have become quite ludicrous. As Captain A.G. Course points out in his *Pirates of the Western* Seas, the crews:

> lived and slept together in the 'tween decks, they bathed with water in a bucket standing naked on deck [...] There were no lavatories on board, although 'Mark' Read said that she 'learned to restrain natural functions until such time as they could be performed in secret.' [...] There were no cubicles or small rooms allocated for this and no doors could be locked or secured in any way. The 'heads', the open space on each side of the bow, where the bowsprit passes into the fo'c'sle head, was the open space used as a lavatory. One had to climb over a rail to get there and it was open to the view of anyone standing on the fo'c'sle head above.

It was by no means unknown for women to disguise themselves as men to go to sea. David Cordingly, in his *Life Among the Pirates,* cites the example of a girl by the name of Hannah Snell who in 1745 took to the sea in search of her husband, James Summs. Summs was a Dutch sailor who had abandoned Snell while she was pregnant. Not one to take such a snub lightly, she found employment on a British sloop, the HMS *Swallow*, which was commanded by Captain Rosier.

Mary Anne Arnold also joined a naval vessel, the *Robert Small*, which was commanded by Captain Scott. She worked as an able seaman for several months before being unmasked. However, even when Captain Scott knew her true identity, it didn't spell the end of her career. 'I have seen Miss Arnold,' he later wrote, 'among the first aloft to reef the mizzen-top-gallant sail during a heavy gale in the Bay of Biscay.'[4]

Fewer women opted to become pirates, though it is known a fair number existed. As well as Bonny and her shipmate Mary Read, there was the Irish pirate Grace O'Malley (see pages 17-27) and the Chinese pirate Cheng I Sao (see pages 159-169). There was also a Scandinavian woman by the name of Alwilda who first appears in Charles Ellms' *The Pirates Own Book: Authentic Narratives of the Most Celebrated Sea Robbers*.

Alwilda was the daughter of a 'Gothic' king called Synardus who pledged his daughter's hand in marriage to the son of King Sygarus of Denmark – Prince Alf.

Anne Bonny (left) was every bit as ruthless as any other pirate. When one of her shipmates began an argument one day about her being female, she is said immediately to have snatched a dagger and stabbed him straight through the heart.

Mary Read (opposite) had been brought up as a boy and worked for a French nobleman as a footman before serving aboard a man-of-war and even joining the army, where she fell in love with one of her fellow soldiers.

Unwilling for the union to go ahead, Alwilda 'embraced the life of a rover; and attired as a man, she embarked in a vessel of which the crew was composed of other young women of tried courage, dressed in the same manner'. This band of women then traveled far and wide, only to meet up one day with a band of pirates who had lost their commander. Talking to Alwilda and liking her 'agreeable manners', they decided she would be the perfect choice to take over as captain. Ellms then goes on to describe how Alwilda became so formidable a pirate that eventually Prince Alf was dispatched to chase her. This he did, finally catching up with his prey in the gulf of Finland. Alf boarded her ship and, having killed most of her crew, then went on

to capture Alwilda herself (although at this point he had no idea who she was). Shortly afterwards, Alf removed the pirate captain's helmet only to discover it was his 'beloved Alwilda; and it seems that his valour had now recommended him to the fair princess, for he persuaded her to accept his hand, married her on board, and then led her to partake of his wealth, and share his throne'.

But while Alwilda's story feels more than a little like a fairytale, Anne Bonny's is far less salubrious – for having joined Captain John Rackham's crew, she enjoyed a life where the killing of others became second nature. One story has it that another crew member challenged Anne one day about her being a female, at which point she is said to have picked up a dagger and stabbed him through the heart. It was also around this time that Mary Read joined Calico Jack's ship, also dressed up as a man. Shakespeare would have been proud of the ensuing turmoil (not to mention the comic potential of such a situation) for, according to Charles Johnson, Anne Bonny found herself drawn toward this new crew member and eventually, sitting down with Mary Read, revealed that she, Anne, was actually a woman. Mary Read then 'knowing what she would be at, and being sensible of her own capacity in that way, was forced to come to a right understanding with her, and so to the great disappointment of Anne Bonny, she let her know that she was a woman also'.[5]

The two women were remarkably similar, not only in their disguise, but in other less obvious ways. For instance, just as Anne Bonny had suffered a turbulent childhood so too had Read. According to Johnson, she was born in England, the second child of a young woman whose husband was a sailor. Shortly after the two were married, this man went to sea, never to return, leaving Mary's mother to bring up their child. Mary's mother then began a liaison with another man and fell pregnant. Ashamed at carrying a bastard child, she retired to stay with friends in the countryside. Soon after Mary was born, her elder child – a boy – died. Penniless, mourning the loss of her firstborn, Mary's mother decided to dress Mary up as a boy and visit her mother-in-law whom she duped into giving her an allowance of one crown a week to look after her 'grandchild'.

Brought up as a boy, when Mary reached the tender age of thirteen her mother secured her a job as a footman to a French noblewoman. But Mary was not the type of child who was born to serve, 'for growing bold and strong, and having also a roving mind, she entered herself on board a man-of-war, where she served some time, then quitted it, went over to Flanders, and carried arms in a regiment of foot, as a cadet'.[6] During this time, Mary met and fell in love with a handsome Flemish soldier who, according to A.G. Course, was called Jules Vosquin. Smitten, she began to neglect her duties, causing the rest of the troops (who didn't know she was a woman) to suspect she was mad. Mary, meanwhile, had to find a way to demonstrate to the soldier that she was not a man, but a woman. With this aim in mind, she saw to it that she and her Flemish paramour were given the same tent to share. During the night she then made sure he was fully aware of her sex. Naturally, the young man was surprised (and no doubt delighted). Unlike all the other soldiers in his regiment he now had a woman all to himself. But Mary played her hand well. Rather than succumb straightaway to his entreaties, she made it clear she wanted a more formal arrangement.

Mary and her Flemish soldier were married shortly thereafter. They both left the army and are said to have settled down to run a hostelry called the Three Trade Horses near Breda. But Mary's happiness was not to last long – soon after their wedding her husband died. Trade at the hostelry tailed off and Mary was forced to return to the army as a foot soldier. After this it is thought she grew weary of the regimented lifestyle she had once so adored. Deciding to change her life once and for all, she bought herself passage on board a ship bound for the West Indies. Of course, some might argue that this story sounds more like fiction than fact and, given that Captain Charles Johnson (whose book this account relies upon heavily) was once thought to be none other than Daniel Defoe (see Glossary), this charge is not so strange as it might first appear. After all, Defoe was the author of such ribald tales as *Moll Flanders* and *Roxanne* so if he was the author of *A General History of the Robberies and Murders of the Most Notorious Pirates*, he probably did indeed spice up his account of Mary's life. And, even if he wasn't the author, who is to say that the real Charles Johnson wasn't himself prone to making things up?

The problem is that there are no other accounts of either Anne Bonny's or Mary

Read's early lives to rely on. Johnson/Defoe's book is the only record available. What is certain, because there are naval records and eyewitness accounts to prove it, is that once Mary reached the West Indies and joined Calico Jack and Anne Bonny on board their ship, the three companions were inseparable (notwithstanding Mary later falling in love with a sailor called Tom Deane). They lived together and they fought together and nowhere was this better demonstrated than in 1720 when the trio, along with the rest of Calico's crew, set out to capture a twelve-ton sloop called the *William*.

The ship was moored in Nassau Harbor on Providence Island and was owned by a local man called Captain John Ham. Well stocked with ammunition and much else besides, she was easy pickings for anyone with a view to piracy. Rowing alongside her bow, a dozen of Calico's men climbed on board the *William* and, without further ado, raised the anchor and sailed her out toward the high seas. Luckily for John Ham's men, Calico Jack was not quite as bloodthirsty as some of his contemporaries. Most accounts would have it that he tried to treat all his captives if not with respect, then with restraint. But piracy, however nicely it was done, was still piracy and when John Ham lodged a complaint with the authorities that his vessel had been hijacked, the Governor of the Bahamas, Captain Rogers, had no choice but to write a warrant out for Jack's arrest. This was issued on 5 September 1720 and mentioned by name not only Captain John Rackham, but also 'two women […] Ann Fulford alias Bonny and Mary Read'. Further to this, the warrant also declared that 'the said John Rackum [sic] and his said Company are hereby proclaimed Pirates and Enemies to the Crown of Great Britain, and are to be so treated and Deem'd by all his Majesty's subjects.'[7]

In fact Captain Rogers (see Glossary) was a fair individual, albeit a tough one. He had sailed around the world from 1708 to 1711 on a privateering commission so he knew better than most about pirates and piracy. In 1718, with all the experience he had accumulated, he sailed out with three warships to the West Indies, holding a commission from the British government to rid the Bahamas of the infamous colony of pirates who frequented Providence Island. On arrival, he tried his hardest to promote law and order and, as mentioned earlier, initially he issued an amnesty for pirates willing to give up their life of crime. John Rackham was one such, but, now he'd returned to his old ways, Rogers was quite prepared to track him down and see him face justice. After all, other men who had

Alwilda was another female pirate, a Scandinavian princess who took to the high seas to avoid an arranged marriage.

relinquished piracy only to return to it had already been captured and executed by him. No exception could be made for John Rackham. Thus, having issued his warrant, Rogers dispatched a sloop with forty-five men on board expressly for the purpose of bringing Calico Jack back to face justice. So eager was Rogers to capture his man that on 2 September he sent out a second ship for the same purpose – this one armed with twelve guns and a crew of over fifty men.

The chase was on. Rackham had been busy attacking small fishing vessels in the vicinity of Harbor Island, but when he got wind of Rogers' plan, he promptly sailed south. On the way he ransacked two merchant sloops, afterwards returning to Jamaica where, near to Port Maria Bay, he captured a schooner which was commanded by Captain Thomas Spenlow. A few days later, on 20 October 1720, Rackham and his crew captured a second sloop, this time in Dry Harbor Bay. After these two successes, he then sailed the *William* westward, along the Jamaican coastline, until he reached Negril Point, but it was here that he encountered a fully operational privateering sloop commanded by Captain Jonathan Barnet, who had a commission from the Governor of Jamaica to arrest as many pirates as possible.

After a short exchange of gunfire which left the *William* disabled, Barnet and his men quickly boarded, at which point it might be expected that the pirates would have put up a good fight – indeed, that all of their number would have fought tooth and nail to repel the invaders. But this was not the case for, according to eyewitness accounts, only two pirates took up arms against Barnet and his men: Anne Bonny and Mary Read.

Dressed in their usual male attire, the two women picked up cutlasses and pistols and tried as hard as they could not only to fight off the intruders, but also to encourage their fellow pirates to act accordingly. The rest of the crew, however, were either too weary or too frightened to take up arms. They retreated to the hold, after which 'Mary and Anne were so disgusted at this exhibition of cowardice, that they rushed to the hatchways and shouted to their dastardly companions to come up and help defend the ship, and when their entreaties were disregarded they were so enraged that they fired down into the hold, killing one of the frightened pirates and wounding several others.'[6] Outnumbered, Anne and Mary eventually had to join their shipmates in surrender and the following day all of Calico Jack's crew were taken under armed guard to Davis' Cove. From there the pirates were escorted by a Major Richard James across the island to Spanish Town, where they were incarcerated.

On 16 November 1720 Captain John Rackham, alongside ten members of his crew (George Fetherston, Thomas Bourn, Patrick Carty, Richard Corner, John Fenwick, James Dobbins, John Howell, Thomas Earl, John Davies and Noah Harwood), was put on trial for piracy. The judge in charge of proceedings was the Governor of Jamaica, Sir Nicolas Lawes, who was accompanied by twelve commissioners.

The two women were tried separately, with their first court appearance (in front of the same judge, Sir Nicolas Lawes) occurring later, on 28 November 1720. It is from transcripts taken during these proceedings – which were later published in Jamaica by Robert Baldwin in 1721 under the title *The Tryals of Captain John Rackham and other*

Pirates – that we get the clearest picture of Anne Bonny and Mary Read. For example, the statement of Dorothy Thomas, who was in a small boat sailing down the north coast of Jamaica when she was attacked, states the following: 'the two women, prisoners at the bar, were then on board the said sloop, and wore mens [sic] Jackets, and long trousers, and handkerchiefs tied about their heads; and cursed and swore at the men, to murder the deponent; and that they should kill her, prevent her coming against them; and the deponent further said, that the reason of her knowing and believing them to be women then was by the largeness of their breasts.'[8]

In fact, the charges that were brought against the two women were almost exactly the same as those leveled at Captain Jack and the other pirates – that they 'did piratically, feloniously, and in an hostile manner, attack, engage and take, seven certain fishing boats'. That Rackham and his crew did 'upon the high sea, in a certain place, distance about three leagues from the island of Hispaniola […] set upon, shoot at, and take two certain merchant sloops'. That Rackham and his crew did attack a schooner under the command of Captain Thomas Spenlow, after which they placed Spenlow and his men 'in corporeal fear of their lives'. That not far out of Dry Harbor Bay in Jamaica Rackham and his crew boarded and looted a ship by the name of the *Mary* and afterwards stole her tackle.

Other witnesses against Bonny and Read included two Frenchmen who were on board the schooner commanded by Thomas Spenlow when it was attacked just outside Port Maria Bay in Jamaica by John Rackham and the two women. The Frenchmen (whose statements had to be translated) stated that both women were actively involved in the attack, handing over gunpowder to the men and generally urging them on to fight. In addition to this, one of the men also swore 'that when they saw any vessel, gave chase, or attacked, they wore men's clothes; and at other times, they wore women's clothes'. Further evidence of the two women's involvement in Calico John's piratical activities (if any were needed) was provided by one Thomas Dillon, master of the *Mary*. He stated that when the pirates came aboard his sloop, 'Anne Bonny, one of the prisoners at the bar, had a gun in her hand, that they were both very profligate, cursing and swearing much, and very ready and willing to do anything on board.'

Surprisingly, given the seriousness of the charges against them, neither woman mounted a defense, nor did they call any witnesses and so, without further ado, Judge Lawes dismissed both prisoners and public from the courtroom to consider the evidence along with his fellow commissioners.

In the third and fourth charges brought against them – the attack on Thomas Spenlow's schooner and the attack on Thomas Dillon's sloop – everyone agreed that Anne Bonny and Mary Read were guilty as charged. Judge Nicolas Lawes was left with only one option. Calling the two women back to the courtroom, he sentenced them both to death by hanging. 'You, Mary Read,' he said, 'and Anne Bonny, alias Boon, are to go from hence to the place whence you came, and from thence to the place of execution, where you shall be severally hanged by the neck till you are severally dead. And God of his infinite mercy be merciful to both your souls.'

Only a few days before, the same sentence had been passed down to Captain John Rackham and his fellow crew members, five of whom were hanged at Gallows Point outside Port Royal. The rest of the convicts, including Captain Jack, were executed in Kingston the following day.

But Bonny and Read, unlike their male counterparts, still had a trick up their sleeves. Only minutes after Judge Lawes had pronounced the death sentence both women announced they were pregnant. The furor this must have caused can only be imagined, but Lawes had no other course but to take their claims seriously. He was forced to delay their executions in order to send them for a medical examination – the result of which was that both women were indeed declared to be with child. No one, not even the bloodthirsty British courts, could execute a pregnant woman and therefore both Bonny and Read had their sentences overturned, but in Read's case the story still did not end happily.

A few months after her trial Mary Read is said to have contracted a fever and, after several days' illness, she and her unborn child died in prison. Records from the Parish Register for the district of St Catherine in Jamaica show that she was buried (presumably in a pauper's grave) on 28 April 1721.[9]

As for Bonny, very little else is known about her, for she seems to have disappeared from all public records. Johnson, in his brief account of her, merely says that, 'She was continued in prison, to the time of her laying in, and afterwards reprieved from time to time; but what became of her since, we cannot tell; only this we know, that she was not executed.'[10]

1 Ellms, *The Pirates Own Book*.

2 Ibid.

3 Black, *Pirates of the West Indies*.

4 Wheelright, *Amazons and Military Maids*.

5 Johnson, *A General History…*

6 Ibid.

7 *The Boston Gazette*, taken from Rogers, *A Cruising Journey Round the World*.

8 *Tryals of Captain John Rackham and Other Pirates*, Robert Baldwin, 1721. Colonial Office Records 137/14, Public Record Office. These extracts also appear in Cordingly, *Life Among the Pirates*.

9 Cordingly, ibid.

10 Johnson, op. cit.

WILLIAM LEWIS
fact and fiction

He was the mildest manner'd man,
That ever scuttled ship or cut a throat;
With such true breeding of a gentleman,
You never could discern his real thought.
Pity he loved an adventurous life's variety,
He was so great a loss to good society.

Charles Ellms, *The Pirates Own Book –*
Authentic Narratives of the Lives, Exploits,
and Executions of the Most Celebrated Sea Robbers

There has always been some confusion over the life of Captain William Lewis, a confusion that can be traced back to Charles Johnson's book, *A General History of the Robberies and Murders of the Most Notorious Pirates*. Here, inserted among the factual biographies, lies a fictional chapter on a Captain Lewis who was apparently active in the Caribbean around 1700. The real Captain Lewis was a former prizefighter who was hanged in 1718, aged about thirty-four, having lived a short but eventful life raiding ships around the Bahamas. On his death, this Captain Lewis is said to have shown little, if any, remorse, but instead ordered a toast be drunk at the gallows to his fellow prisoners and all those who had come to see him die. Little else is known about this real-life pirate, but his namesake, the Captain Lewis who lives on in the pages of Charles Johnson's book, more than makes up for this.

Why did Johnson feel it necessary to insert a fictional biography into a book that otherwise concentrated on real-life pirates? The answer that most readily springs to mind is that with a fictional biography Johnson could highlight the precise qualities that made a pirate's life so enthralling to the general public. Thus Lewis' 'life' is made up of a series of adventures in which ships are captured and afterwards looted, in which prisoners are badly treated, in which rum is drunk and pacts are made with the Devil. Indeed the chapter on Lewis almost becomes *more* interesting because it is fictional. It is also ironic to note that much debate has also been had over the identity of Charles Johnson himself (see Glossary) who at one point in history was said to have been Daniel Defoe, author of, among other fictional biographies, *Robinson Crusoe* (first published in 1719). If Charles Johnson were Daniel Defoe then it would make absolute sense for him to have included a fictional life in his otherwise non-fiction book, but if Defoe wasn't the author of *A General History*, then perhaps Johnson's Lewis really did exist. If he did, he was most certainly among the most evil of all pirates.

William Lewis was brought up in the company of pirates from an early age. According to Charles Ellms, who based much of *The Pirates Own Book* on Charles

One of the most authoritative books about pirates, The General History of the Robberies and Murders of the Most Notorious Pirates, *was first published in England in 1724 but little is known about its author, Charles Johnson. One theory is that it was actually written by* Robinson Crusoe *author Daniel Defoe (above).*

Johnson's study of pirates, he was first discovered as a boy in the company of a pirate called Banister (also fictional), 'who was hanged at the yard arm of a man-of-war, in sight of Port Royal, Jamaica'. When young Lewis was brought ashore, it was discovered that he had a great aptitude for languages, being able to converse in several tongues including French, Spanish, English and the language spoken by the Mosquil Indians. Returning to sea, he was captured by some Spaniards who took him back to Havana, where he spent the next few years in a variety of menial jobs until finally, having befriended six other boys of about the same age as him, he ran away to sea. Not long afterwards, Lewis and his new companions left the ship they were aboard and captured a small Spanish fishing vessel, three of whose crew they persuaded to join them on their adventures. Soon the group of nine were raiding coasters and turtlers and gradually more and more men joined them until the group numbered about forty men.

At this point, Lewis mounted his boldest and most sophisticated attack to date, namely that of a large 'pink'-built ship (see Glossary) which was bound from Jamaica to Campeachy on the coast of South America. Having captured this vessel, Lewis then learnt that not far distant lay a Bermuda-built brigantine mounted with ten guns that was commanded by a Captain Tucker. Lewis wanted more than anything else to capture this ship, so he sent the captain of the pink over to the brigantine with a letter saying that he would give Captain Tucker 10,000 pieces of eight in return for his vessel. He also said that if Tucker wasn't prepared to hand over his vessel, he would nonetheless lose his ship because he, Lewis, would fight him for it and eventually overthrow him.

Not unnaturally, Captain Tucker wasn't impressed by this threat and, instead of handing over the brigantine, he sent for the captains of all the other ships that were at anchor in the bay beside him. He told them that if they would give him fifty-four of their best men, he would fight the pirates on their behalf. But the other captains weren't interested in the proposal. The most they would do was all sail out together in a small flotilla, saying that there was safety in numbers and that Lewis would never dare attack so many vessels at once.

They duly sailed out – but Lewis was a clever young man and a brilliant mariner and consequently managed to slip his ship among theirs without them noticing. And even when they did realize what had happened, their actions were next to useless – one of their number, Joseph Dill, had one of his guns fired at Lewis' ship, but instead of hitting its target the gun split and killed three of Dill's own men. Meanwhile, Tucker was still trying to get the rest of the captains to lend him more crew, but again they refused, so eventually, his being a much faster vessel than theirs, he left them to their own devices and sailed off.

Lewis could now pick and choose from the remaining vessels and soon enough he had captured one and ordered her captain to step aboard the pirate ship. 'As soon as he was on board, he asked the reason of his lying by, and betraying the trust his owners had reposed in him, which was doing like a knave and coward, and he would punish him accordingly; for, said he, you might have got off, being so much a better sailer [sic] than my vessel. After this speech, he fell upon him with a rope's end, and then snatching up his cane, drove him about the decks without mercy.'¹ During this ordeal the captain was said to have offered Lewis a large amount of money that was on board his sloop, if only Lewis would stop beating him, but the revelation had the opposite effect – Lewis beat the man twice as hard. Afterwards, he sent one of his men over to the captain's ship not only to retrieve the money, but also to offer a place on board his own vessel for anyone wanting to join his pirate crew. Several of the men did so – indeed, by the end of this little adventure Lewis' crew numbered in the region of eighty men.

Captain Lewis now sailed toward the Gulf of Florida, where he lay in wait for the West India homeward-bound ships – several of which he captured, looted and afterwards released. A while later he then sailed for the coast of Carolina, where he had his sloop cleaned and took on fresh provisions, before heading for the coast of Virginia. Here he resumed his piratical activities by not only plundering several merchant vessels, but also by forcing several crew members into his service. It was around this time that Lewis became aware of a conspiracy against him – that his English crew were plotting to throw him and all the French crew overboard. Acting immediately on this information, Lewis had the ringleaders arrested and, together with the rest of the English sailors, placed in a tiny boat with only 'ten pieces of beef' to feed them. The boat was then set adrift and, according to Charles Ellms, those on board were all presumed to have died. Of course, as with the pirate practice of marooning (see for example the chapter on Edward England), setting people adrift in the middle of the sea with little or no food or water on board was tantamount to murder, but as a punishment it was frequently used by pirates.

Moving from Virginia, Lewis and his now almost exclusively French crew then sailed to Newfoundland, where they harbored in Conception Bay. While there, they captured a twenty-four-gun galley called the *Herman*, which was commanded by a Captain Beal. Beal, who was on shore at the time of the raid, got word to Lewis that if he sent his quartermaster over to the harbor, he would have him return with more riches in exchange for the *Herman*, which he wanted back. But when the quartermaster arrived on shore, he was immediately seized and carried to Captain Rogers (see Glossary), who had the man chained to a landbound sheet anchor in full view of Lewis' ship. Guns were then mounted around the harbor in the hope that Lewis would try to save his quartermaster, in which attempt Rogers and Beal could capture or shoot him. But Lewis decided his best course of action was to quietly quit his ship, climb into a sloop and have his men row him out of the harbor under cover of darkness.

Once he was clear of the harbor, he swore to get his vengeance on Rogers and Beal, and to this end he intercepted two small fishing vessels whose captains he kidnapped, sending word to Rogers that if his quartermaster was not returned forthwith, he would put his prisoners to death. No sooner was the message received than the quartermaster was released. 'Lewis and the crew inquired how he had been used, and he answered, very civilly. "It's well," said the pirate, "for had you been ill treated, I would have put all these rascals to the sword."'² Instead, Lewis sent them back to shore, but once they were there, they ganged together and sent word to a Captain Tudor Trevor, who was

William Lewis is said to have made a pact with the Devil when being pursued by another ship. His main mast was damaged, making the ship too slow to escape, so he climbed the mast, ripped out a handful of his own hair and threw it in the air as an offering to the Devil until it was time for the Devil to claim the rest of him. Lewis's ship sped up and escaped.

anchored at St John's in a large man-of-war, to come and capture the pirates. As soon as Trevor received the message he sailed as fast as he could, but missed Lewis by a mere four hours.

Lewis now sailed along the coast, capturing French and English vessels as he went, until he came across a particularly fine specimen – a French privateer that was mounted with twenty-four guns. The captain of the privateer hailed Lewis and asked where he was from, to which Lewis replied that he was 'from Jamaica with rum and sugar'. Half satisfied by this answer, the captain warned Lewis to be on his way as quickly as possible for there was a pirate sloop in the vicinity, and for all he knew Lewis might be that pirate. If Lewis didn't leave immediately, the captain continued, then he would fire a broadside into him. Lewis retreated, but instead of sailing away he remained at a distance from the French vessel, resolving to take it at the first opportunity.

The French sloop, meanwhile, put into harbor and, still being uncertain as to Lewis' intentions, the captain raised the alarm and had harbor officials place guns around the walls. After a fortnight Lewis captured yet another couple of fishing vessels which he loaded up with pirates and sailed into the harbor. One crew attacked the battery of guns,

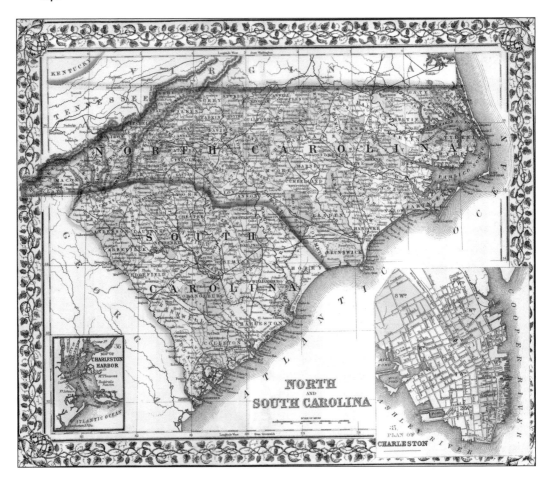

Lewis was sailing off the Carolina coast when violent arguments broke out between his English and French crewmen. Although he may have thought that he had settled the disputes, the ill feeling that was generated is what led to his murder.

while the other attacked and boarded the French ship. 'In the engagement the owner's son was killed, who made the voyage out of curiosity only. The ship being taken, seven guns were fired, which was the signal, and the sloop came down and lay alongside the ship. The captain told him he supposed he only wanted his liquor; but Lewis made answer he wanted his ship, and accordingly hoisted all his ammunition and provision into her.'[3] Lewis then gave the captain his own vessel, which was a fairly generous gesture given that he needn't have provided this man with any replacement ship.

Afterwards Lewis sailed for the coast of Guinea, where he captured and looted further vessels, some of which were English, some Dutch and some Portuguese. But among these ships was one that was commanded by a certain Captain Smith who gave chase to Lewis' ship. It was at this point – or so it is cited in Johnson's account – that Captain Lewis made a pact with the Devil. Seeing that his fore and main-top mast had been ripped off, Lewis ran up the shrouds (ropes stretching from the masthead to the ship's sides) to the main-top, where he tore out a handful of hair and, throwing it up into the air, shouted out to the Devil to take it 'till I come'. Immediately it was observed that the ship suddenly sailed twice as fast as before, thus outrunning those chasing it.

The pirates now sailed down the coast of Carolina, but once again fighting broke out between the French and the English crewmen until such a time as they thought it best to part company. The French chose a large sloop they had recently captured and filled her with provisions and ammunition, after which they chose a new captain, a man by the name of Le Barre. But Lewis appeared less than satisfied by this arrangement and soon gave chase to Le Barre's vessel, eventually running it to ground and ordering all the Frenchmen ashore. The French begged Lewis not to abandon them, or at least to give them some guns and provisions, but he refused. Instead, he took all the goods that had been loaded on to the sloop and reloaded them back onto his own ship, after which he sank the sloop.

The French continued to beg Lewis not to abandon them until finally he gave way and allowed a couple of crewmen and Le Barre on board his own vessel, whereupon everyone began to drink heavily. But later, deep in the middle of the night, some of Lewis' crewmen came to him and warned him that the French were plotting to murder him. Lewis – obviously drunk – was said to have replied that he couldn't withstand destiny and that the Devil had already told him that he was going to be killed that night. A little later, those Frenchmen who had been abandoned ashore found canoes and rowed out to the ship, sneaked into Lewis' cabin and stabbed him to death. Later still the French tried to overcome the rest of the English crew, but, after a bloody fight in which men on both sides were killed, the English beat off their attackers.

Fact or fiction, the adventures of Captain William Lewis make fascinating reading with even his violent death, met while in a drunken slumber rather than in the heat of battle, typical of the less-than-heroic demise suffered by so many pirates.

1 Ellms, *The Pirates Own Book*.
2 Ibid.
3 Ibid.

JEAN LAFITTE
The Terror of the Gulf

Lafitte was handsome; the idol of the women in New Orleans and
was also popular with men. [...] With his pirates he was a strict
disciplinarian and fraud and disobedience were severely
punished. He had a gallows set up on the island. Disputes between
pirates were settled by duels.

Captain A.G. Course, *Pirates of the Western Seas*

Variously known as 'The Corsair', 'The King of Barataria' and 'The Hero of New Orleans' as well as 'The Terror of the Gulf', Jean Lafitte was a man whose many names matched his many personae. Often claimed to be more businessman than sailor, lauded for his bravery during the Battle of New Orleans in which he fought alongside the Americans against the British, he was equally condemned by these same Americans for his acts of piracy in the Mexican Gulf. A charming, complicated individual, Lafitte inspired Lord Byron to sketch a poem about him and centuries later was immortalized in film by none other than Cecil B. DeMille. A National Historical Park and Preserve is named after him, and there is also a Cajun fishing village in Louisiana that bears his name.

According to Charles Ellms in *The Pirates Own Book*, Jean Lafitte was born in St Maloes, France, around 1781 (although other authorities say he was born in Haiti), and went to sea at the age of thirteen. Having sailed for several years around Europe and the coast of Africa, Lafitte was appointed mate on board a French East Indiaman bound for Madras. During the journey the ship was caught up in a storm off the Cape of Good Hope, so the captain changed course to Mauritius. Arriving there safely, Lafitte left the French East Indiaman (having fallen out with the captain) and found employment as the captain of his own privateering vessel.

He was soon out raiding vessels from Britain and Spain as well as from France, but ran into difficulties when one of these ships gave chase and drove Lafitte as 'far north as the equator'. With not enough provisions on board to make it back to Mauritius, Lafitte decided to head for the Bay of Bengal in the hope that he could loot a few English ships there, particularly of their food and water. His vessel was not well equipped, having only two guns and twenty-six men aboard, but Lafitte managed to capture the first English ship they came across, an armed schooner. Putting nineteen of his own men on board this vessel, Lafitte now proceeded to cruise the coast of Bengal where he came across a ship called the *Pagoda*, which belonged to the English East India Company. Pretending to be the kind of pilot boat that guided larger vessels up and down the Ganges, Lafitte maneuvered his vessel close to the *Pagoda*, 'whereupon he suddenly darted with his brave followers upon her decks, overturned

The adventure movie The Buccaneer *was released in 1938, directed by Cecil B. DeMille and starred Fredric March as the swashbuckling Jean Lafitte.*

As a Frenchman, Lafitte had no great love of the British, demonstrating great cunning and bravery not only in the defense of New Orleans against British invaders, but also in engaging British warships at sea. He once captured a forty-gun British warship off the coast of India despite being vastly out-gunned and outnumbered.

all who opposed them, and speedily took the ship'.[1]

After this success, Lafitte and his crew sailed back to Mauritius, where he took command of a new vessel called *La Confiance*. He then sailed for the coast of British India, where, in October 1807, he set his sights on another British vessel, this one carrying a crew of about 400 men together with forty guns. The British ship was far and away superior to Lafitte's privateering sloop, but, inspired by the kind of confidence that only a man like Lafitte possesses, the pirates attacked the ship head on. Even when the crew of the British vessel fired a broadside, the pirates weren't deterred from their mission. Instead, Lafitte ordered them all to lie flat on the deck till the assault was over, after which his men began lobbing grenades and bombs at their target, an assault that killed and maimed several of the British crew – limbs were torn from bodies, wounds bled profusely, one sailor's head was torn off by a bomb blast. Surviving crew were thrown into a state of utter confusion – many of them abandoned ship.

Lafitte, seeing his main chance, then ordered forty of his crew to board the enemy ship with pistols and daggers. This accomplished, Lafitte ordered a second division of men on to the British ship, shortly after which the ship's captain was slaughtered. Lafitte then ordered a group of his pirates to load up one of their cannons with grapeshot and point it in the direction of the enemy ship. This was the last straw for the British sailors, who, seeing that further resistance would prove futile, surrendered.

Seemingly overnight, Lafitte's name became the terror of British commerce in that region, and subsequently any British vessel attempting to cross the Indian Ocean took with it a heavily armed guard. In fact, so well defended were the British vessels in this latitude that eventually Lafitte decided richer pickings could be had elsewhere. Sailing up the Gulf of Guinea and into the Bight of Benin, he captured two vessels carrying large cargoes of ivory, gold dust and palm oil. He then sailed to St Maloes, where he purchased a brigantine which he furnished with twenty guns and a crew of about 150 men, then on to Guadeloupe in the West Indies.

After several successful raids, Lafitte decided to take himself to New Orleans, where he and his brother Pierre set themselves up ostensibly as blacksmiths on the Rue de St Philippe – in reality, a front for a fencing business, buying and selling goods smuggled into Louisiana by pirates. It is also believed that the brothers traded in slaves – selling them on to the cotton and sugar plantation owners in the Mississippi area far more cheaply than the official 'flesh-traders'.

Jean, in particular, was considered not only an astute businessman, but also a very well-educated individual – certain contemporary accounts have it that he was well read and could speak four languages fluently: English, French, Italian and Spanish. Yet despite their apparent success in New Orleans (or perhaps because of it), in 1809 the brothers decided to move out of the city to nearby Barataria Bay in the Gulf of Mexico, in which were situated three islands: Grande Terre, Grande Isle and Cheniere Caminada.

At that time a band of pirates was established there who had started as privateers commissioned and supplied with Letters of Marque by the government of Cartagena, now Columbia, which early in the nineteenth

century was struggling for its independence against Spain. When Lafitte became their leader he was thirty years of age, tall and well built. His pirates were attacking English, French and American ships. A fort had been built on the island and he was given excellent quarters within its walls although most of the pirates' houses were little more than shacks with thatched roofs of palmetto leaves. The harbour was guarded with a battery of twenty guns and look-out posts were built giving a good view of the approach of any likely-looking prizes, the news being signaled immediately to the fort which Lafitte seldom left.'[2]

Lafitte evidently made a very successful life for himself on Barataria, a tropical paradise with long sandy beaches and palm trees growing alongside beautiful, deep blue lagoons. The islands were teeming with fish – flounder, shrimp and crab were abundant – and rich in tropical fruits and vegetables. Lafitte was in his element: king of all he surveyed. With almost a thousand pirates operating out of Barataria, and Lafitte demanding a cut of everything these men plundered from passing merchant ships, sloops and brigantines, he soon became a very rich man. The booty included wine and cheese, cocoa and brandy, silks and crinolines, silver plate, furniture, clothing, embroideries and gold dust, as well as jewelry and pieces of eight – all of which, with his many contacts in New Orleans, he could dispose of easily.

Lafitte constructed a unique transportation system through the bayous and levees that surrounded Barataria and New Orleans – an area which even today is almost impassable given its jungle-like plants and swamps and dangerous animals. A man such as Lafitte, however, wasn't daunted by this landscape. He had his men build canoes and barges out of fallen tree trunks, and developed a system of waterways on which they could travel daily to and from New Orleans with their contraband. And the goods he didn't sell to his old merchant friends back in the city, he auctioned off at a special market on Grand Terre. 'From all parts of Lower Louisiana, people resorted to Barataria [sic], without being at all solicitous to conceal the object of their journey. The most respectable inhabitants of the state, especially those living in the country were in the habit of purchasing smuggled goods coming from Barrataria.'[3]

But the good life wasn't to last long. In 1812 a dispute began between the United States and Great Britain over who owned and therefore controlled the access to various sea-channels in the Louisiana region – an argument that soon saw both sides trying to blockade each other's commercial shipping lanes. Worse still, when the American Congress heard that the British were using native Indians to fight Americans and American settlers, President James Madison declared war on Britain. This was bad news for Lafitte, for the Americans got wind of the fact that the British were planning to seize the lower half of the Mississippi River via the Gulf of Mexico and New Orleans – both Lafitte-dominated territories – and were afraid Lafitte would side with the British. With this in mind, Governor Claiborne of Louisiana issued a warrant for Lafitte's arrest, putting Captain Andrew Holmes from US Customs in charge of the operation.

Lafitte, however, knowing the geography of the bayous and swamps intimately, managed to evade capture for months. Even when he was eventually caught by Captain Holmes and detained along with his brother Pierre, his imprisonment lasted only one night, after which, due to a clerical error, he was released. Posters were put up all over New Orleans for his re-arrest, but to no avail. Governor Claiborne even went so far as to offer a reward of $750 for Lafitte's arrest, but shortly afterwards new posters appeared offering twice as much for Governor Claiborne. Lafitte managed to evade capture and the cat-and-mouse game continued – until finally the matter of war with England became more pressing.

On 2 September 1814 a lookout in Lafitte's colony spied an armed English brigantine, the *Sophia*, sailing close to port. The *Sophia* was commanded by a Captain Lockyer, who had brought a letter from the senior British officer in the Gulf, Captain William Henry Percy, offering Lafitte the chance of serving His Majesty the King. Lafitte would have the rank of post captain, in command of a forty-four-gun frigate, and be paid $30,000 if he would take up arms against the Americans and help the British negotiate the swamps and bayous of the region with the aim of attacking New Orleans.

Lafitte prevaricated for several days, during which time several of his men placed Captain Lockyer under arrest with the intention of murdering him. But Lafitte would not countenance such insurrection and eventually had Lockyer returned to his ship along with a letter asking for yet more time to consider what was being offered him.

TO CAPTAIN LOCKYER

Barrataria, 4th Sept. 1814.

Sir – The confusion which prevailed in our camp yesterday and this morning, and of which you have a complete knowledge, has prevented me from answering in a precise manner to the object of your mission; nor even at this moment can I give you all the satisfaction that you desire; however, if you could grant me a fortnight, I would be entirely at your disposal at the end of that time. This delay is indispensable to enable me to put my affairs in order. You may communicate with me by sending a boat to the eastern point of the pass, where I will be found. You have inspired me with more confidence than the admiral, your superior officer, could have done himself; with you alone I wish to deal, and from you also I will claim, in due time the reward of the services, which I may render you

Yours, &c

J. LAFITTE[4]

Essentially, the object of this letter was to give the appearance of seriously considering Lockyer's offer, but in truth Lafitte was buying time in order to communicate with his arch-enemy, Governor Claiborne, to whom he also wrote on 4 September, to the effect that he and his pirates – rather than fight with the British against the Americans – would far rather fight with the Americans against the British. 'The point of Louisiana, which I occupy, is of great importance in the present crisis. I tender my services to defend it; and the only reward I ask is that a stop be put to the proscription against me and my adherents, by an act of oblivion, for all that has been done hitherto.'[5]

The letter was a clever ploy, one that Lafitte hoped would flatter the Americans into agreeing a settlement. And indeed, after a few days a reply was forthcoming – but not the one Lafitte had hoped for.

Early on the morning of 16 September 1815, three large naval vessels loaded not only with soldiers, but also hundreds of rounds of ammunition, as well as six gunboats and the warship *Carolina*, appeared in Barataria Bay and immediately opened fire on Lafitte's fort and the surrounding houses. Lafitte was stunned by the attack. Cannonball after cannonball was fired at his fort, exploding around him – so many in fact that, fearing for his safety, he fled the town and escaped once again into the surrounding swamps.

Meanwhile, the Americans captured thirteen of Lafitte's vessels and about fifty pirates. Not only that, but they confiscated an estimated $50,000-worth of contraband goods. It was a wonderful victory for them, although Claiborne was disappointed to find Lafitte wasn't among the prisoners.

Despite being on the run, all was not lost for Lafitte. With those pirates who weren't killed in Claiborne's onslaught, he regrouped at a known rendezvous point on Last Island in Bayou Lafourche.[6] One of Lafitte's many informants had told him that General Andrew Jackson was on his way to defend New Orleans against the British. Seeing this as his opportunity to impress the Americans with his good intentions, Lafitte employed the services of an attorney, John Randolph Grymes, to seek a meeting with the General when he arrived.

Jackson duly reached New Orleans on 2 December 1814 and immediately blockaded all the bayous between New Orleans and the Gulf in preparation for the British invasion. When he heard of Lafitte's willingness to fight on the side of the Americans, Jackson was said to merely have scoffed. He had no intention of allowing the 'banditti' Lafitte to join forces with him. Lafitte, however, was not giving up so easily.

History doesn't relate how exactly he got to Jackson, but the most popular account is that he simply barged into the General's headquarters one day and, after half an hour's argument, persuaded Jackson to allow him and his men to fight alongside him. After all, as Lafitte was at pains to point out, the pirates had tons of ammunition at their disposal and weapons and gunpowder – all of which the General was sorely in need. It would be ludicrous to turn Lafitte down, so eventually Jackson agreed to his terms and thereafter petitioned Governor Claiborne to invite Lafitte and his pirates to join the standard of the United States.

On 8 January 1815 the British advanced on New Orleans. They far outnumbered Jackson and Lafitte's forces and were to a man professional soldiers – that is to say, well-trained, well-armed men who comprised 'the Royal North Britain Fusiliers, the Old Fighting Third, the Royal Highlanders and other noted British units which had fought under the Duke of Wellington.'[7] As they advanced, news of their progress was sent back via messenger to the city governors who began to panic and talk of surrender even before one shot was fired. Claiborne and Jackson, however, wouldn't countenance such

Lafitte and his brother, Pierre, set up a blacksmith's shop in this building in New Orleans from where they handled stolen and smuggled goods as well as trading in slaves whom they sold to plantation owners in Mississippi.

a move. Instead, they dispatched officers to try to recruit as many civilian men as possible to take up arms against the enemy. Several hundred new recruits were eventually mustered and supplied with flints and gunpowder, but still the British far outnumbered the Americans.

Advancing in a column of sixty men in front – shouldering muskets and carrying ladders and fascines (bundles of sticks used to fill ditches) – the British were preceded by a volley of rockets and gunfire, the noise of which was likened to a ceaseless roll of thunder. For their part, the Americans, together with Lafitte, had the use of a twenty-four-pound gun that they fired continuously at the British and which Charles Ellms declares became 'one of the points most dreaded by the advancing foe'. Lafitte and his men were positioned behind this cannon and acquitted themselves as if they were veteran soldiers. Indeed they were said to have 'fought with unparalleled bravery,'[8] pushing the enemy back not once, but twice. In the first assault Lafitte, seeing the enemy surge forward between the levee and the river, rushed into their midst, cutlass in hand. Astonished by his bravery, the British tried to fight back, but in the event Lafitte killed two of their officers. Nor was Lafitte the only pirate who fought well that day – many hundreds of his men put up such a good defense that soon the British, realizing it was impossible to take New Orleans, retreated, leaving the battlefield strewn with the dead and the dying.

Afterwards General Jackson wrote of the victory to the Secretary of War, stating that the conduct of the 'Corsairs of Barrataria [sic]' was second to none. 'Their zeal, their courage and their skill, were remarked by the whole army, who could no longer consider such brave men as criminals.'[9] Indeed, so grateful was Jackson to Lafitte that shortly afterwards, on 6 February 1815, President James Madison granted Lafitte and his men a free and full pardon for their past crimes. The proclamation declared that having exhibited rare courage and fidelity in the defense of New Orleans, having turned down the advances of the enemy to fight against the Americans, it was only fair that he, James Madison, granted Lafitte and his followers an unequivocal pardon.

Lafitte and his fellow pirates were overjoyed by the news. They had served their country well and in return their country had honored them. But the celebrations were short-lived, for having allowed the Americans free run of Barataria there was no possible way that Lafitte's pirate community could continue to live there without government interference. The pirates would have to move on, either that or settle down to an honest, peaceful life – something Lafitte wasn't prepared to do. Instead, he and his brother Pierre, with a large number of followers, sailed up to an island in Galveston Bay (otherwise known as Snake Island or by its older name of Campeche) near Texas.

Galveston was Spanish-owned, but Mexico – of which Texas was a province – was fighting for its independence. Lafitte accepted a privateering commission from the Mexicans to capture and loot as many Spanish ships as possible in return for being allowed to stay on the island.

Soon Lafitte, together with his pirates, had built a fort on Galveston which he christened Maison Rouge or the Red House after the color it was painted.

More buccaneers arrived, bringing their women with them; an ever-increasing number of traders came to the settlement; and there was a constant infusion of men of all nations – gamblers, thieves, murderers and other criminals who joined Lafitte's colony in order to escape punishment for crimes committed within the borders of the United States. Numerous rich prizes were brought in, including several captured slavers loaded with Africans. 'Doubloons,' says one writer, 'were as plentiful as biscuits.'[10]

Lafitte's coffers grew larger and larger, but in turn this increasingly brought him and his pirate comrades to the attention of the authorities who once again tried to curb his activities. Lafitte – believing that there was a new-found determination to sweep both him and his ships from the face of the planet – was said to become more ruthless in his dealings with prisoners. Any ship resisting his pirates' advances was given no quarter. When the crews were finally captured they would be taken on to the mainland rather than on to Galveston, where they would be imprisoned and often put to death. Not only that, but Lafitte began ruling over his own mob with an iron hand, interviewing every single man he employed in his fleet. Successful candidates were made to take an Oath of Allegiance in which they swore to acknowledge Lafitte as their supreme leader and promised to share all plunder fairly with their fellow pirates. During this time Lafitte also insisted that only Spanish vessels be attacked – indeed, when his men began attacking American vessels he had the offenders court-martialed and hanged, afterwards sending a letter of apology to the American shipping authorities.

But the pirate community on Galveston was not to last for ever, and in the main this was Lafitte's own fault. Over the years he had allowed huge numbers of fugitives to set up home on Galveston and eventually it was impossible to control their behavior. Neighbors murdered and looted each other and when they weren't doing this they were going out and looting U.S. and Mexican merchant vessels, which resulted in constant interference from both these nations' officials. Not only that, but the native Indians of Galveston – the Karankawa – were forever raiding Lafitte's many properties and killing his men. In late 1818 a huge hurricane hit the island, devastating the vast majority of properties, but all this could have been overcome if Lafitte had so wanted. The truth was, however, that he'd made the best part of his living out of looting Spanish ships for the Mexicans, and now that the Mexicans had made peace with Spain, they no longer required Lafitte's services. President Madison – the very same man who had previously pardoned Lafitte – now declared an all-out war on piracy.

In November 1820 a U.S. naval ship, the *Enterprise*, entered Galveston Bay. On board was Lieutenant Larry Kearney, who ordered Lafitte and his pirates to leave Galveston immediately. Lafitte wasn't so easily moved; in fact, for months he refused to go anywhere until finally Kearney returned with a war fleet and this time issued the pirate with an ultimatum: either leave the island immediately or be blown to smithereens.

Lafitte chose the former option, but not before wreaking as much havoc as possible. 'That night, Lafitte set fire to Campeche. Men aboard the U.S.S. *Enterprise* saw it burst into flames [...] When they went to shore at dawn they found only ashes and rubble. The ships of Lafitte were gone.'[11]

And 'gone' they appear to have remained, for what happened to Lafitte after he and his crew left Galveston is uncertain. According to Captain A.G. Course in his book *Pirates of the Western Seas*, having sailed away from Texas in his brig the *Pride*, nothing was heard of Lafitte again until he died around 1826 of plague in a small Indian town near Merida in the Yucatán. Other stories suggest he settled for a while in Charleston, South Carolina, while still more say he fought with Bolivar's rebels against the South American nationalists.

Charles Ellms, in his account of Lafitte, is alone in saying that far from slinking away from Galveston under cover of darkness, Lafitte instead procured a large brigantine which he equipped with sixteen guns and, together with a crew of 150 men, started over again as a pirate – only this time, instead of capturing just Spanish vessels, he went after ships of all nationalities. Before long, a British man-of-war spied a 'long dark looking vessel, low in the water, but having very tall masts, with sails white as the driven snow'. Soon the man-of-war was chasing Lafitte, until the two ships closed in on each other. Lafitte blasted the British ship's foretopmast, but in return the British fired a broadside that not only toppled Lafitte's foretopmast, but also brought down a large portion of the rigging, killing ten pirates outright. The British sailors then jumped aboard Lafitte's brigantine and hand-to-hand combat began.

'Lafitte received two wounds at this time which disabled him, a grape shot broke the bone of his right leg and he received a cut in the abdomen, but his crew fought like tigers and the deck was ankle deep in blood and gore; the captain of the boarders received such a tremendous blow on the head from the butt end of a musket, as stretched him senseless on the deck near Lafitte, who raised his dagger to stab him in the heart.' But unfortunately for Lafitte, he was losing blood so rapidly that instead of stabbing the captain through the chest, he missed his aim and cut him through the thigh instead. Again Lafitte tried to raise his arm to stab and kill the captain, but this time fell back in defeat and, having lost too much blood, died.

Shortly thereafter, the British claimed victory. All the pirates who had survived the carnage were taken away to Jamaica where they were put on trial before a Court of the Admiralty. Sixteen of their number were condemned to death, although in the event only ten of them were executed, while the other six were pardoned and afterwards released.

'Thus,' writes Ellms in the sort of elegiac terms usually reserved for men of much greater account, 'perished Lafitte, a man superior in talent, in knowledge of his profession, in courage, and moreover in physical strength; but unfortunately his reckless career was marked with crimes of the darkest dye.'

1 Ellms, *The Pirates Own Book.*
2 Course, *Pirates of the Western Seas.*
3 Ellms, op. cit.
4 Ibid.
5 Ibid.
6 www.crimelibrary.com
7 Davis, *Louisiana.*
8 Ellms, op. cit.
9 Ibid.
10 Saxon, *A Collection of Louisiana Folk Tales.*
11 Tallant, *The Pirate Lafitte and the Battle of New Orleans.*

CHENG I SAO

queen of China's seas

And now comes the most remarkable passage in the history of
these pirates [...] On the death of Ching-yih, his legitimate wife
had sufficient influence over the freebooters to induce them to
recognize her authority in the place of her deceased husband's
[...] Ching's widow was clever as well as brave[...].

Charles Ellms, *The Pirates Own Book:*
Authentic Narratives of the Lives, Exploits and Executions
of the Most Celebrated Robbers

If anyone is in any doubt whether a woman can be as cruel as a man, they need look
no further than the Chinese pirate Cheng I Sao (also spelt Ching Yih Saou).
Married to the infamous Cheng I (Ching Yih), who was one of the nineteenth-
century's most notorious sea rovers, she was equal to her husband in both the manner
of her leadership and her thirst for blood.

Little is known of Cheng I Sao's early life; in fact she doesn't seem to figure in the
history books at all – except for a brief mention that she worked as a prostitute in
Canton before she married Cheng I in 1801 and joined him on board his ship as both
wife and pirate companion.

Cheng I, as Charles Ellms deftly illustrates in his study of pirates, was one of China's
foremost rebels: 'by these commanders a certain Ching-Yih had been the most
distinguished by his valor and conduct.' Born into a long line of pirates, Cheng is
believed to have fought with rebel forces in Vietnam before returning to China around
1801 and setting about making himself the supreme commander of the entire Chinese
pirate fleet in the province of Kwang-tung. This was no small feat, given that the pirate
fleet is thought to have numbered no fewer than 800 large vessels and 1,000 smaller
ones. The fleet was then divided into six smaller squadrons, which each had a colored
flag to distinguish it from the other – red, yellow, blue, green, black and white. Each
squadron also had a different sea lane to patrol, usually located near the squadron-
leader's home base.

For his part, Cheng I controlled the Red Flag Fleet, which comprised 200 large
vessels and between 20,000 and 40,000 men. In fact, so large and so efficient was
Cheng I's squadron that it was said to more than match the strength of China's Imperial
Navy, and by 1805 it dominated Canton's coastline to such an effect that even when
British frigates such as HMS *Phaeton* and HMS *Bellona* showed up in 1807, Cheng I's
fleet was not intimidated. But such efficiency and resolution come at a price – and in
the case of Cheng I that price was the brutality of his regime.

John Turner, chief mate on board the *Tay*, fell into the hands of Cheng I and his cohorts around 1806, and for five long months was held prisoner. At night he was kept below decks in a tiny space measuring a mere eighteen inches across and four feet long, while during the day he was regularly beaten and threatened with death. His food consisted of minute portions of rice to which was occasionally added some salt fish. But if his conditions were bad, they were nothing in comparison to those inflicted on Cheng I's Chinese prisoners, most of whom were officers in the Chinese Navy. Barbaric is the only word that adequately describes these poor creatures' treatment. As Turner wrote:

> **I saw one man [...] nailed to the deck through his feet with large nails, then beaten with four rattans twisted together, till he vomited blood; and after remaining some time in this state he was taken ashore and cut to pieces. [While a second prisoner] was fixed upright, his bowels cut open and his heart taken out, which they afterwards soaked in spirits and ate [...] The dead body I saw myself.**[1]

Apart from such stomach-turning scenes of violence, Turner's account included details of how Cheng I's fleet operated. The biggest of his ships were armed with twelve guns and carried with them several rowboats that could accommodate up to twenty men each. These smaller vessels were armed with swivel guns, and were used to board ships more stealthily than would otherwise have been possible. As for what happened once the pirates had boarded a vessel, there were strict rules. Much like other pirates worldwide, if a ship surrendered immediately and handed over its cargo then the crew were allowed to go free, but if a ship retaliated then no quarter was given. Captives would be taken back to the pirate ships where they would be tortured and subsequently killed. Little wonder that Cheng I was feared not only by his enemies, but also by his own men. He ran his water-based fiefdoms with a rod of iron, but eventually even he could not overcome those elements that wielded even more power than himself – it is said that Cheng I died in 1807 when a typhoon swept him overboard. With his fleet lacking a commander, the vacancy had to be filled quickly. Cheng I's widow, Cheng I Sao, stepped into the breach.

It was not unusual for women to attain positions of authority in China, particularly in close-knit communities where divisions between men's work and women's work were by no means rigid. All along China's southern coastline floating villages proliferated, with entire communities living on board junks and other small vessels. Junks were a favorite of the Chinese, particularly of the pirates. The larger vessels normally sported three masts and were about 80 feet long and 18 feet wide, while smaller junks had only two masts and were about half the size of the larger vessels. The captain of each vessel would live in the poop alongside his wife and children, while his crew and their families would be accommodated in long dormitories either in the holds or on the after-deck.[2]

Women worked alongside their menfolk, often going out to sea to catch fish or to trade with other passing vessels. Many women could rise to a position where they were in charge of an entire fleet of vessels – some of which engaged in piratical activities, which necessarily meant going into battle. As the Chinese historian Yuan Yun-lun

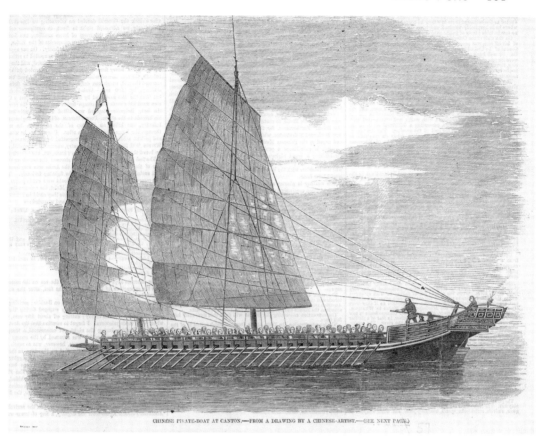

CHINESE PIRATE-BOAT AT CANTON.—FROM A DRAWING BY A CHINESE ARTIST.—(SEE NEXT PAGE.)

Many of the pirate vessels of Cheng I Sao's fleet were fast, twin-masted junks like the one illustrated here. On larger, three-masted junks the captain would live in a cabin on the poop deck at the stern of the ship while his crew and their families lived in the holds or on the afterdeck.

reported: 'There was a pirate's wife in one of the boats, holding so fast by the helm that she could scarcely be take away. Having two cutlasses, she desperately defended herself, and wounded some soldiers; but on being wounded by a musket-ball, she fell back into the vessel and was taken prisoner.'[3]

While women could be promoted to pirate commander, Cheng I Sao still had to move swiftly after her husband's death to secure the position she felt was owed her. She ensured that the most powerful of her husband's remaining allies – a twenty-one-year-old man by the name of Chang Pao – was on her side. She then appointed Pao commander of her husband's former squadron, the Red Flag Fleet, the most powerful unit in the entire pirate task-force. This was an inspired move on her part. When Chang Pao, who had begun life as a lowly fisherman, was captured at the age of fifteen by Cheng I Sao's husband and forced to take up arms as a pirate, he had proved himself to be an exceptional leader – so much so, in fact, that 'before that pirate's death, he had been made a captain.'[4] Cheng I Sao consolidated her strategy by quickly starting an affair with him – an affair that several years later ended in marriage.

Cheng I Sao, together with her new consort, ran the pirate task-force as successfully as Cheng I had done, if not more so. They were both great sticklers for rules and

This photograph of the harbor at Canton shows what it would have looked like when Cheng I Sao ran a gambling den there, the picture having been taken less than sixty years after her death.

regulations and between them devised a system of punishments for anyone daring to step out of line. Among the rules were:

> No pirate might go ashore without permission. Punishment for a first offence was perforation of the ears; a repetition attracted the death penalty. All plundered goods must be registered before distribution. The ship responsible for the taking of a particular piece of booty received a fifth of its value, the remainder became part of the general fund. Abuse of women was forbidden, although women were taken as slaves and concubines. Those not kept for ransom were sold to the pirates as wives for $40 each. Country people were to be paid for provisions and stores taken from them.[5]

Other punishments included death by beheading for anyone disobeying a direct order or found stealing from the pirates' common treasure. For holding back stolen property a pirate would be given the lash. If the same pirate repeated the offence, he/she would be executed (usually by beheading). Rape (particularly of a female) was also punishable by death, but if the prisoner was found to have been complicit in the affair, the man would be beheaded while the woman would have her legs bound and weighted and be thrown into the sea.

In this manner, Cheng I Sao, with Chang Pao at her side, dominated the pirate fleet and for three glorious years kept government forces from destroying the pirates' stranglehold over China's southern seas. Cheng I Sao was also said to be a brilliant businesswoman – as canny with figures as she was with battle strategies. Nor was this gift an insignificant one for, unlike many pirates who captured ships on an ad hoc basis, Cheng I Sao's pirate fleet was highly organized and put as much emphasis on selling looted goods as it did on capturing them. Ransoming was also integral to Cheng I Sao's overall business plan, with not just people being detained for a price, but also vessels and indeed whole communities. 'Vessels of no use to the pirates were ransomed at standard rates of fifty silver yuan for fishing junks and 130 yuan for cargo carriers. Human captives were seldom released for less than ninety taels each, while for foreigners the sum might go as high as seven thousand Spanish dollars.'[6]

Extortion and 'protection' were also popular with Cheng I Sao. The salt trade was one such business that quickly discovered it was easier to pay the pirates protection money rather than see its ships looted and their crews slaughtered. Usually, extortion money was paid once a year, the merchant receiving a 'pass' from the pirates, after which, if he was stopped by any of them, he only had to produce this paperwork for the pirates to allow him free passage. An average payment would be in the region of fifty yuan of silver for every hundred packages of salt – quite a steep price even in those days. With regular payments coming in, it is easy to see how Cheng I Sao slowly but surely built up her business empire. Keeping records of each and every transaction that was made, she knew exactly who owed her what, when payments were overdue, by how much they should be increased every year and numerous other important details. Indeed, in comparison to western pirates, Cheng I Sao was a professional – someone who ran her fleet with one aim in mind: to increase her profit margin every year.

But of course at the heart of all operations were the attacks on trade vessels and the counter-attacks by the government forces. In January 1808, for instance, it is recorded that General Li-Ch'ang-keng, the commander-in-chief of Chekiang province, mounted an offensive against Cheng I Sao in the waters of Kwangtung. The ensuing conflict was bloody in the extreme and finally prompted Li-Ch'ang-keng to send in fire-vessels,[7] but these had little or no effect. Victory went to the pirates, with Li-Ch'ang-keng suffering a horrible death, his throat ripped apart by gunfire.

Later that same year Chang Pao decided to sail up China's Pearl River in order not only to attack the city of Canton, but also to intercept trading vessels between Canton and Macao. Government forces besieged the pirates' vessels on all sides with the intention of starving them into surrender. But Chang Pao wasn't defeated so easily and soon found ways of reaching the shoreline, where he and his men then proceeded to pillage every village and community they came across. Indeed, so cunning were Cheng I Sao's pirate crews, so successful was she in mounting both attacks and defensive actions, that by the end of 1808 government naval forces had reportedly lost in the region of sixty-three ships.

Nor was the civilian population untouched – although many hundreds of communities tried to repel the invaders and stop them looting their goods by building barricades and forming militia groups, by and large these measures were ineffectual. By sheer force of numbers the pirates overwhelmed their civilian targets, wreaking terrible damage. In August 1809, it was recorded that the village of Sanshan was burned to the ground while eighty people who lived there were beheaded. Afterwards, the heads were hung on a banyan tree as a warning to other villages not to defy the pirates' commands. It is also documented that in September 1809 Chang Pao attacked the island of Tao-chiao, during which action his men slaughtered a thousand civilian islanders and abducted twenty of their womenfolk.[8]

The number of people involved in these attacks is staggering, as are the number of casualties – one of whom happened to be a Mr Glasspoole, an English lieutenant on board an East India Company vessel, the *Marquis of Ely*, which was attacked by Cheng I Sao. Glasspoole, according to Charles Ellms' account, was stationed on board the *Marquis of Ely* when he was ordered to proceed to Macao by way of a cutter. Taking seven crew members with him, he reached Macao safely enough and the following day set out to return to the ship. But during the night bad weather set in, forcing the *Marquis of Ely* to up anchor and move. Glasspoole couldn't reach the ship fast enough and so was left on the high seas with little or no protection. He and his men survived for three days like this before reaching a narrow channel in which they spied three large ships. One of them seemed to be an English vessel and they sailed toward it, only to find it was a pirate ship. Luckily, Glasspoole and his men discovered this in time and managed to escape, but only a few days later they were captured by another pirate vessel. "'About twenty savage-looking villains," says Mr Glasspoole, "who were stowed at the bottom of the boat, leaped on board us. They were armed with a short sword in either hand, one

The junks of Cheng I Sao's armada could attack shipping or coastal settlements almost at will, so numerous was her fleet. The Chinese pirates were even bolder when they sprinkled themselves with garlic water, believing that it protected them against being shot in battle.

of which they layed upon our necks, and pointed the other to our breasts, keeping their eyes fixed on their officer, waiting his signal to cut or desist.'"[9]

Luckily for Glasspoole and his fellow crew members, the officer in question, seeing that the captives were in no position to retaliate, decided to spare their lives and take them prisoner instead. The pirates dragged all of the English men, save Glasspoole and one other man who could speak Chinese, on to their boat and bound and shackled them with chains that were attached to the deck. Glasspoole and his interpreter, meanwhile, were taken on to the chief pirate's ship for interrogation. Glasspoole explained that he and his men were Englishmen 'in distress', having been at sea for four days without adequate food or water. But the pirate captain refused to believe this story and told Glasspoole he would be executed. Nevertheless, Glasspoole was fed some rice, after which he was told that he had to write to the captain of the *Marquis of Ely*, telling him that if a ransom of £100,000 was not paid within ten days, then all the captured men would be executed.

Glasspoole did as he was requested and the letter was dispatched, but no reply came. Instead, Glasspoole was witness to several of the pirates' skirmishes with other vessels and communities. 'The Ladrones,' he wrote 'now prepared to attack a town with a formidable force, collected in row-boats from the different vessels. They sent a messenger to the town, demanding a tribute of ten thousand dollars annually, saying, if these terms were not complied with, they would land, destroy the town, and murder all the inhabitants [...]'[10] But things did not go to plan and eventually the pirates returned to wreak havoc. 'The old and the sick, who were unable to fly, or make resistance, were either made prisoners or most inhumanly butchered! The boats continued passing and repassing from the junks to the shore, in quick succession laden with booty, and the men besmeared with blood! Two hundred and fifty women and several children, were made prisoners, and sent on board different vessels.' These unfortunates were held to ransom and those whose money wasn't procured were then sold to the pirate crew at $40 apiece.

Finally Glasspoole did receive word from the commander of the *Marquis of Ely*, Captain Kay, to the effect that he would pay the pirates $3,000 for his men's safe return. But this offer didn't satisfy the pirates' greed. According to Glasspoole, they went on to wreak more havoc on another village along the coastline where, much to his horror, he observed it was a rule among them that for every enemy head they returned with, they would each receive a handsome payment. 'The Ladrones were paid by their chief ten dollars for every Chinaman's head they produced. One of my men turning the corner of a street was met by a Ladrone running furiously after a Chinese; he had a drawn sword in his hand, and two Chinamen's heads which he had cut off, tied by their tails, and slung round his neck. I was witness myself to some of them producing five or six, to obtain payment!'

Again and again the pirates – under Cheng I Sao's supreme command – looted villages and slaughtered their inhabitants. In addition, the pirates also attacked any Mandarin vessel they came across. Indeed, by sheer force of number the pirate fleet was practically unassailable, outnumbering as it did many countries' entire naval forces.

All this time Glasspoole, a prisoner on board one of Cheng I Sao's larger vessels, was made to operate one of the main guns. How he felt about this is not fully explored in his writings. He was obviously horrified by what he saw and yet there is also a note of awe in his observations, perhaps even one of respect, which might explain how he became such a favorite of the pirate chief herself. As Glasspoole notes, Cheng I Sao was in the habit of sprinkling him with garlic water – a practice the Chinese believed would protect them against being shot.

By December, negotiations for Glasspoole's release were almost complete. Glasspoole received a letter from a Lieutenant Maughn who was in command of an East India Company ship called the *Antelope*. The letter stated that in accordance with Cheng I Sao and Chang Pao's demands, the ransom money was ready and consequently, after much maneuvering and further negotiation, the pirates received what they wanted – although at this point Glasspoole wasn't released. Instead, Cheng I Sao inspected the ransom, which comprised 'two bales of superfine cloth; two chests of opium; two casks of gunpowder, and a telescope; the rest in dollars'.[11] The pirates apparently objected to the fact that the telescope was second-hand, but the matter was soon settled with Maughn handing over an extra $100.

The prisoners, including Glasspoole, were returned to the *Antelope*, after a captivity that had lasted an astonishing eleven weeks and three days. Historically speaking, without Glasspoole's testimony our knowledge of Cheng I Sao and how she ruled over her fleet would be all the poorer. He had observed both Cheng and her pirates intimately, and therefore his account is invaluable. For instance, he reported on Ladrones' attitude to women, and how they regarded rats as a delicacy:

With respect to the conjugal rights they are religiously strict; no person is allowed to have a woman on board, unless married to her according to their laws. Every man is allowed a small berth, about four feet square, where he stows with his wife and family. From the number of souls crowded in so small a space, it must naturally be supposed they are horridly dirty, which is evidently the case, and their vessels swarm with all kinds of vermin. Rats in particular, which they encourage to breed, and eat as great delicacies.

When Glasspoole was released in December 1809, Cheng I Sao was at the height of her powers. Her fleet was enormous, the loyalty of her crews unquestionable and the support of her second-in-command, Chang Pao, unstinting. But by the beginning of 1810 Cheng I Sao's nautical empire was in serious danger of collapsing.

The problems began with dissension among the pirates themselves. Ever since Cheng I Sao had promoted Chang Pao to second-in-command, there had been general discontent among the other squadron leaders. One in particular had taken great exception to Chang Pao's promotion, a man called O-potae, 'who commanded one of the flags or divisions of the fleet'.[12] It was only because both men respected Cheng I Sao so much that internecine warfare hadn't already broken out, but at length things came to a head.

Early in 1810, Pao and his fleet found themselves blockaded by the Emperor's ships. Knowing that the situation was perilous, Cheng I Sao commanded that O-potae go to his rival's rescue, but O-potae refused. Chang Pao eventually broke through the blockade and escaped, but, on hearing of O-potae's conduct, he flew into a rage, boarded O-potae's ship and demanded an explanation. According to Ellms, O-potae pretended that his fleet wasn't strong enough to oppose the Emperor's ships – an explanation that further infuriated Pao, who then declared war on his opponent. Fighting broke out, during which Pao lost hundreds of men and eventually had to slink away in defeat. But the battle did not end there. Knowing that Pao would unite forces with Cheng I Sao and return to kill him, O-potae and his men petitioned the Chinese government for a pardon if they surrendered.

In nineteenth-century China (much as in nineteenth-century England), it was not unusual for criminals to beg a pardon from the government, in return for changing their ways and adopting a lawful lifestyle. In most cases these pardons were granted, and O-potae was no exception – the government looked leniently on his request and in due course he was made an imperial officer in the Chinese Navy, while 8,000 of his men were granted their freedom.

Her forces greatly reduced, Cheng I Sao nonetheless continued to pillage villages and loot Chinese and Mandarin ships. But things were growing more difficult for her – as well as the loss of O-potae and his 8,000 crew members, the Chinese Navy had begun enlisting the help of both the British and the Portuguese against the pirates. Larger and larger forces were being assembled to deal with the pirates, and Cheng I Sao began to wonder whether or not it would be better to follow O-potae's lead and beg a pardon from the government. In the end, however, it was not a decision she had to make, for the government pre-empted her by offering all the pirates an amnesty.

Having weighed up her options, Cheng I Sao decided to go to Canton and hold talks there with the Governor-General. On 18 April 1810 she arrived in the city and proceeded to the Governor's residence along with a delegation of seventeen women and children. It was a bold move and some thought a foolhardy one, but Cheng I Sao was well aware that the Governor-General wanted a swift end to the pirates' stranglehold over Chinese waters – he would do anything to find a peaceful solution to the problem.

After several hours' negotiation, it was agreed that the pirates would surrender their vessels and weapons to the government, although they would be allowed to keep any plunder they had already amassed. Furthermore, any of Cheng I Sao's men who wanted to join the Imperial Army were free to do so. Cheng I Sao also negotiated a full pardon for her partner Chang Pao, and requested that he be given the rank of a lieutenant in the Imperial Navy and that he be allowed to keep a private fleet of twenty junks. This was granted on 20 April 1810, and about 17,400 pirates were granted an amnesty.

Not that all the pirates got off so lightly. Sixty of their number were banished from China for a period of two years; 151 were exiled indefinitely; while 126 received the death penalty.[13]

In retirement, Cheng I Sao and Chang Pao set up home first in Canton, but later moved to Fukien where Cheng I Sao gave birth to a baby boy. Chang Pao continued to work for China's armed forces, reaching the rank of colonel before dying in 1822 at the age of thirty-six. After his death Cheng I Sao returned to Canton, where it is said she bought and ran a gambling establishment before she too died in 1844, aged sixty-nine.

Sadly, for all the detailed descriptions Glasspoole gave in his book on being a captive on board a Ladrone vessel, he failed to give any clue as to what Cheng I Sao might have looked like. Nor are there any documents giving a description of her partner Chang Pao. What is known, however, is that she ruled over one of the largest pirate empires the world has ever seen – if not the largest – and she did this for three long years, during which she was never once defeated in battle. For a pirate of either sex, Cheng I Pao's mastery of the sea and of her fleet is second to none.

1 *Sufferings of John Turner, chief mate of the ship* Tay *bound for China... and their seizure and captivity among the Ladrones* (London 1809).

2 Cordingly and Falconer, *Pirates: Fact and Fiction.*

3 Neumann, *History of the Pirates Who Infested the China Sea from 1807 to 1810.*

4 Ellms, *The Pirates Own Book.*

5 Cordingly and Falconer, op. cit.

6 Cordingly (ed.), *Pirates.*

7 Cordingly, *Life Among the Pirates.*

8 Ibid.

9 Ellms, *The Pirates Own Book.*

10 Glasspoole, *A Brief Narration of My Captivity and Treatment Amongst the Ladrones,*

11 Ibid.

12 Ellms, op. cit.

13 Cordingly, op. cit.

BENITO DE SOTO

the last pirate of the Western Seas

[...] when I saw him in his cell and at his trial, although his frame was attenuated almost to a skeleton, the colour of his face a pale yellow, his eyes sunken, and hair closely shorn; he still retained his erect and fearless carriage, his quick, fiery, and malevolent eye, his hurried and concise speech, and his close and pertinent style of remark.

Charles Ellms, *The Pirates Own Book: Authentic Narratives of the Lives, Exploits and Executions of the Most Celebrated Sea Robbers*

According to the author Captain A.G. Course, Benito de Soto was one of the last pirates ever to sail the Western Seas. A man with a particularly vicious personality, de Soto nowadays would no doubt be labeled a psychopath. Born in a village near to Corunna (a Galician city in north-western Spain) to Portuguese parents, little is known of his childhood. He began his career proper as a pirate by operating mainly in the southern seas of the North Atlantic, targeting the trade routes that ran between Britain and the Cape of Good Hope.

In November 1827 de Soto joined a Portuguese brigantine called the *Defensor de Pedro* tasked with picking up and transporting slaves from the Guinea coast to America. The ship's captain was an officer in the Portuguese Navy, a man by the name of Dom Pedro de Maria de Susa Sarmiento who had taken on most of his crew in Buenos Aires – including not only de Soto, but also twelve Cuban pirates.

Trading in slaves was not a gentle occupation and, as Charles Ellms points out in *The Pirates Own Book* (in an account supposedly taken from another document, one written by someone who knew de Soto well), those who engaged in it were rarely fair-minded or moral. Captain Dom Pedro was no exception. 'Those who deal in evil,' writes Ellms, 'carry along with them the springs of their own destruction, upon which they will tread, in spite of every caution, and their imagined security is but the brink of the pit into which they are to fall.' And so it was with Captain Dom Pedro for, shortly after joining the crew of his ship, de Soto grew friendly with the first mate, Miguel Mercuro, and together the two men contrived a plan whereby they would mutiny and take over the ship. To do this, they needed to persuade at least half the ship's crew to join them, so they quickly began canvassing everyone on board.

Eventually twenty-two men conceded that they were ready to overthrow the captain (including a Frenchman by the name of St Cyr Barbazon, of whom more later) because they all disliked Dom Pedro intensely. The plan settled and the men ready, de Soto waited until the ship was anchored ten miles off shore at the entrance to the harbor of

Rio Muni, close by the Guinea coast. When the captain was taken in to harbor by the ship's agent, the mutineers quickly took over the *Defensor de Pedro* (renaming her the *Black Joke*), and turned out eighteen sailors who were unwilling to participate in the mutiny. These men were put into a small boat without provisions or firearms and were later declared missing 'presumed dead'.

The newly named *Black Joke* then sailed onwards to the West Indies, but all was not calm on board. No sooner had the mutiny occurred, than the pirates broke into the liquor store and quickly became drunk. In this atmosphere they tried to decide who their new captain should be – a process that Ellms vividly describes: 'The drunken uproar which that night reigned in the pirate ship was in horrid unison with the raging elements around her; contention and quarrelling followed the brutal inebriety of the pirates; each evil spirit sought the mastery of the others, and Soto's, which was the fiend of all, began to grasp and grapple for its proper place – the head of such a diabolical community.' Eventually Miguel Mercuro was chosen as leader, but de Soto – unhappy at this decision – waited until nightfall when Mercuro was in a drunken stupor and crept into his cabin along with another man by the name of Antonio Biscayo. De Soto and Biscayo then put pistols to Mercuro's head and shot him point blank. Later de Soto excused himself to the crew by saying that he had killed their captain because it was in their best interests and that as their new leader he, Benito de Soto, would bring them untold riches wherever they went.

But de Soto's first act as pirate commander was hardly propitious,

Benito de Soto became involved in a mutiny aboard the slave ship Defensor de Pedro *when the captain was ashore. Eighteen of the crew were cast adrift and the mutineers renamed the ship* Black Joke *before getting drunk and fighting over who was to be her captain.*

In 1832 de Soto attacked the ship Morning Star, *bound from Ceylon to England and the English press reported in great detail how the female passengers had been cruelly abused and raped by the pirates while their husbands were locked in the hold below.*

for shortly after killing the first mate, he and his crew turned their attention to their slave cargo. Cowering below decks, these poor, unfortunate creatures were now dragged up onto the main deck where the vast majority were thrown overboard. Nor did those who survived meet a much better fate, for it was proposed that at the next port of call they should be sold to the highest bidder. This proposition was swiftly agreed upon and as soon as de Soto's ship entered harbor in the West Indies the remaining slaves (all except a small boy whom de Soto kept back to act as a servant for himself) were taken to a market and sold.

Afterwards de Soto and the rest of his pirate crew 'entered freely into their villainous pursuit, and plundered many vessels'.[1] One of the latter was an American brigantine which, having fallen into de Soto's hands, had been stripped of its valuables. The pirates now devised an evil plan for it. Locking all the ship's crew and passengers below decks – all except one black man who was allowed to stay above deck for the sole purpose of the pirates' amusement – de Soto set fire to the ship and afterwards retreated to watch her burn from a distance:

> and as the miserable African bounded from rope to rope, now climbing to the mast head – now clinging to the shrouds – now leaping to one part of the vessel, and now to another – their enjoyment seemed raised to its heighest [sic] pitch. At length the hatches opened to the devouring element, the tortured victim of their fiendish cruelty fell exhausted into

the flames, and the horrid and revolting scene closed amidst the shouts of the miscreants who had caused it.'[2]

Shortly after this horrendous attack, de Soto was once again capturing merchant vessels, looting and plundering any ship that crossed his path. Around 1832, his men spied a convoy of ships that was sailing from Ceylon to England. The largest ship was an East Indiaman called the *Susan*, which weighed 600 tons, while the smallest (and slowest) ship in the convoy was a barque called the *Morning Star*. This was carrying a cargo of cinnamon and coffee (both highly valuable commodities in the nineteenth century), as well as a number of male and female passengers, including an assistant surgeon, a major and his wife, twenty-five invalided soldiers and two civilian merchants. The moment de Soto spied this ship he called all the pirates on deck and ordered them to prepare for an attack.

Meanwhile, on board the *Morning Star*, one of the sailors had spied a large brigantine heading toward them, bearing a long gun. As it approached, the *Black Joke* raised a pirate flag. No sooner was this spotted then the *Susan* began preparing four out of the eight guns she carried, but de Soto, seeing this, deliberately maneuvered his vessel out of their range and kept out of sight until finally the *Susan* – believing the threat to be over – returned to guarding the other ships in the convoy.

On the morning of 21 February 1832 the *Morning Star* sighted the *Black Joke* on the horizon. Thinking they were far enough away to be safe, the captain relaxed – but unfortunately for him it was at this point that the winds changed and suddenly the *Black Joke* switched direction and headed straight for its quarry. The captain of the *Morning Star* – a man by the name of Souley – tried to make an escape, but to no avail. Soon the *Black Joke* was up alongside them. 'The pirate vessel overhauled the British barque quickly and fired a gun as an order to Captain Souley to heave-to. But the *Morning Star* sailed on although the *Black Joke* was so near that the pirate crew could be seen on their deck with de Soto standing by the mainmast, head and shoulders above his "company". Then suddenly the long-gun was fired.'[3] The shot wounded several of the *Morning Star*'s crew as well as toppling the ship's rigging. Captain Souley, knowing he couldn't defend himself against such an onslaught, surrendered.

De Soto now drew the *Black Joke* up to within forty yards of his prey and ordered Souley to climb aboard, bringing with him all the ship's papers. But Souley was unwilling to do this and instead sent over his first mate. De Soto soundly beat the man and cut him with his cutlass, saying that if Souley didn't attend his ship, he would have it sunk. The first mate returned to the *Morning Star* with this message and Souley, left with no other option, joined de Soto on the deck of the *Black Joke*. But no sooner had Souley arrived than de Soto, who was still holding a cutlass in his hand, delivered a blow to Souley's head which killed him outright. At the same time another pirate – St Cyr Barbazon who had joined de Soto's crew during the *Defensor de Pedro* mutiny – killed the *Morning Star*'s second mate, after which a gunful of grapeshot was fired at the *Morning Star*'s passengers who were all standing on deck surveying the carnage. Several of their number were killed while others ran for cover, but de Soto did not stop there –

he had six of his men (including Barbazon) board the *Morning Star* with strict instructions not only to loot her, but to kill everyone on board and afterwards sink the ship so that no witnesses or evidence remained. 'The six pirates, who proceeded to execute his savage demand, were all armed alike – they each carried a brace of pistols, a cutlass and a long knife. Their dress was composed of a sort of coarse cotton chequered jacket and trowsers, shirts that were open at the collar, red woollen caps, and broad canvas waistbelts, in which were the pistols and knives.'[3]

On seeing the pirates approaching them, all the women on board the *Morning Star* were said to have started screaming and clinging to their husbands, who in turn tried to calm them by saying that all the pirates were interested in was the money and jewelry on board – nothing else. Sadly, however, this was far from the truth. No sooner had de Soto's men boarded the ship, than they ordered the major, together with his wife and the twenty-five injured soldiers, to strip down to their underwear, after which every last one of them was thrown into the hold. The hatches were firmly battened down and heavy pieces of equipment dragged over them so that no one could escape. Then those men who remained on deck were slashed by the pirates with their cutlasses while all the remaining women were locked up in the fo'c'sle.

Just these six pirates could accomplish all this. While of course they were outnumbered, the *Morning Star*'s passengers were unarmed, and the twenty-five soldiers were either sick or injured. What's more, de Soto had trained the *Black Joke*'s long gun on the ship so that at a moment's notice he could sink her. Little wonder that no one attempted to challenge the pirates, who set about looting the ship of every valuable she possessed. Charles Ellms writes:

> **Every trunk was hauled forth, every portable article of value heaped for the plunder; money, plate, charts, nautical instruments, and seven parcels of valuable jewels, which formed part of the cargo; these were carried from below on the backs of those men whom the pirates selected to assist them, and for two hours they were thus employed, during which time Soto stood upon his own deck directing operations.**

Afterwards the pirates turned to drinking and abusing the passengers – one of whom was a Frenchman who was made to serve the pirates their alcohol. This man did everything that was asked of him, but still he was treated abominably, at one point having a knife held to his throat when one of the pirates thought he was trying to poison him. A little later another of the pirates asked the Frenchman where Captain Souley kept his money, but the Frenchmen was unable to answer the question. In response, the pirate cocked a pistol, held it to the Frenchman's chest and fired. Miraculously, the shot missed its target. Undeterred, the pirate then reloaded the weapon and once again pointed it at the Frenchman, who was certain he was about to die. It was only due to Barbazon's interference that the Frenchman survived, after which he was sent to the hold along with all the other prisoners.

The pirates now turned their attention to the women who, one by one, were dragged from the fo'c'sle on to the main deck. Ellms says their cries and screams could be heard

The port of Cadiz in Spain as it looked around the time when de Soto presented himself and his men to the authorities, masquerading as honest, shipwrecked sailors. Eventually, suspicions were aroused, six of his men were arrested and de Soto fled to Gibraltar.

by their husbands and the other male passengers who were below deck. Nor was the abuse short-lived for it went on for hours, with many of the women being raped – or so it was reported in the press back in England where stories about pirates were often made more salacious in order to satisfy the reading public's demand for tales of this nature. Indeed, many historians now believe that far from raping their female captives, in general pirates preferred to treat them if not kindly then at least not barbarically. 'Women were almost invariably well treated,' writes Peter Earle in his book, *Corsairs of Malta and Barbary*. 'Anyone who touched a woman in a sensual manner ran a very great risk of being bastinadoed [beaten on the souls of his feet].'

In fact it was Captain Charles Johnson – the man behind so many pirate myths – who did most to promote the idea of pirates harassing their female prisoners and this he probably did in order to spice up his book, *A General History of the Robberies and Murders of the Most Notorious Pirates*. That said, when it comes to Captain Henry Morgan, doubt still remains as to his claims that he treated his female captives fairly. After Morgan's attack on Portobello in 1668, there were several reports on the Spanish side to the effect that terrible tortures had been meted out by the pirates. 'A woman,' says one report, 'there was by some set bare upon a baking stove and roasted, because she did not confess of money which she had only in their conceit. This he heard some declare boasting, and one that was sick confess with sorrow.'[5]

But it is highly debatable whether de Soto's men treated their women captives so heinously – after all, their main goal was to haul the *Morning Star*'s cargo over to the *Black Joke*, after which de Soto was eager that his men begin boring holes in the bottom part of the *Star* so that she would sink. Once this was done the pirates were swiftly ordered to leave the ship to her fate. Undoubtedly, both she and her passengers would have sunk if it hadn't been for the women on board managing to free the men, who in turn swiftly plugged up the holes. Even then, however, their ordeal wasn't over because the pirates had cut down all the ship's rigging, thus making it impossible for the *Star* to catch up with her sister ships or sail for dry land. It was only by chance that the following day a passing ship saw the *Star* and, recognizing she was in distress, came to her rescue.

De Soto, meanwhile, had sailed some distance from the scene of his crime when he was apprised of the fact that his plan to sink the *Morning Star* had failed and that all aboard her had survived. Infuriated by what he saw as his men's incompetence, he had them turn the *Black Joke* round to where they had left the *Morning Star* to sink her properly. But it was too late, for by the time they had reached the place where they had left her, the *Morning Star* had disappeared without a trace, leading de Soto to believe that she had sunk after all, and there was nothing to worry about. The Admiralty would not come looking for him if there were no witnesses left to his crime and so, convinced he had escaped justice, de Soto continued on his way – this time heading for Europe.

On the journey the *Black Joke* encountered several vessels, including an outward-bound East Indiaman. On board were 200 passengers, including women and children and more than fifty soldiers. Having left London shortly after the *Morning Star* had returned with her tales of pirates and their terrible treatment of everyone on board, the brigantine's captain was very concerned that the same fate did not befall his ship. To this end, the moment he spied the *Black Joke* he ordered that all the guns be made ready to fire, while all the soldiers on board were told to assemble on deck with their weapons loaded and ready for use. '*The Black Joke* came up with them quickly. She first made to come up to windward and then de Soto decided to approach to leeward. The captain of the Indiaman hailed her with his trumpet and asked her name.'[6] He received no reply. Even after a second request no reply was forthcoming; consequently he fired two guns over the *Black Joke*'s bow, after which de Soto ordered her starboard guns raised.

Just then a sudden storm whipped up, forcing both ships to attend to the elements rather than each other. The brigantine sailed in one direction, de Soto in another. It was a narrow escape, but soon enough de Soto had another brigantine in his sights – this time one that wasn't so well armed and was duly boarded by the pirates.

After the ship was plundered, de Soto – recalling the debacle with the *Morning Star* and not wanting any live witnesses – had the crew slaughtered, all except one man whom he kept alive because he had particular knowledge of the course the *Black Joke* had to steer in order to reach Corunna. Not that this man survived for long. On reaching the port, de Soto is said to have thanked his guide for his help before drawing out a pistol and shooting the man in the head and throwing his body into the sea.

At Corunna the *Black Joke* was careened and restocked, while de Soto disposed of a large amount of his booty. He then set sail for Cadiz, where he wanted to dispose of the rest of his loot. But not everything went according to plan. Sailing out of Corunna, the *Black Joke* ran into a storm. 'The gale increased – the night grew pitchy dark – the roaring breakers were on his lee-beam – the drifting vessel strikes, rebounds, and strikes again – the cry of horror rings through the flapping cordage, and despair is in the eyes of the demon-crew.'[7] By daybreak the *Black Joke* was little more than a wreck, and the crew took to the boats and rowed to shore.

De Soto then devised a plan whereby he and the rest of the pirates would return to Cadiz, where they would present themselves to the shipping authorities as law-abiding, ship-wrecked mariners who, in order to return to the sea, had to sell their wrecked vessel so that they could purchase another. And, for a few days all went according to plan. The authorities believed de Soto's story and he received an offer of $1,750 for the *Black Joke*, but then someone became suspicious and six of the crew were arrested. Immediately, de Soto and one other pirate fled Cadiz and headed for Gibraltar. However, when they arrived they were told that only those people who had written permission from the Governor were allowed to enter the fortress of Gibraltar. Not wanting to arouse suspicion, de Soto and his companion took up accommodation in Posade. From here the pirate captain began devising a plan to enter the garrison and steal some of the gold kept there; with this he could purchase a new vessel. His companion thought the mission too dangerous, so de Soto had to carry out the plan on his own.

Having obtained a fake pass into the garrison, he found himself a room at a tavern located just off the main street of the town. The tavern was owned by a man called Basso, and in Ellms' account it was a very dark, dingy place, mostly frequented by 'Spaniards, Moors and Jews, their sallow countenances made yellow by the light of dim oil lamps'. De Soto stayed at this tavern for several days, apparently telling Basso that he had come to Gibraltar on his way to Cadiz and was only staying in the town while he waited for a friend to join him. But luck wasn't on de Soto's side – at the tavern he was recognized by some of the soldiers who had been on the *Morning Star* when it was taken by the pirate. In fact, despite his disguise (for at the time de Soto was said to have smartened up his appearance by wearing a blue frock coat, white trousers, white hat and silk stockings), he was easily identifiable. Not only that, on his arrest he was also found to be in possession of several nautical instruments and firearms that had once belonged to the *Morning Star*. On top of this, a chambermaid at the tavern come forward with further evidence as to de Soto's identity by handing a dirk (dagger) over to the authorities as well as several items of clothing, all of which were believed to have belonged to passengers on board the same looted ship. But perhaps the most damning piece of evidence of all was a notebook found in his room that had once belonged to Captain Souley and which had his own handwriting inside.

Benito de Soto was arrested and immediately flung into jail, where he remained for nineteen months while the authorities collected as much evidence as they could against him. Once again it is the account in Charles Ellms' book that gives the best description of the pirate at this point in his life, the most vivid portrait of a man teetering on the brink of destruction. 'When I visited the pirate in the Moorish castle where he was confined, he was sitting in his cold, narrow, and miserable cell, upon a pallet of straw, eating his coarse meal from a tin plate. I thought him more an object of pity than vengeance; he looked so worn with disease, so crushed with suffering […].'

But this downtrodden demeanor was not to last long, for on appearing in front of Sir George Don in court, in Cadiz, de Soto was said to once again stand tall and proud. Indeed, so proud was he that he spoke in a loud, domineering voice, closely following all the evidence against him, occasionally stopping the proceedings so that he could cross-examine witnesses. Not only that, but he was seen to talk and joke with his guards, even when this behavior was inappropriate – as when witnesses were giving accounts of the horrors they had had to endure at de Soto's hands. The prosecution had lined up several people to give evidence during the trial, one of whom was St Cyr Barbazon who turned Queen's Evidence in the hope that his sentence might be lessened.

In his deposition he claimed that while on board the *Defensor de Pedro* he had fallen under the spell of Benito de Soto, who had suggested that he and twenty-one other sailors mutiny and take over the vessel. 'That in the first two days of the Mutiny Miguel Mercuro also commanded jointly with Benito and it appearing to Benito that he wished to command more than himself fired two pistols at him & Antonio Biscayo one, both of them at the same time whilst Miguel was in his bed asleep and they left him dead by which the said Benito remained sole commander.'[8] In his deposition Barbazon also said that they then went on to capture the *Morning Star* and not only plunder her, but that, having locked the men below decks, they subsequently assaulted the females on board, after which Benito de Soto handed him (Barbazon) a pistol with which to kill two of the *Morning Star*'s crew.

> [...] and afterwards he [Barbazon] did the same with the 2 English sailors that came up from the hold filling them with 2 other Pistols the said Benito gave him, upon which 2 other sailors that had come in the boat and remained in it to take care of themselves threw themselves into the sea fearful that the same would be done to them and he [Barbazon] does not know whether they were drowned although he believes they perished as the distance was very great to allow them to arrive safe on board the English vessel.[9]

If this testimony weren't damning enough, the Prosecution then produced the dirk, the trunk of clothes, the notebook and the weapons that had all been found in de Soto's possession at the time of his arrest and which all linked him directly to the crime aboard the *Morning Star*. The maid at the tavern testified that every morning when she made de Soto's bed she had found the dirk under his pillow, and another domestic also testified to the fact that de Soto was in the habit of wearing clothes from the trunk.

Finally the day of judgment arrived: the defendant was found guilty and sentenced to death. Not that Sir George Don's words intimidated de Soto – it is said the pirate 'looked daggers at his heart, and assumed a horrid silence, more eloquent than words'.[10]

For several weeks afterwards de Soto persisted in telling anyone who was interested that not only was he innocent, but that his trial had been a total farce. It was only as the day of his execution drew near that he changed his mind and eventually confessed to his crimes, begging God's forgiveness. Somewhat unusually – given his predicament – Charles Ellms' account also has de Soto handing his guards a razor blade that he had kept hidden in the sole of his shoe because – having found God – he didn't want to add suicide to the list of his crimes. Not that it mattered much, for several days later he was taken from his prison cell to face the hangman's noose.

'I witnessed his execution,' writes the anonymous author of Charles Ellms' account, 'and I believe there never was a more contrite man than he appeared to be; yet there were no driveling fears upon him – he walked firmly at the tail of the fatal cart, gazing sometimes at his coffin, sometimes at the crucifix which he held in his hand.'

The gallows were erected on barren land next to a wide stretch of water, and when the small procession finally reached it, de Soto is said to have climbed into the gallows' cart as bravely as he had walked behind it. But even then things did not run smoothly, for when he mounted the cart it was found that the gallows' noose was too high up for his neck, so de Soto, not wanting to keep the crowds waiting, climbed up on to his coffin (which was also in the cart) and afterwards placed his head in the noose himself. No sooner was this accomplished then the cart began moving, at which point de Soto is said to have murmured '*Adios todos*' ('Farewell everyone') before leaning forwards to facilitate his own death.

So ended the career of one of the most evil pirates ever to have sailed the world's oceans. De Soto's passing was not mourned and neither was that of the rest of his crew who were, to a man, captured (even those who had escaped as far as Carraccas) and afterwards tried and hanged. Later their bodies were quartered and their limbs hung on hooks as a warning to others.

1 Ellms, *The Pirates Own Book*.
2 Ibid.
3 Course, *Pirates of the Western Seas*.
4 Ellms, op. cit.
5 Earle, *The Sack of Panama*.
6 Course, op. cit.
7 Ibid.
8 PRO CO91/94 Jose de Aymerich y Vacas [Military and Civil Governor of Cadiz], to Don [Governor of Gibraltar] 15 May 1828 enclosing Deposition of St Cyr Barbazon (translated by British translator in Gibraltar). Public Record Office, London.
9 Ibid.
10 Ellms, op. cit.

Glossary

Brethren of the Coast It was around 1640 that the buccaneers (q.v.) of the island of Tortuga (q.v.) began calling themselves the Brethren of the Coast. In order to join this elite band of brothers, members had to vow to subscribe to a strict code of conduct called the Custom of the Coast. Before setting out on any expedition, members also had to attend a council aboard ship to negotiate the exact destination of their forthcoming voyage, where to stop off for provisions, what their exact target would be and how the booty would be divided up between them. The pirate-turned-writer Alexander Oliver Exquemelin (q.v.) gives a fascinating account of the negotiations in his book *The Buccaneers of America*:

> In the first place, therefore, they mention how much the Captain ought to have for his ship. Next the salary of the carpenter, or shipwright, who careened, mended and rigged the vessel [...] Afterwards for provisions and victualling they draw out of the same common stock [...] Also a competent salary for the surgeon and his chest of medicaments. Lastly, they stipulate in writing what recompense or reward each one ought to have, that is either wounded or maimed in his body, suffering the loss of any limb, by that voyage. Thus they order for the loss of a right arm 600 pieces of eight, or six slaves; for the loss of a left arm 500 pieces of eight,

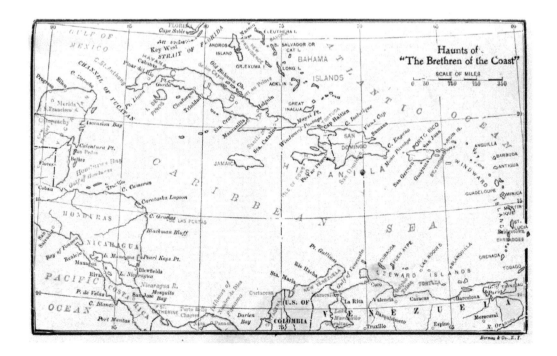

or five slaves; for a right leg 500 pieces of eight; or five slaves; for the left leg 400 pieces of eight, or four slaves; for an eye 100 pieces of eight or one slave; for a finger of the hand, the same reward as for the eye.

After all the above had been paid out, whatever was left over was then divided into shares. The pirate leader would always receive five to six times the amount of an ordinary crew member, while the higher-ranking officers would receive portions commensurate with their rank. Any pirate found stealing from another member of the crew would have his nose and ears cut off. If a man repeated the offence then he would be stranded either on an island or a deserted piece of shoreline with only one pitcher of water, a musket and shot. The most notorious leader of the Brethren of the Coast was Henry Morgan who famously attacked Panama City in 1671.

BRIGANTINE A brigantine was a two-masted vessel that had a fully square-rigged foremast and a fore-and-aft-rigged mainmast with square sails on the main mast. Brigantines were the favored vessels of Mediterranean pirates.

BUCCANEER Originally the term 'buccaneer' referred to the hunters of wild cattle and swine that roamed the pastures and forests on the island of Hispaniola (which is now the Dominican Republic and Haiti). The word comes from the French for barbecue – *boucan* – mainly because the buccaneers tended to roast and/or cure their meat over open fires, something they had learnt from the Arawak Indians of that region. As these *boucaniers* grew in number, eventually the Spanish authorities became alarmed by their rowdy ways and unruly habits and sent hunters in to exterminate the island's animal population. Without food the *boucaniers* couldn't survive and therefore turned to a different type of quarry – the merchant vessels and coastal towns of the West Indies and along the coastlines of South and Central America.

CAREEN To careen a ship means to heel her over and clean the weed and barnacles from her bottom.

COLORS Colors were the flags flown by a vessel to show her nationality.

CORSAIR A corsair was a pirate or privateer operating in the Mediterranean. The most famous corsairs were those based on the Barbary Coast of North Africa.

CUTLASS This weapon was originally used by buccaneers to slaughter animals and cut up meat, but it later evolved into the short sword favored by pirates of all nations.

EAST INDIAMEN These merchant ships were a favorite prey among pirates, mainly because they usually carried luxury cargo that often included gold and silver, silks, spices and jewels.

ELLMS, CHARLES The author of *The Pirates Own Book: Authentic Narratives of the Lives, Exploits, and Executions of the Most Celebrated Sea Robbers*, which was first published in Boston, Massachusetts, in 1837. For the most part Ellms (like Charles Johnson, q.v.) relied on contemporary newspaper accounts and trial transcripts for his information, as well as documents provided by the Admiralty. One interesting note: Ellms is one of the few writers to have mentioned the pirate practice of 'walking the plank', but there is little evidence to prove that this punishment was ever implemented, either by pirates or other seamen.

EXQUEMELIN, ALEXANDER OLIVIER He was most likely a native of Harfleur in Normandy, France, although the date of his birth is unknown. As a young man he was employed by the French West India Company and sailed to the small island of Tortuga (q.v.) around 1666. He served with the company for three years, after which time he changed allegiances, deciding to join up with the buccaneers (q.v.) as a barber-surgeon. He is believed to have sailed back to Europe in 1674, but once again returned to the Caribbean in 1697, again as a surgeon. Later Exquemelin switched professions for a third time and became a writer, penning the highly successful (and exceedingly bloodcurdling) *Buccaneers of America*, which was first published in Dutch in 1678 (*De Americaensche Zee-Rovers*) and in English in 1684. Indeed, so successful was the English edition that a second printing was ordered after only a few months, prompting the publisher to write an advertisement in the frontispiece: 'The first edition of this History of the Buccaneers was received with such general applause of most people, but more especially of the learned, as to encourage me toward obliging the public with this second impression.'

HISPANIOLA Nowadays this island is better known as the Dominican Republic and Haiti.

JOHNSON, CHARLES Johnson was the author of one of the most authoritative and well-cited books on pirates, *The General History of the Robberies and Murders of the Most Notorious Pirates*, first published in England in 1724. His name, however, was thought to be a pseudonym; in 1939 the American academic J.R. Moore announced that the real man behind the book was none other than Daniel Defoe – author of, among other works, *Robinson Crusoe, Moll Flanders, The Journal of the Plague Year* and *Roxanne*. For nearly fifty years Moore's theory went unchallenged until in 1988 P.N. Furbank and W.R. Owens questioned it in their book *The Canonization of Daniel Defoe*. Nowadays it is thought that *The General History* was written by a real Captain Charles Johnson – although who he was, where he lived and when he died, still remain a mystery.

LADRONES The name given to Chinese pirates and thieves.

LETTER OF MARQUE An official document issued by either the sovereign or governing body of a nation, which commissioned the holder to legally attack an enemy vessel. Letters of marque were recognized by international law and therefore a privateer (q.v.) in possession of one could not, in theory, be charged with piracy. One of the first letters of marque ever to have been issued was from King Henry III in 1243: 'Know ye,' it said, 'that we have granted and given license to Adam Robernolt and William le Sauvage [...] to annoy our enemies at sea or by land so that they shall share with us half of all their gain.'[1]

MADAGASCAR This tropical island off the east coast of Africa was popular with those pirates who principally targeted ships in the Indian Ocean. According to Captain Johnson (q.v.), pirates who chose to live on Madagascar were treated like kings: 'They married the most beautiful of the Negro women, not one or two but as many as they liked.'

NASSAU The capital of New Providence (q.v.) island (sometimes known simply as Providence island) in the Bahamas.

NEW PROVIDENCE By 1716 the island of New Providence (sometimes known simply as Providence island) in the Bahamas had become so notorious that it was best known as the 'Nest of Pyrates'. Boasting a harbor that could accommodate up to 500 pirate vessels at any one time (although it was too shallow for naval battleships), it was also the perfect place for pirate ships to take on provisions. Several administrators were sent to New Providence to try to bring the island under control, but the abundance of thieves and rogues soon sent these men packing. Instead, English pirates Benjamin Hornigold and Thomas Barrow declared the island a pirate republic and themselves its governors. Soon they were joined by other captains, among whose number were men such as Calico Jack, Charles Vane and the infamous Blackbeard. It was said that every pirate's wish after he died was not to go to heaven but to New Providence, whose recreational comforts such as grog shops, whorehouses and gambling establishments were second to none.

PINK An extremely narrow-sterned sailing vessel.

PORT ROYAL In the mid seventeenth century the island of Jamaica was wrested from the Spanish by the English, and afterwards achieved notoriety by becoming a leading buccaneer base. Port Royal in particular was colonized by buccaneers (q.v.) from as far afield as France, Portugal, Holland and England, all of whom were actively encouraged to the place by its governors with the express purpose of protecting it from the Spanish and looting as much Spanish gold as possible. It was the perfect location – boasting a harbor capable of holding several hundred ships at any one time, Port Royal was also right in the centre of the main Caribbean shipping routes. In fact, by 1662, so much Spanish gold had been brought into Port Royal that a proposal was made to build a mint on the island. The loot was incalculable: 'gold and silver in bullion and coins. Bars and cakes of gold, wedges and pigs of silver, Pistoles, Pieces of Eight and several other coins of both metals, with store of wrought Plate, jewels, rich pearl necklaces, and of Pearl unsorted and drilled [...] bushels.'[2]

But the port wasn't famous only for the amount of booty that came its way, for with the arrival of the buccaneers the town was soon attracting other businesses to its streets. For instance, in its heyday the town included thirteen doctors, ten tailors, four goldsmiths, twenty-five carpenters and 125 merchants. In addition to this there were also the less salubrious haunts: 'brothels, gaming houses, taverns and grog shops'.[3] The favorite drink among the buccaneers was a type of rum punch called 'kill-devil', which was so potent it prompted Governor Modyford to write that 'the Spaniards wondered much at the sickness of our people, until they knew the strength of their drinks, but then wondered more that they were not all dead.'

Not that it was all drinking and carousing – far from it, for in the six years after the British took over the island, Port Royal buccaneers wreaked havoc among the region's towns and cities, looting many of these settlements over and over again until, in 1692, Port Royal became subject to an even greater force than that wielded by the buccaneers: an apocalyptic visitation of a combined earthquake and tidal wave that wiped out what had commonly become known as the 'Sodom of the New World'.[4] Port Royal was never rebuilt.

PRIVATEER The line between pirates and privateers was always a thin one, most often delineated by a 'letter of marque' (q.v.) which was an authorized document given out by a sovereign or a government allowing privateers to capture enemy merchant vessels without fear of being labeled a pirate. The word 'privateer' can also be applied to the ships that these men sailed in. Initially called private men-of-war, they and their crews soon became known as privateers. Sir Francis Drake, Thomas Cavendish and John Hawkins were all privateers.

PYLE, HOWARD Author of *Howard Pyle's Book of Pirates*, he is probably best remembered for his illustrations of pirates' lives that often appeared in *Harper's Monthly Magazine* in the early part of the twentieth century.

ROGERS, WOODES Best known for his highly successful privateering voyage around the world, which took place between 1708 and 1711 and netted him not only silks and jewelry, but also vast amounts of Spanish bullion. Rogers wrote up an account of his journey in the book *A Cruising Voyage Round the World*, which was first published in 1712. Later, in 1718, Rogers was made Governor of the Bahamas with strict instructions from the British government to wipe out piracy in that region. He died in 1732.

SCHOONER A schooner was a two-masted vessel; both masts would be fore-and-aft rigged.

SLOOP A smallish sailing vessel with one, two or three masts which was favored by Caribbean buccaneers and Atlantic pirates.

ST MARY'S ISLAND Lying on the north-east coast of Madagascar, this island proved the perfect pirate stopover point for careening (q.v.) and restocking their vessels. Among the most notorious pirates to use St Mary's were Edward England and Captain Kidd.

TORTUGA The island of Tortuga lay off the north coast of Hispaniola (q.v.) and made for a perfect pirate haven, possessing as it did good anchorage and adequate shelter for ships while also being positioned on the ever-popular Windward Passage between Hispaniola and Cuba.

1 Platt, *Pirate*.
2 Marx, *Pirate Port*.
3 Konstam, *Buccaneers*.
4 Ibid.

Bibliography

Black, Clinton V., *Pirates of the West Indies*, Cambridge University Press, Cambridge and New York, 1989

Breverton, Terry, *Admiral Sir Henry Morgan: King of the Buccaneers*, Pelican Publishing Company Inc., Louisiana, 2005

Brooks, Graham, *The Trial of Captain* Kidd, Gaunt Inc., London and Toronto, 1995,

Chambers, Anne, *Granuaile: Ireland's Pirate Queen*, Wolfhound Press, Dublin, 2003

Cordingly, David, *Life Among the Pirates: The Romance and the Reality*, Little, Brown and Company, London, 1995

Cordingly, David, and John Falconer, *Pirates: Fact and Fiction*, Collins & Brown Ltd, London, 1992

Cordingly, David (consultant ed.), *Pirates: Terror on the High Seas from the Caribbean to the South China Sea*, World Publications Group Inc., Massachusetts, 1998

Course, Captain A.G., *Pirates of the Western Seas*, Frederick Muller, London, 1969

Davis, Edwin Adams, *Louisiana: A Narrative History*, Claitors Book Store, Baton Rouge, 1965

Defoe, Daniel, *The Life and Strange Surprising Adventures of Robinson Crusoe, of York, Mariner*, London 1719

Earle, Peter, *Corsairs of Malta and Barbary*, Sidgwick & Jackson, London, 1970

Earle, Peter, *The Sack of Panama*, Viking Press, New York, 1981

Ellms, Charles, *The Pirates Own Book: Authentic Narratives of the Lives, Exploits, and Executions of the Most Celebrated Sea Robbers*, Dover Publications 1993. Dickinson, Boston 1837. New edition Marine Research Society, Salem, Massachusetts, 1924

Exquemelin, Alexander Oliver, *Buccaneers of America*, London 1684

Glasspoole, Richard, *A Brief Narrative of My Captivity and Treatment amongst the Ladrones*, London, 1935. In *History of the Pirates Who Infested the China Sea from 1807 to 1810*, translated by K.F. Neumann, London 1831

Grey, Charles (ed. Lieutenant-General Sir George MacMunn), *Pirates of the Eastern Seas*, Sampson Low, Marston & Co, London, 1933

Gosse, Philip, *The Pirate's Who's Who*, 1924, Reprinted Glorieta, New Mexico, 1988

Gosse, Philip, *The History of Piracy*, 1932, Reprinted Rio Grande Press, New Mexico, 1990

Hill, Charles, *Notes on Piracy in Eastern Waters*, Bombay, 1923

Johnson, Charles, *A General History of the Robberies and Murders of the Most Notorious Pirates*, Conway Maritime Press, London, 1998 (first published 1724)

Konstam, Angus, *Buccaneers 1620–1700*, Osprey Publishing Ltd, Oxford, 2000

Lee, Robert E., *Blackbeard the Pirate: A Reappraisal of His Life and Times*, John F. Blair, North Carolina, 2004

Leslie, Charles, *New History of Jamaica*, printed for J. Hodges, London, 1740

Leslie, R.G, *A British Privateer in the Time of Queen Anne*, Chapman and Hall Ltd, 1889

Marx, R.F, *Pirate Port: The Story of the Sunken City of Port Royal*, World Publication Company, Cleveland, 1967

Murphy, Theresa, *Old Bailey: Eight Centuries of Crime, Cruelty and Corruption*, Mainstream Publishing, Edinburgh, 1999

Neumann, Karl F., *History of the Pirates who infested the China Sea from 1807 to 1810*, London 1831 (in translation)

Norman, C.B, *The Corsairs of France*, Sampson Low & Co, London, 1887

Pawson, Michael, and David Buisseret, *Port Royal, Jamaica*, University Press of the West Indies, Kingston, 2002

Platt, Richard, *Pirate*, Dorling Kindersley Eyewitness Guides, London, 1995

Pope, Dudley, *Harry Morgan's Way: The Biography of Sir Henry Morgan 1635–1684*, Secker & Warburg, London, 1977

Pyle, Howard, *Howard Pyle's Book of Pirates: Fiction, Fact & Fancy concerning the Buccaneers & Marooners of the Spanish Main*, Harper & Brothers, USA 1921 (see below for websites)

Ritchie, Robert C., *Captain Kidd and the War against the Pirates*, Harvard University Press, Cambridge, Massachusetts, and London, 1986

Rogers, Captain Woodes, *A Cruising Voyage Round the World* (ed. G.E. Manwaring), Bell and Lintot, London, 1712

Rogozinski, Jan, *The Wordsworth Dictionary of Pirates*, Wordsworth Editions Ltd, Hertfordshire, 1997

Saxon, Lyle; Tallant, Robert; Dryer, Edward, *Gumbo Ya-Ya: A Collection of Louisiana Folk Tales*, Bonanza Books, New York, 1975

Stockton, Frank R., *Buccaneers and Pirates of Our Coasts*, Grosset & Dunlap, 1897–8

Tallant, Robert, *The Pirate Lafitte and the Battle of New Orleans*, Pelican Publishing Co., Gretna, LA, 1998

Wheelright, Julie, *Amazons and Military Maids*, Pandora, London, 1989

Whipple, Addison, *Pirate Rascals of the Spanish Main*, Doubleday & Co, New York, 1957

Zacks, Richard, *The Pirate Hunter: The True Story of Captain Kidd*, Review, Headline Book Publishing, London, 2003

PICTURE ACKNOWLEDGEMENTS

© Corbis: pages 32, 123

© Bettman / Corbis: pages 81, 132, 172

Hulton Archive / Getty Images: pages 42, 53, 58, 111, 134, 135, 142, 149, 162, 175
Time & Life Pictures / Getty Images: page 45

Bill Manning / Istockphoto: page 114
Klaas Lingbeck van Kranen / Istockphoto: page 155

Mary Evans Picture Library: pages 127, 161

North Wind Picture Archives: page 165

Carol Gregory / www.photographersdirect.com: page 19

Amon Ayal / www.shutterstock.com: page 107
Randi Utnes / www.shutterstock.com: page 119
Steven Wright / www.shutterstock.com: pages 101, 146

© The British Library / HIP / TopFoto.co.uk: pages 26, 89
TopFoto.co.uk: pages 72, 150

Other illustrations from private collections.

ACKNOWLEDGEMENTS

First and foremost I would like to thank Robert Bulgin for the
loan of several books which I have used in my research.

I would also like to thank Rod Green and the whole editorial
team at Michael O'Mara Books for all their help and support.

grzimek's
Student Animal Life Resource

• • • •

grzimek's
Student Animal Life Resource

• • • •

Amphibians
volume 3

African treefrogs to Caecilians

**Leslie A. Mertz, PhD, and
Catherine Judge Allen, MA, ELS, authors**

**Madeline S. Harris, project editor
Neil Schlager and Jayne Weisblatt, editors**

THOMSON

GALE

Detroit • New York • San Francisco • San Diego • New Haven, Conn. • Waterville, Maine • London • Munich

Grzimek's Student Animal Life Resource: Amphibians

Leslie A. Mertz, PhD, and Catherine Judge Allen, MA, ELS

Project Editor
Madeline S. Harris

Editorial
Stephanie Cook, Heather Price, Lemma Shomali

Indexing Services
Synapse, the Knowledge Link Corporation

Rights and Acquisitions
Margaret Abendroth, Timothy Sisler

Imaging and Multimedia
Randy Bassett, Michael Logusz, Dan Newell, Chris O'Bryan, Robyn Young

Product Design
Tracey Rowens, Jennifer Wahi

Composition
Evi Seoud, Mary Beth Trimper

Manufacturing
Wendy Blurton, Dorothy Maki

LIBRARY OF CONGRESS CATALOGING-IN-PUBLICATION DATA

Mertz, Leslie A.
Grzimek's student animal life resource. Amphibians / Leslie A. Mertz and Catherine Judge Allen, authors; Neil Schlager and Jayne Weisblatt, editors.
    p. cm.
  Includes bibliographical references and index.
  ISBN 0-7876-9407-X (set hardcover : alk. paper) — ISBN 0-7876-9408-8 (volume 1) — ISBN 0-7876-9409-6 (volume 2) — ISBN 0-7876-9410-X (volume 3)
   1. Amphibians—Juvenile literature. I. Allen, Catherine Judge. II. Schlager, Neil, 1966– III. Weisblatt, Jayne. IV. Title.
  QL644.2.M4263 2005
  597.8—dc22   2005015192

This title is also available as an e-book
Contact your Thomson Gale sales representative for ordering information.

Printed in Canada
10 9 8 7 6 5 4 3 2 1

Contents

Reader's Guide

Grzimek's Student Animal Life Resource: Amphibians offers readers comprehensive and easy-to-use information on Earth's amphibians. Order entries provide an overview of a group of families, and family entries provide an overview of a particular family. Entries are arranged by taxonomy, the science through which living things are classified into related groups. Each entry includes sections on physical characteristics; geographic range; habitat; diet; behavior and reproduction; animals and people; and conservation status. All entries are followed by one or more species accounts with the same information as well as a range map and photo or illustration for each species. Entries conclude with a list of books, periodicals, and Web sites that may be used for further research.

ADDITIONAL FEATURES

Each volume of *Grzimek's Student Animal Life Resource: Amphibians* includes a pronunciation guide for scientific names, a glossary, an overview of amphibians, a list of species in the set by biome, a list of species by geographic location, and an index. The set has 221 full-color maps, photos, and illustrations to enliven the text, and sidebars provide additional facts and related information.

NOTE

Grzimek's Student Animal Life Resource: Amphibians has standardized information in the Conservation Status section. The IUCN Red List provides the world's most comprehensive inventory of the global conservation status of plants and animals. Using a set of criteria to evaluate extinction risk, the IUCN recognizes the following categories: Extinct, Extinct in the Wild, Critically Endangered, Endangered, Vulnerable, Conservation Dependent, Near Threatened, Least Concern, and Data Deficient. These terms are defined where they are used in the text, but for a complete explanation of each category, visit the IUCN web page at http://www.iucn.org/themes/ssc/redlists/RL cats2001booklet.html.

ACKNOWLEDGEMENTS

Gale would like to thank several individuals for their assistance with this set. Leslie Mertz and Catherine Judge Allen wrote the text for the volumes. At Schlager Group Inc., Jayne Weisblatt and Neil Schlager coordinated the writing and editing of the set.

Special thanks are also due for the invaluable comments and suggestions provided by the *Grzimek's Student Animal Life Resource: Amphibians* advisors:

- Mary Alice Anderson, Media Specialist, Winona Middle School, Winona, Minnesota
- Thane Johnson, Librarian, Oklahoma City Zoo, Oklahoma City, Oklahoma
- Debra Kachel, Media Specialist, Ephrata Senior High School, Ephrata, Pennsylvania
- Nina Levine, Media Specialist, Blue Mountain Middle School, Courtlandt Manor, New York
- Ruth Mormon, Media Specialist, The Meadows School, Las Vegas, Nevada

COMMENTS AND SUGGESTIONS

We welcome your comments on *Grzimek's Student Animal Life Resource: Amphibians* and suggestions for future editions of this work. Please write: Editors, *Grzimek's Student Animal Life Resource: Amphibians*, U•X•L, 27500 Drake Rd., Farmington Hills, Michigan 48331-3535; call toll free: 1-800-877-4253; fax: 248-699-8097; or send e-mail via www.gale.com.

Pronunciation Guide for Scientific Names

Acanthixalus spinosus ay-kan-THICK-sal-us spy-NO-sus

Adelotus brevis ay-deh-LO-tus BREH-vis

Adenomus kandianus ay-deh-NO-mus kan-die-AY-nus

Albericus siegfriedi al-BEAR-ih-kus SIG-freed-eye

Alexteroon jynx ay-LEKS-tih-roh-on jinks

Allophryne ruthveni ah-lo-FRYN rooth-VEN-eye

Allophrynidae ah-lo-FRY-nih-dee

Alytes obstetricans ah-LYE-tes ob-STET-trih-kanz

Ambystoma tigrinum am-bih-STOH-ma tih-GRIH-num

Ambystomatidae am-bih-stoh-MA-tih-dee

Amphiuma tridactylum am-fee-U-ma try-DAK-tih-lum

Amphiumidae am-fee-U-mih-dee

Aneides lugubris ay-NEE-ih-deez lu-GU-bris

Ansonia longidigita an-SOH-nee-aye lon-jih-DIJ-ih-ta

Anura ann-UR-uh

Arenophryne rotunda ah-ree-no-FRYN roh-TUN-da

Arthroleptidae ar-throh-LEP-tih-dee

Arthroleptis stenodactylus ar-throh-LEP-tis sten-oh-DAK-tih-lus

Ascaphidae as-KAF-ih-dee

Ascaphus montanus as-KAF-us mon-TAN-us

Assa darlingtoni AY-suh dar-ling-TON-eye

Atelognathus patagonicus ay-teh-log-NAYTH-us pat-ah-GO-nih-kus

Atelopus varius ay-teh-LO-pus var-ee-us

Atelopus vogli ay-teh-LO-pus vohg-lye

Barbourula busuangensis bar-bo-RU-la bus-u-an-JEN-sis

Bolitoglossa pesrubra bo-LYE-toh-glos-sah pes-ROO-bra

Bombina bombina BOM-bin-ah BOM-bin-ah

Bombina orientalis BOM-bin-ah oh-ree-en-TAL-ihs

Bombina variegata BOM-bin-ah vay-ree-GA-ta

Bombinatoridae BOM-bin-ah-TOR-ih-dee

Brachycephalidae brak-ee-sef-FAL-ih-dee

Brachycephalus ephippium brak-ee-SEF-fal-us ee-FIP-ee-um

Brachycephalus nodoterga brak-ee SEF-fal-us no-DOE-tur-ga

Brachycephalus pernix brak-ee-SEF-fal-us PER-nicks

Brachycephalus vertebralis brak-ee-SEF-fal-us ver-teh-BRA-lis

Brachytarsophrys intermedia brak-ee-TAR-so-frys in-tur-ME-dee-uh

Bufo marinus BOO-foe MAYR-ih-nus

Bufo periglenes BOO-foe pair-ee-GLEH-nees

Bufonidae boo-FOH-nih-dee

Bymnophiona bim-no-fee-OH-nuh

Caecilian seh-SILL-ee-uhn

Caeciliidae seh-SILL-ee-eye-dee

Caudata kaw-DAY-tuh

Centrolene geckoideum SEN-troh-lean gek-oh-EYE-dee-um

Centrolenidae sen-troh-LEN-ih-dee

Ceratophrys cornuta seh-RAT-oh-fris kor-NEW-ta

Chioglossa lusitanica chee-oh-GLOSS-ah loo-sih-TAN-ih-ka

Cochranella ignota kok-ran-ELL-ah ihg-NO-ta

Cochranella saxiscandens kok-ran-ELL-ah saks-ee-SKAN-denz

Colostethus caeruleodactylus coh-loh-STETH-us see-RUE-lee-oh-DAK-til-us

Conraua goliath kon-RAH-u-ah go-LYE-eth

Cophixalus riparius co-FIX-ah-lus rih-PAIR-ee-us

Cryptobranchidae KRIP-toe-BRAN-kih-dee

Cryptobranchus alleganiensis krip-toe-BRAN-cus al-lee-GAY-nee-en-sis

Cyclorana platycephala sy-klo-RA-na plat-ee-SEF-fa-la

Cynops pyrrhogaster sy-NOPS pie-roh-GAS-ter

Dendrobatidae den-droh-BA-tih-dee

Dermophis mexicanus der-MO-fis meks-ih-KAN-us

Desmognathus fuscus dez-mog-NATH-us FUS-cus

Dicamptodon tenebrosus di-CAMP-toe-don ten-eh-BROH-sus

Dicamptodontidae di-CAMP-toe-DON-tih-dee

Discoglossidae dis-ko-GLOSS-ih-dee

Discoglossus pictus dis-ko-GLOSS-us PIK-tus

Edalorhina perezi ed-dah-LOR-heena PER-ez-eye

Epicrionops marmoratus eh-pee-KREE-oh-nops mar-moh-RA-tus

Epipedobates tricolor eh-pee-ped-oh-BA-tees tri-KUL-or

Eurycea bislineata u-REE-see-uh bis-LIN-ee-ah-ta

Eurycea rathbuni u-REE-see-uh rath-BUN-eye

Gastrophryne carolinensis GAS-troh-fryn kay-roh-LIN-en-sis

Gastrotheca riobambae gas-troh-THEH-ka ree-oh-BAM-bee

Gymnophiona jim-no-fee-OH-nuh

Heleophryne natalensis heh-lee-oh-FRYN nay-TAL-en-sis

Heleophrynidae heh-lee-oh-FRYN-ih-dee

Hemiphractus proboscideus heh-mee-FRAK-tus proh-BOSS-kid-day-us

Hemisotidae heh-mee-SAW-tih-dee

Hemisus barotseensis heh-MEE-sus bare-aht-SEEN-sis

Hemisus marmatorus heh-MEE-sus mar-mah-TOR-us

Hemisus sudanensis heh-MEE-sus soo-dan-EN-sis

Hyalinobatrachium valerioi high-ah-LIN-oh-bah-TRAK-ee-um vah-LAIR-ree-oh-eye

Hyla leucophyllata HIGH-lah loo-ko-fye-LAT-ta

Hylidae HIGH-lih-dee

Hynobiidae high-no-BEE-eye-dee

Hynobius retardatus high-NO-bee-us ree-tar-DAT-tus

Hyperoliidae high-per-OLE-lee-eye-dee

Hyperolius marginatus high-per-OLE-lee-us mar-jin-AT-tus

Hyperolius marmoratus high-per-OLE-lee-us mar-more-AT-tus

Hyperolius viridiflavus high-per-OLE-lee-us vir-rid-ih-FLA-vus

Ichthyophiidae ik-thee-oh-FYE-eye-dee

Ichthyophis glutinosus ik-thee-OH-fis gloo-tin-OH-sus

Kaloula pulchra kah-LOW-oo-la PULL-kra

Kassina senegalensis kah-see-na sen-ee-gall-EN-sis

Leiopelma hamiltoni lay-oh-PEL-ma ham-il-TO-nye

Leiopelma pakeka lay-oh-PEL-ma pa-KEY-ka

Leiopelmatidae lay-oh-pel-MAH-tih-dee

Lepidobatrachus laevis lep-ee-doh-bah-TRAK-us lay-EH-vis

Leptobrachium banae lep-toh-BRAK-ee-um BAN-nee

Leptodactylidae lep-toh-dak-TIL-ih-dee

Leptodactylus pentadactylus lep-toh-dak-TIL-us pen-ta-DAK-til-us

Limnodynastidae lim-no-dye-NAS-tih-dee

Lithodytes lineatus lih-thoh-DYE-teez lin-ee-AT-tus

Litoria caerulea lih-TOR-ree-uh seh-RU-lee-uh

Mantidactylus liber man-ti-DAK-til-us LEE-ber

Megophryidae me-go-FRY-ih-dee

Megophrys montana me-go-FRIS mon-TAN-ah

Micrixalus phyllophilus my-krik-SAL-us fye-LO-fil-us

Microbatrachella capensis my-kro-bah-trak-ELL-la cap-PEN-sis

Microhyla karunaratnei my-kro-HIGH-la kare-roo-nah-RAT-nee-eye

Microhylidae my-kro-HIGH-lih-dee

Myobatrachidae my-oh-bat-TRAK-ih-dee

Nasikabatrachidae nas-SIK-ka-bat-TRAK-ih-dee

Nasikabatrachus sahyadrensis nas-SIK-ka-bat-TRAK-us sa-HIGH-ah-dren-sis

Necturus maculosus nek-TOO-rus mak-u-LOH-sus

Neobatrachus pictus nee-oh-bat-TRAK-us PIK-tus

Notaden melanoscaphus NO-tah-den mel-an-oh-SKAF-us

Nyctixalus pictus nik-TIK-sal-us PIK-tus

Occidozyga lima ock-sih-DOZE-ih-gah LEE-ma

Onychodactylus japonicus on-ik-oh-DAK-til-us ja-PON-ih-kus

Oreolalax schmidti oh-ree-oh-LA-laks SCHMIDT-eye

Otophryne pyburni oh-toe-FRYN pie-BURN-eye

Parhoplophryne usambarica par-HOP low-fryn u-sam-BAR-ee-ka

Pelobatidae pel-low-BA-tih-dee

Pelodytes punctatus pel-low-DYE-teez punk-TAH-tus

Philautus papillosus fil-LAW-tus pa-pill-OH-sus

Philoria pughi fil-LOW-ree-uh PYU-eye

Phrynomantis bifasciatus fry-no-MAN-tis bi-FAS-see-at-tus

Phyllobates terribilis fye-low-BA-teez ter-rib-BIL-iss

Pipa pipa PIE-pa PIE-pa

Pipidae PIE-pih-dee

Plethodontidae pleth-oh-DON-tih-dee

Pleurodema bufonina PLOOR-oh-dee-ma boo-fo-NEE-na

Proteidae pro-TEE-ih-dee

Proteus anguinus PRO-tee-us AN-gwin-us

Pseudis paradoxa SOO-dis pair-ah-DOKS-sa

Pseudoeurycea bellii soo-doe-yur-EE-see-ah BELL-ee-eye

Rachophorus arboreus rak-OH-for-us ar-bor-EE-us

Rana catesbeiana RAH-nah kat-TEEZ-bee-eye-an-uh

Rana temporaria RAH-nah tem-po-RARE-ee-uh
Ranidae RAH-nee-dee
Ranodon sibiricus RAH-no-don sib-EAR-ee-kus
Rhacophoridae rak-oh-FOR-ih-dee
Rhinatrematidae rye-na-tree-MA-tih-dee
Rhinoderma darwinii rye-no-DER-ma dar-WIN-ee-eye
Rhinodermatidae rye-no-der-MA-tih-dee
Rhinophrynidae rye-no-FRY-nih-dee
Rhinophrynus dorsalis rye-no-FRY-nus DOR-suh-lis
Rhyacotriton cascadae rye-YA-koh-try-ton KAS-kah-dee
Rhyacotritonidae rye-ya-koh-try-TON-nih-dee
Salamandra salamandra sal-a-MAN-dra sal-a-MAN-dra
Salamandridae sal-a-MAN-drih-dee
Scaphiophryne calcarata skaf-FEE-oh-fryn kal-ka-RAT-ta
Scaphiophryne gottlebei skaf-FEE-oh-fryn got-LEB-ee-eye
Scaphiophrynidae skaf-fee-oh-FRYN-nih-dee
Scarthyla goinorum skar-THIGH-la go-in-OR-um
Scolecomorphidae skoh-lee-kom-MOR-fih-dee
Scolecomorphus kirkii skoh-lee-kom-MOR-fus KIRK-ee-eye
Silurana tropicalis sil-u-RA-na trop-ih-KAL-is
Siren intermedia SIGH-ren in-ter-ME-dee-uh
Sirenidae sigh-REN-nih-dee
Sooglossidae soo-GLOSS-sih-dee
Sooglossus sechellensis soo-GLOSS-sus say-shell-EN-sis
Stumpffia helenae STUM-fee-uh hell-LEN-ah-ee
Taudactylus eungellensis taw-DAK-til-us ee-u-jel-LEN-sis
Thoropa miliaris thor-OH-pa mil-ee-AIR-iss
Trichobatrachus robustus try-koh-ba-TRAK-us roh-BUS-tus
Triprion petasatus TRIP-pree-on pet-TAS-sah-tus
Triturus cristatus TRY-ter-us krih-STAT-us
Triturus vulgaris TRY-ter-us vul-GARE-iss
Tylototriton verrucosus tie-LOW-tow-try-tun ver-ruh-KOH-sus
Typhlonectes compressicauda tie-flo-NEK-teez kom-press-sih-KAW-duh
Uraeotyphlus oxyurus u-ray-ee-oh-TIE-flus oks-ee-YUR-us
Uraeotyphylidae u-ray-ee-oh-tie-FIE-lih-dee
Vibrissaphora ailaonica vie-brih-saf-FOR-uh ale-la-ON-nik-ah
Xenopus laevis zee-NA-pus lay-EH-vis

Words to Know

A

Adaptable organism An organism that can adjust to various living conditions.

Ambush A style of hunting in which a predator hides and waits for an unsuspecting prey animal to come to it.

Amphibian A vertebrate that has moist, smooth skin; is cold-blooded, meaning the body temperature is the same as the temperature of the surroundings; and, in most instances, has a two-stage life cycle.

Amplexus In frogs, a mating position in which the male clings to the female's back.

Amphipods Beach fleas, water lice, and other small water-living invertebrates.

Aposematic coloration Warning colors that advertise something about an animal, possibly its bad-tasting, poisonous skin.

Aquatic Living in the water.

Arboreal Living in trees.

Arthropods Insects, spiders, and other invertebrates that have jointed legs.

B

Balancers Structures on the sides of the head of some salamander larvae that support the head until the legs develop.

Barbels Little bits of flesh sometimes seen dangling from the mouth or chin of animals, such as some frogs and fishes.

Bask Sunbathe; often seen in reptiles and amphibians to help warm up their bodies.

Bioindicator species An organism that people can use to tell whether or not the environment is healthy.

Bromeliads Plants of warm, usually tropical, forests that often grow on other plants. Their leaves typically overlap into cup shapes that can hold water.

C

Cannibalistic Describing animals that eat other members of their own species.

Carnivorous Meat-eating.

Cartilage A flexible material in an animal's body that is often associated with bones.

Chorus In male frogs, a group that calls together.

Chromosomes The structures in a cell that hold the DNA.

Cloaca The chamber in some animals that holds waste from the kidneys and intestines, holds eggs or sperm about to be released to the outside, holds sperm entering a female's body, and is the passage through which young are born.

Coniferous forest Land covered with trees that bear their seeds inside cones.

Crepuscular Describing animals that are active only at dawn and at dusk.

Crustaceans Water-dwelling animals that have jointed legs and a hard shell but no backbone.

Cryptic coloration Colors and often patterns on an animal that help it blend into its environment.

Cutaneous respiration Breathing through the skin

D

Deciduous forest Land covered by trees that lose their leaves during cold or dry seasons.

Direct development Process by which frog eggs develop right into froglets and skip the tadpole stage.

Diurnal Active during the day.

DNA A chain of chemical molecules that is the instruction booklet for making a living thing; scientists can tell one species from another by comparing the DNA.

E

Ectothermic Describing animals whose body temperature changes when the outside air warms up or cools down.

Embryo A developing animal that has not yet hatched or been born.

Estivation As seen in some animals, a period of inactivity during dry spells.

Explosive breeders Members of a species that breed together in a large group, usually over a very short time.

F

Fertilization The joining of egg and sperm to start development.

Filter feeder An animal that strains water for bits of food.

Foraging Searching for food.

Fossorial Living underground.

Froglet The life stage of a frog right after the tadpole stage.

G

Gill An organ for obtaining oxygen from water.

Granular glands Poison glands, which in frogs are typically in noticeable bumps, often called "warts," on the back.

H

Herbivorous Plant-eating.

Herpetologist A person who studies amphibians and reptiles.

Hibernation A state of deep sleep that some animals enter in the winter to help them survive the cold weather.

Hybrid Describing the young produced by parents of two different species.

I

Indirect development Process by which frog eggs develop first into tadpoles and then into froglets.

Infertile eggs Eggs that will never develop into young.

Introduced species An animal, plant, or other species that is brought to a new location, usually by humans, either on purpose or by accident.

Invertebrate An animal, such as an insect, spider, or earthworm, without a backbone.

L

Larva (plural, larvae) An animal in an early stage that changes form before becoming an adult.

Lateral line system A row of tiny dot- or stitch-shaped organs, seen in fishes, tadpoles, and some other water-living organisms, that allow the animal to feel vibrations in the water.

M

Marsupium Found in some animals, a pouch in the adult where the young develop.

Metamorphosis The changes in form that some animals make to become adult, such as tadpole to frog.

Microorganisms Living things that are too small to see.

Mimic To copy.

Mollusk An animal with a soft, unsegmented body that may or may not have a shell.

N

Nocturnal Active mostly at night.

Nuptial pads Seen in some frogs, thick pads that form on the forelegs, on the front feet, on the toes of the front feet, and sometimes on the chest to help the male grip onto the female during mating.

O

Ocelli In frogs, small dots of color.

Opportunistic feeder An animal that will eat just about anything that it can capture and swallow.

Ovary The organ that makes eggs.

P

Palate The roof of the mouth.

Paratoid glands In some frogs, a pair of enlarged poison-containing sacs found at the back of the head.

Permanent body of water A body of water that is filled with water year-round.

S

Silt Dirt that is washed from land and collects in rivers and streams.

Sperm Microscopic cells from a male that trigger eggs from a female to start development.

Spicules Seen on the snout of a Mesoamerican burrowing toad, small, hard, sometimes pointy bumps.

Spine Backbone; also known as the vertebral column.

Spiracle In a tadpole, a tiny hole that lets water out.

Sternum A bone in the middle of the chest between the ribs; breastbone.

Symmetrical Describing a pattern that has two sides that are mirror images of one another.

T

Temporary body of water A body of water that is only filled with water for part of the year.

Terrestrial Living on land.

Toxin Poison.

Toxicity The level of poison.

Transparent See-through.

Tubercles Bumps.

Tympanum Eardrum, which in many frogs is visible as a round spot on the side of the head.

U

Utraviolet radiation A type of light that humans cannot see, but that scientists believe may be harming some frog species, especially those that live high in mountains where the radiation is strongest.

Unken reflex Seen in some frogs and salamanders, a stiff backbend pose that serves to warn predators that the animal is bad-tasting or poisonous.

Urostyle A long, rod-shaped bone in the hip area of a frog.

V

Vernal pool A body of water that forms in the spring but then dries up for the rest of the year.

Vertebrae The bones that make up the spinal column.

Vertebrates Animals, such as birds, frogs, snakes, and mammals, with backbones.

Vocal sac Extra flesh on the throat of most male frogs that expands like a balloon when they make their calls.

W

Wart In frogs, a wart is a lump in the skin that contains poison and helps protect the frog from predators. In humans, a wart results from a virus and sometimes requires medical care.

Getting to Know Amphibians

AMPHIBIANS

Three different types of amphibians (am-FIB-ee-uhns) live on Earth today:

- Frogs are the often-slimy creatures almost everyone has seen hopping into a pond or heard calling on a spring evening. The smallest species reach less than one-half an inch (1.3 centimeters) long, while the largest can grow to more than a foot (30.5 centimeters) in length. Frogs are in the order Anura (ann-UR-uh). Toads are included in this order, too. They are simply one kind of frog. Frogs are different from other amphibians because they do not have tails when they are adults. Some frogs, called the tailed frogs, have little taillike bits of tissue, but they are not really tails. Many frogs have long and strong hind legs for hopping, but a few have short hind legs and typically get around by walking or running.

- Salamanders are the four-legged, tailed animals that hikers or gardeners sometimes surprise when they turn over a rock or log. The smallest salamanders are less than 1.2 inches (3 centimeters) long, while the largest can grow to 4 feet 11 inches (150 centimeters) in length, or more. Salamanders have bodies in the shape of a pipe with a tail at the rear. Most have small legs that are all about the same size. They hold their legs out to the side of the body when they are scrambling around on the ground. A few species have only two legs. The name of the salamanders' order is Caudata (kaw-DAY-tuh).

- Caecilians (seh-SILL-ee-uhns) come in many sizes, ranging from just 4.5 inches long to more than 5 feet 3 inches (160 centimeters) in length, but most people have never seen them in the wild. Caecilians look rather like earthworms, even having similar rings around their bodies, but caecilians have many things that earthworms do not, including jaws and teeth. A caecilian's tail is actually quite short, but since it blends into the rest of the body, this can be difficult to see unless the animal is flipped over. The tail in a caecilian begins at the vent, a slitlike opening on its underside. The caecilians are in the order Gymnophiona (jim-no-fee-OH-nuh).

In all, the world holds at least 4,837 species of frogs and toads, 502 of salamanders, and 165 of caecilians. Scientists are still discovering new species, so those numbers grow larger and larger as the years pass.

WHAT MAKES AN AMPHIBIAN AN AMPHIBIAN?

Although frogs, salamanders, and caecilians are usually not mistaken for one another, they still share several features that make them all amphibians.

Illustration of a frog skeleton. (Illustration by Marguette Dongvillo. Reproduced by permission.)

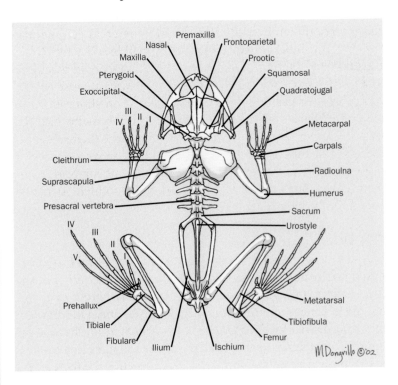

Skin

Some people confuse salamanders with lizards, but lizards are reptiles. An easy way to tell an amphibian from a reptile is to check for scales on the skin. Reptiles have scales, but amphibians do not. The skin of an amphibian is at least a little bit moist, even among the rather-dry toads, and some amphibians are very slippery. Part of the slipperiness comes from the moist or wet places they live, and part of it comes from their mucus (MYOO-kus) glands. Mucus glands are little sacks that ooze a slimy substance.

Amphibians also have another type of glands in their skin that ooze poison instead of mucus. Depending on the species, the poison may be weak or very strong. The poison in some of the poison frogs of South America is even powerful enough to kill a person who gets some in his or her bloodstream. In other species, just a little taste of the poison can turn a person's lips numb or cause extreme sickness.

Body temperature

Like fishes and reptiles, amphibians have body temperatures that become colder when the outside temperature is cold and warmer when the outside temperature is hot. Animals with a changing body temperature like this are known as ectothermic (EK-toe-thur-mik) animals. Sometimes, people call ectothermic animals "cold-blooded," but they are really only cold when the weather is also cold. Many amphibians warm themselves by sunbathing, or basking. Frogs frequently sit on shore in damp but sunny spots to bask. They may also simply swim into the warmer, upper layer of water in a pond to heat themselves up a bit. When they get too hot, they typically move to a cooler place, sometimes even going underground. This not only keeps them cooler but also helps them stay moist, which is important for their breathing.

Breathing

Amphibians breathe in several different ways. Like reptiles, birds, and mammals, most amphibians breathe in air through their nostrils to fill up their lungs. Caecilians have two lungs, but the left one is much smaller than the right one. This arrangement works well for the caecilians, which would not have room for two large lungs in their long and thin bodies. Some salamanders have very small lungs, and a few, such as the red-backed salamander that is common in North American forests, have no lungs at all.

Small or no lungs does not cause a problem for amphibians, however, because they do much of their breathing through their skin. When a person breathes in through the nose, the air travels into the lungs in the chest, where blood picks up the oxygen from the air and delivers it throughout the body. In amphibians, oxygen can pass right through their moist skin and into blood that is waiting in blood vessels just below the skin. The skin must be moist for this process to work: A dry amphibian is a dead amphibian. Using this through-the-skin breathing, which is called cutaneous respiration (kyoo-TAIN-ee-us res-per-AY-shun), amphibians can even breathe underwater. Oxygen that is dissolved in the water can also cross the skin and enter their blood.

Most amphibians go through a phase in their lives when they breathe underwater through gills, just as a fish does. Gill breathing is like cutaneous respiration, because dissolved oxygen in the water is picked up by blood in vessels that are in the gills. Gills are so full of blood vessels that they are typically bright red. Usually an amphibian breathes through gills only when it is young. Frogs, for instance, use gills when they are still tadpoles. A young salamander, which also has gills, is called a larva (LAR-vuh). The plural of larva is larvae (LAR-vee). Some amphibians, however, skip the gill-breathing phase and hatch right from the egg into a lung- and/or skin-breather. Others, however, keep their gills throughout their entire lives. Mudpuppies are examples of a salamander that has gills even as an adult. Since they live in the water, gills work well for them. In a few species, like the eastern newt, the animal goes through several phases: a gill-breathing larva, then a gill-less juvenile, and finally a gilled adult.

Hearing

Besides hearing sounds like humans do, frogs and salamanders can hear vibrations in the ground. When the ground vibrates, the movement travels up their front legs to the shoulder blade and then to a muscle that connects to the ear, so the amphibian can hear it. This type of hearing can be very sensitive. Not only can amphibians hear the footsteps of an approaching predator, like a raccoon, but they can also hear something as slight as an insect digging in the soil.

WHERE AMPHIBIANS LIVE

Amphibians live around the world. The only places where they do not live are in the extremely cold polar regions of the Earth, most of the islands in the ocean, and some desert areas. The three major groups of amphibians—the frogs, the caecilians, and the salamanders—each have their own favorite climates. Caecilians stay in warm, tropical climates and nowhere else. Although frogs live just about anywhere an amphibian can live, the greatest number of species make their homes in the tropics. Salamanders, on the other hand, tend toward cooler areas. Most salamanders live north of the Equator, and many exist in areas that have all four seasons, including a cold winter.

Because amphibians must keep their skin moist, they are always tied to water. That water may be a lake or river, a little puddle, a clammy spot under a log, or even a slightly damp burrow underground.

In the water

Most amphibians live at least part of their lives in the water. Many frogs and salamanders lay their eggs in the water. The frog eggs hatch into tadpoles, and the salamander eggs hatch into larvae. Both the tadpoles and the salamander larvae have gills that they use to breathe underwater. Eventually, the tadpoles turn into baby frogs, and the salamander larvae turn into young salamanders, and both can then leave the water to live on land. Scientists do not have all of the details about caecilians, but they think the typical caecilian lays its eggs on land; the eggs hatch into young that are also called larvae and have gills; and the larvae wriggle into water. The caecilian larvae grow in the water before losing their gills and moving onto land.

Those species that live on land for much of the year and only have their young in the water, often choose small pools that are only filled with water part of the year. Such pools are called temporary pools. Temporary pools, since they dry up later in the year, usually do not contain fish, which often eat amphibian eggs

THE RISE OF THE AMPHIBIANS

The oldest fossil amphibian is about 250 millions years old, but amphibians were around even before that. These animals lived when the Earth had only one large land mass that was surrounded by ocean. That land mass was called Pangaea (pan-JEE-uh). When Pangaea began to break up about 190 million years ago, the amphibians were split up, too. The land masses continued to move around the globe and split up into the continents as they are today. While these movements were taking place, the amphibians were changing and becoming new species. Some had features that made them well-suited to life in certain temperatures or certain areas. Today, the Earth holds thousands of different species.

and young. The only problem with laying eggs in a temporary pool is that the pools sometimes dry up too fast for the eggs to hatch into the tadpoles or larvae and for these to turn into land-living amphibians. When this happens, the young may die.

In each major group of amphibians, some species remain in the water for their entire lives. These are known as fully aquatic (uh-KWOT-ik) animals. The word *aquatic* means that an organism lives in the water, and the word *fully* means that it can always live there. Some caecilians from South America live in the water. Sirens and mudpuppies are types of salamanders that live in the water as eggs, larvae, and adults. As adults, both have bodies that are well-designed for swimming instead of walking on land. They have strong, flattened tails to move swiftly through the water but very tiny legs. The sirens only have two small front legs and have neither back legs nor hip bones.

Many frogs are fully aquatic. The clawed frogs and Surinam toads, for instance, live in just about any kind of freshwater, including swamps, slow streams, and ponds. They have very large and webbed hind feet, which make excellent paddles. One very unusual frog is the hairy frog. Adults of this species live on land most of the year, but the males will stay with the eggs underwater until they hatch. During this time, the male develops "hairs" all over the sides of its body. The hairs are actually thin fringes made of skin. This gives him more skin area and makes it easier for him to breathe. With his "hairs," he is able to stay underwater for days with his eggs without ever coming up for air.

Tadpoles, aquatic larvae, and some aquatic adult amphibians have lateral (LAT-eh-rul) line systems. Fishes have lateral line systems, too. The lateral line system looks like a row of stitch-like marks or dots that runs down each side of the body. Inside each mark or dot are tiny hairs that sway one way or the other with the movements of the water. When another animal swims past or enters the water nearby, the hairs lean and send a message to the amphibian's brain that it is not alone in the water. This helps amphibians to escape predators or, if they eat insects or other water-living prey, to find the next meal.

Along the ground

Many adult frogs and salamanders live on land and along the ground. Since they have to keep their skin moist, they often huddle under a rotting log, inside a crack in a rock, in piles of dead leaves, under the low-lying leaves of plants, or in some other damp place. Once in a while, a caecilian is also found snuggled between a leaf and stem in a low plant. In many cases, amphibians only move about on the ground during or after a heavy rain. Some, like the American toads, can survive under a bit drier conditions than other amphibians and hop or walk around the forest floor even on warm and dry summer days.

Above the ground

Some frogs and salamanders will venture into the trees. Animals that spend part of their lives off the ground and in plants or trees are known as arboreal (ar-BOR-ee-ul) animals. Among the salamanders, only some lungless salamanders are arboreal. One, which is known as the arboreal salamander, may crawl under tree bark or climb into tree holes to escape hot and dry weather. Many more frogs than salamanders are arboreal. Hundreds of these are called treefrogs and have sticky, wide pads on the tips of their toes to help them scramble up plants and trees. Some of the arboreal frogs live in humid forests that are

Life cycle of a salamander (Ambystoma opacum) and frog (Rana temporaria); a. and b.— adults; c.—eggs laid in water; d.— —terrestrial salamander eggs laid in a moist area on land; e, f, g, h—larval stage; i and j—juvenile stage. (Illustration by Jacqueline Mahannah. Reproduced by permission.)

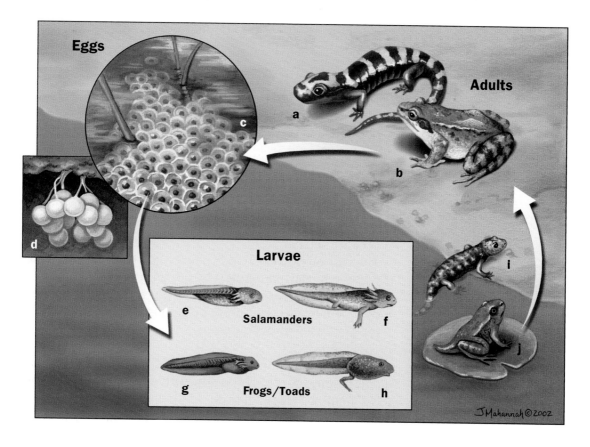

moist enough for them to sit out on leaves most of the time. Others need more moisture and find it in bromeliads (broh-MEE-lee-ads), which are plants that often grow on the sides of trees and have tube-shaped leaves that catch rainwater. There, the frogs find tiny pools where they can dip their bodies or float.

Under the soil

Since amphibians need to keep their skin moist, many of them find dampness under the soil. Animals that live underground are called fossorial (faw-SOR-ee-ul) animals. Most of the caecilians remain underground, only coming up to the surface once in a while to feed. They typically have tiny eyes and are nearly blind, although they can tell light from dark. They make their own burrows, digging headfirst into moist soil. Among the salamanders, the best-known burrowers are the mole salamanders. These salamanders, which live through much of North America, usually do not make their own burrows, instead borrowing them from mice and other small rodents. They stay inside these underground hideaways until rains wet the ground. At that time, they climb out and look for food to eat. Many of the mole salamanders, such as the blue-spotted salamander, also may live under rotting logs. The larger spotted salamander sometimes hides under rocks or deep in a damp well.

Numerous frog species, including the spadefoot toads, live underground for much of their lives. They, like many other burrowing frogs, have a hard bump that looks like the edge of a shovel blade on each of their digging feet. Some burrowing frogs do not have hard bumps on their feet. They do, however, have powerful digging legs and usually wide feet to move away the soil as they burrow.

HOW DO AMPHIBIANS MOVE?

Since amphibians may have four legs, two legs, or no legs at all, and they may spend most of their time on the ground, in the water, or in trees, they move in many different ways. Some walk or run; some hop or leap; some swim; some burrow; and some even glide through the air.

Walking and running

The land-living, or terrestrial (te-REH-stree-uhl), salamanders travel from one place to another by walking or running. They do this with their bodies very close to the ground and their upper legs held out from the body in the same position that a person takes when starting to do a push-up. Lizards, which people often confuse with salamanders, typically hold their bodies higher off the ground. The arboreal salamanders use these same movements to climb trees. Some frogs, especially those frogs with short hind legs, also get around mainly by walking. The Roraima bush toad is an example. This little toad walks slowly over the rocks where it lives. If it needs to escape quickly, it tucks in its legs so it forms a little ball and rolls off the face of the stone.

Hopping

The frogs and toads are the hoppers and leapers among the amphibians. They have two especially long ankle bones in their hind legs, as well as a long rod of bone in the hip where the jumping muscles attach. These bones give the frog's leaps added boost. They also have a strong but springy chest that can catch the frog safely as it lands on its front feet. Not all frogs and toads hop, but most do. Some, like most of the frogs in the family called true toads, have short hind legs and can only hop a short distance. Others, like most of those in the family called true frogs, have long and powerful hind legs that help them leap several times their body length. Some people even hold frog-leaping contests and bet on the frog they think will jump the farthest.

Swimming

Adult frogs swim much as they leap, shoving off with both hind feet at the same time. The frogs that are the best swimmers typically have large hind feet with webbing stretched between the toes and to the toe tips or close to the tips. Tadpoles do not have any legs until they start to turn into froglets, but they can swim by swishing their tails. Salamander larvae and the aquatic adult salamanders may or may not have tiny legs, but they all use their tails to swim. The aquatic caecilians swim much as snakes do, waving their bodies back and forth in "s" patterns to slither-swim through the water.

Burrowing

Caecilians burrow head-first into the moist soil where they live. Frogs may burrow head-first or hind feet-first. The spadefoot toads are one of the groups of frogs that dig backwards into the soil, scraping through the soil with their back feet while wriggling backward. This buries the frog deeper and deeper into the soil. The sandhill frog that lives in Australia is one of the frogs that digs head-first by paddling its front feet and making it look as if it is swimming down into the sand.

Gliding

A few of the frog species, including the flying frogs in the family known as the Asian treefrogs, can soar through the air. They do not flap their front legs or have feathers like a bird, but they do have long toes that are separated by webbing that reaches the toe tips. When they widen their toes, the feet look almost like fans. These treefrogs can leap off a tree branch high above the ground and glide safely to earth by using their fan-shaped feet to keep from falling too fast. They are also able to steer by moving their feet one way or the other.

WHAT DO AMPHIBIANS EAT?

Meat eaters

Many amphibians eat meat or are carnivorous (kar-NIH-vor-us). For most of them, their meals are insects, spiders, and other invertebrates (in-VER-teh-brehts), which are animals without backbones. Often, larger species will eat larger prey. Most caecilians eat earthworms, termites, and other invertebrates that live underground. Mexican caecilians, which may grow to 19.7 inches (500 centimeters) in length, sometimes eat other animals, such as small lizards and baby mice that crawl on top of the leaf-covered ground where the caecilians live. Most salamanders eat earthworms or small arthropods (AR-throe-pawds), which are insects and other invertebrates with jointed legs. Adult frogs also usually eat invertebrates, but if they are able to capture a larger prey and swallow it, many will. The bullfrog, which is common in much of North America, will eat anything and nearly everything from other frogs to small snakes, rodents, and even small birds.

Many amphibians hunt by ambush, which means that they stay very still and wait for a prey animal to happen by. Some amphibians hunt by foraging (FOR-ij-ing), when they crawl, hop, or swim about looking for something to eat. Many amphibians simply snap their mouths around the prey and swallow it. Some flick their tongues out to nab it and then reel their tongues and the prey back into their mouths. Many salamanders have especially long tongues.

Plant eaters

Tadpoles are usually herbivorous (urh-BIH-vor-us), which means that they eat plants. Many have beaklike mouths that scrape algae (AL-jee) and other scum from rocks and underwater plants. Some, like the tadpoles of spadefoot toads, will eat invertebrates in addition to plants.

AMPHIBIANS AS PREY

A wide variety of animals attack and eat amphibians. Birds, snakes, raccoons and other mammals, fishes, and other amphibians are their predators. Even insects, like diving beetles, can kill a tadpole. For most amphibians, the best defense against their predators is to remain still and let their camouflage colors help them stay out of sight. Frogs, in particular, are often the same color as their surroundings. Some, like the horned frogs,

Amphibian behavioral and physiological defense mechanisms; a. Marine toad (Bufo marinus) inflates its lungs and enlarges; b. Two-lined salamander (Eurycea bislineata) displays tail autotomy (tail is able to detach); c. Eleutherodactylus curtipes feigns death; d. Echinotriton andersoni protrudes its ribs; e. Bombina frog displays unken reflex. (Illustration by Jacqueline Mahannah. Reproduced by permission.)

have large and pointy heads that look much like dead leaves. Other amphibians are very brightly colored. The juvenile eastern newt, for example, is bright orange red. This newt also is very poisonous, and its bright colors advertise to predators that they are dangerous to eat.

When numerous amphibians are attacked, they will stiffen their bodies, arch their backs, and hold out their feet. This position is called the unken (OONK-en) reflex. The fire-bellied frogs use this position, which shows off their bright red, yellow, or orange undersides and the similarly colored bottoms of their feet. The colors may remind predators that these frogs have a bad-tasting poison in their skin and convince them to leave the frogs alone.

Although it is not very common, some amphibians will fight back if attacked. Adult African bullfrogs will snap at large predators, even lions or people, who come too close to the frogs or their young. Among salamanders, the large hellbenders can give a painful bite.

REPRODUCTION

In all three groups of amphibians, mating involves both males and females. The females produce the eggs, and the males make a fluid that contains microscopic cells called sperm. An egg will only develop into a baby amphibian if it mixes with sperm. This mixing is called fertilization (FUR-tih-lih-ZAY-shun). In almost all frogs, the male climbs onto the back of the female, and as she lays her eggs, he releases his fluid so that the eggs are fertilized outside. In the caecilians, the male adds his fluid to the eggs while they are still inside the female's body. Salamanders fall in between these two types of fertilization. In most salamanders, the male puts drops of his fluid along the ground, and the female follows along behind to scoop up the droplets and put them inside her body with the eggs. All amphibians either lay their eggs in the water or in a moist place where the eggs will not dry out.

Most amphibian eggs hatch into tadpoles or larvae before becoming miniature versions of the adults. Often, these eggs, tadpoles, and larvae develop in the water. In some species, the adults lay the eggs on land but near water; the eggs hatch into tadpoles or larvae that squirm into the water or scramble onto the parent's back for a ride to the water. A number of species have young that never enter the water. In many of these amphibians,

the eggs skip the tadpole or larvae stage and hatch right into miniature adults.

These aglypto frogs are engaging in a behavior known as "explosive breeding." (Photograph by Harald Schüetz. Reproduced by permission.)

ACTIVITY PERIODS

Amphibians often have certain times of day or times of year when they are active. Some may even enter states of deep sleep for parts of the year when the weather is too cold or too dry.

Day and night

Most amphibians are nocturnal (nahk-TER-nuhl), which means they are active at night. Nocturnal animals hide someplace during the day. Sirens, which are the two-legged salamanders, spend their days buried in mud. Many frogs likewise stay out of sight during the day, sometimes hidden underground, in a rock crevice, or in some other hiding place, and come out at night to look for food or to mate. By being active at night instead of the daytime, these amphibians can avoid many predators that rely on their eyesight to find prey. Nights are also usually more humid than days, so the amphibians can keep their skin moist better if they are only active at night.

Some species are diurnal (die-UR-nuhl), which means that they are active during the day. In many cases, these species have especially poisonous or bad-tasting skin that protects them from daytime predators. Many of the poison frogs of South America, for example, are diurnal. On rainy days, some of the nocturnal amphibians will come out of hiding and wander about. With the wet weather, they can keep their skin moist.

During the seasons

Many species of amphibians are active only during some times of year. Those that live in climates with a cold winter often spend the winter underground or in another sheltered spot and enter a state of deep sleep, called hibernation (high-bur-NAY-shun). The bodies of some species, like the wood frog in the family of true frogs, actually freeze in the winter, but they are able to thaw out the following spring and continue living. Many other cold-climate species become active again when the spring arrives. Salamanders in the northern United States, for instance, start to move about on land even before the snow melts. Frequently, in these species, the spring also is the time for mating.

Besides the cold-weather species, some other amphibians enter a state of deep sleep when the weather becomes too dry. For species that live in deserts or dry grasslands, such as the water-holding frog of Australia, many burrow down into the ground and wait there until the next rainy season arrives. A period of deep sleep during a dry period is known as estivation (es-tih-VAY-shun). In these species, the rainy season marks the beginning of the mating period.

Amphibians that live in warm and wet tropical areas usually are active all year long, but they often mate only on rainy days.

AMPHIBIANS AND PEOPLE

Of all the amphibians, frogs are the most familiar to people. Nearly everyone has seen a frog or heard one calling during its mating season. Because neither salamanders nor caecilians have mating calls, and both usually stay out of sight during the day, many people have seen few, if any, of these two types of animals. Frogs are also much more common pets than salamanders or caecilians. In addition, many people eat frogs and some even eat tadpoles, but few people eat caecilians or salamanders.

Scientists are interested in amphibians for many reasons. In some species, their skin poisons or other chemical compounds have been made into or studied as medicines. Scientists also use amphibians to learn how their bodies work and therefore learn more about how human bodies function. Perhaps most importantly, ecologists see amphibians as living alert systems. Since amphibians live on land and in the water, and often are very sensitive to changes in the environment, they are excellent alarms that can warn humans about problems, such as water or air pollution.

ENDANGERED AMPHIBIANS

Through the World Conservation Union, which goes by the initials IUCN, scientists keep track of how well amphibians, along with other organisms, are surviving on Earth. They separate the species into different categories based on the number of individuals in the species and anything that might make them lose or gain numbers in the future. One of the categories the IUCN uses is called Data Deficient. This category means that scientists do not have enough information to make a judgment about the threat of extinction. The number of amphibians listed as Data Deficient is quite large: 1,165 species of frogs, 62 species of salamanders, and 111 caecilians. Many of these species are rare and/or live underground or in some other hard-to-reach location where they are difficult to study.

Amphibians in danger

The IUCN lists 367 species of frogs and forty-seven species of salamanders as Critically Endangered and facing an extremely high risk of extinction in the wild; 623 frog species, 106 salamanders, and one caecilian are Endangered and facing a very high risk of extinction in the wild; 544 frogs, 86 salamander species, and three caecilians are Vulnerable and facing a high risk of extinction in the wild; and 302 frogs and fifty-nine salamanders are Near Threatened and at risk of becoming threatened with extinction in the future.

Many of these species are at risk because the places where they live or breed are disappearing or changing, perhaps as

EXTRA LEGS?

In 1995, a group of students at the Minnesota New Country School were outside hiking when they found frogs with odd legs, including extra feet. In all, half of the frogs they saw had some type of deformity. After this discovery, many other people began reporting other deformed frogs. Scientists immediately started tests and experiments to learn why the frogs were deformed. Today, many believe the deformities were the result of disease, pollution, and/or some of the sun's rays, called UV radiation.

Amphibian morphological defense mechanisms; a. Darwin's frog (Rhinoderma darwinii) uses camouflage and cryptic structure; b. Pseudotriton ruber and Notophthalmus viridescens display mimicry; c. Bufo americanus has poison parotid glands; d. Poison dart frog (Dendrobates pumilio) has warning coloration; e. Physalaemus nattereri has eye spots on its hind quarters. (Illustration by Jacqueline Mahannah. Reproduced by permission.)

people cut down trees for lumber or otherwise clear the land to put in farms, homes, or other buildings. Some of the other problems for amphibians come from air and water pollution, infection with a fungus that is killing amphibians around the world, and global warming. Global warming changes weather patterns, sometimes causing especially dry conditions in some places. Since frogs need to keep their skin moist, especially dry weather can be deadly to them.

Saving endangered amphibians

To help many of the at-risk amphibians, governments, scientific organizations, and other groups are protecting some of the areas where the animals live. These may be national parks, preserves, or other natural areas. Many local, state, and national governments have also designed laws to protect the amphibians from being hunted or collected. In a few cases, conservationists are trying to raise amphibians in captivity and then releasing them into the wild with the hopes that they will survive, breed, and increase the size of the natural populations.

Too late to save

The efforts to protect the Earth's amphibians are important, because many species have already become extinct in recent years. An extinct species is one that is no longer in existence.

Leopard frogs with missing, deformed or extra legs started appearing near St. Albans Bay of Lake Champlain in St. Albans, Vermont. Biologists are not sure if pollution, a parasite, disease, or something else is causing the frogs to develop abnormally. Photograph AP/World Wide Photos. Reproduced by permission.

This includes two species of salamanders and thirty-two species of frogs. In addition, the IUCN lists one frog as Extinct in the Wild, which means that it is no longer alive except in captivity or through the aid of humans.

FOR MORE INFORMATION

Books:

Behler, John. *Simon and Schuster's Guide to Reptiles and Amphibians of the World.* New York: Simon and Schuster, 1989, 1997.

Clarke, Barry. *Amphibian.* New York: Dorling Kindersley, 1993.

Florian, Douglas. *Discovering Frogs.* New York: Charles Scribner's Sons, 1986.

Halliday, Tim, and Kraig Adler, eds. *The Encyclopedia of Reptiles and Amphibians (Smithsonian Handbooks).* New York: Facts On File, 1991.

Harding, J. H. *Amphibians and Reptiles of the Great Lakes Region.* Ann Arbor: The University of Michigan Press Institution Press, 1997.

Lamar, William. *The World's Most Spectacular Reptiles and Amphibians.* Tampa, FL: World Publications, 1997.

Maruska, Edward. *Amphibians: Creatures of the Land and Water.* New York: Franklin Watts, 1994.

Miller, Sara Swan. *Frogs and Toads: The Leggy Leapers.* New York: Franklin Watts, 2000.

O'Shea, Mark, and Tim Halliday. *Smithsonian Handbooks: Reptiles and Amphibians (Smithsonian Handbooks).* New York: Dorling Kindersley Publishing, 2002.

Periodicals:

Hogan, Dan, and Michele Hogan. "Freaky Frogs: Worldwide Something Weird Is Happening to Frogs." *National Geographic Explorer* (March–April 2004): 10.

Masibay, Kim Y. "Rainforest Frogs: Vanishing Act? Frog Populations Around the World Are Dying Off Mysteriously. Can Scientists Save Them—Before It's Too Late?" *Science World* (March 11, 2002): 12.

Sunquist, Fiona. "The Weird World of Frogs." *National Geographic World* (March 2002): 14.

Walters, Mark Jerome. "Spotting the Smallest Frog: As Hopes Fade for One Species, a Tiny Frog Comes into View." *Animals* (May–June 1997): 8.

Web sites:

"North American Reporting Center for Amphibian Malformations." *National Biological Information Infrastructure.* http://frogweb.nbii.gov/narcam/index.html (accessed on May 15, 2005).

Stoddard, Tim. "Island hoppers: Sri Lankan tree frogs end game of hide-and-seek." *BU Bridge.* http://www.bu.edu/bridge/archive/2002/10-18/frogs.htm (accessed on February 12, 2005).

Trivedi, Bijal P. "Frog Fathers Provide Transport, Piggyback Style." *National Geographic Today.* http://news.nationalgeographic.com/news/2002/08/0807_020807_TVfrogs.html (accessed on February 12, 2005).

"Weird Frog Facts." *Frogland.* http://allaboutfrogs.org/weird/weird.html (accessed on February 12, 2005).

AFRICAN TREEFROGS
Hyperoliidae

Class: Amphibia

Order: Anura

Family: Hyperoliidae

Number of species: 240 species

PHYSICAL CHARACTERISTICS

African treefrogs are also known as reed and sedge frogs. The typical African treefrog has a slender body, large and often bulging eyes usually with horizontal pupils, and rounded pads on the ends of its webbed toes. Its back legs are long and thin, and its front legs are also quite thin. The treefrogs with this appearance are good climbers and leapers. Some of the African treefrogs look quite different. These species, which are often called running frogs, remain on the ground; have no toe pads or toe webbing; have shorter hind legs, frequently only a bit longer than the front pair; and walk or run rather than hop.

The males of this family have large vocal sacs, which are pouches in the throat area that blow up and then deflate when they call. Male African treefrogs have a vocal sac, which may blow up to be three or more times as big as the head. In many species, this sac is covered with an oval-shaped flap that can be seen even when the frog is not calling.

The African treefrogs come in many different colors and patterns. In some cases, even members of the same species do not look alike. One member of the species known as the painted reed frog, for example, may be green with a few dozen, tiny, black-centered, yellow spots on its back, orange toes, and orange upper legs. Another might be greenish gray with large black blotches, tan with black and yellow markings on its sides, or cream with black and orange stripes. The following examples will show the varying colors among different species within this family:

phylum

class

subclass

order

monotypic order

suborder

▲ **family**

- Greater leaf-folding frog, also known as the spiny leaf-folding frog—Chocolate brown with a wide silvery to light brown back, which is sometimes split down the middle with a chocolate brown stripe; also with silvery to light brown color on the top of the hind legs
- Yellow-striped reed frog—Light green with a yellow stripe on each side of its body from the snout over the large, orange-colored eye to the rump; orange toes and a yellow underside with orange on its rear legs
- Yellow-legged kassina, also known as the yellow-legged treefrog—Beige with many brown spots on its back, brown bands on its legs and toes, and yellow on the underside of upper rear leg
- White-spotted reed frog—White, covered with small yellow dots that are outlined in dark brown
- Transparent reed frog, also known as the water lily reed frog—Light green with orange toes
- Malagasy variable reed frog—Orange yellow with small brown spots on the head and front half of the back and a narrow brown stripe on each side of the snout
- Madagascar reed frog, also known as the blue-back frog—Baby blue head and back, orange yellow underside, dark orange toes, two black stripes from the snout to the eyes, and a few black spots on both sides between the eye and the front leg and on the front leg

Depending on the species, African treefrogs may have eyes that are all brown, gold, whitish, or some other solid color, or that are one color on the top half and another on the bottom half. The Malagasy variable reed frog, for instance, has large eyes that are white on the bottom and pinkish on the top. Most of the treefrogs have large eyes, but in some species they are enormous. The Seychelles treefrog is an example. Its pearly white eyes look almost like big headlights.

Often the color of the frog changes as it grows older. Young froglets in many species are yellow or brown with dark markings down the back, while the adults are brightly colored and patterned. In some species, the youngsters are green, while the adults are brownish. Scientists call these colors the "juvenile phase." Sometimes, many of the adult males have the juvenile colors during the breeding season, too.

Adult African treefrogs may be as small as 0.5 inches (1.2 centimeters) long from the tip of the snout to the end of the rump or as large as 4.3 inches (11.0 centimeters) in length. While males and females are the same size in many species, the females are larger in others. The African wart frog and the greater leaf-folding frog are two species in which the males and females reach the same size. Adult African wart frogs grow to 1.4 inches (3.6 centimeters) long, and adult greater leaf-folding frogs reach 1.6 inches (4.1 centimeters) in length. Female toad-like treefrogs, on the other hand, are larger than males. In this species, females grow to 1.4 to 1.6 inches (3.6 to 4.1 centimeters), while males reach only 1.1 to 1.3 inches (2.9 to 3.3 centimeters) in length. The difference between the sexes is even more noticeable in the big-eared forest treefrogs. Here, females reach up to 3.3 inches (8.4 centimeters) long, while males are about half that size at 1.6 to 1.8 inches (4.1 to 4.6 centimeters) in length.

GEOGRAPHIC RANGE

African treefrogs live in most of central and southern Africa. Some species are also found on the large island of Madagascar and the tiny island of Seychelles, which are in the Indian Ocean east of southern Africa.

HABITAT

Many species in this family live in often dry and hot grassy fields or in areas that are humid and covered in thick bushes and trees. In addition, some live in rainforests, and others tend to make their homes in land that is currently being farmed or in abandoned and overgrown farmland. Some of the African treefrogs live high in mountains, but many others do not. Many species are arboreal (ar-BOR-ee-ul), which means that they live above the ground in trees. Other species stay on the ground, and some are able to dig beneath it.

DIET

They eat mainly invertebrates (in-VER-teh-brehts), which are animals without backbones. They especially eat insects and other arthropods (AR-throe-pawds), which are invertebrates with jointed legs, but they will often add any other animal they can capture and swallow. Usually treefrogs and other species of frogs only eat things that are moving, but at least one of the African treefrogs will eat non-moving things. This treefrog, called the greater leaf-folding frog, will eat the eggs of other frogs that make foam nests for their young. The greater leaf-folding frog pokes its head through the nest and eats the eggs inside.

BEHAVIOR AND REPRODUCTION

African treefrogs are active at night, which is when they look for food and mate. During the day, some of the species that live in hot, open areas dig down into the soil where it is cooler and moister. Scientists are not sure, but they think that some of them, including the toad-like treefrog, either remain underground for the entire dry season in a state of deep sleep, known as estivation (es-tih-VAY-shun), or come out on humid mornings to search for food. Some of these burrowing species shed their skin when they are underground, and this skin dries into a sort of cocoon. The frog remains inside the cocoon, which helps to keep the frog moist. Other species of treefrogs are outdoor types and stay outside even on very hot and dry days. They are not active during the day, however, and simply sit still on leaves until the evenings arrive. The painted treefrog survives hot and dry days by oozing mucus from its skin. This mucus is waterproof, but instead of keeping moisture out, it keeps the moisture in. Even so, they often lose some water from their bodies. Some young painted treefrogs are able to survive even after their bodies have lost half their weight in water. The sharp-nosed reed frog protects itself from dry weather simply by staying down low in grasses on hot days. There, the air is more humid.

The typical African treefrog mates during the rainy season. Males head to the water, often a small pool formed by the rains, and begin calling. Sometimes, the males reach the mating area even before the rains have filled the pools. Not all species mate in new pools on the ground. The African wart frog and others mate inside a tree hole above a puddle of water. Scientists still do not know where some species, such as the toad-like treefrog, mate.

Using their often-enormous vocal sacs, the males make a variety of calls. The greater leaf-folding frog, for instance, calls with a creaking sound followed by several clicks in a row. The bubbling kassina makes a sound like tiny bubbles popping. The males of the *Afrixalus brachycnemis* and other similar species are unusual because their calls have two parts. In this species, the first part is a zipping sound, and the second is a trill. The zipping sound tells other males of the same species to stay away, and the trill is an invitation to females interested in mating. The males of a few species, including the African wart frog, may not be able to call at all.

For those species that mate at tree holes, only one male uses each tree hole, and the female follows his call to him. It is not so easy for those that mate in ground pools. There, many males of several different species of African treefrogs may use the same pool for mating and call at the same time. Despite the confusion of calls and the large number of frogs, a female can pick out the call of a male from her own species and follow that call to a mate. In some species, the female is stopped on her way to a calling male by another male that is not calling, and she mates with him instead. These quiet males that hang around a calling male waiting for a chance to meet a female are called satellite (SAT-eh-lite) males.

The majority of the species in this family lay their eggs on leaves that hang over pools of water on the ground. For example, the female Betsileo reed frog of Madagascar lays her sticky eggs on leaves just above the water. These eggs hatch into tadpoles, and the tadpoles use their tails to wriggle off the leaves and fall into the water. The leaf-folding frogs also lay their eggs on grass blades or other leaves above a pool of water, but then fold the leaf around the eggs. Since the gel-covered eggs are sticky, the leaf stays folded. When the eggs hatch into tadpoles, the tadpoles wriggle off the leaf and into the water below. In at least one species of leaf-folding frogs, known as the delicate spiny reed frog, the female may mate with more than one male in a night, so the young in her batch of eggs may have different fathers.

The gray-eyed frog is the only species of African treefrog in which the parents provide a foamy nest inside the folded leaf for their eggs. The female makes mucus and then beats it with her hind legs until it turns into foam. She lays her eggs in the foam, and the male folds the leaf around them. The foam helps keep the eggs moist. The eggs hatch, and the tadpoles fall off the leaf and into the water below. Some species of treefrogs, including the kassinas and the sharp-nosed reed frog, lay their eggs right in pools of water along the ground. They typically stick their eggs, sometimes one at a time, onto underwater plants.

Several species, such as the African wart frog, mate in tree holes that hold water. The female lays her eggs on the inside wall of the hole just above the water. The eggs are coated in a gel and stick to the wall. When they hatch into tadpoles, the tadpoles drop into the water. The big-eared forest treefrog and a few other species do not lay their eggs in the water. Instead, these frogs

NOW, THAT'S A SUPER SPECIES!

To some scientists, the painted reed frog should actually be divided into several species. This is because painted reed frogs from one area can look much different than painted reed frogs from another area and because frogs from these separate groups sometimes will not mate with one another even when they live together in the same place. For now, the painted reed frog is often called a super-species, which means that it is a group of two or more species instead of just one.

bury their eggs in moist soil that may be 33 feet (10 meters) or more away from any water. Their eggs are large and filled with yolk, which provides food for the young. Eventually, the tadpoles are strong enough to wriggle along the ground to the water, where they continue to grow. In at least one egg-burying species, known as the giant big-eyed treefrog, the eggs do not hatch into tadpoles at all but hatch right into froglets.

Depending on the species, the number of eggs that a female lays may be as few as a dozen or as many as two hundred or more. The female sharp-nosed reed frog and the Seychelles treefrog are two examples of African treefrogs that lay large numbers of eggs. A typical clutch for a sharp-nosed reed frog is about two hundred eggs, while that of the Seychelles treefrog may be as many as five hundred. In most species of African treefrogs, the adult females lay the eggs and leave them to develop on their own. The African treefrog species known as the midwife frogs are different. The females stay with the gel-covered eggs until they hatch and then help the tadpoles escape from the gel.

The tadpoles of many African treefrogs change into froglets within weeks. Some, like the African wart frog, may wait until they are about three months old before going through the change, which is known as metamorphosis (meh-tuh-MOR-foh-sis). They may need this much time to grow because they live in small pools of water inside tree holes, where food may be very scarce. The sharp-nosed reed frog, on the other hand, lays its eggs in larger pools on the ground. When the tadpoles hatch from the eggs, they find plenty of food and grow so quickly that they can turn into froglets and be ready to mate and have their own young before the end of the breeding season in which they were born.

AFRICAN TREEFROGS AND PEOPLE

Some people keep African treefrogs as pets, but most people are happy to enjoy the frogs only by listening to them calling in the wilds of Africa.

CONSERVATION STATUS

The World Conservation Union (IUCN) lists one species as Critically Endangered and facing an extremely high risk of extinction in the wild; nineteen species as Endangered and facing a very high risk of extinction in the wild; twenty-nine that are Vulnerable and facing a high risk of extinction in the wild; sixteen that are Near Threatened and at risk of becoming threatened with extinction in the future; and fifty-three that are Data Deficient, which means that scientists do not have enough information to make a judgment about the threat of extinction.

The one Critically Endangered species is known by its scientific name of *Alexteroon jynx*. It has only been found in two small areas on hillsides in southwestern Cameroon. This frog lives among thick plants along forest streams that are shaded by overhead trees. It lays a few eggs together in a group on leaves above the water. These eggs hatch into tadpoles, which slide off the leaf and into the stream. Ecologists are concerned not only because it lives in such a small area but also because the forests are not protected and are disappearing as people cut down the trees. Unless the area is protected soon, they fear that the frogs will become extinct.

The Knysna banana frog, Pickersgill's reed frog, and the long-toed treefrog are examples of the Endangered species in this family. All three live in South Africa. The Knysna banana frog is a rare species that lives along the southern coast of South Africa in shrubs, forests, and sometimes farmland; it mates among plants that grow in small pools of water and dams. Pickersgill's reed frog lives in shrubby areas and grasslands farther up the coast of South Africa and uses small pools of water that may dry up later in the year. The home of the long-toed treefrog is in inland grasslands, often on mountainsides between 3,280 to 6,000 feet (1,000 to 1,830 meters) above sea level. It mates in marshes and other grassy pools that may dry up later on.

Human activity, such as the construction of buildings, cutting of trees, and draining of water from wetlands for farms, is causing problems for all three species. In the case of the Pickersgill's reed frog, people are also using the insect-killing chemical known as DDT to control mosquitoes. These mosquitoes can bite people and spread a sometimes-fatal disease called malaria (muh-LAIR-ee-uh). DDT, however, can also kill frogs. Besides this threat, the frogs are in danger because people have brought in eucalyptus (yoo-cuh-LIP-tus), a new plant that can soak up much of the water in a wetland. Water-loving introduced plants, as well as fires, are causing a problem for the long-toed treefrogs. Although each of these species is endangered, some of them make their homes at least partially inside a protected area, such as a national park or nature reserve.

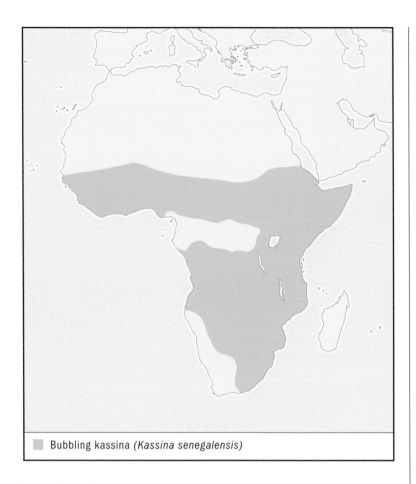

Bubbling kassina (*Kassina senegalensis*)

BUBBLING KASSINA
Kassina senegalensis

Physical characteristics: The bubbling kassina, also known as the Senegal running frog, is a light greenish gray to tan frog with wide, dark, often brown or black striping or spots on its head and back and dark blotches on its front and rear legs. In many, the markings on the back and head include one long stripe beginning between the eyes and continuing almost to the rump, one broken stripe on each side, a stripe from the tip of the snout to at least the shoulder, and another blotch or several spots low on each side. On its head, the large eyes may look light olive gray to tan or gold, and each has a vertical pupil. Most other African treefrogs have horizontal pupils. Its front legs are not overly long, and its hind legs are only a bit lengthier than the

With its small hind legs, the bubbling kassina does not hop but instead walks or runs, which is why it is sometimes called the Senegal running frog or simply a running frog. (© K. H. Switak/ Photo Researchers, Inc.)

front pair. Both have a pattern of dark bars on lower legs and onto the feet. The front toes have no webs between them; the rear toes have a little webbing. Its belly is white.

Males and females are about the same size. They each reach about 1 to 1.9 inches (2.5 to 4.9 centimeters) long from the tip of the snout to the end of the rump. In some areas, the size of the frogs is on the small side, but in others, most grow closer to the maximum size of 1.9 inches (4.9 centimeters) in length.

Geographic range: It lives over the southern two-thirds of Africa from South Africa north to parts of Sudan, Mali, Ethiopia, Senegal, Niger, and Chad.

Habitat: These frogs are terrestrial (te-REH-stree-uhl), which means they live along the ground. For much of the year, they are usually found in grassy areas, although some make their homes in more shrubby areas, in pastures, or in country gardens. They mate in shallow spots in ponds or swamps, usually those places with a good deal of plants living in the water.

Diet: These frogs probably eat arthropods.

Behavior and reproduction: With its small hind legs, the bubbling kassina does not hop but instead walks or runs, which is why it is sometimes called the Senegal running frog or simply a running frog. When it sits still, this small striped frog almost disappears against the blades of grass in the grasslands where it lives. It becomes much more noticeable when the rainy season arrives and the males begin calling. The male's call is a high "poink" sound that is rather similar to a bubble bursting or a drop of water landing in a small, metal tub. The male only makes one "poink" sound at a time, usually waiting a while between the sounds. Males call at night while sitting in grass, often on the shore of a pond or swamp and under an overhang, such as a low, dirt cliff. They may also call from a spot in shallow water and surrounded by grass. Females join the males to mate with them in the water. A female lays her eggs one at a time on underwater plants. Each egg has a gel coating, and groups of them may stick together in a clump on the plants. The eggs hatch into tadpoles, which have wide fins, and pointy tails.

Bubbling kassinas and people: Many people in the grasslands of Africa enjoy the call of the bubbling kassina. Yet they very rarely actually see one. As a person nears a calling frog to find it, the frog stops calling and sits still. When the frog is not moving, its color and pattern help it to blend into the grass and make it very difficult to spot.

Conservation status: The IUCN lists this species in the category of "least concern," which means that it is under no known threat of extinction and the animal does not qualify for any of the Threatened categories. The bubbling kassina is a common species that lives over a large part of Africa, including numerous parks and other protected areas. ■

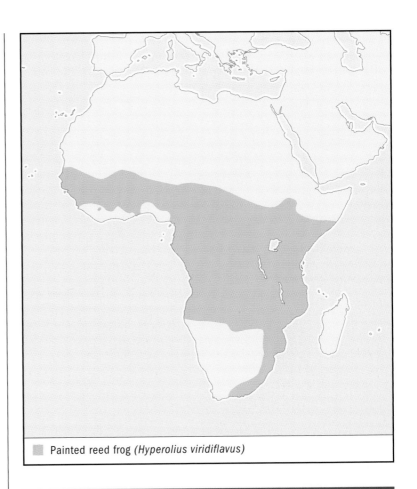

Painted reed frog (*Hyperolius viridiflavus*)

PAINTED REED FROG
Hyperolius viridiflavus

Physical characteristics: Painted reed frogs, also known as common reed frogs, are hard to describe because they come in so many colors and patterns. Some of them are striped in black and yellow from head to rump and on their legs. Some are speckled in green and black on a cream background or have a black-and-white spotted back and brown sides. Others are tan to brown with wide yellow and black bands on their sides and dark gray toes with orange tips. They have many different common names based on what they look like and where they live.

Despite the differences in colors and patterns, all painted reed frogs share certain features. They all have slender bodies, no noticeable

neck separating the short head from the body, two large eyes with one on either side of the head, and thin legs. Their pupils are horizontal, and no eardrum shows on the side of the head. Their snouts narrow toward the front and are rounded at the end. The front and hind feet have webbing between the toes, and the toes have rounded pads at the ends. Their bellies are usually white, but sometimes may be pink. Male painted reed frogs have one large, dark gray vocal sac on their throats that blows up and deflates like a balloon when they call. Sometimes the vocal sac has tiny orange spots. The females do not have this sac, but they do have a side-to-side fold across the throat. They typically grow to about 1.2 inches (3 centimeters) in length.

Geographic range: They live over most of the southern two-thirds of Africa.

Habitat: Many of the painted reed frogs live in grasslands, but one group found in central Africa and a small area in West Africa makes its home in forests. They mate and lay their eggs in ponds and sometimes in swamps and even slow-moving streams.

Diet: These frogs probably eat arthropods.

Behavior and reproduction: Unlike most frogs that hide during the daytime, some of the painted reed frogs sit out in the open. Often, the frogs that sit in plain view are those that are brightly colored. These colors may be a warning sign to the predators that the frogs are not good to eat because they have poisonous skin. Many of the painted reed frogs that live in dry, hot grasslands are able to rest in the sun without drying out and dying because they can make a thin layer of mucus to cover their bodies. This mucus hardens into a waterproof coat that keeps the frog's skin moist inside. Some, especially the younger frogs, are also able to survive even if their bodies lose up to half of their weight in water. In particularly dry weather, many of the frogs become white. Darker colors soak up more heat from the sun, so the white color helps to keep the frog a bit cooler.

Painted reed frogs mate during the rainy season. The males sing together in choruses (KOR-us-es) or groups, which sounds like the ringing of small bells and can make a lovely music in the African grasslands and forests. Males call from tall grass-type plants, called reeds and sedges, along the shores of ponds, but sometimes also call from taller bushes and trees. Females lay up to a dozen eggs underwater on plants. In captivity, the frogs will often mate and lay eggs every few weeks during the breeding season, but this behavior has not been seen in the wild. The eggs hatch into tadpoles that turn into froglets. The young froglets may be quite large, and they may be able to become parents themselves later that same year. At least one research team reported that a female painted reed frog may sometimes turn into a male.

Painted reed frogs and people: The frogs may have poisonous skin, and some people in Africa believe that a cow will die if it eats a frog.

Conservation status: In its listing, the IUCN has split up the painted reed frog into several different species, which include the "main" species *Hyperolius viridiflavus*, the marbled or painted reed frog with the scientific name *Hyperolius marmoratus*, *Hyperolius marginatus*, and several others. The IUCN lists these three to be of "least concern," which means that they are under no known threat of extinction and the animals do not qualify for any of the Threatened categories. According to the IUCN, all three are very common, and one (the marbled reed frog) is even spreading into new areas, especially any new water pools that people make. These three frogs also make their homes inside various protected areas, which should limit the clearing of land where they live. ■

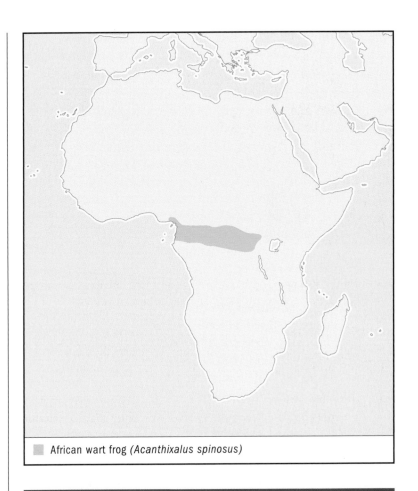

■ African wart frog (*Acanthixalus spinosus*)

AFRICAN WART FROG
Acanthixalus spinosus

Physical characteristics: The African wart frog is covered with warts on its head, back, and the tops of its legs. It is an olive green, gray, or brown frog with dark bands—sometimes broken bands—that run from one side of its back to the other. It has thin legs, some webbing between the toes of its front and hind feet, and round pads on the tips of its toes. It has large brownish eyes and a rather long snout that narrows toward the front. This frog has an orange tongue. It can grow to 1.4 inches (3.6 centimeters) long from its snout to its rump. Young frogs are orange and maroon.

The African wart frog is active at night. During the day, it typically sits in a puddle of water that has formed inside a tree hole or a pocket on a branch. (Illustration by Emily Damstra. Reproduced by permission.)

Geographic range: It lives in west-central Africa, including Cameroon and the Democratic Republic of the Congo.

Habitat: This frog makes its home in rainforests that are thick with trees and plants. It spends most of its time in water-filled holes of either living or dead trees, sometimes in holes of large branches.

Diet: Although scientists are not sure what they eat, they suspect that these frogs probably eat arthropods, as do many other species in this family.

Behavior and reproduction: The African wart frog is active at night. During the day, it typically sits in a puddle of water that has formed inside a tree hole or a pocket on a branch. Usually, the frog floats underwater with just its nostrils sticking out into the air. The frog may hop out of the water at night to find food. Its body colors and patterns help to hide it from predators, but if a predator does see the frog and comes too close, the African wart frog closes its eyes, tucks its legs in tight against its body, and thrusts out its tongue. This may startle a predator enough that it leaves the frog alone.

This frog mates near the water of its tree hole or branch. Unlike other frogs, the male African wart frog does not have a vocal sac and does not make a call, so a female cannot find him by hearing him. Instead, scientists think the male and female locate each other by smell. The pair mate above the water, and the female lays eight to ten yellow-colored eggs that attach with a sticky gel to the wall of the tree or branch hole barely above the water. The eggs hatch into tadpoles, and the tadpoles drop down into the water, where they live and grow for about three months. During that time, they eat little bits of food that they find in the water, such as pieces of plants. They then turn into froglets.

African wart frogs and people: People rarely see this frog. Since the males make no calls, people never hear them either.

Conservation status: The IUCN lists this species in the category of "least concern," which means that it is under no known threat of extinction and the animal does not qualify for any of the Threatened categories. With many species of frogs, scientists estimate the size of the population during the mating season when the males are calling and the frogs are easiest to find. Since the males in this species of frog are quiet, scientists have not been able to make good estimates about the frogs' numbers. Nonetheless, they believe the frogs are quite common. Since the frogs mate and lay their eggs in the holes of trees, the logging of these trees may cause a problem for the frogs in the future. ■

FOR MORE INFORMATION

Books:

Halliday, Tim, and Kraig Adler, eds. *The Encyclopedia of Reptiles and Amphibians (Smithsonian Handbooks).* New York: Facts On File, 1991.

Lovett, Sarah. *Extremely Weird Frogs.* Santa Fe, NM: John Muir Publications, 1991.

Mattison, Chris. *Frogs and Toads of the World.* New York: Facts On File Publications, 1987.

Miller, Sara Swan. *Frogs and Toads: The Leggy Leapers.* New York: Franklin Watts, 2000.

Schiotz, Arne. *Treefrogs of Africa.* Frankfort am Main, Germany: Edition Chimaira, 1999.

Showler, Dave. *Frogs and Toads: A Golden Guide.* New York: St. Martin's Press, 2004.

Wager, Vincent A. *The Frogs of South Africa.* Johannesburg, South Africa: Purnell and Sons (S.A.) Pty., Ltd., 1965.

Web sites:

"African Tree Frogs (Hyperoliidae): Herpetology." *Chemistry Biology Pharmacy Information Center.* http://www.infochembio.ethz.ch/links/en/zool_kriecht_froesche_laub_afrikan.html (accessed on May 10, 2005).

"Family Hyperoliidae (African tree frogs)." *Animal Diversity Web.* http://animaldiversity.ummz.umich.edu/site/accounts/pictures/Hyperoliidae.html (accessed on May 10, 2005).

Heying, H. "Family Hyperoliidae (African tree frogs)." *Animal Diversity Web.* http://animaldiversity.ummz.umich.edu/site/accounts/information/Hyperoliidae.html (accessed on May 10, 2005).

Opisthothylax immaculatus. AmphibiaWeb. http://elib.cs.berkeley.edu/cgi-bin/amphib_query?query_src=aw_lists_alpha_&where-genus=Opisthothylax&where-species=immaculatus (accessed on May 10, 2005).

Razzetti, Edoardo R., and Charles Andekia Msuya. *Field Guide to the Amphibians and Reptiles of Arusha National Park (Tanzania).* http://www.gli.cas.cz/SEH/files/tanzie2002.pdf (accessed on May 16, 2005).

ASIAN TREEFROGS

Rhacophoridae

Class: Amphibia

Order: Anura

Family: Rhacophoridae

Number of species: 341 species or more

family

CHAPTER

phylum

class

subclass

order

monotypic order

suborder

▲ family

PHYSICAL CHARACTERISTICS

Asian treefrogs come in many sizes and colors, but they have a few common features. Almost all have sticky pads on the tips of their front and rear toes, which help them to move through trees and on leaves, even when they have to climb straight up. Most Asian treefrogs also have heads that are attached to the body with a noticeable neck. In many other frogs, the head blends back into the body without an obvious neck. The typical Asian treefrog has large eyes with horizontal pupils. Some members of this family have full webbing between all of their toes. In these frogs, which are known as flying or gliding frogs, the webs reach all the way to their toe tips. When their toes are spread wide, the feet almost look like fans. In a few species, including Wallace's flying frog, the frog also has a flat body and flaps of skin or fringe down the sides of the legs. These features give the frog's body a shape rather like that of a kite.

Asian treefrogs may be colored green, brown, gray, black, or white, often with markings on their backs. The underside may be a lighter version of the back color, or it may look completely different. Buerger's frog, for instance, is brown to gray on its back, but white on its belly. The Betsileo golden frog has a gray to brown back, but its underside is black. Most Asian treefrogs can hide well against their surroundings. Perhaps the species with the best camouflage is the Vietnamese mossy frog, which not only has a back and head that are the same green and brown as the moss on the ground, but also has spines and tall bumps, or tubercles (TOO-ber-kulz) that stand up just like the stems and leaves of the moss do. When this frog sits still on moss-covered rocks near streams or at the entrance of caves, a person could walk right past without ever seeing it.

The mantellas look different than most other members of this family. They do not have the toe pads that are common to other species, and they are very brightly colored. Some have red, orange, or yellow backs, while others have black backs and bright-colored legs. The painted mantella is an example. This frog has a black body, a white stripe on its head, legs that are orange on top and yellow underneath, and yellow shoulders.

Depending on the species, Asian treefrogs may be as small as 0.6 inches (1.5 centimeters) long from the tip of the snout to the end of the rump, or as much as 4.9 inches (12 centimeters) in length. The female is a bit longer than the male in many species, but in others, they are about the same size.

GEOGRAPHIC RANGE

Asian treefrogs live in southeastern Asia, the southern half of Africa, and Madagascar. In southeastern Asia, species live in southern India, Sri Lanka, central and southern China, Japan, Taiwan, the Philippines, Vietnam, Cambodia, and Indonesia. In Africa, they live in a stretch of land across the center of the continent from about the Ivory Coast in the west to Somalia in the east, and then down the eastern side.

HABITAT

Some species in this family live in forests. These include such frogs as Buerger's frog, the forest bright-eyed frog, Eiffinger's Asian treefrog, and the Luzon bubble-nest frog. Others, like the gray treefrog, prefer very dry grasslands. This gray treefrog, which is also known as the foam nest frog, is different from the eastern gray treefrog and Cope's gray treefrog of North America. Both of the North American species are members of a separate family, called the Amero-Australian treefrogs.

Some species in this family live near the water and use it to breed. They also use the water to lay their eggs. Buerger's frog is an example. The adults live in forests near rocky streams and enter the water to mate and lay their eggs. The eggs hatch into tadpoles, which remain in the water until they turn into froglets. Other species, like the free Madagascar frog, mate on the leaves of branches that overhang swamps or other water, and the female lays her eggs there on the leaves. As they hatch, the tadpoles plop down into the water, where they continue growing. Some Asian treefrogs live close to people. The golden treefrog, also sometimes called the banana frog, is often seen on the sides of trees in city parks and on bathroom walls.

DIET

Scientists know little about the diet of many species in this family. In those frogs that they have studied, the adult frogs eat ants, fruit flies, tiny spiders, and other small invertebrates (in-VER-teh-brehts), which are animals without backbones. They suspect that the other Asian treefrogs have a similar diet. Their tadpoles, however, are mostly vegetarian. They nibble at bits of algae (AL-jee) and dead plants that are stuck to and lying on underwater rocks or the water bottom. The tadpoles of two species, the Burmese bubble-nest frog and Eiffinger's Asian treefrog, also eat the eggs of other frogs.

BEHAVIOR AND REPRODUCTION

The Asian treefrogs are perhaps best known for three reasons: Some can glide through the air; some are poisonous; and some build foam nests. Although they are often called flying frogs, they can actually only glide. In other words, they cannot flap their legs to go higher in the air as a bird can with its wings, but they are able to soar from tree to tree. They do this by stretching out the webbing between their toes into a fan shape and using these large web-fans to catch the air and prevent them from falling too quickly. To glide, the frog typically reaches out in a Superman-like pose, but with the legs slightly bent. They adjust the angle of their feet to change direction in flight. Wallace's flying frog is an excellent glider. When this frog leaps from a height of 17.7 feet (7.3 meters), it can soar through the air for a distance of up to 24 feet (7.3 meters). Other gliding frogs include such species as the jade treefrog and the Himalaya flying frog. Besides being a quick way to get around the forest, gliding helps the frogs escape predators that cannot soar or fly.

The poisonous members of this family are called mantellas. Like the poison frogs of South and Central America, they have poison in their skin. Most of the other members of this family are active at night, which helps hide them from would-be predators. The mantellas, on the other hand, are not only active in the daytime, but they also sit right out in the open. Their bright colors draw even more attention to them. The golden mantella, for example, is bright yellow to orange, while the Betsileo golden frog is gold or orange gold with black sides. Scientists think the bright colors warn predators to leave the frogs alone. The poison in the mantellas is like that found in many of the poison frogs of South and Central America, but it is not as strong. It is, however, powerful enough to convince predators to pass by the frogs and look for something else to eat.

Some of the Asian treefrogs build foam nests. The gray treefrog is an example. First, a pair of frogs finds a spot in a tree branch that hangs over the water. Next, the female oozes a fluid before she lays her eggs, and she alone, or she and her mate, kick the fluid with their hind legs to whip it into foam. Once they have made a large amount of foam, she lays her eggs inside. The outside of the foam nest dries and hardens, but the inside stays moist. The eggs soon hatch into tadpoles inside the nest. By this time, the nest's bottom has become soft, often dissolving in a rain storm, and the tadpoles drop out of the bottom to the water below.

Except for the mantellas, mating in Asian treefrogs is mainly a nighttime activity. The males call to keep other males away and to attract females. The male common treefrog has a call that sounds like a deep quack; the male golden mantella makes quick, clicking noises; and males of other species have their own calls. In most species, the males call from or near a hidden spot or from a place where predators cannot easily reach. The male Buerger's frog calls from rocks in fast-moving streams, for instance, and the male Eiffinger's Asian treefrog does his calling next to the tree hole where he will mate. The mantellas, however, are very bold. These brightly colored males call loudly from open places in plain sight. Their colors serve them well at this time of year. They not only continue to warn predators of their poisonous skin and usually keep the frog safe, but they also tell other male frogs that an area is already taken. Sometimes two males fight over a good calling site. One will grab the other around the head and upper legs and try to push it away. This same type of fighting sometimes happens with female mantellas, but it is less common.

During mating, males typically climb onto the female's back and slowly squirt a fluid, which contains microscopic cells called sperm, onto the eggs while the female lays them. In the foam-nesting species, the male adds his fluid to the foam. In the gray treefrog, more than one male may add fluid. The eggs all have the same mother, but the father is whichever male added the sperm to the egg. In this way, the eggs in one nest may have several fathers.

In those species of Asian treefrogs that do not make foam nests, only one male mates with each female, and her young all have the same father. Sometimes, however, one male may mate with more than one female, and therefore be the father to several clutches of eggs. Depending on the species, the frogs may lay their eggs in foam nests, as described above, in tree holes, on the ground, or in still water. The painted Indonesian treefrog is one of the species that uses tree holes. A male and a female mate inside the tree hole over a puddle of water inside. The eggs stick to the inside wall of the tree. When they hatch, the tadpoles fall out of the eggs and into the water below. The Luzon bubble-nest frog is one of many species in which the female lays her eggs on the ground. In these species, the female usually lays only one dozen to three dozen eggs at a time. The Luzon bubble-nest frog, for instance, lays between five and nineteen large eggs. Like many other ground layers, she actually lays her eggs on the base of a leaf. Her eggs develop right into froglets there on the leaf, never becoming tadpoles in between.

Although the male golden mantellas usually do their calling from spots where they can be seen, male and female pairs mate in secret. Once a female approaches a calling male, the two find a hiding spot under a piece of bark or a rock that is next to some water. The eggs hatch into tadpoles, which then wriggle over the ground a short way until they plop into the water. The arboreal mantella, which is also sometimes known as the Folohy golden frog, mates differently. In this species, the female lays only one egg, which she sticks on an object above a puddle of water. Often, this puddle is inside a broken, standing piece of bamboo. The arboreal mantella is one of the only frogs in the world that lays one egg at a time.

Other frogs in this family breed in water. These include Buerger's frog and the forest bright-eyed frog, which both mate and lay their eggs in streams. The eggs hatch into tadpoles that continue growing in the water and eventually change into froglets.

Most of the frogs in this family breed over many weeks each year, but a few species mate during a very short period of only a few days. After they mate and lay their eggs, the males and females of many species leave their young to develop on their own. In a few species that do not lay their eggs in the water or in foam nests, the males will sit atop the clump of eggs while they develop. This may help to keep them moist or may help protect them from predators that might otherwise eat them. Some females of the foam-nesting species also stay nearby, sometimes returning to the nest to add more foam if necessary. They may even urinate on the nest to keep it moist enough for the eggs to survive.

The female Eiffinger's Asian treefrog lays her eggs on the inside of a tree hole and cares for her young. Instead of protecting them from predators or making sure they are moist, she feeds them. The water in the tree hole sometimes has little to feed the growing tadpoles, so she lays extra eggs in the water for her tadpoles to eat. Since these extra "blank" eggs have never mixed with sperm from a male, they would never have developed into young frogs, even if the tadpoles did not eat them. Arboreal mantellas do something similar. The female will drop a "blank" egg into the water for her tadpole to eat. Sometimes, however, the male becomes involved and leads another female to the water where one of his tadpoles is developing. If she lays her egg there, it may hatch into a tadpole that will become food for its older sibling.

The tadpoles of the common treefrog get no extra food from their parents. When they drop from their foam nests into the water, these hungry youngsters use their sharp and powerful beaks to eat almost anything in sight. If the water is just a small puddle, they may even eat their nest mates. Sometimes, only one tadpole is left in the puddle by the time it changes into a froglet.

Depending on the species, tadpoles take different amounts of time before they change into froglets. The western white-lipped treefrog usually needs one or two months. Golden mantellas also take one-and-a-half to two months, but other mantella species may need a longer time to change into froglets.

JUST HOW MANY?

The number of species in the Asian treefrog family is uncertain. Some people separate out a group of the frogs into a separate family, called Mantellidae, but even when they are included, the overall number of species may differ by nearly one hundred. For example, the World Conservation Union (IUCN), which keeps track of risks facing different species, has a different total number than AmphibiaWeb, which is an online system offered through the University of California at Berkeley. The IUCN lists 156 species in the Mantellidae family and another 262 Asian treefrogs for a total of 418 species. AmphibiaWeb, on the other hand, counts 150 species in Mantellidae and 224 Asian treefrogs, which adds up to 374 species.

ASIAN TREEFROGS AND PEOPLE

People rarely see most of the species in this family, which live in forests and other areas away from human activity. Some of the Asian treefrogs, like the Kinugasa flying frog, often turn up in gardens where people notice them. A few species, including the beautifully colored mantellas, are popular in the pet trade.

CONSERVATION STATUS

The World Conservation Union (IUCN) lists eighteen species that are Extinct, which means that they are no longer in existence; twenty-five species that are Critically Endangered and face an extremely high risk of extinction in the wild; fifty-six species that are Endangered and face a very high risk of extinction in the wild; forty-nine that are Vulnerable and face a high risk of extinction in the wild; thirty-eight that are Near Threatened and at risk of becoming threatened with extinction in the future; and ninety-four that are Data Deficient, which means that scientists do not have enough information to make a judgment about the threat of extinction.

The eighteen Extinct species have not been seen in the wild for at least fifty years, and some of them for more than one hundred years, even though scientists have searched for many of them again and again. One of the Critically Endangered species is the Chalazodes bubble-nest frog. Scientists had thought this species was extinct for 125 years when a population was discovered in a small area of moist forest on a hillside in India. It is still in danger, however, because it only appears to live in this one spot, and the forests are disappearing as people turn them into farms.

The Shillong bubble-nest frog, which is also Critically Endangered, lives in a different small area of India. The frog was quite common in its forest as late as the 1970s, but it has now become so rare that scientists have not even been able to hear a single male calling during the frog's breeding season. Like the Chalazodes bubble-nest frog, the Shillong bubble-nest frog's forests are disappearing as people cut the trees for lumber or firewood or to make room for houses and buildings. Another of the Critically Endangered species, known only by its scientific name of *Philautus papillosus*, is also facing habitat loss, but this time it is mainly due to mining for gemstones. Miners cut down trees that are in the way of their work. The endangered

Romer's treefrog, which lives in Hong Kong, has lost some of its habitat as people move into its forests and marshes but has also been pushed out by the building of a new airport. Ecologists tried to protect the frog by moving some populations. As of 2004, they had moved the frogs to eight new locations in protected areas, and seven of these populations were doing well.

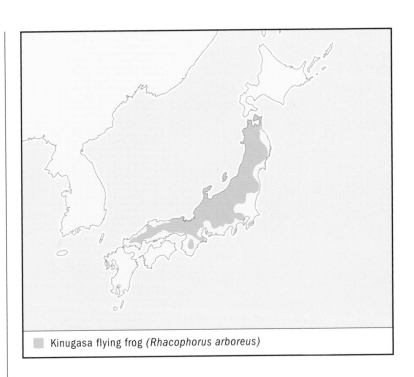

Kinugasa flying frog (*Rhacophorus arboreus*)

KINUGASA FLYING FROG
Rhacophorus arboreus

Physical characteristics: Also known as the forest green treefrog or the Japanese treefrog, the Kinugasa flying frog may be a solid, lime-green color, dark green, or green with many reddish brown, brown, or black speckles. The reddish brown and brown speckles are outlined with black. The frog's back, head, and legs are rough and covered with small bumps, or tubercles. Whether solid or speckled, its underside is white or cream-colored, often with somewhat-faded, brown blotches on the chest and throat. They have two large eyes bulging from the sides of a rather flattened, but large head. The eyes, which are orange to brown, often have a noticeable dark band running between them. They also have a noticeable ridge on each side of the head, stretching from the end of the snout to the middle of the eye and continuing on the other side of the eye where it curves down toward the top of the shoulder. The snout narrows toward the front. The legs are slender, and the underside of the rear legs has black lines and blotches near the body. The front toes are slightly webbed, but the hind toes are fully webbed. The toes on all four feet are long and

have very large, triangular-shaped pads on the tips. Females are larger than males. Females reach 2.3 to 3.2 inches (5.9 to 8.2 centimeters) from the tip of the snout to the end of the rump, while males grow to 1.7 to 2.4 inches (4.2 to 6.0 centimeters) in length.

Geographic range: Its home is in Honshu, the largest of the islands that make up Japan, as well as on a small island, called Sado, just to the northeast of Honshu. In addition, it has been introduced to two other areas in Japan.

Habitat: Although they can live in lowland forests, Kinugasa flying frogs usually prefer wooded locations high in the mountains, sometimes more than 6,560 feet (2,000 meters) above sea level. Tadpoles develop in the water of rice fields, marshes, and other wetland ponds.

Diet: Its diet is made up of insects.

Behavior and reproduction: Usually found in mountains, the Kinugasa flying frog sits among trees or under piles of leaves along the ground for much of the year. It sometimes also enters people's gardens and makes its home there. In the cold winters of this area of Japan, the frog finds a spot under a layer of moss or buried just under the ground and enters a state of deep sleep, called hibernation (high-bur-NAY-shun), until the weather warms again the following spring. The breeding season for this frog is about four months long, from April to July. The breeding season begins when males hop to the edge of a pool or wet rice field and start calling. Each male makes a similar call, which is two to six clicking noises followed by several lower clucks. After a female follows a call to a male, he climbs on her back, and she releases a fluid rather like the raw egg white from a chicken's egg. She then kicks the fluid with her feet, beating it into a foam. Sometimes the male helps her in whipping up the fluid. The longer the foam is beaten, the larger it grows. When it reaches an oblong shape about 3.5 inches (8.8 centimeters) wide and 4.7 inches (12.0 centimeters) long, she lays her eggs inside the frothy nest. As she does, the male adds his own fluid, which is filled with microscopic cells, called sperm. When the sperm combine with the eggs, the eggs can start to develop into young frogs. A female may lay three hundred to eight hundred eggs in the nest.

Sometimes, the mating pair is not alone. Other males may join in by beating up the foam and by adding their own sperm-filled fluid to the nest. In this way, the eggs in one nest may not all get sperm from the same male. When this happens, the young frogs from one nest may have different fathers. Once all the eggs are laid, the outside of the nest starts to dry into a hard shell. The shell protects the eggs from other animals that might want to eat them, and it also keeps the foam inside from drying out. The eggs eventually hatch into tadpoles inside the nest. By this time, the bottom of the nest becomes soft, and the tadpoles fall out, dropping into the water below. There, they continue their growth and turn into froglets.

Kinugasa flying frogs and people: In some ponds in Japan, the frogs have become a tourist attraction. Here, hundreds of male and female frogs arrive together to mate at night and during the day, and people come from miles away to watch this natural scene. Away from these busy ponds, people who live in the countryside also enjoy hearing smaller groups of males calling from rice fields and pools of water on summer nights.

Conservation status: This frog is quite common, and the IUCN lists it as being of Least Concern, which means it has no known threat of extinction and does not qualify for any of the "threatened" categories. It lives in numerous protected areas, and because some populations are tourist attractions, people keep a careful watch over them. ■

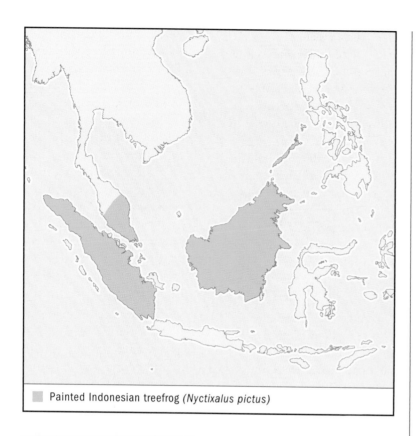

Painted Indonesian treefrog (*Nyctixalus pictus*)

PAINTED INDONESIAN TREEFROG
Nyctixalus pictus

Physical characteristics: The painted Indonesian treefrog, also known as Peter's treefrog or the cinnamon treefrog, may be bright orange, red, orange brown, or brown in color and looks as if it has been painted with tiny white dots. This dotted pattern gives the frog another of its common names, the spotted treefrog. Sometimes the dots form a broken line from the snout over the eye and to the back. The frog has a rough back with small and pointy bumps on its upper surface. On its underside, the frog is a paler orange or orange brown color. The head is flat like the body and narrows to a dull point at the end of its fairly long snout. It has two very large eyes, one on each side of the head. The eyes are white on top and brown on the bottom.

This species is a slender frog with very long and thin hind legs that fold neatly against its flattened body when it is sitting still. Its

front legs are also quite thin, and the frog likewise holds them tucked close to its body. On the front feet, the toes may be unwebbed or may have a small amount of webbing between them. The toes of the rear feet have more webbing. Females are larger than males. Females reach 1.46 to 1.54 inches (3.7 to 3.9 centimeters) from the tip of the snout to the end of the rump, while males grow to 1.12 to 1.5 inches (3.0 to 3.7 centimeters) long.

Geographic range: It lives in southeastern Asia, including Sumatra and Borneo in Indonesia, Palawan Island of the Philippines, Malaya, Sumatra, Singapore, and the southern edge of Taiwan.

Habitat: Adults live in moist forests either in lowlands or high in mountains up to 5,400 feet (1,650 meters) above sea level. For the frogs to survive, the forests must not be disturbed by humans. Tadpoles develop in puddles of water inside tree holes.

Diet: Although they do not know for sure, scientists believe they probably eat the same types of food as other members of this family: small invertebrates.

Behavior and reproduction: Scientists know little about this frog's behavior. Some adult frogs have been spotted from 3.3 to 9.8 feet (1 to 3 meters) above the ground on the leaves of small trees and shrubs, but they may climb even higher in the trees. The frogs breed in tree holes and rotting logs that contain puddles of water from the rain. Females lay about ten eggs at a time in a clump of gel that sticks to the inside wall of the tree hole or hollow log just above the puddle. The eggs hatch into tadpoles, which drop down into the water. They are able to survive by eating little bits of dead leaves or other material that is in the puddle. The tadpoles grow inside the puddle and eventually turn into froglets.

Painted Indonesian treefrogs and people: This frog does not survive well in forests that have been changed by people. Even a small amount of logging can cause a population to die off.

Conservation status: The IUCN considers this species to be Near Threatened, which means that it is at risk of becoming threatened with extinction in the future. Although the frogs live in many areas of southeastern Asia, they are not common anywhere. Ecologists are concerned about the future of this frog because more and more of its forests are being cut down by local people and by loggers. Some populations of the painted Indonesian treefrog live in areas that are protected from logging. ■

Free Madagascar frog *(Mantidactylus liber)*

FREE MADAGASCAR FROG
Mantidactylus liber

Physical characteristics: This is a slim frog with slender front and rear legs and extremely thin toes. Its front legs, including the long toes, would be about as long as the frog's body if they were stretched out. The toes on all four feet end in large pads. The front toes have no webbing between them; the back toes are slightly webbed. The frog's back, head, and legs are red, gray, or green, often smeared with patches of a slightly different second color. For example, a frog may have a pinkish brown back colored with light brown or greenish brown patches. A faint light line runs from the snout over the head and down the back. Some white or yellow spots may be noticeable low on the sides, especially toward the rump, and a few white speckles may show on the sides of the head and neck. The underside of the frog may be black. Its head has a rather long snout that narrows

This little known genus from Madagascar has many color variations of color, even within the same species. (Photograph by Harald Schüetz. Reproduced by permission.)

toward the front, and one eye of the large, gold to copper-colored pair of eyes on either side. A dark bar may show between the eyes. A narrow ridge runs from the back of the head to the shoulder.

Males have a flat structure, called a gland, under the skin on the upper rear leg, and a large, white vocal sac in the throat region. The vocal sac, which is also seen in other species of Asian treefrogs and many other types of frogs, blows up like a balloon when the male makes his call. Males are often a bit smaller than females, but both can grow to the same size. Males reach 0.8 to 1.1 inches (2.1 to 2.9 centimeters) from the tip of the snout to the end of the rump, while females grow to 1.06 to 1.1 inches (2.7 to 2.8 centimeters) long.

Geographic range: They live on the eastern side of Madagascar, as well as in the central region of the country.

Habitat: They live in moist rainforests from lowland areas at sea level to mountain locations up to 3,900 feet (1,200 meters) above sea level. Tadpoles develop in shallow water of swamps and other wetlands.

Diet: The diet is probably like that of many other treefrogs: small arthropods, including insects and spiders.

Behavior and reproduction: Most of the time, this frog sits in or near plants with cup- or tube-shaped parts that fill with water. The rainiest time of year is the mating season for the free Madagascar frog, and males begin calling from plants around the still or slow-moving water of small pools and swamps. The male's call is a ticking sound. When a female answers his call, she approaches him and may even give him a little push from behind. He then climbs onto her back and begins to wiggle. As he does, she lays her eggs onto the leaves. Each female may lay thirty to ninety eggs. When the eggs hatch into tadpoles, the tadpoles drop off the leaves and plop into the water below. They stay in the water until they develop into froglets.

Free Madagascar frogs and people: This frog survives quite well in rainforests that humans have not disturbed and in rainforests that have seen a good deal of human activity, such as the cutting of some trees for farming or other purposes.

Conservation status: This frog is quite common, and the IUCN lists it as being of Least Concern, which means it has no known threat of extinction and does not qualify for any of the "threatened" categories. Scientists are, however, watching this and other frog species as the rainforest disappears. Fortunately, the free Madagascar frog lives in many places that are protected from habitat destruction. ■

FOR MORE INFORMATION

Books:

Alcala, A. C., and W. C. Brown. *Philippine Amphibians: An Illustrated Field Guide.* Makati City, Philippines: Bookmark, Inc., 1998.

Channing, A. *Amphibians of Central and Southern Africa.* Ithaca, NY: Comstock Publishing Associates, 2001.

Glaw, F., and M. Vences. *A Fieldguide to the Amphibians and Reptiles of Madagascar.* Frankfurt, Germany: Edition Chimaira, 1999.

Halliday, Tim, and Kraig Adler, eds. *The Encyclopedia of Reptiles and Amphibians (Smithsonian Handbooks).* New York: Facts on File, 1991.

Inger, R. F., and R. B. Stuebing. *A Field Guide to the Frogs of Borneo.* Kota, Indonesia: Natural History Publications, 1997.

Maeda, N., and M. Matsui. *Frogs and Toads of Japan.* Tokyo, Japan: Bun-Ichi Sogo Shuppan Co., 1990.

Mattison, Chris. *Frogs and Toads of the World.* New York, NY: Facts on File Publications, 1987, pp. 177–179.

Miller, Sara Swan. *Frogs and Toads: The Leggy Leapers.* New York: Franklin Watts, 2000.

Passmore, N. I., and V. C. Carruthers. *South African Frogs: A Complete Guide.* Johannesburg, South Africa: Witwatersrand University Press, 1995.

Showler, Dave. *Frogs and Toads: A Golden Guide.* New York: St. Martin's Press, 2004.

Schiøtz, A. *Treefrogs of Africa.* Frankfurt, Germany: Edition Chimaira, 1999.

Zug, G. R., L. J. Vitt, and J. P. Caldwell. *Herpetology: An Introductory Biology of Amphibians and Reptiles.* San Diego, CA: Academic Press, 2001.

Periodicals:

Milius, Susan. "Lifestyles of the Bright and Toxic Overlap." *Science News* (April 14, 2001): 230.

Williams, Wendy. "Flash and Thunder." *Animals* (July 2000): 25.

Web sites:

"Common Tree Frog." *Wetlands, a publication of Sungei Buloh Nature Park.* http://wetlands.sbwr.org.sg/text/99-6-2-1.htm (accessed on May 6, 2005).

"Frog Wrestling." *American Museum of Natural History.* http://www.amnh.org/exhibitions/frogs/featured/wrestling.php (accessed on February 1, 2005).

"Golden Mantella." *St. Louis Zoo.* http://www.stlzoo.org/animals/abouttheanimals/amphibians/frogsandtoads/goldenmantella.htm (accessed on May 6, 2005).

"Golden Mantella." *theBigZoo.com.* http://www.thebigzoo.com/Animals/Golden_Mantella.asp (accessed on May 6, 2005).

"*Mantellidae.*" *AmphibiaWeb.* http://elib.cs.berkeley.edu/aw/lists/Mantellidae.shtml (accessed on May 6, 2005).

"*Mantidactylus liber.*" *Naturalia.* http://www.naturalia.org/ZOO/ANFIBI/e_24.html (accessed on May 6, 2005).

"Parachuting/Defying Gravity." *American Museum of Natural History.* http://www.amnh.org/exhibitions/frogs/featured/parachuting.php (accessed on February 1, 2005).

"Rhacophoridae." *Frogs of the Malay Peninsula.* http://frogweb.org/Families.aspx?FamilyID=22 (accessed on May 6, 2005).

"Spotted Tree Frog." *Ecology Asia.* http://www.ecologyasia.com/verts/amphibians/spotted_tree_frog.htm (accessed on May 6, 2005).

CHAPTER

PHYSICAL CHARACTERISTICS

With 362 species, this large family of narrow-mouthed frogs comes in many shapes and sizes. Most species are brown, tan, or yellow-brown on their backs, sometimes with brighter colors on their undersides. The horned land frog, for example, has a brown back and gray sides, but may have an orange or red underside. The saffron-bellied frog has a black back with yellowish to silvery flecks, and large, bright yellow spots on its black sides and belly. Some, like the rubber frog, stand out even more. The rubber frog has a dark brown to black body with pink or red markings on its back.

Many, but not all, of the narrow-mouthed frog species have a round, wide, often chubby-looking body and a short head that ends in a narrow or pointed snout. This gives these species an overall shape that resembles a pear or a teardrop. Others do not have this body shape. Some are long and thin, and others have rounded bodies with fairly wide heads. The New Guinea bush frog, for example, has a head that is just as wide as its body. Rain frogs of the genus *Breviceps* are also plump and round. They have such tiny legs that they cannot hop, and walk instead. Another rather plump frog, known as the ornate narrow-mouthed frog, has longer legs than *Breviceps* and is an excellent hopper.

Many, but not all, of the narrow-mouthed frogs have noticeable, small warts on their backs and legs. The typical member of this family has little or no webbing on its toes. Many have pads on their toe tips. The horned land frog, for instance, has large pads, especially on the toes of its front legs. The eyes of species in this family are frequently small, but some, like Boulenger's callulops frog, have large eyes. A few, including the New Guinea bush frog and the horned land frog, have eyelids decorated with small spines that almost look like thick eyelashes.

The majority of the frogs in this family share a few somewhat hidden characteristics. Unlike other frogs, most species of narrow-mouthed frogs have two or three zigzag folds on the roof of the mouth. The roof of the mouth is called the palate (PAL-ett). The majority of the species in this family also have no teeth. In addition, most narrow-mouthed frogs have smaller bones in the shoulder and chest than other frogs typically have. Some, like the Malaysian painted frog, have no neck bones and, therefore, no neck. In this case, the head almost blends in with the body, which makes the frog look quite chubby. In fact, the nickname of the Malaysian painted frog is chubby frog.

The typical narrow-mouthed frog grows to 1.6 inches (4 centimeters) long from snout to rump, and some never even reach 0.5 inches (1.3 centimeters) long as adults. The largest species, like the Malaysian painted frog, can top 3 inches (7.5 centimeters) long, and some can reach 4 inches (10 centimeters) in length. In most species of narrow-mouthed frogs, females are at least a little larger than the males. In some cases, like Bushveld's rain frog, the female is almost twice the size of the male.

GEOGRAPHIC RANGE

Depending on the species, narrow-mouthed frogs may live in southern North America, central and northern South America, Central America, southern Africa and Madagascar, southeast Asia including the Philippines and the East Indies, and/or northern Australia and New Guinea.

HABITAT

The members of this family live in many different habitats. Most prefer hot and humid rainforests, where many live in underground burrows. Some live along but above the ground, and others spend at least part—and sometimes all—of their lives in the trees. A few species, like those with the scientific genus names of *Oreophryne* and *Oxydactyla*, live high in the mountain grasslands of New Guinea. The rain frogs of southern Africa, on the other hand, survive the dry, almost desert-like sand dunes by spending much of their time in underground burrows. These odd frogs, with their exceptionally plump bodies and four tiny legs, will venture out of their burrows during the rain or on humid nights.

DIET

Most narrow-mouthed frogs eat only small invertebrates (in-VER-teh-brehts), which are insects and other animals without backbones. Many species have small mouths that come to a point at the end and can only eat tiny invertebrates. Ants are a favorite food for these frogs, but they will also eat other insects that are small enough to fit in their mouths. The Bolivian bleating frog is one of many species that are especially fond of ants. Other narrow-mouthed frogs have slightly larger mouths and are able to eat larger invertebrates. The New Guinea bush frog has a large head and especially wide mouth, which allows it to eat insects, as well as larger animals, like other frogs and lizards.

Scientists have not seen most of the frogs feeding, so they have to guess about how they go about eating. Some of the frogs probably eat insects that they find while they move about in trees or along the ground, but scientists think that many of these frogs may hunt by ambush. In this type of hunting, the frog sits very still. An insect that does not notice the frog may approach closely enough for the frog to grasp it and eat it.

Not all narrow-mouthed frog species have a tadpole stage, but in those that do, the tadpoles suck in water, sift out tiny microorganisms, and eat them. Microorganisms (MY-crow-OR-gan-izms) are living things that are too small to see. Scientists call this type of eating filter feeding, because the tadpoles sift, or filter, their food from the water. Some of the tadpoles have funnel-shaped mouths that are perfectly designed for filtering food from the surface of the water.

BEHAVIOR AND REPRODUCTION

Most of the narrow-mouthed frogs are active at night, but they sometimes come out during the day. Those that live high in mountains are more likely to be active in the day time. Many of the narrow-mouthed frogs are burrowers and use flat scoops, or spades, on the heels of their feet to help them dig backward into the soil. The Bushveld rain frog, for example, has spades on each of its hind feet to help it dig. This frog can burrow as far as 20 inches (50 centimeters) below the surface. Others that burrow do not have the spades and instead use their front feet to dig into the soil head first. A few, like Boulenger's callulops frog, make their homes in burrows that they probably take from other animals, rather than build themselves. Many of the burrowing frogs stay underground during dry periods, only coming out during heavy rains. This behavior allows desert-living frogs to survive, but even the burrowing species that live in rainforests will crawl underground when the weather is dry.

Like many other frogs, most narrow-mouthed frogs defend themselves from predators by quickly jumping off, perhaps into a shrub where they can hide or into a nearby pond where they can dive out of sight. Some will also disappear into a burrow or try to dig down into the soil. A few narrow-mouthed frogs have more unusual defense tactics. One of the most bizarre is the tomato frog, a plump frog that lives on the northeast coast of Madagascar, a large island that lies east of southern Africa. The males are orange and grow to about 2.5 inches (6.5 centimeters), but the females are red and can reach 4 inches (10.1 centimeters) long and weigh half a pound (227 grams). Like many other frogs, the tomato frogs have skin that oozes, or secretes, a poisonous substance that tastes bad to predators. The substance in the tomato frog's skin goes a step farther. When a snake or other predator bites a frog, not only does the predator get a mouthful of white, bad-tasting goop, but the goop is exceptionally sticky—so sticky, in fact, that it can seal shut the mouth and eyelids of the retreating predator for several hours, sometimes days. Studies have shown that the substance is five times stronger than rubber cement.

Another narrow-mouthed frog with an unusual way of protecting itself is a broad-headed frog of New Guinea, near Australia. When it feels threatened, it holds its ground rather than running away, blows up its body, and opens its mouth to show off its bright, blue tongue. If the predator is not already frightened off by this display, the frog clamps its jaws on the predator and hangs on for several minutes. When the frog finally lets go, the predator often has had enough and leaves the frog alone.

Most of the frogs in this family mate when the weather is warm and rainy. In tropical rainforests, where it is almost always wet and warm, some species may be able to mate any time of the year. Those that live in very dry areas, however, mate only during the very short rainy season. The Bushveld rain frog spends most of its life underneath the dry ground of the desert-like areas where it lives. When the rains come, it comes out, usually at night, to search on land for termites and eat until it is fat. This fat helps the frog survive underground until the next rainy season. It also mates during this rainy period.

Depending on the species, narrow-mouthed frogs may mate in or near the water or on land. In both cases, the males begin calling when they are ready to mate. Some call with single or groups of ringing notes, while some have harsher voices. Many males have a bag of skin, called a vocal sac, on the throats. The vocal sac fills with air and deflates when the male calls. Other species have no vocal sacs, but still manage to call. In 2002, scientists reported that one narrow-mouthed frog, called the Borneo tree-hole frog, actually practices and adjusts its call, making it higher or lower to get the best echo from the tree cavity where it does its singing. The scientists said this was the first time any animal had ever been shown to change its call or song based on the place from which it calls. For other narrow-mouthed frogs, the males simply call. The females hear the calls and follow them to find the males. In the species that mate on land, a male's call may not only attract a female, but may also tell other males to find somewhere else to mate. The male horned land frog is such a frog. Males will often call back and forth, apparently to set up and keep their territories.

Species that mate on land usually do so in various hidden-away spots. These may include burrows that the males dig themselves, piles of leaves on the ground, tree holes, or plants that grow on the sides of the trees. The male Fry's whistling frog, for example, moves to the top of the pile of leaves where it lives and calls from there. Boulenger's callulops frog, on the other hand, calls from inside or near the entrance to its burrow, which it does not make but instead takes over from another burrowing animal. More than half of the narrow-mouthed frogs mate in or near water. The water may be a stream or other body of water that remains filled with water all year, or it may be a pool of water that dries up once the rainy season ends. Some frogs use very small pools of water that they find inside tree holes or within plant leaves that grow together to form small cups. Boulenger's climbing frog is an example of a frog that makes use of puddles inside tree holes.

Little information is available about reproduction in most of the 362 species in this family. Scientists assume, however, that the males and females of most if not all narrow-mouthed frogs mate like many other frogs: the male climbs onto the female's back as she lays her eggs. This piggyback position is called amplexus (am-PLEK-sus). In some species, like Bushveld's rain frog, the females are much larger than the males of the same species, which would make it difficult for the male to hold on if he didn't have some help. The help comes in the form of a sticky substance that oozes from the skin. It glues the pair together while they mate. In other species, like Boulenger's climbing frog, the males have sharp spines on one toe of each front foot. They probably use the spine to hang onto the females during mating.

In the species that mate on land, the females lay their eggs in a moist spot. In the Bushveld rain frog, the stuck-together male and female pair dig backward into the soil until they find a moist spot and she lays her eggs there. The eggs of this frog and most other land-mating species of narrow-mouthed frogs develop right into froglets, rather than turning into tadpoles first. The froglets usually look like miniature versions of the adults. Scientists use the term direct development to describe the growth of eggs right into froglets instead of tadpoles and then froglets. The food for each developing egg comes from a large yolk. Because the yolk is so large, the females usually lay only a few eggs at a time. A female Fry's whistling frog lays seven to twelve eggs, while a female Timbo disc frog lays just four to six eggs at a time. The males typically stay behind to watch over the young, sometimes even carrying them around on their backs. The males nab and gulp down insects that would otherwise eat the eggs and may also huddle with the eggs to keep them moist.

In the species of narrow-mouthed frogs that mate in the water, the females of some species drop their eggs in a pond or stream, while others lay their eggs in a pool of water inside a tree hole or within water held in plant leaves. The saffron-bellied frog is a species that mates around small pools that fill with water after a heavy rain. The females lay their eggs in the pools. The eggs of water-mating species may clump together as they do in the

FREAKY FRIENDS

A tarantula could easily kill a frog, so why does the Great Plains narrow-mouthed toad make its home inside the large spider's burrow? This frog, which lives in parts of the United States, has formed an unusual relationship with the spider. The tarantula does not bother the frog, which is quite safe from other predators in the spider's home. At the same time, the frog eats ants and other insects inside the burrow that might harm and possibly devour the tarantula's eggs.

A GOOD YOLK

Even when scientists have never actually seen a particular frog species' eggs develop, they can predict whether they will turn into tadpoles or whether they will skip the tadpole stage and change right into froglets. The clue is in the yolk. Some frogs, including many of the narrow-mouthed frogs, lay eggs with a lot of yolk. This yolk feeds the frog developing inside. If the yolk is large enough, it can contain enough food for the developing frog to hatch right into a froglet. If the egg has a small yolk, scientists assume that the egg hatches into a tadpole, which must then find food on its own.

Bolivian bleating frog; they may float on the surface as they do in the ornate narrow-mouthed frog, or they may sink or float in other patterns. Frogs that mate in the water often lay hundreds of eggs at a time. One of these frogs, the ornate narrow-mouthed frog, lays several hundred. The Bolivian bleating frog lays about two hundred at a time, but the female may lay several clutches in a single season. One female Bolivian bleating frog was found with more than two thousand eggs in her body.

Once most water-mating narrow-mouthed frogs lay their eggs, both adults leave the eggs to hatch on their own. The females that lay their eggs in larger bodies of water, like streams or ponds, lay small eggs. For instance, two hundred eggs of the Bolivian bleating frog can fit into a cluster just 4 inches (10 centimeters) in diameter. These eggs hatch into tadpoles, sometimes in as little as a day and a half, and the tadpoles search for food in the water. In some species, like the ornate narrow-mouthed frog, the tadpoles have see-through bodies that make them nearly invisible. This helps them avoid predators.

Those water-mating frogs that use small pools of water for mating have eggs with yolks that are larger than the pond or stream species. Even after the tadpoles hatch from the eggs, they continue to rely completely on the egg yolk for food. This is important, because their tiny pools would likely not have enough food in them to keep the tadpoles alive. In some species, like Boulenger's climbing frog, the male stays in the tree hole with the eggs until they develop into froglets.

NARROW-MOUTHED FROGS AND PEOPLE

Some native people in South America, New Guinea, and perhaps some other areas eat narrow-mouthed frogs, but they do not take enough of the frogs to threaten the survival of any species. A few species, such as the Malaysian painted frog, are fairly common in the pet trade. Most, however, are rarely seen by humans in the wild or in the pet trade.

CONSERVATION STATUS

The World Conservation Union (IUCN) considers six species are Critically Endangered, which means that they face an extremely high risk of extinction in the wild; twenty-five species are Endangered and face a very high risk of extinction in the wild; thirty-six are Vulnerable and face a high risk of extinction in the wild; seventeen are Near Threatened and at risk of becoming threatened with extinction in the future; and 155 are Data Deficient, which means that scientists do not have enough information to make a judgment about the threat of extinction.

The Critically Endangered species include the beautiful nursery frog, which is also known as the elegant frog, and five others known only by their scientific names. These are *Albericus siegfriedi, Microhyla karunaratnei, Parhoplophryne usambarica, Scaphiophryne gottlebei,* and *Stumpffia helenae.* Most of these live in very small areas that are changing as people clear the land for purposes such as farming. Often, the frogs cannot survive these changes. Some of the species are also in danger from pollution and from global warming. Scientists believe that global warming in the future will cause weather-related problems, such as especially long-lasting, dry spells, that will harm the frogs and may lead to extinction for some species.

Since many of the narrow-mouthed frogs live in rainforests, and people continue to cut down rainforests, many environmentalists are worried about the future of these frogs, many of which scientists know little about. If the frogs have no place left to live, they will likely die off.

The U.S. Fish and Wildlife Service does not list any United States species of narrow-mouthed frogs to be at risk.

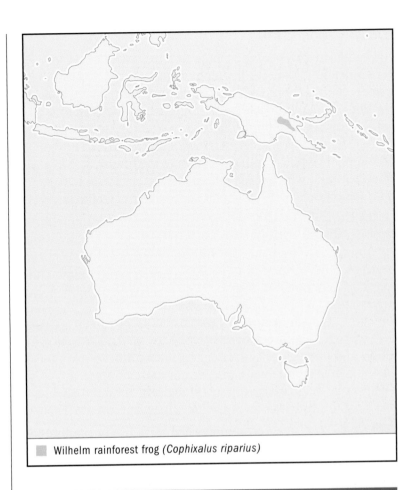

Wilhelm rainforest frog (*Cophixalus riparius*)

WILHELM RAINFOREST FROG
Cophixalus riparius

Physical characteristics: The Wilhelm rainforest frog has a dark brown or purplish brown body with yellowish tan spots and blotches on its back and legs. The snout is short and slightly upturned at the end. Its long, thin legs have lengthy toes that are tipped with wide, triangular-shaped pads. This species grows to 2 inches long (5 centimeters) from snout to rump.

Geographic range: The Wilhelm rainforest frog lives in the mountains of Papua, New Guinea, between 6,000 to 9,000 feet (1,900 to 2,800 meters) above sea level.

Habitat: This species hides among rainforest trees and in holes along the ground in steep areas, especially on the edges of roads, and sometimes in grass near streams.

Diet: Scientists are not sure what specific kinds of food these frogs eat. If they are like many other members of the family, however, they eat some types of invertebrates.

Behavior and reproduction: Wilhelm rainforest frogs may be found in many areas in the rainforest. They often climb high into trees, where they hide away in tree holes or inside plants that grow on the sides of the trees. They may also spend time along the ground, frequently tucked into burrows on the sides of stream banks or other steep areas. The males call females from inside ground burrows or from hiding spots high in the trees. They mate in either place. Females lay strings of two dozen or so eggs in the burrow or high in the trees. Scientists have little information on their reproduction, but one report noted a string of 27, 0.2-inch (5-millimeter) eggs in a burrow, along with a frog—probably the male—staying with them. Instead of hatching into tadpoles, the eggs hatch right into froglets.

Wilhelm rainforest frogs and people: People rarely see this frog in the wild. It is not common in the pet trade.

Conservation status: The World Conservation Union (IUCN) does not consider Wilhelm rainforest frogs to be at risk. This frog lives in a fairly small area, but the area is in good shape and the frog is quite common. ■

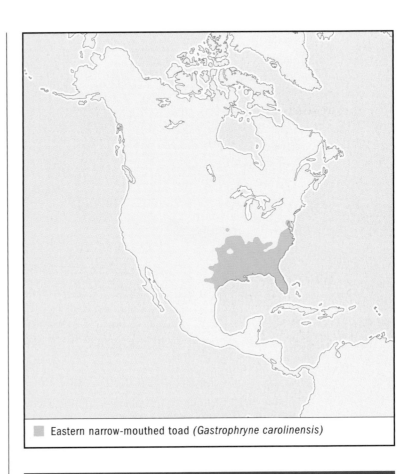

■ Eastern narrow-mouthed toad (*Gastrophryne carolinensis*)

EASTERN NARROW-MOUTHED TOAD
Gastrophryne carolinensis

Physical characteristics: The eastern narrow-mouthed toad has the typical teardrop-shaped body common to many members of this family. Its back and legs are light brown, gray, or reddish brown with patterns of darker brown lines or spots. The sides have a more faded color than the back. The frog's snout comes to a point, and it has a fold of skin that crosses the head just behind its small eyes. Its feet are unwebbed, and each of the hind feet has a spade for digging. Males have a dark throat, but the females do not. The frogs can reach 1.5 inches (3.8 centimeters) long from snout to rump.

Geographic range: Eastern narrow-mouthed toads live in the southeastern quarter of the United States. They have also been

introduced to two islands in the Bahamas and to Grand Cayman Island.

Habitat: Although members of this species can survive in many on-land habitats, they prefer areas along the coastline. They usually stay off mountains and out of dry places.

Diet: Eastern narrow-mouthed toads eat mainly small invertebrates, especially ants, termites, and beetles that are 0.25 inches (6 millimeters) long at most.

Behavior and reproduction: During the day, eastern narrow-mouthed toads usually stay beneath leaves, under stones, or in other hidden spots along the ground. When discovered, they typically try to hop quickly away. They come out at night, which is when they eat. By remaining active at night and hiding during the day, the toads can avoid many of their predators, including garter snakes, bullfrogs, and large wading birds called egrets. When they are attacked, however, the toads can ooze a bad-tasting substance from their skin. This substance may be poisonous to a predator. The substance provides protection from the predators as well as the biting ants that the toad eats.

During wet periods of the year, the males begin calling for females from ponds and small rain-filled pools of water or from hidden places on land along shore. In southern areas, such as Florida, the males call from April to October. In cooler areas, they begin calling later and stop earlier. The calls last about 4 seconds and sound like the "baa" of a lamb. When a female finds a male, he holds onto her back with his front arms and makes a gluey substance with his belly that helps him stick to her. The female then lays her approximately five hundred eggs in several batches. The eggs float on the top of the water, hatch into tadpoles, which then turn into froglets. In warmer areas, the tadpoles may change into froglets in as little as twenty days, but in colder places, they may need as long as sixty-seven days to make the change.

Eastern narrow-mouthed toads and people: For most of the year, people only see this species in the wild if they search for them by flipping over rocks, logs, and piles of leaves that lay on the ground. The toads' loud mating calls, however, may help people find them during the mating season.

Conservation status: Neither the World Conservation Union (IUCN) nor the U.S. Fish and Wildlife Service consider this species to be at risk. It is very common throughout the southeastern United States, including suburbs where people live.   ■

Malaysian painted frog (*Kaloula pulchra*)

MALAYSIAN PAINTED FROG
Kaloula pulchra

Physical characteristics: The Malaysian painted frog is also known as the painted or Asian bullfrog, chubby frog, rice frog, and bubble frog. It has the teardrop-shaped body common to many narrow-mouthed frogs. This frog has no neck bones and, therefore, no neck, which gives it a chubby look. Its back is mostly chocolate brown with a wide, light yellowish to cream-colored band on each side of the body. The band is outlined with a thin, dark brown line. The yellowish cream color also covers the top of its snout between its large eyes. The frog has rather short legs, which are mottled with brown, light gray, and cream colors, and barely webbed feet. Each of its back feet has a spade for digging. The toes on its feet end in small pads. Malaysian painted frogs are one of the largest species in this family and grow to 3 inches (7.5 centimeters) long from snout to rump.

Geographic range: The Malaysian painted frog lives in southeastern Asia, including China and Taiwan, and parts of Indonesia. Populations also live in Borneo and Sulawesi, but people probably brought the frogs to these areas.

Habitat: The Malaysian painted frog is different from most frogs, which tend to stay away from towns and other places where people have moved in and made changes to the environment. Instead, this species lives in and around towns and avoids quiet, people-free areas.

Diet: The Malaysian painted frog eats a variety of small insects, especially ants.

Behavior and reproduction: For much of the time, the frogs stay out of sight by digging backward into underground burrows, into piles of trash, and into other secretive spots they find along the ground. When the rains come, however, the frogs come out to mate in pools that have filled with water. The males float in the pools and blow up their bodies to make calls that sound like loud honks. Females arrive and mate with the males. The female's eggs quickly turn into tadpoles, which rapidly change into froglets. This speedy growth is important because the water in their pools usually dries up in a very short time after the rains end.

Malaysian painted frogs and people: This species is fairly common in the pet trade. Although it lives near homes and buildings, people rarely see this usually underground frog in the wild. Some people, however, do hunt it for food.

Conservation status: The World Conservation Union (IUCN) does not consider the Malaysian painted frog to be at risk. This frog lives in a large area, and the area is in good shape. Moreover, even though it is collected as food and is seen in the pet trade, the frog remains very common in the wild. ■

Pyburn's pancake frog (*Otophryne pyburni*)

PYBURN'S PANCAKE FROG
Otophryne pyburni

Physical characteristics: Pyburn's pancake frog has a wide rather flat back and a pointy snout that makes it look somewhat like a dead leaf. The frog is brown to yellowish gray with scattered, tiny, blue to cream speckles and sometimes dark stripes or other markings. It also has two, thin, light yellow to cream stripes, each of which begins at the snout and runs down the side of the body to the hind leg. The stripe widens onto the back where it has a ragged edge. The pancake frog's legs are short. The females can reach 2.2 inches (5.6 centimeters) long from snout to rump, while the males are a bit smaller.

Scientists know little about this frog outside of its breeding behavior, but they think the frog remains tucked away underground most of the time. When it breeds, the males call females from hidden spots near a stream. (Illustration by Brian Cressman. Reproduced by permission.)

Geographic range: Pyburn's pancake frog lives in northern South America, from southeastern Colombia in the west to French Guiana in the east.

Habitat: For most of the year, this frog moves along sandy ground in the rainforest. When it breeds, however, it enters the water of a nearby stream, which is also where the eggs hatch and tadpoles grow.

Diet: Scientists are not sure exactly what this frog eats, but they think it probably eats ants, which is what other closely related frogs eat.

Behavior and reproduction: Scientists know little about this frog outside of its breeding behavior, but they think the frog remains tucked away underground most of the time. When it breeds, the males call females from hidden spots near a stream. These hiding places may be underneath piles of leaves or inside tangles of plant and tree roots that poke up from the ground. The females lay eggs, which can be 0.2 inches (5 millimeters) across, in the quiet ponds of water or nearby. The eggs hatch into tadpoles that have sharp teeth, which they perhaps use to sift out sand as they suck water into their mouths. They then filter out tiny organisms from the water and eat them. The tadpoles scoot among leaves in the small stream where they were born until they develop into froglets and hop onto land.

Pyburn's pancake frog and people: People very rarely see this frog in the wild.

Conservation status: The World Conservation Union (IUCN) does not consider Pyburn's pancake frog to be at risk. This frog lives in a fairly large area. Logging, farming, and other activities are under way in part of its area and may be hurting the frogs that live there, but people have still not bothered most of the frog's habitat. Currently, Pyburn's pancake frog remains a common species. ■

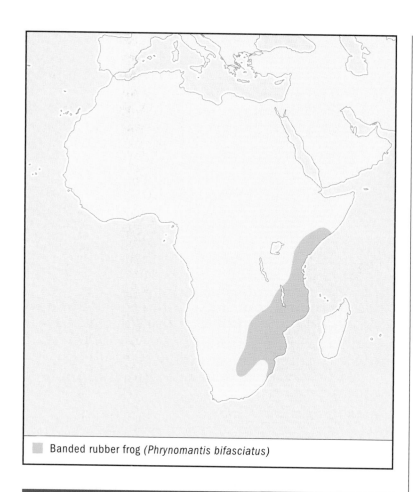

Banded rubber frog (*Phrynomantis bifasciatus*)

BANDED RUBBER FROG
Phrynomantis bifasciatus

Physical characteristics: The banded rubber frog is black and pear-shaped with a wide body that becomes increasingly narrow toward the head. Two wide, red to orange red stripes run down the sides of the body from the snout over the eye and to the front of the hips. A red to orange red splotch also colors the rump. The body is smooth and quite shiny. Its short, front and back legs have numerous red spots. Its toes, which have almost no webbing, end in small pads. The front toes are quite long. Its underside is decorated with small white spots. Banded rubber frogs grow to about 2.75 inches (6.8 centimeters) long from the tip of the snout to the end of the rump. The tadpoles have a rather fish-like look, because their eyes are on the sides

of the head rather than on top, like many other tadpoles' eyes are.

Geographic range: The banded rubber frog lives along the far eastern side of central to southern Africa.

Habitat: Even though they do not have spades on their feet like many other digging frogs have, banded rubber frogs are burrowers. They spend much of their time in underground burrows that they dig themselves.

Diet: The adults eat small insects, especially ants and termites. Tadpoles suck in water and sift out tiny organisms, which they eat.

Behavior and reproduction: During the day, they dig backward into the soil or into termite hills. Sometimes, they simply climb into holes in trees. They are active at night, when they come out on land. Instead of hopping, they either walk or run. By remaining underground during the day, they avoid most predators. When necessary, however, they can also protect themselves by oozing a substance from their skin that predators find to be bad-tasting.

In rainy times of year, the males move into or alongside puddles and small pools of water and begin making their calls. The call is a high-pitched trill that lasts several seconds and then repeats. Like other frogs, the males and females mate when the male crawls up onto the female's back. The female can lay up to 1,500 eggs, which drop into the water and stick to underwater plants. The eggs hatch into tadpoles that float heads up in the water, while wiggling their whip-like tails below. In about a month, the tadpoles change into half-inch (1.3-centimeter) tadpoles.

Banded rubber frogs and people: People rarely see this burrowing frog, except in the pet trade, where it is fairly common. If a person handles the frog, it may ooze from its skin the same substance it uses to protect itself from predators. This substance may bother human skin.

Conservation status: The World Conservation Union (IUCN) does not consider the banded rubber frog to be at risk. This frog lives in a large area and has a large population, even though it is a fairly common pet species. ■

FOR MORE INFORMATION

Books:

Halliday, Tim, and Kraig Adler, eds. *The Encyclopedia of Reptiles and Amphibians (Smithsonian Handbooks)*. New York: Facts on File, 1991.

Mattison, Chris. *Frogs and Toads of the World*. New York: Facts on File Publications, 1987.

Parker, H. W. *A Monograph of the Frogs of the Family Microhylidae*. London: British Museum, 1934.

Passmore, N. I., and V. C. Carruthers. *South African Frogs*. Johannesburg: Witwatersrand University Press, 1979.

Showler, Dave. *Frogs and Toads: A Golden Guide*. New York: St. Martin's Press, 2004.

Periodicals:

Milius, Susan. "Frogs Play Tree: Male tunes his call to specific tree hole." *Science News,* December 7, 2002 (vol. 162): 356.

Web sites:

"Chubby Frog." *Frogland.* http://allaboutfrogs.org/info/species/chubby .html (accessed on March 26, 2005).

"Eastern Narrow-Mouthed Toad *Gastrophryne carolinensis*." *USGS Northern Prairie Wildlife Research Center.* http://www.npwrc.usgs.gov/ narcam/idguide/gcarolin.htm (accessed on March 26, 2005).

"The Fragile World of Frogs: Paternal Instincts." *National Geographic.* http://www.nationalgeographic.com/ngm/finaledit/0105/ (accessed on April 8, 2005).

"*Gastrophryne carolinensis*, Eastern Narrowmouth Toad." *Herps of Texas — Frogs and Toads.* http://www.zo.utexas.edu/research/txherps/ frogs/gastrophryne.carolinensis.html (accessed on March 26, 2005).

"Painted Chorus Frog, *Microhyla butleri*." *Wildlife Singapore.* http:// www.wildsingapore.per.sg/discovery/factsheet/frogpaintchorus.htm (accessed on March 26, 2005).

"Red-banded rubber frog, *Phrynomerus bifasciatus*." http://www .calacademy.org/research/herpetology/frogs/list22.html (accessed on March 26, 2005).

"Tomato Frog." *Woodland Park Zoo.* http://www.zoo.org/educate/ fact_sheets/day/tomato.htm (accessed on March 26, 2005).

MADAGASCARAN TOADLETS
Scaphiophrynidae

Class: Amphibia

Order: Anura

Family: Scaphiophrynidae

Number of species: About 9 species

PHYSICAL CHARACTERISTICS

The Madagascaran toadlets are small frogs that look like toads. Many come in shades of brown or green, as do many toads. One of the toadlets is called the green burrowing frog. It, for instance, is green with brown blotches on its back, head, and legs. The red rain frog, however, is a more brightly colored member of this family. This species, which is also known as the rainbow burrowing frog, is red, orange red, or pink on its back and the top of its head, but white or light yellow green on its sides, legs, lower face, and underside. It also has considerable black markings on its body, along with a few yellow or whitish blotches on the back and head. Many of the toadlets have detailed, darker brown patterns on their backs. From one side of the back to the other, the patterns are usually mirror images of each other. This type of mirror-image pattern is known as a symmetrical (sim-MET-rih-kul) pattern.

Most Madagascaran toadlets have small warts. In some species, like Mocquard's rain frog, the warts may be as little as grains of sand, if they are there at all. The red rain frog has no warts on its back. Madagascaran toadlets have short back legs, but both their front and back legs have rather long toes. Each of the back feet has a noticeable bump, or tubercle (TOO-berkul). Their toes are either unwebbed or barely webbed. A few species, like the red rain frog and green burrowing frog have large pads on the tips of their front toes. The undersides of the frogs may be light or dark-colored. Mocquard's rain frog is a species with a white underside. It does, however, have red or dark purple patches on the undersides of its upper legs. The red rain frog, on the other hand, has a dark underside that is usually a dark grayish purple.

The web-foot frog, also known as the narrow-headed frog, looks different from the other eight species of Madagascaran toadlets. This frog has a teardrop-shaped, pudgy-looking body with a snout that comes to a point. Its hind legs are rather long. It has very small eyes that only barely bulge from the sides of the head. The toes on the back feet are fully webbed.

Males and females look much alike, although the males in some species may have darker throats and be a bit smaller than females. Depending on the species, adults may be 0.8 to 2.4 inches (2 to 6 centimeters) long from the tip of the snout to the end of the rump. Red rain frogs can grow to 1.4 inches (3.6 centimeters) long as adults. Mocquard's rain frogs are a bit smaller, and the males are even smaller than the females. Female Mocquard's rain frogs grow to 1.1 to 1.3 inches (2.8 to 3.3 centimeters) long, while males only reach 0.8 to 1.1 inches (2 to 2.7 centimeters) long. Adult web-foot frogs reach to 0.8 to 1 inches (2 to 2.4 centimeters) long. In this species males are a bit larger than females.

This family contains about nine species. Some scientists count more, mostly by splitting one or more of these nine species into two, or count fewer by grouping two into one species. Although this volume lists the Madagascaran toadlets in their own separate family, some scientists believe they should be grouped with the family of narrow-mouthed frogs.

GEOGRAPHIC RANGE

All of the species in this family live in Madagascar, a large island nation in the Indian Ocean off southern Africa.

HABITAT

Madagascaran toadlets live in many areas of Madagascar from low areas at sea level to slopes up to 6,600 feet (2,000 meters) above sea level. Although the tadpoles of all species are found in the still waters of swamps and pools of water that dry up later in the year, the adults live in a variety of different habitats. Some, like the brown rain frog and the red rain frog, prefer hot, dry places in the western and southern regions of the country. The red rain frog spends the daytime hours under stones scattered along the ground of rather humid forests that cover slopes and

AN ANCIENT LINK

Scientists are interested in the Madagascaran toadlets because they think the toadlets may be a link between two major groups of frogs. One group, called the Ranoidea, includes the true frogs of the family Ranidae and others. The second group, called the Microhyloidea, includes the narrow-mouthed frogs and others. The skeletons of the adult Madagascaran toadlets include some bones that are like those found in both of these two groups. Madagascaran toadlet tadpoles also have a few features of each group. Because of the similarities between Madagascaran toadlets and the two major groups, scientists believe that both the Ranoidea and Microhyloidea probably had the same ancestor—one that, like the Madagascaran toadlets, had a combination of their characteristics. The species in Ranoidea kept some of those characteristics, and the species in Microhyloidea kept others.

canyons in the dry area. Other members of this family live in much colder places high on mountains where even the trees do not survive. These frogs, including the Madagascar rain frog, which is also known as the green rain frog, exist in grassland habitats. Rainforests, on the other hand, are the surroundings for the green burrowing frog and the web-foot frog. The web-foot frog, for instance, usually stays among fallen, rotting, and damp leaves lying on the forest floor.

DIET

Scientists know very little about the diet of Madagascaran toadlets, but they believe the frogs are mainly insect-eaters. Although toadlets, like the red rain frog, will eat crickets in captivity, this does not necessarily mean that they normally eat crickets in the wild. The tadpoles are filter-feeders, which means that they strain out tiny bits of food from the water.

BEHAVIOR AND REPRODUCTION

The Madagascaran toadlets usually remain hidden during the day, staying out of sight underground, often beneath stones or logs. The green burrowing frog sometimes comes out during the day. This frog's color and pattern help it to blend in as it wanders about on leaves along the ground or climbs up green moss-covered trees. The color and pattern of the web-foot frog is also an excellent camouflage. Unless the frog moves, most people cannot see the brown and yellowish frog against the muddy ground, plants, and trees of its habitat.

Scientists have learned most of the information about this family during the frogs' mating seasons and believe that the frogs bury themselves underground and rest for much of the rest of the year. This resting period is known as estivation (es-tih-VAY-shun).

The frogs mate during the summer's rainy season, which usually begins in Madagascar in December, January, or February.

After heavy rains soak the ground and fill pools and swamps with water, males will group together at the watering holes and begin calling together. Group calling is known as a chorus. The sound of the loud choruses can carry over long distances and attract females. Each male calls by using his body and his vocal sac, which is extra flesh on his throat. He sucks in air, blows up both his body and his vocal sac, and lets out the air to make his call. This can be a dangerous time for the male frogs, which not only call in females with their calls, but may call in predators. While the males are calling and their bodies are full of air, the frogs cannot dive down into the water to escape, and this makes them easy targets for predators.

Mating in each of these frog species typically occurs all at once and over a very short time. A frog species that mates together and over a short time is known as an explosive breeder. To mate, the male holds onto the female's back by grasping her near her front legs. From this position, she lays her eggs. Many species, including the web-foot frog and Mocquard's rain frog, lay several hundred tiny eggs measuring just 0.04 inches (1 millimeter) in diameter. Usually, the eggs float together and form a film on the water surface. The eggs hatch into tadpoles. The warmer the temperature outside, the faster the tadpoles turn into froglets.

MADAGASCARAN TOADLETS AND PEOPLE

The more colorful Madagascaran toadlets are common in the pet trade.

CONSERVATION STATUS

The World Conservation Union (IUCN) considers one species in this family to be Critically Endangered, which means that it is facing an extremely high risk of extinction in the wild. All of the members of this species, the red rain frog, live in two tiny spots in south-central Madagascar. One of these spots is inside a national park. People sometimes collect this beautiful species to sell in the pet trade, but this could be hurting the species because its numbers are so low.

According to the IUCN, other species in this family are at risk. It lists the species known only by its scientific name of *Scaphiophryne boribory* as Endangered and facing a very high risk of extinction in the wild; the green burrowing frog as Vulnerable and facing a high risk of extinction in the wild; and the

Madagascar rain frog as Near Threatened and at risk of becoming threatened with extinction in the future. Two other species known by the scientific names of *Scaphiophryne obscura* and *Scaphiophryne verrucosa* are Data Deficient, which means that too little information is available to make a judgment about the threat of extinction. Some scientists think that these two species are actually one and the same and often list them both as *Scaphiophryne verrucosa*.

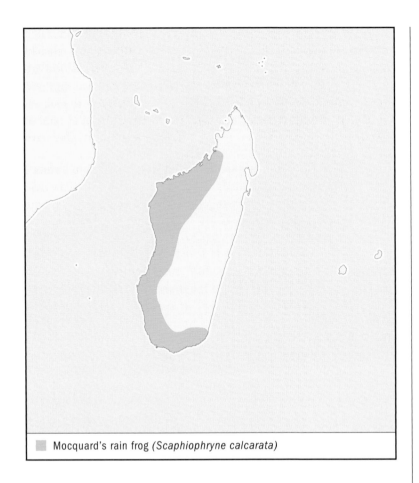

Mocquard's rain frog *(Scaphiophryne calcarata)*

MOCQUARD'S RAIN FROG
Scaphiophryne calcarata

Physical characteristics: Mocquard's rain frog is a tiny species with small legs, a slightly pointy snout, and smooth to slightly warty skin on its back. Its back and head may be brown, gray, or green, often with a dark brown and symmetrical pattern on its back. Many also have a light-colored stripe running from head to rump down the middle of the back. Their legs are brown, usually with noticeable dark brown bands. Their sides are dark brown, the belly is white, and the undersides of the thighs are red or purple. The back toes have very little webbing between them, and the front toes have none at all. Males have a black throat, while females' throats are white with brown markings. Males and females are also a bit different in size. Males grow to

00.8 to 1.1 inches (2 to 2.7 centimeters) long from snout to rump, and females reach 1.1 to 1.3 inches (2.8 to 3.3 centimeters) in length. This species, along with the web-foot frog at 0.8 to 1.0 inches (2 to 2.4 centimeters) long, are the smallest Madagascaran toadlets.

Geographic range: They live in western and southern Madagascar.

Habitat: Mocquard's rain frogs live in dry areas up to 1,000 feet (300 meters) above sea level. They can survive in forests, shrubby or grassy spots, and even farmland.

Diet: Scientists know little about the frog's diet, but the stomach of one captured frog was filled with large ants.

Behavior and reproduction: Like other Madagascaran toadlets, Mocquard's rain frog is active at night during the rainy season and likely spends the dry season buried underground. Heavy rains soak the earth during the summer in Madagascar, and males of this species group together at newly water-filled pools and swamps. The males begin calling in choruses for females and create quite a racket. When a female approaches a male, he calls even faster before climbing onto her back to mate. He holds on near her front legs as she lays several hundred small eggs. The eggs hatch into tadpoles. The tadpoles, which are almost completely see-through, sift food out of the water or pick small particles out of the water to eat. The tadpoles change into froglets in a few weeks, not long before their watering hole dries up for another year. The tiny newborn froglets are just 0.2 to 0.3 inches (5.5 to 7.5 millimeters) long from snout to rump.

Mocquard's rain frogs and people: This frog disappears underground in all but the rainy season, when some may hop into people's homes.

Conservation status: The World Conservation Union (IUCN) does not consider this species to be at risk. Mocquard's rain frog is quite common in its habitat, some of which is located in protected areas. ■

FOR MORE INFORMATION

Books:

Glaw, Frank, and Miguel Vences. *A Fieldguide to the Amphibians and Reptiles of Madagascar.* 2nd ed. Köln: Vences & Glaw Verlag, 1994.

Web sites:

"How Animal Camouflage Works." *How Stuff Works.* http://science. howstuffworks.com/animal-camouflage.htm (accessed on April 15, 2005).

"Narrow-headed frog." *Madagascar Biodiversity and Conservation.* http://www.mobot.org/mobot/madagascar/image.asp?relation=A56 (accessed on April 15, 2005).

"*Paradoxophyla palmata.*" *AmphibiaWeb.* http://elib.cs.berkeley.edu/ cgi-bin/amphib_query?query_src=aw_lists_alpha_&where-genus= Paradoxophyla&where-species=palmata (accessed on April 15, 2005).

"Species: *Scaphiophryne marmorata.*" *Naturalia.* http://www.naturalia .org/ZOO/ANFIBI/e_39.html (accessed on April 15, 2005).

Staniszewski, Marc. "Madagascan Burrowing Frogs FAQ." *Marc Staniszewski's Amphibian Information Centre.* http://www.amphibian .co.uk/scaphiophryne.html (accessed on April 15, 2005).

Class: Amphibia
Order: Caudata
Number of families: 10 families

order

PHYSICAL CHARACTERISTICS

Caudata (kaw-DAY-tuh) is the group of animals most people call salamanders but that also includes newts, sirens, hellbenders, olms, mudpuppies, and amphiumas (AM-fee-yoo-muhs). Salamanders are four-legged amphibians that have a long tail and short legs. Amphibians (am-FIB-ee-uhns) are vertebrates (VER-teh-brehts), or animals with a backbone, that have moist, smooth skin; are cold-blooded, meaning their body temperature is the same as the temperature of their surroundings; and, in most instances, have a two-stage life cycle. The word "amphibian" comes from a Greek word that means "having a double life." One of the life stages is a larva (LAR-vuh) that lives in water and has gills, and the other is an adult that lives on land and has lungs. Larvae (LAR-vee, the plural of larva) are animals in an early stage that go through metamorphosis (meh-tuh-MOR-foh-sus), or a change in body form, before becoming adults. Other amphibians are frogs, toads, and caecilians (sih-SILL-yuhns).

The head of a salamander is the same width as or narrower than the trunk. The trunk has twelve to eighteen vertebrae (ver-teh-BREE), which are the bones that make up the spinal column, also called the backbone even though it is made up of more than one bone. The tail of a salamander usually is about the same length as the head and body combined. Most salamanders are 1.5 to 8 inches (4 to 20 centimeters) long, but some can be as long as 5 feet (1.5 meters). Sirens and amphiumas look different from other salamanders in that they have a long, snakelike body, a short tail, and tiny legs.

The moist skin of a salamander contains many glands. Some of these glands make mucus, and some make poison. Most salamanders have camouflage coloring, but some are brightly colored. The brightly colored ones are poisonous or look like the poisonous ones in order to trick predators. Salamander skin is thick and tightly attached to the bone and muscle under it. Salamanders get 90 percent of their oxygen through their skin and also drink through their skin. Salamanders cannot survive if their skin dries out.

Salamanders have a long, fast tongue that contains as many as eleven bones. The tongue shoots from the mouth through the action of specialized muscles. The muscles that bring the tongue back into the mouth are extremely long, being anchored on the animal's hip bones. Salamanders have large eyes they use mainly for finding prey and watching out for predators. Salamanders also have an excellent sense of smell. Although they can hear, salamanders have no outer ears, and sound appears to play little role in their lives.

IS IT A SALAMANDER OR A LIZARD?

Many people confuse salamanders and lizards. In the southern parts of the United States, salamanders often are called "spring lizards." Salamanders are amphibians, but lizards are reptiles. Salamanders have smooth, moist skin, but lizards have dry, scaly skin. Salamanders have rounded toes, but lizards have claws.

GEOGRAPHIC RANGE

Almost all salamanders live in the Northern Hemisphere. One species even lives north of the Arctic Circle. Only a few species of salamanders live south of the equator, and those live in North and South America as far south as Bolivia.

HABITAT

Salamanders live in cool, damp places. Most live on land, some live in water, and some move between water and land. Salamanders live in areas ranging from northern forests to tropical rainforests and from sea level to high mountains. Some salamanders live in trees, and some live in caves. Salamanders that live on land often spend long periods in underground burrows, especially when they are not breeding and during cold winters and dry summers.

DIET

Adult salamanders eat spiders, insects, worms, crustaceans such as crayfish, mollusks such as slugs and snails, fish and fish eggs, tadpoles, other salamanders, and even small rodents.

WORLD CONSERVATION UNION CATEGORIES

Extinct   No longer in existence.

Extinct in the Wild   No longer alive except in captivity or through the aid of humans.

Critically Endangered   Facing extremely high risk of extinction in the wild.

Endangered   Facing very high risk of extinction in the wild.

Vulnerable   Facing high risk of extinction in the wild.

Lower Risk/Conservation Dependent If the conservation program were to end, the animal would be placed in one of the threatened categories.

Low Risk/Near Threatened   At risk of becoming threatened with extinction in the future.

Least Concern   There is no known threat of extinction, and the animal does not qualify for any of the threatened categories.

Data Deficient   There is not enough information to make a judgment about the threat of extinction.

Not Evaluated   The species has not been evaluated for the threat of extinction.

Crustaceans (krus-TAY-shuns) are water-dwelling animals that have jointed legs and a hard shell but no backbone. Mollusks (MAH-lusks) are animals with a soft, unsegmented body that may or may not have a shell.

BEHAVIOR AND REPRODUCTION

Adult salamanders live alone rather than in groups. They hide during the day under leaves, rocks, or logs and are active at night but sometimes come out on rainy days. Salamanders hunt mainly by sight but also by smell. They sit and wait for prey to come close and then capture it with an explosive motion of their tongues. The tongue action is so fast it cannot be seen by human eyes.

Salamanders live as long as thirty years in the wild. The type of life cycle and method of development vary from species to species. In many species female salamanders lay eggs in the water, and the male releases sperm on them. Fertilization (FUR-teh-lih-ZAY-shun), or the uniting of egg and sperm to start development, takes place outside the female's body. The eggs hatch into larvae that have gills and live in the water, sometimes for years, before going through metamorphosis. During the transformation the larvae lose their gills, develop lungs, grow legs, and crawl onto land. After metamorphosis, the adult salamanders spend all or most of their time on land. In some species, female salamanders guard their nests of eggs in order to protect them from predators and to keep them from drying out.

About one-half of salamander species do not have a water-dwelling larva stage. When they hatch from eggs laid on land, the young salamanders have the same body form as adults and continue to live the rest of their lives on land. In some species of salamanders, larvae that hatch from eggs laid on land wriggle to nearby water or are caught up by rising waters in the spring. They live in water for a while and then undergo metamorphosis. Still other species of salamanders live their entire lives in water with their bodies in the larva body form. Their reproductive organs do mature, however, and these salamanders do produce young.

Some male salamanders do not spread sperm on eggs but deposit a sperm packet in or near the water. The female takes the sperm into her body, and fertilization takes place inside her. In a few species of salamanders, the developing larvae stay inside the female for one or two years or even longer. These larvae go through metamorphosis inside the female. The young animals are quite large when they are born, having received their nourishment first by eating their siblings and later by eating secretions in the female.

Most salamander larvae can be classified as the pond type or the stream type. The pond type usually change form in one season and have large, feathery gills and a large tail fin. Stream-type larvae have a small tail fin, very short gills, and a flat body with short, fat legs and hard toes. These larvae may live for several seasons before going through metamorphosis.

SALAMANDERS, NEWTS, AND PEOPLE

Some people keep salamanders as pets. Salamanders also have been the subjects of myth, folklore, and literature. According to

U.S. FISH AND WILDLIFE SERVICE CONSERVATION CATEGORIES

Endangered In danger of extinction throughout all or a significant portion of its range.

Threatened Likely to become endangered in the near future.

Aztec myth in Mexico, a god trying to escape from his enemies dove into water and changed himself into a salamander. From at least the time of the ancient Romans people have believed that salamanders cannot be harmed by fire. This belief arose because salamanders were seen crawling out of the flames after people placed logs on a fire. People also once believed that salamanders had magical powers. In the play *Macbeth* by William Shakespeare, three witches brew a potion using "eye of newt."

CONSERVATION STATUS

The World Conservation Union (IUCN) lists two species of salamanders as Extinct, forty-six as Critically Endangered, 105 as Endangered, eighty-one as Vulnerable, and fifty-six as Near Threatened. Extinct means no longer in existence. The U.S. Fish and Wildlife Service lists six species of salamanders and newts as Endangered and five as Threatened.

FOR MORE INFORMATION

Books:

Bernhard, Emery. *Salamanders*. New York: Holiday House, 1995.

Lawlor, Elizabeth P. *Discover Nature in Water and Wetlands*. Mechanicsburg, PA: Stackpole, 2000.

Llamas Ruiz, Andres. *Reptiles and Amphibians: Birth and Growth*. New York: Sterling, 1996.

Petranka, J. W. *Salamanders of the United States and Canada*. Washington, DC: Smithsonian Institution Press, 1998.

Web sites:

Hawes, Ales. "On Waterdogs, Mudpuppies, and the Occasional Hellbender." *Zoogoer*. http://nationalzoo.si.edu/Publications/ZooGoer/2000/2/waterdogsmudpuppieshellbender.cfm (accessed on March 28, 2005).

"Order Caudata (Salamanders)." *Animal Diversity Web*. http://animaldiversity.ummz.umich.edu/site/accounts/classification/Caudata.html (accessed on March 28, 2005).

"Order Caudata: Salamanders." Northern Prairie Wildlife Research Center. http://www.npwrc.usgs.gov/narcam/idguide/index.htm#ambystom (accessed on March 28, 2005).

SIRENS AND DWARF SIRENS

Sirenidae

Class: Amphibia

Order: Caudata

Family: Sirenidae

Number of species: 4 species

PHYSICAL CHARACTERISTICS

Sirens and dwarf sirens are salamanders with eel-like bodies, no hind legs, and front legs that are extremely small. The jaws are covered with a hard, beaklike structure. The gills are large and stick up from the head like feathers. The body is shaped like a tube with a flat tail. Young sirens have a clear fin on their back that extends to the tip of the tail. On older sirens the part of the fin on the back disappears, and the tail fin that is left becomes solid rather than clear. The legs of sirens have three or four toes that have hard tips.

Sirens and dwarf sirens never leave the water. They get oxygen from water passing through their gills and skin, but they also have lungs. These salamanders live their entire lives with a larva body form. A larva (LAR-vuh) is an animal in an early stage that changes form, or goes through metamorphosis (meh-tuh-MOR-foh-sus), to become an adult. Sirens and dwarf sirens do not respond to the environmental signals that tell other salamanders to start metamorphosis.

Sirens and dwarf sirens are 5 to 40 inches (12 to 100 centimeters) long. Newly hatched sirens and younger larvae (LAR-vee, the plural of larva) are deep black with yellow, red, or silvery white markings. There is a band across the nose and another on the top of the head. Many of these animals have stripes on the body. When the animals are older the markings become dull or disappear.

phylum

class

subclass

order

monotypic order

suborder

▲ **family**

GEOGRAPHIC RANGE

Sirens live in North America from the far northeastern part of Mexico north to the southwestern part of Michigan and east to Maryland. Dwarf sirens live in the southeastern part of the United States from Florida to South Carolina.

HABITAT

Sirens and dwarf sirens live in still to slowly flowing, often swampy, water with a muddy bottom and sometimes with floating and rooted plants.

DIET

Sirens and dwarf sirens eat any water animal small enough for them to swallow.

BEHAVIOR AND REPRODUCTION

Sirens and dwarf sirens hide in burrows near the water's edge during daylight hours and come out at night to look for food along the water bottom and among plants. These salamanders swim by making wavy movements of their body and tail, but they also move their small legs in walking motions when they are near the bottom.

To find food, sirens and dwarf sirens poke around with their snouts and find prey using their sense of smell. They suck food into their mouth by rapidly expanding their throat and opening the mouth so that the food is sucked inside with a rush of water. Gill rakers keep the food inside the throat, and the water passes to the outside through gill slits. Sirens and dwarf sirens are greedy eaters. They shake their prey vigorously and swallow larger animals in a series of gulps without breaking the prey into pieces.

Even though they look like larvae, adult sirens and dwarf sirens have reproductive organs and produce young. Scientists do not know how fertilization (FUR-teh-lih-ZAY-shun), or the joining of egg and sperm to start development, takes place in these salamanders. They believe it happens outside the body because males do not have glands for making a sperm packet, and females do not have a sac for sperm storage. The large eggs are laid singly, sometimes attached to plants, or in groups.

SIRENS, DWARF SIRENS, AND PEOPLE

Dwarf sirens have been sold as fishing bait.

CONSERVATION STATUS

Sirens and dwarf sirens are not considered threatened or endangered.

Lesser siren (*Siren intermedia*)

LESSER SIREN
Siren intermedia

Physical characteristics: In addition to having a long, tubular body, no hind legs, and very short front legs, lesser sirens have thirty-one to thirty-seven grooves along their sides, four toes, and three gill slits. They are 7 to 27 inches (18 to 69 centimeters) long. The head is broadly rounded when looked at from the top. Newly hatched larvae are densely black and have bright red bands across the tip of the snout, across the head, and on the body. Older lesser sirens may keep a pale snout band, but the other markings disappear. The adult color pattern appears to vary from place to place in the geographic range, but there is always a greenish to gray background color with different amounts of shimmery speckling. The clear fin on the young siren's back and tail becomes solid in older lesser sirens and is present only on the tail.

Lesser sirens eat almost any water animal they can catch and fit into their mouths. (Illustration by Joseph E. Trumpey. Reproduced by permission.)

Geographic range: Lesser sirens live in North America from the far northeastern part of Mexico north to the southwestern part of Michigan and east to Florida and the southeastern part of Virginia.

Habitat: Lesser sirens live in many types of still or slowly flowing water, such as swamps, ponds, and ditches.

Diet: Lesser sirens eat almost any water animal they can catch and fit into their mouths, including small crustaceans such as crayfish, worms, mollusks such as snails, insect larvae, and small fishes. Crustaceans (krus-TAY-shuns) are water-dwelling animals that have jointed legs and a hard shell but no backbone. Mollusks (MAH-lusks) are animals with a soft, unsegmented body that may or may not have a shell.

Behavior and reproduction: Lesser sirens spend all their time in the water. Large numbers of them may live in one place. These salamanders spend the daylight hours burrowed into the water bottom or near the water's edge. They look for food along the water bottom at night. They suck the prey into their mouths and swallow it whole.

Salamanders usually do not make a sound, but when bitten or forced from a hiding spot by another salamander, lesser sirens yelp. Lesser sirens placed in unfamiliar surroundings may make several types of sounds. If there is not enough oxygen in the water, these lesser sirens come to the surface to gulp air.

If their pond, ditch, or mud hole dries out, lesser sirens move into burrows at the bottom and wait for water. They make a cocoon by shedding their skin several times and become inactive until water returns. The gills do not work unless the salamander is underwater, and they become small nubs while the lesser siren is in its burrow and breathing with its lungs.

Female lesser sirens lay as many as fifteen hundred eggs in a nest at the water bottom. Scientists believe one of the parents guards the nest. Each egg is enclosed in four jelly envelopes. The eggs hatch forty-five to seventy-five days after being laid. At this point the larvae are about 0.4 inches (10 millimeters) long.

Scientists do not know how lesser sirens find their mates or how the eggs are fertilized (FUR-teh-lyzed). They have found that during the breeding season most lesser sirens large enough to reproduce have a number of bite marks on them that match the size of the mouth of this species. Scientists believe males and females may bite each other during mating or that males bite one another while fighting over females or over territory.

Lesser sirens and people: Lesser sirens have no known importance to people. Some people are afraid of these salamanders because they confuse them with amphiumas (AM-fee-yoo-muhs), which give a dangerous bite.

Conservation status: Lesser sirens are not considered threatened or endangered. ■

FOR MORE INFORMATION

Books:

Bernhard, Emery. *Salamanders*. New York: Holiday House, 1995.

Llamas Ruiz, Andres. *Reptiles and Amphibians: Birth and Growth*. New York: Sterling, 1996.

Petranka, J. W. *Salamanders of the United States and Canada*. Washington, DC: Smithsonian Institution Press, 1998.

Web sites:

Gabbard, J. *"Siren intermedia." Animal Diversity Web.* http://animaldiversity.ummz.umich.edu/site/accounts/information/Siren_intermedia.html (accessed on March 28, 2005).

Class: Amphibia

Order: Caudata

Family: Hynobiidae

Number of species: 43 species

family
CHAPTER

PHYSICAL CHARACTERISTICS

Asiatic salamanders are small to medium-sized salamanders. Most of these salamanders are 4 to 10 inches (10 and 25 centimeters) long, although some species grow to a length of 12 inches (30 centimeters). Most of these salamanders are dull sandy brown to dark olive, but a few species have colorful spots on their backs.

There are two main groups of Asiatic salamanders. One group lays a large number of eggs, and the larvae (LAR-vee), or animals in an early stage, spend one year in development before metamorphosis (MEH-tuh-MORE-feh-sis), or a change in body form to become an adult, is finished. The other group lays a much smaller number of eggs, and the larvae take two to three years to go through metamorphosis.

Some Asiatic salamanders that live in mountain streams have a hard structure on their toes. One species has claws. Some species have a horny covering on their feet. These structures and coverings help the salamanders grasp the ground. Some Asiatic salamanders have four instead of five toes. The arrangement of the teeth, which are located on the roof of the mouth, is an important characteristic for identifying the genus (JEE-nus) and species (SPEE-seez) of Asiatic salamanders. Some species of Asiatic salamanders have very small lungs, and others have no lungs at all. The small size or lack of lungs may be part of the salamanders' water-dwelling lifestyle. The larvae of Asiatic salamanders have four pairs of gill slits. Gills are organs for obtaining oxygen from water.

phylum

class

subclass

order

monotypic order

suborder

▲ **family**

EYE OF NEWT, BREAKFAST OF BAT?

Paghman mountain salamanders have the most bizarre diet of all Asiatic salamanders. Baby bats have been found in their stomachs. The salamanders live in caves, which they share with bats. The baby bats fall into the water, where they are caught and eaten by the salamanders.

GEOGRAPHIC RANGE

Asiatic salamanders live only in Asia. Their range extends from Japan, Taiwan, and the mainland of China westward to Afghanistan, Iran, and Kazakhstan in central Asia. To the north, Asian salamanders live on the Kamchatka peninsula, the island of Sakhalin, and in Siberia and Mongolia westward beyond the Ural Mountains. Siberian salamanders are the only Asiatic salamanders that enter European Russia and are the only salamanders that live north of the Arctic Circle.

HABITAT

Some Asiatic salamanders, such as clouded salamanders, live only in lowlands. Others live only in the mountains. Many live 6,600 to 13,000 feet (2,000 to 4,000 meters) above sea level. The record for highest home belongs to the Tibetan stream salamander, which lives in western China at a height of 14,000 feet, or about 2.5 miles (4,250 meters).

Some Asiatic salamanders live in water all year. These salamanders live mainly in mountain streams with cool, fast-flowing water. During daylight hours, they stay under rocks in the water. Sometimes they hide under large rocks on shore, but they are never far from water. In some species of Asiatic salamanders the adults spend most of the year on land, but in the breeding season (February to June) they travel to and gather at breeding sites, which are either ponds or mountain streams with running water. Most species breed in only one of the types of water. For example, Korean salamanders breed only in ponds. Some species, however, such as Chinese salamanders, breed in both ponds and streams. They have been found under rocks and grass and in burrows. Some species have been dug out of soil.

DIET

Asiatic salamanders, both larvae and adults, eat insects and other invertebrates (in-VER-teh-brehts), which are animals without backbones. Hokkaido salamanders and Longdong stream salamanders eat others of their own species.

BEHAVIOR AND REPRODUCTION

Asiatic salamanders hunt for food at night. Scientists know little else about how these salamanders behave outside of breeding season. The breeding season varies from late winter to early summer. Some Asiatic salamanders breed in late winter and early spring. The eggs develop in ice-cold water mixed with ice and snow. Others breed in early summer. The breeding season may be as late as July for some species in western China.

Males of all but one species of Asiatic salamanders release sperm into the water while the females are laying sacs of eggs. The exception is male Semirechensk salamanders, which place sacs of sperm on rocks or plants. In all species, fertilization (FUR-teh-lih-ZAY-shun), or the joining of egg and sperm to start development, takes place outside the body. The females lay two groups of eggs, one batch of eggs coming from each ovary. The ovaries (OH-vuh-reez) are the organs that make eggs. The eggs are contained in jelly-like sacs, which attach to rocks or plants in ponds, streams, or marshes. Egg sacs that do not attach to something usually are not fertilized (FUR-teh-lyzed). The number of eggs in each sac varies, ranging from three in Japanese clawed salamanders to 105 in Siberian salamanders.

In most species of Asiatic salamanders the female chooses an object such as a rock or plant, grasps it firmly, and lays her egg sacs on it. The sacs stick to the rock or plant. After she releases part of the egg sac, the female lets go of the plant or rock and floats backward. A male waiting nearby immediately moves onto the egg sac. The male often pushes and kicks the female with its legs and presses on the egg sacs with its cloaca to fertilize the eggs. The cloaca (kloh-AY-kuh) is a chamber in both males and females that holds waste from the kidneys and intestines as well as eggs and sperm before they are released to the outside. The male's activity may help to speed up egg laying. Male clouded salamanders guard and vigorously defend the egg sacs they have fertilized.

Most Asiatic salamander eggs hatch in three to five weeks, depending on the temperature. The larvae of some salamander species that are not well developed when they hatch have a balancer on each side of the head. The balancers, which look like whiskers, support the head until the front legs develop, and then they fall off. The larvae of most stream-breeding Asiatic salamanders are well developed when they hatch and do not have balancers.

ASIATIC SALAMANDERS AND PEOPLE

Asiatic salamanders have no known importance to people.

CONSERVATION STATUS

The World Conservation Union (IUCN) lists five species of Asiatic salamanders as Critically Endangered, ten as Endangered, twelve as Vulnerable, and two as Low Risk/Near Threatened. Critically Endangered means facing extremely high risk of extinction in the wild. Endangered means facing very high risk of extinction in the wild. Vulnerable means facing high risk of extinction in the wild. Low Risk/Near Threatened means at risk of becoming threatened with extinction in the future.

The primary threats to the survival of Asiatic salamanders are their small geographic ranges and small numbers. Many Asiatic salamanders live in only a small area on one island or mountain. These areas in Japan and China are getting smaller and are being separated from one another. Damage to habitat caused by people is another problem for these salamanders.

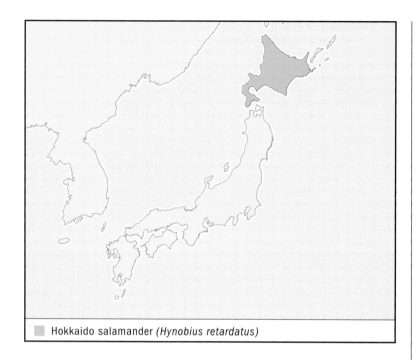

Hokkaido salamander *(Hynobius retardatus)*

HOKKAIDO SALAMANDER
Hynobius retardatus

Physical characteristics: Hokkaido salamanders are 4 to 7 inches (10 to 18 centimeters) long. There are eleven or twelve grooves along the sides of the body, and the tail is long. The legs and toes are long compared with those of other Asiatic salamanders. The back is dark brown with a few blurry spots. Some Hokkaido salamanders keep the larval body form even though they grow to adult size.

Geographic range: Hokkaido salamanders live on Hokkaido, the northernmost of the main islands of Japan.

Habitat: Hokkaido salamanders live less than 6,600 feet (2,000 meters) above sea level. During the breeding season they live in slow-moving streams and ponds. When they are not breeding, these salamanders live on land under grass, rocks, and leaf litter on the forest floor but often visit bodies of water.

Diet: The larvae of Hokkaido salamanders eat small water-dwelling invertebrates. Adults eat insects, crustaceans, water worms, and,

Hokkaido salamander larva finish metamorphosis within one year, but if the water is cold, metamorphosis can take two or even three years. (Photograph henk.wallays@skynet.be. Reproduced by permission.)

sometimes, fish. Crustaceans (krus-TAY-shuns) are water-dwelling animals that have jointed legs and a hard shell but no backbone. Hokkaido salamander larvae packed close together in large groups sometimes eat other Hokkaido salamander larvae but usually do not eat their brothers and sisters.

Behavior and reproduction: Scientists know how Hokkaido salamanders reproduce but little else about how these salamanders behave. Breeding starts when the snow begins to melt and the water temperature is 37 to 41°F (3 to 5°C). In most areas, the breeding season is in April, but at higher elevations, breeding may not start until early June. Both male and female Hokkaido salamanders travel to and gather at their breeding sites. Mating and egg laying take place at night. The females lay two egg sacs, which attach to twigs and grass. Each egg sac usually contains thirty to fifty eggs, but there may be as many as ninety-three eggs in a sac. Larvae finish metamorphosis within one year, but if the water is cold, metamorphosis can take two or even three years.

Hokkaido salamanders and people: Hokkaido salamanders have no known importance to people.

Conservation status: Hokkaido salamanders are not considered threatened or endangered. ■

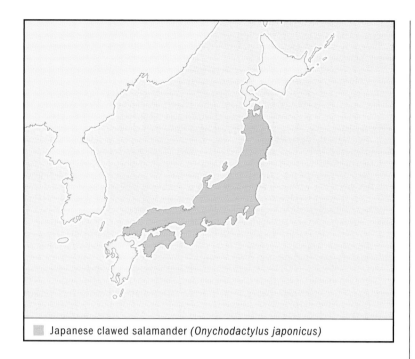

Japanese clawed salamander (*Onychodactylus japonicus*)

JAPANESE CLAWED SALAMANDER
Onychodactylus japonicus

Physical characteristics: Japanese clawed salamanders are 4 to 7 inches (10 to 18 centimeters) long. The body is thin, and the tail is long. The back is brown with orange spots. There also are orange spots on the back of the head and on the legs. Orange stripes run along the center of the back. The larvae have clawlike structures on their toes. Adults have these "claws" only during the breeding season. Japanese clawed salamanders do not have lungs.

Geographic range: Japanese clawed salamanders live on two Japanese islands, Honshu and Shikoku.

Habitat: Japanese clawed salamanders live more than 3,300 feet (1,000 meters) above sea level. When they are not breeding, these salamanders live on land but very close to water. Their favorite places are under wet rocks or logs beside a stream. They also live under logs on the forest floor, in tree holes, and in other damp places.

Diet: Japanese clawed salamanders eat insects and their larvae, spiders, millipedes, snails, tadpoles, and fish larvae.

Behavior and reproduction: Scientists know how Japanese clawed salamanders reproduce but little else about how these salamanders behave. The males breed every two years, and the females breed every three years. The breeding season is in May, but in some areas it extends into June. The females lay eggs at night, usually at the source of a mountain stream. Each of the two egg sacs contains three to eight eggs, for a total of seven to fifteen eggs per female. Larvae take three years to finish metamorphosis.

Japanese clawed salamanders and people: Japanese clawed salamanders have no known importance to people.

Conservation status: Japanese clawed salamanders are not considered threatened or endangered. ■

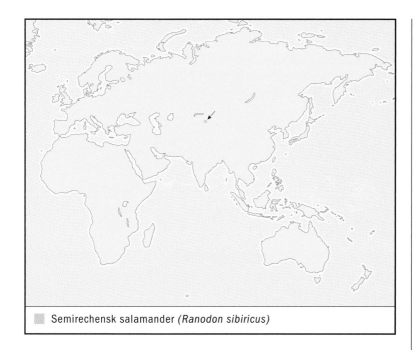

Semirechensk salamander (*Ranodon sibiricus*)

SEMIRECHENSK SALAMANDER
Ranodon sibiricus

Physical characteristics: Semirechensk salamanders are 6 to 10 inches (15 to 25 centimeters) long. The tail is as long as the rest of the body and has a ridge along the top. The body is brown with scattered black spots. Adult Semirechensk salamanders have small lungs.

Geographic range: Semirechensk salamanders live in the Ala Tau mountains and the Tien Shan mountains of eastern Kazakhstan and western China.

Habitat: Semirechensk salamanders live in mountain streams and marshes 5,000 to 9,000 feet (1,500 to 2,750 meters) above sea level.

Diet: Larvae of Semirechensk salamanders and salamanders that have just completed metamorphosis eat the larvae of water-dwelling invertebrates. Adults eat water-dwelling and land-dwelling invertebrates.

Behavior and reproduction: Semirechensk salamanders hunt for food at night. The larvae begin hunting four to eight days after they hatch. These salamanders continue to hunt during metamorphosis.

Semirechensk salamanders live in mountain streams and marshes. (© Joseph T. Collins/ Photo Researchers, Inc.)

The breeding season is May to July. Semirechensk salamanders take two to three years to go through metamorphosis. Male Semirechensk salamanders are the only Asiatic salamanders that make bags of sperm. They attach the sperm bags to the undersides of rocks and plants, and females attach their egg sacs to the same rocks and plants, where fertilization takes place. Male Semirechensk salamanders, not the females, choose the breeding sites.

Semirechensk salamanders and people: Semirechensk salamanders have no known importance to people.

Conservation status: The World Conservation Union (IUCN) lists Semirechensk salamanders as Endangered, or facing very high risk of extinction in the wild. They are under protection in both Russia and China. The small geographic range and damage to their habitat are the main threats to the survival of Semirechensk salamanders. These salamanders do well in captivity, and some scientists are trying to return them to the wild. ∎

FOR MORE INFORMATION

Books:

Bernhard, Emery. *Salamanders.* New York: Holiday House, 1995.

Duellman, William E., and Linda Trueb. *Biology of Amphibians.* Baltimore: Johns Hopkins University Press, 1994.

Gunzi, Christiane. *Amphibians and Reptiles of North America.* San Diego, CA: Thunder Bay, 1995.

Lawlor, Elizabeth P. *Discover Nature in Water and Wetlands.* Mechanicsburg, PA: Stackpole, 2000.

Llamas Ruiz, Andres. *Reptiles and Amphibians: Birth and Growth.* New York: Sterling, 1996.

Petranka, J. W. *Salamanders of the United States and Canada.* Washington, DC: Smithsonian Institution Press, 1998.

Web sites:

Heying, H. "Hynobiidae." *Animal Diversity Web.* http://animaldiversity .ummz.umich.edu/site/accounts/information/Hynobiidae.html (accessed on April 5, 2005).

"Hynobiidae (Cope, 1859) Asiatic Salamanders." *Livingunderworld.org.* http://www.livingunderworld.org/caudata/families/index.htm# hynobiidae (accessed on April 5, 2005).

ASIATIC GIANT SALAMANDERS
AND HELLBENDERS

Cryptobranchidae

Class: Amphibia

Order: Caudata

Family: Cryptobranchidae

Number of species: 3 species

CHAPTER

phylum

class

subclass

order

monotypic order

suborder

▲ **family**

PHYSICAL CHARACTERISTICS

Asiatic giant salamanders and hellbenders are the largest salamanders, and the largest amphibians. Amphibians (am-FIB-ee-uhns) are vertebrates (VER-teh-brehts), or animals with a backbone, that have moist, smooth skin; are cold-blooded, meaning their body temperature is the same as the temperature of their surroundings; and, in most instances, have a two-stage life cycle. Asiatic giant salamanders and hellbenders are born in the water and spend their entire lives there, never moving to land the way many other amphibians do. There are only three species in this group: Chinese giant salamanders, Japanese giant salamanders, and hellbenders. Asiatic giant salamanders grow to a length of almost 6 feet (1.8 meters) and weigh as much as 50 pounds (23 kilograms). The longest hellbender is about half that length. Asiatic giant salamanders and hellbenders have a broad, flat head and body that makes it easy for them to get under rocks. The tail is flat, too, but from side to side rather than from top to bottom, making it look like an eel's tail.

Asiatic giant salamanders and hellbenders have loose flaps of skin along the sides of their bodies and on the legs. This skin is filled with blood vessels only one cell thick that allow oxygen to pass directly from the water into the salamander's blood. This is how these salamanders breathe. They have lungs and go to the surface sometimes to gulp air but use the lungs mainly for staying stable in the water. The skin of these salamanders also makes lots of slime.

Asiatic giant salamanders and hellbenders have many colors and patterns. They can be gray, brown, greenish brown, yellowish brown, orange-red, or, rarely, white. Some of them have dark blotches or speckles. Japanese giant salamanders and Chinese salamanders have bumps on their heads and throats. The bumps on Japanese giant salamanders are large and separate from one another, but those on Chinese giant salamanders are small and paired.

The legs of Asiatic giant salamanders and hellbenders are thick and strong but short. The eyes are small and do not have eyelids. Hellbenders usually keep one pair of gill openings on each side of their head throughout life, but Asiatic giant salamanders lose these openings during metamorphosis, which can take as long as three years. Gills are organs for obtaining oxygen from water. Metamorphosis (MEH-tuh-MORE-feh-sis) is the process by which some animals change body form before becoming adults. The jaws of Asiatic giant salamanders and hellbenders are very flexible. Bundles of elastic tissue called cartilage (CAR-tih-lej) allow each side of the lower jaw bone to move by itself, so these salamanders can open their mouths very wide to suck in large prey.

GEOGRAPHIC RANGE

Asiatic giant salamanders and hellbenders live in the eastern part of China, the southern part of Japan, and the eastern part of the United States.

HABITAT

Asiatic giant salamanders and hellbenders live in cool streams and rivers with gravel- or rock-covered bottoms. Chinese giant salamanders live in mountain streams, usually at heights less than 5,000 feet (1,500 meters) above sea level. Japanese giant salamanders live at heights less than 2,300 feet (700 meters) above sea level. Hellbenders live below 2,500 feet (750 meters) above sea level.

DIET

Asiatic giant salamanders and hellbenders mainly eat crustaceans and fish. They also eat worms, mollusks, insect larvae, crustaceans, lampreys, fish and fish eggs, frogs and toads and their tadpoles, water-dwelling reptiles, and small mammals as well as the meat of dead animals, their own shed skin and eggs, and one another. Mollusks (MAH-lusks), such as slugs and snails, are animals with a soft, unsegmented body that may or may not have a shell. Larvae (LAR-vee) are animals in an early stage that change form before becoming adults. Crustaceans (krus-TAY-shuns), such as crayfish, are water-dwelling animals that have jointed legs and a hard shell but no backbone.

BEHAVIOR AND REPRODUCTION

Asiatic giant salamanders and hellbenders spend their entire lives in water, rarely coming to the surface. They hunt at night. These salamanders capture prey by quickly opening their flexible jaws and sucking in the prey with a rush of water.

WHAT'S IN A NAME?

People believed the side-to-side movements of hellbenders and the wavy motion of their skin made these animals look like they were experiencing the tortures of hell.

Asiatic giant salamanders and hellbenders breed from August through January, as the days get shorter and the water becomes colder. As the breeding season approaches, these salamanders, especially the males, become more active during the day as they look for places to mate and build nests. They usually choose a place under a rock or log that is protected on the upstream side but has an entrance facing downstream. Tunnels and cracks in the stream or river bank also are good places for hellbender nests.

After finding a good breeding place, a male Asiatic giant salamander or hellbender places himself at the entrance to the nest and lures in or forces in one or more egg-filled females. The male fights a female if she tries to leave before laying her eggs. As the female lays two strings of eggs, the male places himself alongside her. He rocks the lower part of his body and releases sperm over the egg masses. Fertilization (FUR-teh-lih-ZAY-shun), or the joining of egg and sperm to start development, takes place outside the body. The male then guards the eggs and the nest from predators, which include other salamanders in the same species. The larvae are usually 1 to 1.3 inches (2.5 to 3.3 centimeters) long when they hatch. In the wild, Asiatic giant salamanders live more than sixty years, and hellbenders live more than thirty years.

ASIATIC GIANT SALAMANDERS, HELLBENDERS, AND PEOPLE

People have eaten Asiatic giant salamanders and hellbenders for centuries. In parts of Asia these animals were used as medicines and in religious ceremonies and were considered delicacies until they gained protected status. In North America hellbenders have been used for food and fish bait. Asiatic giant salamanders and hellbenders usually are harmless but if attacked can give a severe bite to a finger or hand.

CONSERVATION STATUS

The World Conservation Union (IUCN) lists one species of Asiatic giant salamanders and hellbenders as Critically Endangered and two species as Low Risk/Near Threatened. Critically Endangered means facing extremely high risk of extinction in the wild. Low Risk/Near Threatened means at risk of becoming threatened with extinction in the future.

Much of the habitat of Asiatic giant salamanders and hellbenders has been destroyed or damaged by pollution and by people trying to control the flow of rivers by removing rocks and building dams. Rock removal takes away the salamanders' hiding and breeding places. Dam building forms lakes, which do not have enough fast water flow and are too warm for these salamanders. Habitat also is destroyed by the buildup of silt, which is dirt that is almost like sand. When river or stream banks do not have enough plant life on them to keep the soil in place, as happens when livestock eat all the grass away, when all the trees are cut down, or when farmers do not use good planting practices, the soil is washed from the land into streams and rivers. The silt smothers the eggs of salamanders and other animals and also smothers the invertebrates (in-VER-teh-brehts), or animals without backbones, that they eat.

People may be collecting too many Asiatic giant salamanders and hellbenders. Scientists are successfully breeding Japanese giant salamanders in zoos, and they are trying to figure out how to breed hellbenders, so that these animals can be returned to the wild.

Hellbender (*Cryptobranchus alleganiensis*)

HELLBENDER
Cryptobranchus alleganiensis

Physical characteristics: Most hellbenders are 11 to 20 inches (28 to 51 centimeters) long and weigh 4 to 5 pounds (1.8 to 2.3 kilograms). The record length is 29 inches (74 centimeters). Male hellbenders are smaller than females. Hellbenders have a broad, flat body and head, like those of a catfish. The tail, however, is flat from side to side, looking like an eel's tail, and has a ridge along the top and the bottom to help in steering. Hellbenders are brown or gray, but during the breeding season some of them change from greenish brown or yellowish brown during the day to orange at night. The toes have rough pads that help the salamanders keep their traction on slippery rocks. Other names for hellbenders are devil dogs, water dogs, mud devils, mountain alligators, and walking catfish.

Hellbenders have floppy folds of skin along the sides of their bodies and on their legs. This skin is filled with many tiny blood vessels that absorb oxygen from the water flowing over the salamander.

Hellbenders get about 95 percent of their oxygen this way. They have lungs and can gulp air through them if necessary, but they rarely come to the surface. The lungs are used mainly as internal balloons to help keep the hellbender light enough to walk along the bottom. Hellbenders are very slimy. The slime is made in glands in the skin and tastes bad to predators.

Geographic range: Hellbenders live only in North America. Their range is southern New York south to northeastern Mississippi and west to eastern Missouri and Arkansas. The hellbenders that live in this region are called eastern hellbenders. Other hellbenders live only in south central Missouri and a few rivers in north central Arkansas. These are called Ozark hellbenders.

Habitat: Hellbenders live in clear, fast-moving, rocky streams and rivers less than 2,500 feet (750 meters) above sea level. The riffling movement over rocks keeps the water full of oxygen, and the rocks give the hellbenders places to hide and breed.

Diet: Crayfish are the main prey of hellbenders, but these salamanders also eat insects, snails, fish eggs, and worms. Hellbenders eat by sucking in their prey with a rush of water.

Behavior and reproduction: Hellbenders spend their entire lives in the water. They never make the change to land the way many salamanders do. When they are not breeding, hellbenders live alone. They hide during the day, sometimes with their head sticking out from under a rock. Even though they have an eel-like tail, hellbenders almost never swim. They walk slowly along the river or stream bottom on their short legs. When they are too hot or when there is not enough oxygen in the water, hellbenders rock their bodies from side to side to get more water on their loose flaps of skin.

Hellbenders breed in the late summer to early fall. At breeding time, male hellbenders dig nests under rocks or logs and lure in one or more females. The males sometimes fight one another for the best rocks. Each female lays two strands of 150 to 750 round eggs, which end up in clusters in the nest. Because more than one female may breed with the same male, some nests have almost two thousand eggs, which expand to the size of Ping-Pong balls. The larger a female, the larger are her eggs. The male releases a cloud of sperm over the eggs. Fertilization and development take place outside the body. After they lay their eggs, the male forces the females out of the nest. The males then guard their nests from predators until after the larvae hatch.

Larvae hatch in two to three months, when they are about 1 inch (2.5 centimeters) long. When they start eating small invertebrates, the larvae turn dark brown or black. Newly hatched hellbender larvae have gills that stick up behind their heads. These gills disappear when the larvae are 1.5 to two years old and are 4 to 5 inches (10 to 13 centimeters) long. Over the next five to six years the young hellbenders grow about 0.8 inches (2 centimeters) per year while their heads and bodies flatten. Hellbenders can reproduce when they are about seven years old. Hellbenders live more than thirty years.

Hellbenders and people: Hellbenders are harmless to people. Because they can live only in very clean water, the presence of hellbenders is a sign of good water quality. Some people believe hellbenders interfere with fishing, but they are wrong. Some people try to trap hellbenders to sell as pets, but removing these salamanders from the wild is illegal. In Pennsylvania scientists have found evidence of huge piles of hellbender skeletons that date back ten million years. The scientists believe these fossils are evidence that early people used hellbenders for food and in tribal ceremonies.

Conservation status: The World Conservation Union (IUCN) lists hellbenders as Low Risk/Near Threatened, which means they are at risk of becoming threatened with extinction in the future. The main danger to hellbenders is damage to their habitat through silt buildup, which smothers eggs and the animals the hellbender need for food; loss of trees, which allows silt to wash into the water and removes the shade hellbenders need to keep cool; and pollution of river water by chemicals used on crops and from old mines. Hellbenders absorb the chemicals in polluted water through their skin the same way they absorb oxygen. Some scientists believe too many hellbenders are being collected. They are researching the best conditions for breeding hellbenders so that someday these salamanders can be returned to the wild. ■

FOR MORE INFORMATION

Books:

Bernhard, Emery. *Salamanders.* New York: Holiday House, 1995.

Duellman, William E., and Linda Trueb. *Biology of Amphibians.* Baltimore: Johns Hopkins University Press, 1994.

Gunzi, Christiane. *Amphibians and Reptiles of North America.* San Diego, CA: Thunder Bay, 1995.

Lawlor, Elizabeth P. *Discover Nature in Water and Wetlands.* Mechanicsburg, PA: Stackpole, 2000.

Llamas Ruiz, Andres. *Reptiles and Amphibians: Birth and Growth.* New York: Sterling, 1996.

Petranka, J. W. *Salamanders of the United States and Canada.* Washington, DC: Smithsonian Institution Press, 1998.

Web sites:

Anft, Michael. "Amphibian Assault." *Citypaperonline.* http://www.citypaper .com/special/story.asp?id=6657 (accessed on April 19, 2005).

Flanagan, William P., III. "Taxon Management Account: Hellbender Salamander *Cryptobranchus alleganiensis alleganiensis* (Daudin)." *Caudata.org.* http://www.caudata.org/cig/taxon_management_account .html (accessed on April 18, 2005).

"Hellbender, *Cryptobranchus alleganiensis.*" *Northern Prairie Wildlife Research Center.* http://www.npwrc.usgs.gov/narcam/idguide/crypto .htm (accessed on April 19, 2005).

Herman, J. "Cryptobranchus alleganiensis." *Animal Diversity Web.* http://animaldiversity.ummz.umich.edu/site/accounts/information/ Cryptobranchus_alleganiensis.html (accessed on April 19, 2005).

Heying, H. "Cryptobranchidae." *Animal Diversity Web.* http:// animaldiversity.ummz.umich.edu/site/accounts/information/ Cryptobranchidae.html (accessed on April 19, 2005).

Johnson, Tom R., and Jeff Briggler. "The Hellbender." *Missouri Department of Conservation.* http://www.conservation.state.mo.us/documents/ nathis/herpetol/amphibian/hellbend.pdf (accessed on April 16, 2005).

"What's a Hellbender?" *The Hellbender Homepage.* http://hellbenders .sanwalddesigns.com/whats.html (accessed on April 18, 2005).

PACIFIC GIANT SALAMANDERS
Dicamptodontidae

Class: Amphibia
Order: Caudata
Family: Dicamptodontidae
Number of species: 4 species

phylum
class
subclass
order
monotypic order
suborder
▲ **family**

PHYSICAL CHARACTERISTICS

Pacific giant salamanders are large, strong salamanders that live as larvae for several years. Larvae (LAR-vee) are animals in an early stage that change body form in a process called metamorphosis (MEH-tuh-MORE-feh-sis) before becoming adults. After metamorphosis Pacific giant salamanders live on land. These salamanders are 7 to 14 inches (17 to 35 centimeters) long. There are only four species: the Idaho giant salamander, Cope's giant salamander, the California giant salamander, and the coastal giant salamander.

Pacific giant salamanders have a large head, a stout body, well-developed eyes, and large, thick legs. They have strong jaws and many small but well developed teeth. The tail is short for a salamander tail—about an inch (2.5 centimeters) shorter than the length of the head plus the body. The tail is flat from side to side and has a ridge along the top and the bottom. Adult Pacific giant salamanders are dark brown and often have blotches of different shades of gray. The belly is light brown or yellowish white.

The larvae of Pacific giant salamanders are somewhat flat from back to belly and are dark in color. The short, strong tail is flat from side to side and has a small fin. Larvae that live in small, rapidly flowing streams have short, bushy red gills, but those that live in lakes and large streams have large, filmy gills. Gills are organs for obtaining oxygen from water.

GEOGRAPHIC RANGE

Pacific giant salamanders live in the Pacific Northwest of North America from north of San Francisco, California, to the

northern end of the Olympic Peninsula in Washington and from the southern Cascade Mountains of Oregon in the United States into the coastal mountains of southwestern British Columbia, but not on Vancouver and the neighboring islands, in Canada. Idaho giant salamanders are geographically separated from the other species and live in the mountains of northern Idaho and northwestern Montana, west of the Continental Divide in the United States.

HABITAT

Pacific giant salamanders live in wooded areas that have clear streams for larvae. Most of these salamanders live in coniferous woodlands, or those covered with trees that bear their seeds inside cones. These salamanders do especially well in areas with Douglas firs and redwoods. Adult Pacific giant salamanders live under rocks or logs. The larvae usually live in small, trout-free streams, but larger larvae may live in rivers and small lakes.

DIET

The larvae of Pacific giant salamanders eat the larvae of any bottom-dwelling insects they find, but they also eat other stream-dwelling animals. Because they grow to a large size, the salamander larvae feed on larger prey as well, including small fish and the larvae of mole salamanders. Small adult Pacific giant salamanders eat land-dwelling invertebrates (in-VER-teh-brehts), or animals without backbones, which they catch with their long, fast tongue. As they grow larger, Pacific giant salamanders prey on vertebrates, or animals with backbones, such as slender salamanders, lizards, shrews, mice, and even snakes, which they seize with their strong jaws. Pacific giant salamanders travel to find food and can climb as high as 6.6 feet (2 meters) on tree trunks.

BEHAVIOR AND REPRODUCTION

Adult Pacific giant salamanders are active at night, but sometimes they are found walking by day in dark, moist forests.

Large Pacific giant salamanders can be aggressive, head butting and tail-lashing one another and inflicting severe bites to defend themselves from predators. Adult Pacific giant salamanders bark sharply, but scientists do not know why they make this sound.

Scientists are not sure how Pacific giant salamanders mate. They do know that the males place sacs of sperm on land and that fertilization (FUR-teh-lih-ZAY-shun), the joining of egg and sperm to start development, takes place inside the female's body. The females lay eggs one at a time in groups of eighty or more under large rocks and logs. The fertilized (FUR-teh-lyzed) eggs develop slowly, and hatching does not occur for many weeks. Newly hatched larvae probably do not feed for several weeks. Metamorphosis takes at least two years and sometimes as long as four years. Some Pacific giant salamanders do not go through metamorphosis; they keep the body forms they have as larvae. However, their reproductive organs mature, and they can breed.

PACIFIC GIANT SALAMANDERS AND PEOPLE

Pacific giant salamanders are rarely seen by humans, but the rare encounters are remarkable because the animals are impressively large and do not try to escape unless someone pokes them or tries to pick them up. Sometimes people find adult Pacific giant salamanders on the floors of dense coniferous forests during light rains. At other times the larvae are caught on hook and line by people who are fishing.

CONSERVATION STATUS

The World Conservation Union (IUCN) lists one species of Pacific giant salamanders as Low Risk/Near Threatened, or at risk of becoming threatened with extinction in the future. These salamanders depend on forests and clear, unpolluted streams. This habitat is being harmed by excessive logging, road building and other construction, and the spreading of cities. Salamanders are most abundant in old-growth forests, but they survive after logging as long as the streams remain relatively free of silt.

Coastal giant salamander (*Dicamptodon tenebrosus*)

COASTAL GIANT SALAMANDER
Dicamptodon tenebrosus

Physical characteristics: Adult coastal giant salamanders may be the largest land-dwelling salamanders. The head plus body length is more than 7.5 inches (19 centimeters), and the total length is at least 13 inches (34 centimeters). The largest coastal giant salamanders on record were larvae found in large rivers. These larvae were about 8 inches (20 centimeters) in head plus body length and nearly 14 inches (35 centimeters) in overall length. The color of coastal giant salamanders varies. The background color of larvae usually is dark brown to black. As metamorphosis approaches, a silvery or dull golden color appears over the dark base and produces a marbling effect of light on dark. The marbling varies from fine to coarse. In some cases the marbling is so coarse that the underlying color cannot be seen.

Geographic range: Coastal giant salamanders live in an area that extends from southwestern British Columbia, Canada, southward

A pacific giant salamander is eating a large banana slug. (Photograph by Karl H. Switak. Photo Researchers, Inc.)

west of the crest of the Cascade Mountains to northern California, United States. Some of these salamanders live in isolated areas in north central Oregon, east of the Cascade crest.

Habitat: Coastal giant salamanders live in and near clear, cold, rocky streams.

Diet: Coastal giant salamanders mainly eat frogs and small mammals, but they also eat worms, insects, and spiders.

Behavior and reproduction: Adult coastal giant salamanders are active at night and are secretive, but they sometimes are seen walking through leaves on rainy days in densely forested regions. When approached, these salamanders bark. They are one of the few salamanders that make a sound. Coastal giant salamanders also can be found on rainy nights as they try to cross roads in areas near breeding sites.

Scientists know little about the breeding habits of coastal giant salamanders. Eggs are fertilized inside the female's body, so scientists believe males make a sperm sac that the females pick up. Females lay large numbers of large eggs under large rocks that are at least partially underwater in streams. The eggs take several months to hatch, and scientists believe the females guard their nests while the eggs are developing. After hatching, metamorphosis takes about two years.

Some coastal giant salamanders do not go through metamorphosis, but even though they look like larvae, they can reproduce.

Coastal giant salamanders and people: Coastal giant salamanders are rarely found and are little known to people.

Conservation status: Coastal giant salamanders are not considered threatened or endangered. The greatest risk to these salamanders is destruction of forests and the buildup of silt in streams. ■

FOR MORE INFORMATION

Books:

Bernhard, Emery. *Salamanders.* New York: Holiday House, 1995.

Duellman, William E., and Linda Trueb. *Biology of Amphibians.* Baltimore: Johns Hopkins University Press, 1994.

Gunzi, Christiane. *Amphibians and Reptiles of North America.* San Diego, CA: Thunder Bay, 1995.

Lawlor, Elizabeth P. *Discover Nature in Water and Wetlands.* Mechanicsburg, PA: Stackpole, 2000.

Llamas Ruiz, Andres. *Reptiles and Amphibians: Birth and Growth.* New York: Sterling, 1996.

Petranka, J. W. *Salamanders of the United States and Canada.* Washington, DC: Smithsonian Institution Press, 1998.

Web sites:

"Coastal (Pacific) Giant Salamander, *Dicamptodon tenebrosus.*" *Northern Prairie Wildlife Research Center.* http://www.npwrc.usgs.gov/narcam/idguide/diteneb.htm (accessed on April 21, 2005).

"*Dicamptodon* (Strauch, 1870) Giant Salamanders." *Livingunderworld.org.* http://www.livingunderworld.org/caudata/database/dicamptodontidae/dicamptodon (accessed on April 21, 2005).

Guillermo, G.L. "Pacific Giant Salamander." Colegio Franklin Delano Roosevelt, American School of Lima. http://www.amersol.edu.pe/ms/7th/7block/jungle_research/new_cards/11c/report11c_G.html (accessed on April 21, 2005).

MOLE SALAMANDERS
Ambystomatidae

Class: Amphibia
Order: Caudata
Family: Ambystomatidae
Number of species: 33 species

PHYSICAL CHARACTERISTICS

Mole salamanders are small to large, stocky salamanders that live in water as larvae and on land as adults. Larvae (LAR-vee) are animals in an early stage that change form in a process called metamorphosis (MEH-tuh-MORE-feh-sis) before becoming adults. Mole salamanders are 3.5 to 14 inches (9 to 35 centimeters) long from the tip of the snout to the tip of the tail. They have a broad head, small eyes that stick out from the head, deep grooves along the sides of the body, and a long tail that is flat from side to side. Mole salamanders often have bold patterns as adults. Many species are brightly colored with yellow, orange, or silver spots, bars, and frosted patterns on a black background. Some mole salamanders have large poison glands on the head and along the body. All mole salamanders have lungs after metamorphosis.

Mole salamander larvae live in the water and have filmy gills that stick out behind their heads. Gills are organs for obtaining oxygen from water.

The larvae have a large tail fin that extends onto the body. Their small eyes do not have moveable eyelids. Many species of mole salamanders in Mexico and the United States do not go through metamorphosis; as adults they keep the body form they have as larvae. However, their reproductive organs mature, and they can breed.

GEOGRAPHIC RANGE

Mole salamanders live in North America from southern Canada to just south of Mexico City, Mexico.

phylum
class
subclass
order
monotypic order
suborder
▲ **family**

AXOLOTLS

Axolotls (ACK-suh-lah-tehls) are a species of mole salamanders that never go through metamorphosis and never leave the water. According to Aztec legend a god named Xolotl escaped from his enemies by diving deep into a lake and changing himself into a salamander. Mexico City was later built on that lake.

HABITAT

Mole salamanders live in woodlands and grasslands, including partially dry pine and juniper woodland with vernal pools, ponds, or streams for breeding. A vernal (VUHR-nehl) pool is one that forms in the spring but then dries up for the rest of the year. Species that do not go through metamorphosis live in large lakes, as long as there are no predatory fish around.

DIET

Mole salamanders are predators as both larvae and adults. They eat insects, earthworms, crustaceans, frog tadpoles, and even baby rodents. Crustaceans (krus-TAY-shuns), such as crayfish, are water-dwelling animals that have jointed legs and a hard shell but no backbone.

BEHAVIOR AND REPRODUCTION

Mole salamanders spend most of the year in underground burrows and tunnels made by small mammals and come out only on rainy nights to feed or to travel to breeding sites, where they stay for several weeks. This behavior gives these salamanders their name. Moles are small mammals that spend almost all their time in tunnels searching for insects to eat.

Two key types of behavior of mole salamanders are their defenses from predators and their traveling. Many mole salamanders that have gone through metamorphosis take a head-down position and lash their tails when threatened. Both behaviors show predators parts of the salamander's body that are full of poison glands. Mole salamanders are famous for their travels to breeding ponds. In some species hundreds of salamanders may travel on a single rainy night to a breeding site, giving a spectacular display of salamanders crossing the landscape, including roads. In other species the travels take as long as many weeks rather than one night. In general, males travel before females do and stay for a longer time in the breeding pond.

Most mole salamanders breed in the winter or spring, although mountain salamanders breed in the summer. Land-dwelling adults move into vernal pools, ponds, or, more rarely, streams to breed. Two species mate and lay eggs on land. Males often compete for females. The males deposit bags of sperm on the ground, and females take the bags into their bodies, where sperm and egg unite. One male may deposit more than thirty sperm bags in a single night. Females lay the eggs either one at a time or in large clusters. The eggs attach to the pond bottom or to plants. After hatching, larvae spend several months to several years in the water before going through metamorphosis and starting a land-dwelling lifestyle.

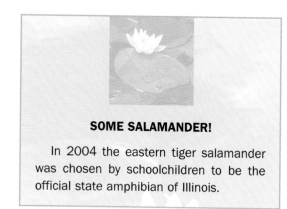

SOME SALAMANDER!

In 2004 the eastern tiger salamander was chosen by schoolchildren to be the official state amphibian of Illinois.

MOLE SALAMANDERS AND PEOPLE

People in Mexico eat mole salamanders. Everywhere they live, mole salamanders give important clues about the health of the environment.

CONSERVATION STATUS

The World Conservation Union (IUCN) lists eight species of mole salamanders as Critically Endangered, two as Endangered, three as Vulnerable, and one as Low Risk/Near Threatened. Critically Endangered means facing extremely high risk of extinction in the wild. Endangered means facing very high risk of extinction in the wild. Vulnerable means facing high risk of extinction in the wild. Low Risk/Near Threatened means at risk of becoming threatened with extinction in the future.

The U.S. Fish and Wildlife Service lists two species of mole salamanders as Endangered and two species as Threatened. Endangered means in danger of extinction throughout all or a significant portion of its range. Threatened means likely to become endangered in the near future.

Large numbers of mole salamanders crossing roads to and from their breeding ponds sometimes are killed by cars. In New York State an underpass was built to help these salamanders. The main dangers to mole salamanders are loss of their land and water habitats, the introduction of predatory fish that eat the salamander larvae, and, possibly, a fungus disease. Mole salamander species that do not go through metamorphosis are especially at risk because they spend their entire lives in a single lake, where introduced fish, pollution, and draining can endanger an entire species.

■ Tiger salamander (*Ambystoma tigrinum*)

TIGER SALAMANDER
Ambystoma tigrinum

Physical characteristics: Tiger salamanders are about 14 inches (35 centimeters) long from the tip of the snout to the tip of the tail, making them the largest land-dwelling salamanders. Tiger salamanders are large, strong salamanders. Adults have many color patterns depending on where they live. The most common pattern is the one that gives them their name: black with bright yellow stripes, spots, or bars. Some tiger salamanders have blurry gold blotches or yellow flecks on a black background. Others are solid olive green, brown, or black. In the central part of the United States and in the Rocky Mountains, some tiger salamanders do not go through metamorphosis.

Geographic range: Tiger salamanders have the widest geographic range of any other salamander in North America. The range extends

A Barred tiger salamander is eating an earthworm. (Photograph by Ken Highfill. Photo Researchers, Inc.)

from southern Canada south roughly to the border between Mexico and the United States.

Habitat: Tiger salamanders live mainly in grasslands in prairie and open, dry woodland, from sea level to a height of more than 11,000 feet (3,350 meters).

Diet: Fearsome predators, tiger salamanders eat just about any animal. As larvae, they eat prey ranging from microscopic plants and animals drifting in the water to tadpoles and even one another. As adults on land, tiger salamanders eat all kinds of invertebrate and small vertebrate prey, including animals almost as large as they are. Invertebrates (in-VER-teh-brehts) are animals without backbones, and vertebrates are animals with backbones.

Behavior and reproduction: Adult tiger salamanders spend almost all of their lives in underground rodent burrows. They come out and travel to breeding ponds during spring rains and sometimes can be found on the surface at night during heavy rains. Tiger salamander larvae are often the top predators in the vernal pools and ponds where they live. To reproduce, male salamanders deposit sperm sacs, and female salamanders take them up into their bodies, where sperm and egg unite. The female then lays the eggs. After hatching, some of the larvae go through metamorphosis, and some do not.

Tiger salamanders and people: In many parts of the United States, tiger salamander larvae are sold as fish bait. Throughout their range tiger salamanders cannot live in the same bodies of water as predatory fish. When people stock these waters with bass, catfish, and other species, tiger salamanders are at risk.

Conservation status: Tiger salamanders are not considered threatened or endangered.   ■

FOR MORE INFORMATION

Books:

Bernhard, Emery. *Salamanders.* New York: Holiday House, 1995.

Bishop, Sherman C. *Handbook of Salamanders: The Salamanders of the United States, of Canada, and of Lower California.* Ithaca, NY: Comstock, 1994.

Duellman, William E., and Linda Trueb. *Biology of Amphibians.* Baltimore: Johns Hopkins University Press, 1994.

Gunzi, Christiane. *Amphibians and Reptiles of North America.* San Diego, CA: Thunder Bay, 1995.

Lawlor, Elizabeth P. *Discover Nature in Water and Wetlands.* Mechanicsburg, PA: Stackpole, 2000.

Llamas Ruiz, Andres. *Reptiles and Amphibians: Birth and Growth.* New York: Sterling, 1996.

Petranka, James W. *Salamanders of the United States and Canada.* Washington, DC: Smithsonian Institution Press, 1998.

Periodicals:

Breisch, Alvin, and Peter K. Ducey. "Woodland and Vernal Pool Salamanders of New York." *New York State Conservationist* (June 2003): 15–18.

Fellman, Bruce. "To Eat or Not to Eat." *National Wildlife* (February-March 1995): 42–45.

Pennisi, Elizabeth. "Kinship Ties Influence Behavior, Morphology." *Science News* (May 1, 1993): 278.

Travis, John. "Starting Over: Some Animals Can Regenerate Limbs or Even Most of Their Bodies." *Science News* (November 1, 1997): 280–282.

Web sites:

"Ambystomatidae (Mole Salamanders)." U. S. Forest Service. http://www
.fs.fed.us/r4/amphibians/family_ambystomatidae.htm (accessed on
April 22, 2005).

Erelli, Mark. "Mole Salamanders." *The Vernal Pool.* http://www.vernalpool
.org/inf_mol.htm (accessed on April 22, 2005).

Heying, H. "Ambystomatidae." *Animal Diversity Web.* http://animaldiversity
.ummz.umich.edu/site/accounts/information/Ambystomatidae.html (accessed on April 22, 2005).

"Tiger Salamander." *BioKIDS.* http://www.biokids.umich.edu/critters/
information/Ambystoma_tigrinum.html (accessed on April 22, 2005).

"Tiger Salamander: *Ambystoma tigrinum.*" *Northern Prairie Wildlife
Research Center.* http://www.npwrc.usgs.gov/narcam/idguide/atigrin
.htm (accessed on April 22, 2005).

NEWTS AND EUROPEAN SALAMANDERS

Salamandridae

Class: Amphibia
Order: Caudata
Family: Salamandridae
Number of species: 59 species

family

phylum
class
subclass
order
monotypic order
suborder
▲ **family**

PHYSICAL CHARACTERISTICS

Newts and European salamanders have long, slender bodies, long tails, sturdy legs, and poisonous skin. Some species have large skin glands that stick out from the head. Newts that have just gone through metamorphosis and begun their life on land are called efts. Metamorphosis (MEH-tuh-MORE-feh-sis) is the process by which some animals change body form before becoming adults. Newts and European salamanders are 3 to 14 inches (7 to 35 centimeters) long. They have four toes on their front legs and four or five toes on their hind legs. These salamanders do not have the grooves on the sides of their body that many other salamanders have. Efts and adults have lungs; larvae have external gills that stick up behind their heads. Larvae (LAR-vee) are animals in an early stage that change body form in metamorphosis. Gills are organs for obtaining oxygen from water. Many newts and European salamanders develop back body and tail fins when they enter the water in the breeding season.

All newts and European salamanders release substances from their skin that are poisonous or bad-tasting to predators. Many of the salamanders that make these poisons are brightly colored. The skin of most species of newts and European salamanders is rough, except during the water-dwelling phase. In the water, the skin becomes smooth, thin, and slimy. In the water, salamanders breathe through their skin, meaning they absorb oxygen directly from the water. In the water-dwelling phase, newts and European salamanders shed their skin frequently. Some newts eat the shed skin.

Because they look for food underwater, newts and European salamanders have eyes that are shaped for seeing prey, and their mouth is shaped for sucking in prey. In the water-dwelling phase, newts have organs in the skin that make up a system called the lateral (LAT-uhr-uhl) line. With these organs the newt feels tiny water currents and thus can detect moving prey, even in the dark and in muddy water.

Some keep the body form of larvae even though they become adults and can reproduce. These adults do not make the move to land and remain in water throughout life.

GEOGRAPHIC RANGE

Newts and European salamanders live in scattered areas across the Northern Hemisphere, including western and eastern North America, Europe, Japan and other areas in Asia, and the northern part of Africa.

HABITAT

Newts and European salamanders live in damp places close to ponds and streams, where breeding takes place. In the land-dwelling phase, newts and European salamanders need damp conditions and live in dense plant cover or in crack in rocks and under logs, where conditions stay moist at the drier times of year. Because the larvae live in water, all newts and European salamanders need water for reproduction. Many of these animals breed in ponds, but some breed in larger lakes and others in mountain streams. Many newts and European salamanders do well in ponds that dry up during the summer, because these ponds cannot support fish, dragonfly larvae, and other water-dwelling animals that prey on newt and salamander larvae.

DIET

Newts and European salamanders eat small invertebrate prey, including insects, earthworms, slugs, and snails. Invertebrates (in-VER-teh-brehts) are animals without backbones. In the water-dwelling phase, newts eat water insects and are fierce predators of frog tadpoles. The larvae of newts and European salamanders eat small invertebrates, such as water fleas.

BEHAVIOR AND REPRODUCTION

Most newts and European salamanders live on land as adults but move to water to breed. Some of these animals stay in the

water for several months around breeding time, but the amount of time spent in the water varies greatly among species and even sometimes within one population of the same species. Newts that lay eggs one at a time have longer breeding seasons and, thus, spend more time in the water, because it takes many weeks for a female to lay all her eggs. Species that lay their eggs in clusters spend little time in the water.

Scientists know little about the behavior of newts and European salamanders during the land-dwelling, because these animals are rarely seen. At least some species, especially eastern newts, have highly developed sensing powers that help them to return to the same breeding ponds each spring. These newts can detect at least one thing in the environment that gives them directional information, such as a smell, the position of the Sun, the pattern of light in the sky, or the direction of the magnetic field of the Earth.

When bothered by predators, some newts raise their heads, chests, and tails to show the bright colors on their bellies. These newts often rock back and forth and release a strong-smelling poison through their skin. The poison of some newts is one of the most powerful natural toxins.

During mating, a male places a sperm bag close to a female and then pushes her over it or uses displays to lure her over it, so that she takes the sperm up into her cloaca, and it is united with eggs inside her body. The cloaca (kloh-AY-kuh) is the chamber in some animals that holds waste from the kidneys and intestines, holds eggs and sperm that are about to be released to the outside, holds sperm entering a female's body, and is the passage through which young are born. The female stores the sperm in special organs in her body until she is ready to lay her eggs. Some females lay single eggs on the leaves of water plants and then wrap the eggs in leaves to hide them from predators such as fish.

Transfer of sperm in a sperm bag has two interesting consequences. First, it is unreliable: In some species, many sperm bags are missed by females. Second, rival males can interfere. For example, in several species rival males mimic female behavior, causing the original males to release sperm bags that are not picked up by females. To make sure this does not happen and to make sure their sperm gets into a female, some males defend females by picking them up and carrying them away if a rival male approaches.

Chemical communication is important in the mating of newts and European salamanders. Males have glands that release scented chemicals that make females receptive to them.

In most species of newts and European salamanders the females lay their fertilized (FUR-teh-lyzed) eggs. The eggs hatch into larvae that live in the water for a while and then go through metamorphosis to become adults. In four species of European salamanders, however, the females keep the fertilized eggs inside their bodies and give birth to large larvae or, in some instances, young salamanders that look like adults but are not ready to reproduce. In these four species only a small number of eggs complete development. In Caucasian salamanders only two fully developed young are born after three or four years inside the female. Fire salamanders, alpine salamanders, and Lanza's alpine salamanders also reproduce this way.

NEWTS, EUROPEAN SALAMANDERS, AND PEOPLE

Because they taste bad and can be poisonous, newts and European salamanders are not eaten by humans. Several species are popular as pets, but they are well known for their ability to escape from all but the most secure tank.

CONSERVATION STATUS

The World Conservation Union (IUCN) lists one species of newts and European salamanders as Extinct, one as Critically Endangered, nine as Endangered, ten as Vulnerable, and eleven as Low Risk/Near Threatened. Extinct means no longer in existence. Critically Endangered means facing extremely high risk of extinction in the wild. Endangered means facing very high risk of extinction in the wild. Vulnerable means facing high risk of extinction in the wild. Low Risk/Near Threatened means at risk of becoming threatened with extinction in the future.

Newts and European salamanders are threatened by loss of habitat as the result of too much cutting of trees, the spread of cities, and poor farming practices. Some of these salamanders can live together with people in areas where farmers use traditional

Even if they don't know much about amphibians, people who do a lot of crossword puzzles know the word "eft." "Young newt" is a common crossword clue.

methods, such as making natural fences out of hedges and digging ponds for livestock. Modern farming methods are dangerous to salamanders. Ponds are filled in, hedges are torn up, and chemical fertilizers as well as the chemicals used to kill insects and weeds also kill salamanders.

Smooth newt (*Triturus vulgaris*)

SMOOTH NEWT
Triturus vulgaris

Physical characteristics: Smooth newts are slender and small, usually less than about 4 inches (11 centimeters) long. The tail makes up about one-half of the total length of the animal. In the land-dwelling phase, smooth newts are brown or dark gray. The skin secretions of smooth newts taste bad to predators, but they are not poisonous, so they provide little protection. Smooth newts are eaten by birds and other animals.

Geographic range: Smooth newts live in Europe.

Habitat: Smooth newts live in woodlands, grasslands, clumps of trees and shrubs, rows of hedges or trees surrounding fields, and yards and gardens. These salamanders breed in small ponds.

During breeding season male and female newts look very different from each other. Males develop a high crest that runs along the back and tail. (Photograph by Adrian Davies. Bruce Coleman, Inc.)

Diet: Smooth newts eat small invertebrates and frog tadpoles.

Behavior and reproduction: Smooth newts return to ponds to breed in early spring and stay in the water for several months. During the breeding season male and female smooth newts look very different from each other. Males develop a high crest that runs along the back and tail. The crest has a jagged edge and, like the rest of the body, is marked with large, dark spots. Stripes of red and blue decorate the lower edge of the male's tail, just behind the greatly swollen, dark cloaca. The toes on the hind limbs of the male develop flaps of skin. These flaps help the male swim fast in pursuit of females.

Female smooth newts lay several hundred eggs during the breeding season. The eggs are laid one at a time, and the female carefully wraps each egg in a folded leaf. The eggs hatch into tiny meat-eating larvae, which grow and go through metamorphosis over the summer months to leave the water in late summer at a length of approximately 0.8 inches (2 centimeters). The young newts spend the next two or three years on land before they return to water to breed as mature adults.

Smooth newts and people: Smooth newts have no known importance to people.

Conservation status: Smooth newts are not considered threatened or endangered. ■

Great crested newt (*Triturus cristatus*)

GREAT CRESTED NEWT
Triturus cristatus

Physical characteristics: Great crested newts get their name from the large, deeply notched crest that runs along the backs of breeding males. The males also have a tail that is thick from top to bottom and is decorated with a bold white stripe. Great crested newts can be as long as 6 inches (16 centimeters). Because of an abnormality in their chromosomes (KROH-muh-sohms), or the parts of a cell that hold the DNA, 50 percent of young great crested newts die before they hatch.

Geographic range: Great crested newts live in Europe.

Habitat: Great crested newts need dense cover during their land-dwelling phase and large, deep ponds for breeding.

Diet: Great crested newts eat small invertebrates, frog tadpoles, and the larvae of other newts.

Behavior and reproduction: Great crested newts live as long as sixteen years. They spend much of their lives on land, and little is known about their habits. When these newts are handled, glands in their skin release a bitter-smelling milky substance that humans and predators, such as water birds and hedgehogs, find highly offensive. The bright orange and black on the belly of great crested newts act as warning colors. Predators associate the color with the bad taste and do not attack the newts.

Adult great crested newts travel to ponds early in the spring. In Sweden they have been observed moving over snow and entering ponds that are still partially covered with ice. Females start the breeding season full of large eggs, but it takes males several weeks to fully develop their thick tails and their back crests. Males that come out of winter hibernation with larger fat reserves develop larger crests, and it is likely they are more attractive to females than are males with small crests.

While in breeding ponds, great crested newts are secretive by day and mate at dusk. A male takes up a position in front of a female and displays to her with rhythmic beats of his tail. The movement sends a chemical released by a large gland in the male's cloaca toward the female's snout. The male also displays his large, white-striped tail, which is bright in the dim light. If the female responds to the displays by moving toward him, the male turns and deposits a sperm bag on the bottom of the pond. The female places herself over it and picks it up with her open cloaca.

Two or three days after mating, female great crested newts begin to lay eggs, which have united with sperm inside them. This process takes many weeks. Great crested newts lay seventy to six hundred eggs, usually 150–200, one at a time, carefully wrapping each egg in the leaf of a water plant. After two to three weeks, the eggs hatch into tiny larvae, which start to feed on water animals such as water fleas. Development and metamorphosis take two to three months, and the young leave the pond in late summer and autumn looking like miniature adults. They grow larger until they are old enough to reproduce. Female newts mate several times during the breeding season, interrupting egg-laying to replenish the supply of sperm.

Great crested newts and people: Great crested newts have no known importance to people.

Conservation status: Great crested newts are not considered threatened or endangered. Their numbers are decreasing, however, as a result of changes in their habitat caused by changes in land use and farming practices. In France, however, the great crested newt is slowly expanding its range. In central France, great crested newts overlap with marbled newts, and mating between the two species is common. In some parts of France, great crested newts seem to be handling new patterns of land use better than marbled newts and are expanding into ponds previously used only by marbled newts, whose numbers are decreasing as a result. ■

European fire salamander (*Salamandra salamandra*)

EUROPEAN FIRE SALAMANDER
Salamandra salamandra

Physical characteristics: European fire salamanders have a variety of colors and skin patterns. Some of these salamanders are black with yellow markings, and some are yellow with black or red or orange spots or stripes. They reach a length of 11 inches (28 centimeters) from tip of snout to tip of tail. Females are slightly larger than males. The legs are short and stout with broad toes, and the tail is tube-shaped and shorter than the body. European fire salamanders have two rows of poison glands along the sides of the body and a cluster of poison glands on each side of the head behind the eyes.

Geographic range: European fire salamanders live in Europe.

Habitat: European fire salamanders live in burrows in deciduous forests and, sometimes, in coniferous forests at heights of 656 to 3,280

feet (200 to 1,000 meters). Coniferous (koh-NIH-fuh-russ) forests are made up of trees that bear their seeds inside cones. Deciduous (dih-SIH-juh-wuhs) forests are made up of trees that lose their leaves during cold or dry seasons.

Diet: European fire salamanders eat worms, insects, insect larvae, and slugs.

Behavior and reproduction: European fire salamanders are active at night. When conditions are damp, these salamanders come out of their burrows to look for food. After metamorphosis European fire salamanders live entirely on land. They defend the ground around their burrows against intrusion by neighbors. The striking color patterns on these salamanders act as warning signs. When attacked, fire salamanders squirt toxin from their skin glands over a great distance.

During mating, which takes place on land, a male European fire salamander grasps a female from below. He stimulates the female with glands on his head, and when the female is ready he deposits a sperm bag. The male then flips his tail to one side so that the female falls onto the sperm bag. The sperm enter the female's body and unite with eggs. Larvae develop inside the eggs, and the female lays the eggs in ponds or streams in batches of twelve to fifty. In a few high-altitude populations, the larvae stay in the female throughout development and are released having the adult body form. During development in the female, larvae may eat smaller siblings. As a result, only a few salamanders in each batch of eggs complete development.

European fire salamanders and people: European fire salamanders have no known importance to people.

Conservation status: European fire salamanders are not considered threatened or endangered. ■

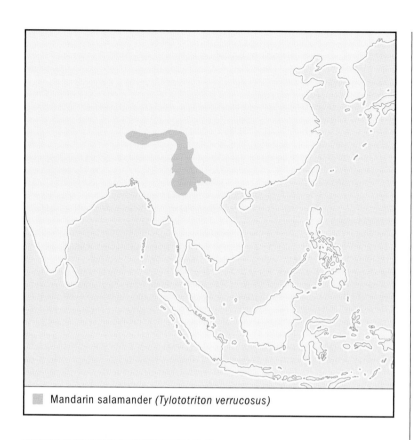

Mandarin salamander (*Tylototriton verrucosus*)

MANDARIN SALAMANDER
Tylototriton verrucosus

Physical characteristics: Mandarin salamanders have a sturdy build. They reach a length of 7 inches (18 centimeters) from tip of snout to tip of tail. These salamanders have a large head with large ridges of skin glands. When mandarin salamanders are in the water-dwelling phase, the tail is long, is flat from side to side, and has a fin. Mandarin salamanders are black or dark brown and are covered with two rows of large brown, orange, or red bumps. These bright colors are a warning sign to predators. Mandarin salamanders release a bad-tasting substance from their skin. The skin has a grainy texture.

Geographic range: Mandarin salamanders live in China, India, Nepal, Thailand, and Vietnam.

Habitat: Mandarin salamanders live in hills and mountains. The natural habitat is damp woodland and forest, but these salamanders also live in habitats made by people, such as rice fields and tea gardens.

Diet: Mandarin salamanders eat small invertebrates.

Behavior and reproduction: Scientists know little about how mandarin salamanders behave. These salamanders live on land for most of their lives and travel to ponds and other water bodies in March or April when the monsoon rains begin. Mating occurs in water. The male clasps the female before transferring his sperm bag. Fertilization takes place inside the female's body. The female lays thirty to sixty eggs in water. Some scientists believe the females guard their eggs. Mandarin salamanders can reproduce when they are three to five years old.

Mandarin salamanders and people: Mandarin salamanders are caught and sold as pets.

Conservation status: Mandarin salamanders are not considered threatened or endangered. ■

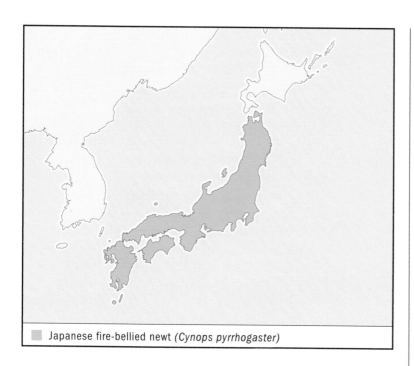

Japanese fire-bellied newt (*Cynops pyrrhogaster*)

JAPANESE FIRE-BELLIED NEWT
Cynops pyrrhogaster

Physical characteristics: Japanese fire-bellied newts reach a length of 5 inches (12 centimeters) from tip of snout to tip of tail. The tail is long and has a large fin that helps the salamanders swim powerfully. The tail of males has a thin string at the tip. Japanese fire-bellied newts have a black back and a bright red, spotted belly that acts as warning. When attacked, these salamanders release poison from their skin, especially from large glands on the head.

Geographic range: Japanese fire-bellied newts live on Honshu, Shikoku, and Kyushu, Japan.

Habitat: Japanese fire-bellied newts live in ponds and pools, their numbers often becoming quite large.

Diet: Japanese fire-bellied newts eat small invertebrates.

Behavior and reproduction: Except for mating practices, scientists do not know how Japanese fire-bellied newts behave. Mating takes

place in water. The males do not grasp the females' bodies but stand in front of the females, sometimes restraining them with one hind foot. In this position a male beats the tip of his tail, producing a current in the water that carries a scented chemical from glands in his swollen cloaca to the female's snout. Fertilization takes place inside the female's body. She lays the eggs in water, and the eggs attach to underwater plants.

Japanese fire-bellied newts and people: Their bright color makes Japanese fire-bellied newts very popular as pets.

Conservation status: Japanese fire-bellied newts are not considered threatened or endangered. ■

Golden-striped salamander (*Chioglossa lusitanica*)

GOLDEN-STRIPED SALAMANDER
Chioglossa lusitanica

Physical characteristics: Golden-striped salamanders reach a length of 6 inches (16 centimeters) from tip of snout to tip of tail. The body and tail are long and thin. The tail makes up about two-thirds of the total length of the animal. Golden-striped salamanders are dark brown and have two golden brown stripes on the back that join to form one stripe on the tail. On some salamanders, the stripes are broken into lines of spots. Golden-striped salamanders have a long, narrow head, large eyes, and a long, sticky tongue for catching prey.

Geographic range: Golden-striped salamanders live in Europe in northern Portugal and the northwestern part of Spain.

Habitat: Golden-striped salamanders live in wet, mountainous areas.

Diet: Golden-striped salamanders eat flies and other insects.

Behavior and reproduction: Golden-striped salamanders are active at night only when it is damp and thus only in areas where there is heavy rainfall. They are dormant underground or in caves during the winter and also are dormant during dry periods in the summer. If attacked, golden-striped salamanders can run quickly. If caught, they can break off their tails. The tail regrows but never reaches its original length. When they are attacked, golden-striped salamanders release a milky poison from their skin.

Golden-striped salamanders spend most of their lives on land but breed in water. Males develop swellings on the upper parts of their front legs during the breeding season. The females lay clumps of as many as twenty eggs in summer or autumn under rocks in springs and streams. The larvae spend the winter in the water.

Golden-striped salamanders and people: Golden-striped salamanders have no known importance to people.

Conservation status: The World Conservation Union (IUCN) lists golden-striped salamanders as Low Risk/Near Threatened because of habitat loss due to land drainage, replacement of natural forest by farms, and pollution from farming chemicals. This means they are at risk of becoming threatened with extinction in the future. ∎

FOR MORE INFORMATION

Books:

Bernhard, Emery. *Salamanders.* New York: Holiday House, 1995.

Duellman, William E., and Linda Trueb. *Biology of Amphibians.* Baltimore: Johns Hopkins University Press, 1994.

Griffiths, R. A. *Newts and Salamanders of Europe.* London: T. & A. D. Poyser, 1996.

Gunzi, Christiane. *Amphibians and Reptiles of North America.* San Diego, CA: Thunder Bay, 1995.

Lawlor, Elizabeth P. *Discover Nature in Water and Wetlands.* Mechanicsburg, PA: Stackpole, 2000.

Llamas Ruiz, Andres. *Reptiles and Amphibians: Birth and Growth.* New York: Sterling, 1996.

Petranka, J. W. *Salamanders of the United States and Canada.* Washington, DC: Smithsonian Institution Press, 1998.

Periodicals:

Breisch, Alvin, and Peter K. Ducey. "Salamanders of New York State." *New York State Conservationist* (April 2003): 15-18.

Horgan, John. "A Nasty Little Squirt: Europe's Fire Salamander Lives Up to Its Legend." *Scientific American* (July 1990): 28.

Nickens, T. Edward. "Herpin' Around: Thought It Just Took a Little Water to Make These Critters Happy?" *American Forests* (Spring 2002): 26–31.

Web sites:

"*Cynops* (Tschudi, 1839) Fire Belly Newts." *Livingunderworld. org.* http://www.livingunderworld.org/caudata/database/salamandridae/cynops (accessed on April 7, 2005).

"Great crested newt (*Triturus cristatus*)." *ARKive.* http://www.arkive.org/species/ARK/amphibians/Triturus_cristatus/more_info.html (accessed on April 7, 2005).

Heying, H. "Salamandridae." *Animal Diversity Web.* http://animaldiversity.ummz.umich.edu/site/accounts/information/Salamandridae.html (accessed on April 7, 2005).

"Newts." *Kids Ark.* http://web.ukonline.co.uk/conker/newts.htm#morenewts (accessed on April 7, 2005).

"Salamandridae (Goldfuss, 1820) Newts and True Salamanders." *Livingunderworld.org.* http://www.livingunderworld.org/caudata/families/#salamandridae (accessed on April 7, 2005).

"Smooth Newt (*Triturus vulgaris*)." *ARKive.* http://www.arkive.org/species/ARK/amphibians/Triturus_vulgaris/more_info.html (accessed on April 7, 2005).

Sydlowski, R. *"Salamandra salamandra." Animal Diversity Web.* http://animaldiversity.ummz.umich.edu/site/accounts/information/Salamandra_salamandra.html (accessed on April 7, 2005).

"Triturus (Rafinesque, 1815), *Mesotriton* (Bolkay, 1927), and *Lissotriton* (Bell, 1839)." *Livingunderworld.org.* http://www.livingunderworld.org/caudata/database/salamandridae/triturus (accessed on April 7, 2005).

Class: Amphibia

Order: Caudata

Family: Proteidae

Number of species: 6 species

family
CHAPTER

phylum

class

subclass

order

monotypic order

suborder

▲ **family**

PHYSICAL CHARACTERISTICS

Olms and mudpuppies are medium-sized to large salamanders with a long, squared-off snout, small legs, and large, bushy, red gills. Gills are organs for obtaining oxygen from water. Most olms are pale and nearly eyeless. Mudpuppies are dark with large spots and have small eyes. Olms and mudpuppies are large for salamanders, more than 16 inches (40 centimeters) from the tip of the snout to the tip of the tail.

Olms and mudpuppies spend their entire lives in water, never making the move to land the way many amphibians do. Amphibians (am-FIB-ee-uhns) are vertebrates (VER-teh-brehts), or animals with a backbone, that have moist, smooth skin; are cold-blooded, meaning their body temperature is the same as the temperature of their surroundings; and, in most instances, have a two-stage life cycle. Olms and mudpuppies have the same body features as adults that they do as larvae. Larvae (LAR-vee) are animals in an early stage that change body form in a process called metamorphosis (MEH-tuh-MORE-feh-sis) before becoming adults. These features include three pairs of large, bushy, red gills; a short tail that is flat from side to side, like an eel's tail; a tail fin; and small eyes.

GEOGRAPHIC RANGE

Olms live in southeastern Europe, and mudpuppies live in eastern North America. The Appalachian Mountains form a wedge separating the coastal waterdogs from the inland mudpuppies. Olms live in the limestone cave systems along the Adriatic Sea from western Slovenia and northeastern Italy in

Mudpuppies are the
most commonly used am-
phibians in college com-
parative anatomy and
physiology classes.

the north to Montenegro in the south. Most of them live in
western Slovenia.

HABITAT

Olms and mudpuppies live in freshwater. Olms live in underground streams and lakes in limestone caves, where it is
always dark and where the water is cold year-round, usually
about 46°F (8°C). These salamanders are thought to group together in deep cracks in the stone. Most sightings and captures
of olms have been in places where they either have been flushed
out by heavy rains or have been hunting for food. Mudpuppies
live in muddy canals; ditches; large, rocky, fast-flowing streams;
reservoirs; and large, cool lakes. Mudpuppies can be found at
all seasons of the year and are even active beneath the ice in
mid-winter.

DIET

Mudpuppies eat fish, fish eggs, crayfish, worms, small mollusks, and water insects, in short, almost anything that moves
and will fit into their mouths. They are especially fond of fish
called sculpins and sometimes can be found gorged with these
fish. Little is known about what olms eat in the wild, except
that they seem to feed on tiny crustaceans, insect larvae, and
other small invertebrates. Olms use chemical sensors to find
prey in total darkness. Mollusks (MAH-lusks) are animals with
a soft, unsegmented body that may or may not have a shell,
such as slugs and snails. Crustaceans (krus-TAY-shuns), such
as crayfish, are water-dwelling animals that have jointed legs
and a hard shell but no backbone.

BEHAVIOR AND REPRODUCTION

Mudpuppies crawl slowly over the bottoms of streams and
lakes, but they can swim rapidly when frightened. In captivity,
mudpuppies are secretive and hide under any available object,
including one another. They appear to be repelled by light. In
water with a low amount of oxygen, mudpuppies constantly
fan their gills, which can become large, bushy, and bright red.
Under such conditions, the mudpuppies often rise to the surface to take gulps of air. In water with plenty of oxygen the
gills tend to be held motionless against the sides of the neck
and eventually shrink. There is some evidence that mudpuppies are capable of homing behavior. Olms are friendly to one
another, at least when they are not breeding, and tend to group

together in deep cracks in the cave walls. Scientists believe olms use chemical sensors to mark and find their home shelters.

Scientists know little about how olms and mudpuppies reproduce. The breeding season for mudpuppies is in the fall or winter, depending on the species and where the animals live. Males that are ready to mate have a swollen cloaca and a pair of enlarged finger-like structures that stick out toward the rear of the body. The cloaca (kloh-AY-kuh) is the chamber in some animals that holds waste from the kidneys and intestines, holds eggs or sperm about to be released to the outside, holds sperm entering a female's body, and is the passage through which young are born.

Breeding in olms does not appear to be related to the seasons, reflecting the stability of their underground habitat. Olms seem to be much more territorial than mudpuppies during breeding. All species for which information is known use some kind of mating ritual in which the males and females stimulate each others' cloacas. The male then releases a bag of sperm, which the female picks up with her cloaca. The female may store sperm in special structures inside her cloaca for six months or more. Fertilization (FUR-teh-lih-ZAY-shun), or the joining of egg and sperm to start development, takes place inside the female's body. When the female lays them, the eggs usually attach to the bottom of an object such as a rock or a log, and the female guards them.

The eggs of olms and mudpuppies hatch two to six months after they are laid, depending on the species and the temperature. The larvae develop gradually into adults without going through metamorphosis. Scientists do not know when mudpuppies are old enough to reproduce, but olms can reproduce when they are seven years old. Scientists believe olms and mudpuppies live nine to sixty years.

OLMS, MUDPUPPIES, AND PEOPLE

Olms and mudpuppies have long been used for scientific studies. Mudpuppies are caught and sold as pets. Olms are a tourist attraction, particularly in Slovenia. Because of their thin skin and dependence on clean water with plenty of oxygen, olms and mudpuppies may be good indicators of water quality.

CONSERVATION STATUS

The World Conservation Union (IUCN) lists one species of olms and mudpuppies as Endangered, one as Vulnerable, and one as Low Risk/Near Threatened. Endangered means facing very high risk of extinction in the wild. Vulnerable means facing high risk of extinction in the wild. Low Risk/Near Threatened means at risk of becoming threatened with extinction in the future.

Olms have been protected in Slovenia since 1949. The main threats to olms are economic development, industrial pollution, and over-collecting. Mudpuppies are threatened by chemical pollution, changes in habitat, and over-collecting.

Olm (*Proteus anguinus*)

OLM
Proteus anguinus

Physical characteristics: Olms are long and thin and have pale, pinkish white skin. The head is flat and narrow, and the eyes are tiny. Three pink gills stick out from each side of the head. The legs are small, and there are only three toes on the front feet and two toes on the rear feet. These features are thought to be adaptations to living in underground waterways. Some olms turn darker when exposed to light. These olms have larger eyes than do olms that never leave their caves. Olms have a squared-off snout and a short tail that is flat from side to side. They reach a length of about 12 inches (30 centimeters) from tip of snout to tip of tail.

Geographic range: Olms live in Europe from the Dinaric Alps of Slovenia and Italy in the north to Montenegro in the south.

Habitat: Olms live in underground lakes and rivers in limestone caves.

Diet: Olms feed at night, using chemical sensors to find small crustaceans and insects and other invertebrates.

Behavior and reproduction: Olms are friendly to one another except during the breeding season, when they defend their territory. Olms are secretive and rarely seen, except when they leave their caves either to feed or because of flooding. Breeding is not related to the seasons. Fertilization takes place inside the female's body after she picks up a sperm bag that has been released by a male. The fertilized (FUR-teh-lyzed) eggs are large and yellowish and are laid under rocks and other cover and guarded by the female. The eggs hatch in about six months. Larvae develop directly into adults without going through metamorphosis. Scientists believe some olms give birth to a pair of well-developed young rather than laying a batch of eggs.

Olms and people: Olms are a tourist attraction. They are popular in the pet trade and are used in scientific research.

Conservation status: The World Conservation Union (IUCN) lists olms as Vulnerable, or facing high risk of extinction in the wild. ■

Mudpuppy (*Necturus maculosus*)

MUDPUPPY
Necturus maculosus

Physical characteristics: Mudpuppies reach a length of 8 to 19 inches (20 to 48 centimeters) from tip of snout to tip of tail. They have small eyes, a short tail, small legs, and a squared-off snout. Mudpuppies have camouflage coloring against the dark bottom of lakes, rivers, and streams. The colors vary from deep rusty brown to gray or even black with scattered black or bluish black spots and blotches. The spots sometimes form two rows along the back. A dark bar extends through the eye to the gills. The belly is paler than the back and may or may not have dark spots. The edges of the tail often are tinged with reddish orange. The colors of mudpuppy larvae can be strikingly different from that of adults.

Mudpuppies have different shapes of gills, depending on their environment. Mudpuppies that live in the fast-moving waters of rivers

Mudpuppies have different shapes of gills, depending on their environment. Mudpuppies that live in the fast-moving waters of rivers and streams have small gills that stay close to the sides of the animal's head. In warm or slow-moving rivers and lakes, the gills are big and bushy. (Photograph by Jack Dermid. Bruce Coleman Inc.)

and streams have small gills that stay close to the sides of the animal's head. In warm or slow-moving rivers and lakes, the gills are big and bushy.

Geographic range: Mudpuppies live in North America in a range that covers essentially the entire Mississippi River drainage system. The range extends from southern Manitoba and Quebec, Canada, in the north to Georgia, Alabama, Mississippi, and Louisiana, United States, in the south.

Habitat: Mudpuppies live in a variety of water habitats, including rivers, streams, canals, and lakes.

Diet: Mudpuppies eat water-dwelling invertebrates and vertebrates, including crayfish and other crustaceans, mollusks, worms, insect larvae, fish, and other amphibians.

Behavior and reproduction: Mudpuppies are active all year and have been seen moving around beneath the ice in mid-winter. Adults are mostly active at night, when they look for food. Mudpuppies hide under rocks and other objects or in burrows during the day. The mating season for mudpuppies is in the autumn or winter, possibly extending into spring, depending on where they live. The fertilized eggs are laid in May or June and attach to the bottoms of large rocks. The female takes care of the eggs and defends them against predators. Hatching takes place in one or two months, depending on the temperature of the water. The newly hatched larvae are approximately

1 inch (2.5 centimeters) long and have two yellow stripes on a dark background. Mudpuppies grow into adults without going through metamorphosis.

Mudpuppies and people: Mudpuppies are collected in large numbers by biological supply companies for use in classrooms and laboratories around the world. They also are caught and sold as pets.

Conservation status: Mudpuppies are not considered threatened or endangered. ■

FOR MORE INFORMATION

Books:

Arnold, E. N., and J. A. Burton. *Field Guide to the Reptiles and Amphibians of Britain and Europe.* 2nd ed. London: HarperCollins Publishers, 1998.

Bernhard, Emery. *Salamanders.* New York: Holiday House, 1995.

Bishop, S. C. *Handbook of Salamanders.* Reprint. Ithaca, NY: Cornell University Press, 1994.

Conant, Roger, and Joseph T. Collins. *A Field Guide to Reptiles and Amphibians, Eastern and Central North America.* New York: Houghton Mifflin, 1991.

Duellman, William E., and Linda Trueb. *Biology of Amphibians.* Baltimore, MD: Johns Hopkins University Press, 1994.

Lawlor, Elizabeth P. *Discover Nature in Water and Wetlands.* Mechanicsburg, PA: Stackpole, 2000.

Llamas Ruiz, Andres. *Reptiles and Amphibians: Birth and Growth.* New York: Sterling, 1996.

Petranka, J. W. *Salamanders of the United States and Canada.* Washington, DC: Smithsonian Institution Press, 1998.

Web sites:

Hawes, Alex. "On Waterdogs, Mudpuppies, and the Occasional Hellbender." *Zoogoer.* http://nationalzoo.si.edu/Publications/ZooGoer/2000/2/waterdogsmudpuppieshellbender.cfm (accessed on April 8, 2005).

Heying, H. "Proteidae." *Animal Diversity Web.* http://animaldiversity.ummz.umich.edu/site/accounts/information/Proteidae.html (accessed on April 8, 2005).

"Mudpuppy and Waterdog." *BioKIDS.* http://www.biokids.umich.edu/critters/information/Necturus_maculosus.html (accessed on April 8, 2005).

"Proteidae (Gray, 1825) Mudpuppies, Waterdogs, and Olms." *Livingunderworld.org.* http://www.livingunderworld.org/caudata/database/proteidae (accessed on April 8, 2005).

Siebert, E. "*Necturus maculosus.*" *Animal Diversity Web.* http://animaldiversity.ummz.umich.edu/site/accounts/information/Necturus_maculosus.html (accessed on April 8, 2005).

TORRENT SALAMANDERS
Rhyacotritonidae

Class: Amphibia
Order: Caudata
Family: Rhyacotritonidae
Number of species: 4 species

PHYSICAL CHARACTERISTICS

Torrent salamanders are small, short-tailed, greenish yellow, large-eyed salamanders. They are 3 to 4.5 inches (8 to 11 centimeters) long with a stocky body, a broad head, eyes that stick out, and a short snout. The legs are small but sturdy. The tail is short, is flat from side to side, and has a small ridge along the top. These salamanders have lungs that do not function.

GEOGRAPHIC RANGE

Torrent salamanders live in the northwestern part of the United States from the Olympic Peninsula in northwestern Washington in the coast ranges to southern Mendocino County in northern California. They live in the Cascade range from the vicinity of Mount Saint Helens, Washington, south to central Oregon.

HABITAT

Torrent salamanders live in densely forested areas near cool water in small, clear, rapidly flowing streams, in rocky areas where water has seeped to the surface, and in cracks in large rocks with thin layers of water cascading over the surface. These habitats almost always are in closed-canopy forests often dominated by coniferous (koh-NIH-fuh-russ) trees, or those that have cones, but some are in river areas dominated by maples and alders, which are deciduous (dih-SIH-juh-wuhs) trees, or those that lose their leaves during cold or dry seasons.

phylum

class

subclass

order

monotypic order

suborder

▲ **family**

WHAT'S IN A NAME?

The scientific name for the torrent salamander family, Rhyacotritonidae, comes from the Greek *rhyakos,* meaning "stream," and Triton, the Greek god of the sea. Despite the common name, a torrent being a violent, rushing stream, these salamanders rarely live in such water, although they may be found nearby.

DIET

Scientists believe torrent salamanders eat insects, especially larvae, and other invertebrates (in-VER-teh-brehts), or animals without backbones. Larvae (LAR-vee) are animals in an early stage that change body form in a process called metamorphosis (MEH-tuh-MORE-feh-sis) before becoming adults.

BEHAVIOR AND REPRODUCTION

Scientists do not know how torrent salamanders behave. These salamanders are secretive and are seldom seen. Fertilization (FUR-teh-lih-ZAY-shun), the joining of egg and sperm to start development, takes place inside the female's body. Large, colorless eggs are laid in cold, clear water under rocks or in cracks. The embryos (EHM-bree-ohs), or young animals in the eggs, develop slowly, as do the larvae, which live for three or four years in the water. The larvae go through metamorphosis when they are close to adult size, but scientists do not know how long it takes the transformed salamanders to mature.

TORRENT SALAMANDERS AND PEOPLE

Torrent salamanders help scientists understand the biological characteristics of the Pacific Northwest region.

CONSERVATION STATUS

The World Conservation Union (IUCN) lists one species of torrent salamanders as Vulnerable and two species as Low Risk/Near Threatened. Vulnerable means facing high risk of extinction in the wild. Low Risk/Near Threatened means at risk of becoming threatened with extinction in the future. Clearing of forests is the greatest risk to torrent salamanders, because it damages their habitat.

Cascade torrent salamander (*Rhyacotriton cascadae*)

CASCADE TORRENT SALAMANDER
Rhyacotriton cascadae

Physical characteristics: Cascade torrent salamanders are 3 to 4.5 inches (7.5 to 11 centimeters) long from tip of snout to tip of tail. The body is stout with a broad head, eyes that stick out, and a relatively short snout. The tail is flat from side to side, has a ridge along the top, and is shorter than the head plus the body. Cascade torrent salamanders usually are rich brown on top and yellowish and sometimes greenish yellow on the belly. The back is marked with darker blotches and speckles. There is a sharp difference between the brown of the back and sides and the yellow of the belly. There are white flecks on the sides above the beginning of the yellow belly. The belly has dark spots, but there are fewer spots than on the back. There are fine gray flecks on the throat and chest. Male Cascade torrent salamanders have swellings on the edges of the belly.

Geographic range: Cascade torrent salamanders live in the United States in the Cascade Mountains. The range extends from near Mount Saint Helens in Washington to central Oregon. These salamanders usually live at a height of less than 2,000 feet (610 meters) above sea level.

Habitat: Cascade torrent salamanders live in streams, usually in heavily forested areas. These salamanders avoid large streams but may be found near them in small, rapidly flowing arms of the streams, where they live under moss-covered rocks, in coarse gravel, in piles of rocks, and in cracks in rocks in areas that are very moist. Water often is flowing through the rocks in thin sheets. Adult Cascade torrent salamanders go onto land but rarely travel more than a few feet (1 meter) from water. The larvae live in the same habitat as adults but stay in the water.

Diet: Scientists believe that Cascade torrent salamanders eat small invertebrates, especially insect larvae and mollusks. Mollusks (MAH-lusks) are animals with a soft, unsegmented body that may or may not have a shell, such as slugs and snails.

Behavior and reproduction: Scientists do not know how Cascade torrent salamanders behave. These salamanders are extremely secretive. They are not seen unless people actively look for them by turning over rocks. Scientists also are not sure how Cascade torrent salamanders reproduce. A related species lays about eight colorless eggs one at a time in cold water flowing through rocks and rock cracks. The eggs probably are slow to hatch in the cold water. Larvae grow slowly, taking three or four years to go through metamorphosis, which they do when they are 1.5 to 1.8 inches (4 to 4.5 centimeters) long.

Cascade torrent salamanders and people: Cascade torrent salamanders have no known importance to people.

Conservation status: The World Conservation Union (IUCN) lists Cascade torrent salamanders as Low Risk/Near Threatened, or at risk of becoming threatened with extinction in the future. The greatest risk to these salamanders is the cutting of forests, which causes the small streams used by these animals to become too hot and to dry up. ■

FOR MORE INFORMATION

Books:

Bernhard, Emery. *Salamanders*. New York: Holiday House, 1995.

Duellman, William E., and Linda Trueb. *Biology of Amphibians*. Baltimore, MD: Johns Hopkins University Press, 1994.

Gunzi, Christiane. *Amphibians and Reptiles of North America*. San Diego, CA: Thunder Bay, 1995.

Lawlor, Elizabeth P. *Discover Nature in Water and Wetlands*. Mechanicsburg, PA: Stackpole, 2000.

Llamas Ruiz, Andres. *Reptiles and Amphibians: Birth and Growth*. New York: Sterling, 1996.

Petranka, J. W. *Salamanders of the United States and Canada*. Washington, DC: Smithsonian Institution Press, 1998.

Web sites:

Heying, H. "Rhyacotritonidae." *Animal Diversity Web*. http://animaldiversity.ummz.umich.edu/site/accounts/information/Rhyacotritonidae.html (accessed on April 8, 2005).

"*Rhyacotriton* (Dunn, 1920) Torrent Salamanders." *Livingunderworld.org*. http://www.livingunderworld.org/caudata/database/rhyacotritonidae/rhyacotriton (accessed on April 8, 2005).

Wallays, Henk. "Observations on Torrent Salamanders (*Rhyacotriton*) in Oregon and California." *Caudata.org*. http://www.caudata.org/cc/articles/Rhyacotriton.shtml (accessed on April 26, 2005).

LUNGLESS SALAMANDERS
Plethodontidae

Class: Amphibia
Order: Caudata
Family: Plethodontidae
Number of species: 346 species

PHYSICAL CHARACTERISTICS

The family of lungless salamanders includes the smallest and nearly the largest land-dwelling salamanders. These salamanders have no lungs and breathe through their skin. They have four toes on their front legs and four or five toes on their rear legs. They have a medium to long tail. Lungless salamanders are 1 to 14 inches (2.5 to 35 centimeters) long. The head is specialized for burrowing and for wedging under rocks and in stream beds. Some lungless salamanders have a long tongue that they can flick rapidly to catch prey. Lungless salamanders that live in caves never have eyes or skin coloring and may have oddly formed limbs and snouts. Other species start life as larvae, but as they go through metamorphosis their eyes disappear, the eyelids fuse together, and their skin loses its color.

Some lungless salamanders live as water-dwelling larvae for a few months to three years. Larvae (LAR-vee) are animals in an early stage that change body form in a process called metamorphosis (MEH-tuh-MORE-feh-sis) before becoming adults. Some species do not go through metamorphosis and spend their entire lives with the body form of larvae, but they can reproduce. At least three species never live as larvae and hatch from their eggs looking like small adults.

Scientists have found large numbers of miniature salamanders, mainly in the family of lungless salamanders. Most of these miniature species live on land throughout their lives, and many are secretive. New species continue to be discovered at a high rate. Many of these species are less than 1.2 to 1.4 inches (3 to 3.5 centimeters) long from tip of snout to tip of tail.

GEOGRAPHIC RANGE

Lungless salamanders live in southern Canada, much of the United States, and Mexico except the north-central parts of these countries. They also live in Central America and central South America. Most of the species live in the eastern and central parts of the United States. Six species live in the middle western Mediterranean region of Europe.

HABITAT

Lungless salamanders live in forest, woodlands, streams, springs, and caves. They thrive in wooded mountain areas. Some species live in deserts that receive fewer than 10 inches (25 centimeters) of rainfall each year. Others live in rainforests. Many species live in trees all or part of the time.

WHERE DID THE LUNGS GO?

Lunglessness is thought to have evolved as an adaptation for life in flowing water. Larvae are small, and lungs would tend to act as air sacs that might make the salamander float in the water. This would dislodge them from their food source and threaten their survival. Water in a stream is constantly being mixed with air, and salamanders can breathe through their skin, so there is little natural selection for keeping lungs.

DIET

Lungless salamanders eat small crustaceans and insects but sometimes eat worms. Larger species sometimes eat smaller species. Lungless salamanders capture prey with an explosive flicking of their tongue. Crustaceans (krus-TAY-shuns), such as crayfish, are water-dwelling animals that have jointed legs and a hard shell but no backbone.

BEHAVIOR AND REPRODUCTION

Lungless salamanders commonly live close together in large numbers and typically are the most numerous vertebrates (VER-teh-brehts), or animals with backbones, in a region. Lungless salamanders are secretive by day and active by night. They have small home ranges. The only ones that make seasonal travels are the few species that breed in water. Lungless salamanders that live in streams are more active than land-dwelling species, but most species can move quickly when disturbed, and they are good at escaping capture. The land-dwelling species, especially the tropical species, rely more on stealth than speed to avoid detection and capture and do not move as quickly as water-dwelling species. Some lungless salamanders are aggressive and fight to defend their territory.

All lungless salamanders have complex mating behavior, and mating can take many hours. More than half of the species are strictly land-dwelling and lay large eggs that they hide in spaces under rocks or logs, in moss mats, in balls of moss hanging in plants, in trees, and in plants that grow in trees. The eggs of these species hatch weeks after being laid, and the young look like small adults. Some species of lungless salamanders lay eggs in or near shallow water, typically moving water, and the eggs hatch into water-dwelling larvae that take a few months to three years to go through metamorphosis. A few species live their entire lives as larvae.

LUNGLESS SALAMANDERS AND PEOPLE

Lungless salamanders are not often seen by people.

CONSERVATION STATUS

The World Conservation Union (IUCN) lists one species of lungless salamanders as Extinct, thirty-one as Critically Endangered, eighty-three as Endangered, fifty-four as Vulnerable, and thirty-six as Low Risk/Near Threatened. Extinct means no longer in existence. Critically Endangered means facing extremely high risk of extinction in the wild. Endangered means facing very high risk of extinction in the wild. Vulnerable means facing high risk of extinction in the wild. Low Risk/Near Threatened means at risk of becoming threatened with extinction in the future.

The U.S. Fish and Wildlife Service lists four species of lungless salamanders as Endangered and three species as Threatened. Endangered means in danger of extinction throughout all or a significant portion of its range. Threatened means likely to become endangered in the near future.

Dusky salamander (*Desmognathus fuscus*)

DUSKY SALAMANDER
Desmognathus fuscus

Physical characteristics: Dusky salamanders are about 5.5 inches (14 centimeters) long from tip of snout to tip of tail. They have short legs and a stocky build. The hind legs are much larger than the front legs. The head is wedge shaped and has large eyes that bulge out. The jaw and neck muscles are thick. The tail has a low fin and ends in a sharp point. The tail grows back if it is pulled off by a predator, but it grows back with a blunt end rather than a sharp tip. Dusky salamanders usually are darker on the back than on the belly, which is cream colored. The back is mottled gray and black, striped with various shades of tan to yellowish brown to brown. A black stripe extends from the eye diagonally back to the angle of the jaw.

Dusky salamanders lay the eggs in clusters of five to thirty in moist, hidden places in seepage pools on rocks or at the edges of springs and small streams. The female guards the eggs until they hatch in about forty-five days. (© E. R. Degginger/Photo Researchers, Inc.)

Geographic range: Dusky salamanders live in Quebec and New Brunswick in eastern Canada. Their range extends south and west as far as Indiana and South Carolina in the United States.

Habitat: Dusky salamander larvae live in springs, in small streams, and in water that has seeped up through the ground and collected in a pool. Adults spend some time on land but spend most of their time in seeped-up water or on the sides of springs and small streams, where they live among rocks or under logs.

Diet: Dusky salamander larvae mainly eat small invertebrates (in-VER-teh-brehts), or animals without backbones, such as the larvae of water-dwelling insects. They also eat tiny crustaceans and clams. Adults eat land-dwelling prey, mainly small insects and crustaceans, but they feed on water-dwelling insects when in the water. Larger dusky salamanders eat larger prey, but they continue to eat small prey. These salamanders sometimes eat one another, especially the larvae of others in their species. Adults capture their prey by rapidly flicking their tongues and snapping their jaws.

Behavior and reproduction: Dusky salamanders are active animals. They move very fast and are hard to catch. Most of their normal activity takes place in the early evening, but when conditions are warm and moist, these salamanders may be active throughout the night. By day dusky salamanders typically stay under cover. Dusky salamanders defend themselves from predators by remaining motionless or by biting.

Dusky salamanders mate on land. The male lures the female by rubbing her head with his body, waving his front legs, and placing himself alongside her and snapping backward. He approaches the female and positions her head at the base of his tail. He then walks forward, moving his tail back and forth while the female follows. The male releases a sperm bag, and the female takes it into her body. The female stores the sperm inside her. The eggs are fertilized when the female is ready to lay them in middle to late summer. She lays the eggs in clusters of five to thirty in moist, hidden places in seepage pools on rocks or at the edges of springs and small streams. The female guards the eggs until they hatch in about forty-five days. When the larvae hatch, they still have plenty of nutrients from the egg and do not feed immediately. Larvae grow slowly in the fall and winter but rapidly in the spring and go through metamorphosis in about nine months.

Dusky salamanders and people: Dusky salamanders have no known importance to people.

Conservation status: Dusky salamanders are not considered threatened or endangered. They are one of the most common salamanders in eastern North America. These salamanders adapt well to changes in their habitat as long as there are enough small streams. ■

Arboreal salamander *(Aneides lugubris)*

ARBOREAL SALAMANDER
Aneides lugubris

Physical characteristics: Arboreal (ar-BOR-ee-ul) salamanders have a heavily muscled head and body; a long, grasping tail; and long, grasping toes. The toes also have widened, somewhat curved tips. Arboreal salamanders are a little longer than 7 inches (18 centimeters) from tip of snout to tip of tail. Their large eyes bulge from the head in front of large jaw muscles. The head is nearly triangular. The upper and lower jaws have large, saber-like teeth with curved tips that can cause a serious wound. These salamanders are grayish brown to brown with yellow spots and a lighter belly. The spots can be small and scattered or large and close together.

Geographic range: Arboreal salamanders live mainly in California, United States, in the coastal mountains and valleys from the northwestern part of the state to the extreme north-western part of Baja California Norte, Mexico. Some of these salamanders live on off-shore islands in the Pacific Ocean. Scattered groups live in the foothills of the Sierra Nevada.

Habitat: Arboreal salamanders live mainly in oak woodlands, where they use holes in the trees for nesting sites and for escape from dry conditions. These salamanders also live in sycamore wood-lands near creeks in the southern parts of their range. Arboreal salamanders are commonly found under the bark of fallen oak logs, under rocks, and in holes in the ground.

Diet: Despite their large jaws and teeth, arboreal salamanders mainly eat small insects and crustaceans. Sometimes they eat slender salamanders.

Despite their large jaws and teeth, arboreal salamanders mainly eat small insects and crustaceans. (Illustration by Gillian Harris. Reproduced by permission.)

Behavior and reproduction: Arboreal salamanders are aggressive. Both males and females have large jaw muscles and teeth that they use in fights over territory and against predators. These salamanders are good climbers, but most of their activity takes place on the ground.

Arboreal salamanders spend their entire lives on land. They do not enter water to breed. The females lay grape-like clusters of large eggs that are suspended from the roofs of underground holes, in large de-caying logs, or in trees. The eggs hatch three to four months after they are laid, just before the fall rains. Young salamanders that look like small adults emerge from the eggs.

Arboreal salamanders and people: Arboreal salamanders have no known importance to people.

Conservation status: Arboreal salamanders are not considered threatened or endangered. ■

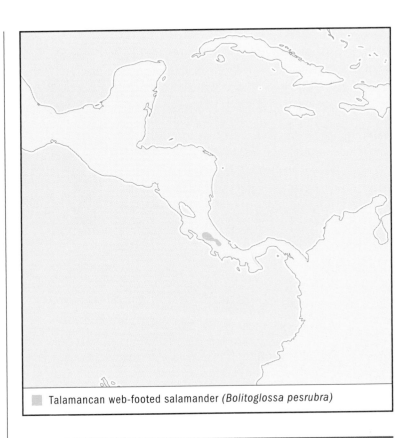

Talamancan web-footed salamander (*Bolitoglossa pesrubra*)

TALAMANCAN WEB-FOOTED SALAMANDER
Bolitoglossa pesrubra

Physical characteristics: Talamancan (tah-lah-MAHNG-kahn) web-footed salamanders are stocky salamanders that reach a length of about 4 inches (11 centimeters) from tip of snout to tip of tail. The tail is about half of the total length. The toes are webbed, meaning there is skin between them, although the tips of the toes stick out beyond the webbing. Most of these salamanders are dark brown with a gray or black blotched or marbled pattern, but some of them are solid brown. The belly is dark gray but is lighter than the back. The throat is much lighter than the back and often has a slight yellow color. The legs are usually dark red or reddish orange.

Geographic range: Talamancan web-footed salamanders live in the Cordillera de Talamanca in central and eastern Costa Rica, generally at heights of 7,500 feet (2,300 meters) above sea level.

Habitat: Talamancan web-footed salamanders live under the bark of logs and under leaf litter in oak forests, but they also have survived in many areas where habitats have been destroyed. Large numbers of these salamanders have been found in local rubbish heaps. Talamancan web-footed salamanders also live in plants that grow in trees, in moss mats on trees, and by the sides of roads. These salamanders once were common at very high elevations, about 10,000 feet (3,050 meters), even in completely open areas, where they were found under rocks, slabs of concrete, and other objects, but in more recent years few have been found.

Diet: Talamancan web-footed salamanders eat small insects, which they catch with a very fast tongue that they flick with great accuracy.

Behavior and reproduction: Talamancan web-footed salamanders hunt and mate at night. Other than that, scientists know little about their behavior. When these salamanders hatch, they look like small adults. They do not hatch as larvae that have to change form before becoming adults. The females lay eggs all year in clusters of thirteen to thirty-eight eggs. The eggs are large and take a very long time to develop, partly because of the cool temperature of their mountain habitat. Females guard the eggs until they hatch.

Talamancan web-footed salamanders and people: Talamancan web-footed salamanders are the best known of the many tropical salamanders because they have been observed by generations of students in classes organized by the Organization for Tropical Studies, a group of scientists from all over the world that has three research stations in Costa Rica. These salamanders once were thought to be extremely tolerant of human activities and thrived even along heavily used roads, but they have disappeared from much of their range. Talamancan web-footed salamanders are still found in deep forests.

Conservation status: The IUCN lists Talamancan web-footed salamanders as Endangered, or facing very high risk of extinction in the wild. ■

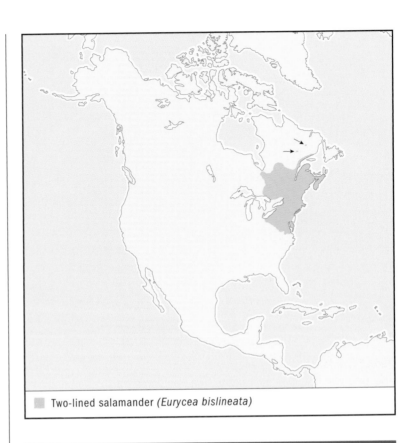

■ Two-lined salamander (*Eurycea bislineata*)

TWO-LINED SALAMANDER
Eurycea bislineata

Physical characteristics: Two-lined salamanders are small, thin salamanders with long, tapered tails. The eyes bulge out from the head. The color of these salamanders ranges from greenish yellow to yellow or orangish brown. Broad bands extend from behind the eyes along the trunk to near the tip of the tail. This band is marked with dark brown or black spots. On each side of the dark brown band is a brown or black stripe that extends from the eye well onto the tail. The sides of the salamanders are light with dark spots, and the belly is bright yellow with scattered dark spots. These salamanders are 5 to 5.5 inches (13 to 14 centimeters) long from tip of snout to tip of tail.

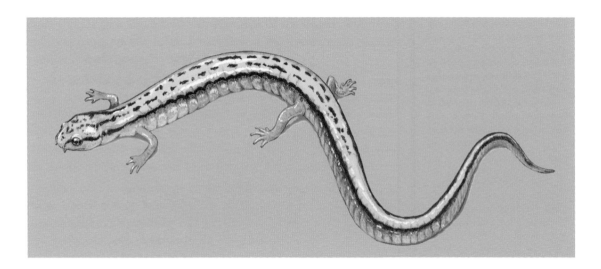

Geographic range: The geographic range of two-lined salamanders extends from northeastern Canada through the northeastern part of the United States to Ohio, West Virginia, and Virginia.

Habitat: The larvae of most two-lined salamanders live in small springs and water that has seeped up through the ground and collected in a pool. They sometimes live in ponds, where they live on the bottom. Young salamanders that have recently gone through metamorphosis and adults usually stay near streams in forested areas but move out into the forest, sometimes quite far from the water. As adults some two-lined salamanders stay on land for much of the year.

Diet: Larvae of two-lined salamanders eat the larvae of small water-dwelling insects but also eat small crustaceans. Adults feed mainly on small insects but also eat snails.

Behavior and reproduction: Two-lined salamanders look for food in the forest at night. Some scientists believe these salamanders guard their territory. Scientists believe two-lined salamanders mate on land and that females store sperm until it is time to lay the eggs. The fertilized eggs are laid one at a time under rocks in small streams. The females form nests but do not guard them. Nests can contain more than one hundred eggs, but there are usually about fifty eggs in a nest. Eggs take as long as ten weeks to hatch. After hatching, most two-lined salamanders live as larvae for about two years before metamorphosis is complete. Two-lined salamanders in the southern parts of the range are larvae for about one year.

These salamanders are 5 to 5.5 inches (13 to 14 centimeters) long from tip of snout to tip of tail. (Illustration by Gillian Harris. Reproduced by permission.)

Two-lined salamanders and people: Two-lined salamanders have no known importance to people.

Conservation status: Two-lined salamanders are not considered threatened or endangered. ■

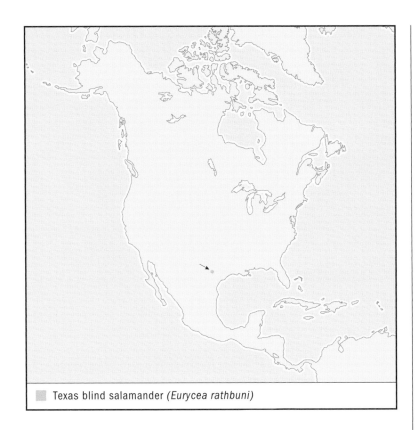

Texas blind salamander (*Eurycea rathbuni*)

TEXAS BLIND SALAMANDER
Eurycea rathbuni

Physical characteristics: Texas blind salamanders have no eyes. They have red, feathery gills and a shiny white body with long, extremely thin legs. Gills are organs for obtaining oxygen from water. These salamanders reach a length of about 5 to 5.5 inches (13 to 14 centimeters) from tip of snout to tip of tail. The head is large and flat and has a broad, blunt snout.

Geographic range: Texas blind salamanders live only in a small area on the edge of the Edwards Plateau, near San Marcos in south-central Texas, United States.

Habitat: Texas blind salamanders live only underground in streams and pools in sinkholes and caves. A sinkhole is an area where the

land over an underground river has collapsed and formed the entrance to a cave.

Diet: Texas blind salamanders eat snails and tiny crustaceans such as water fleas and cave shrimp.

Behavior and reproduction: Scientists know little about the behavior of Texas blind salamanders. These animals have been seen swimming in the water of caves and using their long limbs to grab and cling to the rocky cave walls. Scientists do not know how Texas blind salamanders reproduce.

Texas blind salamanders and people: Texas blind salamanders have no known importance to people.

Conservation status: The IUCN lists Texas blind salamanders as Vulnerable, or facing high risk of extinction in the wild. These salamanders were one of the first species named to the United States federal endangered species list. They become threatened when people remove the water from their habitat and by pollution from the land above the caves. ■

Bell's salamander (*Pseudoeurycea bellii*)

BELL'S SALAMANDER
Pseudoeurycea bellii

Physical characteristics: Bell's salamanders are the largest lungless salamanders and almost the largest land-dwelling salamanders. They reach a length of nearly 14 inches (36 centimeters) from tip of snout to tip of tail. Bell's salamanders are shiny dark black and have a pair of red to reddish orange spots on the back of the head and paired rows of red to reddish orange spots along the back. There is usually a V-shaped mark at the beginning of the paired rows of spots. The tail is large and long. The legs are long and sturdy.

Geographic range: Bell's salamanders live in northern and central Mexico, usually at heights greater than 4,000 feet (1,220 meters) above sea level.

Bell's salamanders are the largest lungless salamanders and almost the largest land-dwelling salamanders. (Illustration by Gillian Harris. Reproduced by permission.)

Habitat: Bell's salamanders live only on land under large surface objects such as logs and rocks in moist woods. They use burrows in the ground and can be found in holes in the sloping mounds of earth that line roadbeds in some areas.

Diet: Scientists believe Bell's salamanders eat insects, which they catch with a flick of their long, fast tongue.

Behavior and reproduction: Bell's salamanders are active at night. The females lay batches of more than twenty large eggs. Other than that scientists do not know how these salamanders behave or reproduce.

Bell's salamanders and people: Bell's salamanders have no known importance to people.

Conservation status: The IUCN lists Bell's salamanders as Vulnerable or facing high risk of extinction in the wild. ■

FOR MORE INFORMATION

Books:

Bernhard, Emery. *Salamanders.* New York: Holiday House, 1995.

Griffiths, R. A. *Newts and Salamanders of Europe.* San Diego: Academic Press, 1996.

Gunzi, Christiane. *Amphibians and Reptiles of North America.* San Diego, CA: Thunder Bay, 1995.

Lawlor, Elizabeth P. *Discover Nature in Water and Wetlands.* Mechanicsburg, PA: Stackpole, 2000.

Llamas Ruiz, Andres. *Reptiles and Amphibians: Birth and Growth.* New York: Sterling, 1996.

Petranka, J. W. *Salamanders of the United States and Canada.* Washington, DC: Smithsonian Institution Press, 1998.

Periodicals:

Cohn, Jeffrey P. "Meet the Salamander." *Americas (English Edition)* (November-December 1993): 3.

Web sites:

"*Aneides lugubris*: Arboreal Salamander." *San Diego Natural History Museum.* http://www.sdnhm.org/fieldguide/herps/anei-lug.html (accessed on April 11, 2005).

"Arboreal Salamander, *Aneides lugubris.*" *Northern Prairie Wildlife Research Center.* http://www.npwrc.usgs.gov/narcam/idguide/aneidelu.htm (accessed on April 11, 2005).

Bartholomew, P. "*Aneides lugubris.*" *Animal Diversity Web.* http://animaldiversity.ummz.umich.edu/site/accounts/information/Aneides_lugubris.html (accessed on April 11, 2005).

Heying, H. "Plethodontidae." *Animal Diversity Web.* http://animaldiversity.ummz.umich.edu/site/accounts/information/Plethodontidae.html (accessed on April 11, 2005).

Munger, M. "*Eurycea rathbuni.*" *Animal Diversity Web.* http://animaldiversity.ummz.umich.edu/site/accounts/information/Eurycea_rathbuni.html (accessed on April 11, 2005).

"Northern Two-lined Salamander: *Eurycea bislineata.*" *Northern Prairie Wildlife Research Center.* http://www.npwrc.usgs.gov/narcam/idguide/eurybis.htm (accessed on April 11, 2005).

Vanwormer, E. "*Eurycea bislineata.*" *Animal Diversity Web.* http://animaldiversity.ummz.umich.edu/site/accounts/information/Eurycea_bislineata.html (accessed on April 11, 2005).

phylum

class

subclass

order

monotypic order

suborder

▲ **family**

PHYSICAL CHARACTERISTICS

Amphiumas (AM-fee-YOO-muhs) are very long, medium-sized to very large salamanders that look like snakes with four very short legs. These animals are dark reddish brown to gray or black on top. The belly is a lighter shade than the back or almost as dark. Adult amphiumas reach a length of 13 to 46 inches (33 to 117 centimeters), depending on the species. The legs usually are less than 0.4 inch (1 centimeter) long, and there are one to three toes on each foot.

Amphiumas have a pointed head, but the snout is somewhat flattened in two species. There are teeth on the jaw bones. Amphiumas have no eyelids and have one gill slit on each side of the body. Gills are organs for obtaining oxygen from water. Unlike the bushy, outside gills of other salamanders, the gills of amphiumas are inside their bodies, just behind the head. Gill slits are openings from the gills to the outside of the body. Gill arches support the gills inside the body.

Adult amphiumas have glands in their skin that ooze out slippery mucus. An amphiuma's tail is flat from side to side and makes up 20 to 25 percent of the total body length. A lateral (LAT-uhr-uhl) line, a system of organs that help some animals sense movement in the water, is present on the body and head of amphiumas. The bodies of these animals have fifty-seven to sixty grooves along the sides, each of which indicates a vertebra (VER-teh-bruh), or one of the bones that make up the spinal column. The vertebrae (VER-teh-bree, the plural of vertebra) are curved in on each end like the inside of a bowl. A few vertebrae near the front of amphiumas have ribs connected to them.

Amphiumas are the longest and largest salamanders in the United States. Even though local people call amphiumas congo eels, lamper eels, ditch eels, lampreys, and congo snakes, these salamanders are amphibians, not fish like eels and lampreys and not reptiles like snakes. Amphibians (am-FIB-ee-uhns) are vertebrates (VER-teh-brehts), or animals with a backbone, that have moist, smooth skin; are cold-blooded, meaning their body temperature is the same as the temperature of their surroundings; and, in most instances, have a two-stage life cycle.

Amphiumas that have gone through metamorphosis keep some features of larvae: a lack of eyelids and tongue and the presence of four gill arches with a single opening to the outside between the third and fourth arches rather than a slit for each gill. Larvae (LAR-vee) are animals in an early stage that change body form in a process called metamorphosis (MEH-tuh-MORE-feh-sis) before becoming adults. Amphiumas have lungs, but they also can breath through their throat and skin. When young amphiumas hatch, they keep their gills for a few days. Hatchlings are a little more than 2 inches (5 centimeters) long. Amphiumas that have just gone through metamorphosis may be as short as 2.5 inches (6 centimeters). Adults reach a length of 46 inches (117 centimeters).

GEOGRAPHIC RANGE

Amphiumas live in an area that extends from southeastern Virginia southward along the coastal plain and throughout Florida, westward along the coastal plain and from southwestern Alabama and all of Mississippi and Louisiana to the easternmost part of Texas and most southeastern part of Oklahoma northward to the extreme southeastern portion of Missouri.

HABITAT

Amphiumas live in swamps, marshes, ditches, lakes, and sluggish streams. One species lives in watery muck. Amphiumas can be quite common in cities, where they live in waterways such as ditches and canals. Amphiumas may hide among water plants, but they prefer crayfish holes. In rainy weather amphiumas may crawl around on wet surfaces.

DIET

Amphiumas eat worms, water insects and their larvae, frogs, salamanders, fish, and any other small vertebrates. A favorite prey is crayfish.

In Florida, amphiuma nests have been found in the nest mounds of alligators.

BEHAVIOR AND REPRODUCTION

Amphiumas are active at night and are most active when water temperatures are higher than 41°F (5°C). These salamanders wait in holes for passing prey, or they prowl in search of prey. The strong teeth and powerful bite are used to subdue prey animals. Amphiumas are eaten by snakes and large wading birds.

If a ditch or pond goes dry, amphiumas hide in holes where they lie dormant. Amphiumas have been dug from holes as deep as 3.3 feet (1 meter). Amphiumas live about twenty-seven years and can go as long as three years without food. Amphiumas periodically shed their skin and sometimes eat it. This behavior helps them stay nourished during dry spells. Amphiumas move with a side-to-side wavy motion. They are sensitive to vibrations that they detect with their lateral line system. Amphiumas out of water sometimes make a whistling sound.

Adult male amphiumas may fight during the mating season, and many have scars to show for it. During the breeding season, the cloaca of male amphiumas swells. The cloaca (kloh-AY-kuh) is the chamber in some animals that holds waste from the kidneys and intestines, holds eggs or sperm about to be released to the outside, holds sperm entering a female's body, and is the passage through which young are born. Male amphiumas make sperm from October to May. A male amphiuma courts a female by rubbing his snout against her. The female then rubs her nose along the male's body and coils her body under his, so that his cloaca is joined to hers. The male produces a sperm sac, and the female picks it up with her cloaca.

Fertilization (FUR-teh-lih-ZAY-shun), the joining of egg and sperm to start development, takes place inside the female's body. The female makes a nest in a moist place, usually under a log, leaves, or other cover. The female lays the eggs in beady strings of fifty to two hundred eggs, but there may be as many as 354 eggs in a chain. The female coils around and guards the eggs. It may take as long as six months for the eggs to hatch. The eggs and their jelly-like outer layers are approximately 0.4 inch (1 centimeter) in diameter in large species. Female amphiumas reproduce every two years.

AMPHIUMAS AND PEOPLE

Amphiuma meat is edible and tastes much like frogs' legs, but few people eat the meat, because the skin is difficult to strip from it. Amphiuma cells, especially the red blood cells, are the largest known cells in vertebrates, and they have long been used in physiological studies and in classrooms. The chromosomes of amphiumas also are very large and useful for study. Amphiumas are captured with dip nets, seines, minnow traps, electroshock equipment, and by hand. The skin is so slippery that cotton gloves must be used to maintain a hold on the animal long enough to place it in a container. Care in handling is recommended, because the bite can be painful.

CONSERVATION STATUS

The World Conservation Union (IUCN) lists one species of amphiumas as Low Risk/Near Threatened, or at risk of becoming threatened with extinction in the future. Although human activity has destroyed much of the habitat of amphiumas, it also has increased habitat through the building of ponds, ditches, canals, lagoons, and lakes. Amphiumas can survive in waters with fish, and they may be major predators in some waters.

Three-toed amphiuma (*Amphiuma tridactylum*)

THREE-TOED AMPHIUMA
Amphiuma tridactylum

Physical characteristics: Three-toed amphiumas have three toes on each foot. Hatchlings are 1.5 to 2.5 (4 to 6 centimeters) long from tip of snout to tip of tail. Young three-toed amphiumas that have recently finished metamorphosis are about 2.5 inches (6 centimeters) long. Adults can be as long as 40 inches (103 centimeters). The back is dark brown to black, and the belly is a lighter shade of the same color. The throat has a dark patch on it.

Geographic range: Three-toed amphiumas live in an area that extends from eastern Texas to southeastern Oklahoma, southeastern Missouri, and southwestern Alabama.

Habitat: Three-toed amphiumas live in swamps, lakes, ditches, and sluggish streams.

Diet: Three-toed amphiumas mainly eat crayfish, but they also eat other water animals.

Behavior and reproduction: Three-toed amphiumas are active at night. Although they usually stay in a small area, some of these salamanders have been known to move as far as 1,300 feet (400 meters) from their main spot.

A male three-toed amphiuma courts a female by rubbing his snout against her. The female then rubs her nose along the male's body and coils her body under his, so that his cloaca is joined to hers. The male produces a sperm sac, and the female picks up the sperm with her cloaca for fertilization inside her body. The female every two years lays 42 to 150 eggs at a time in burrows. Larger females lay larger numbers of eggs. The eggs hatch about five months after being laid. Three-toed amphiumas reach adulthood in three to four years.

Three-toed amphiumas and people: Three-toed amphiumas are edible but are rarely eaten. These salamanders are used for classroom study. Scientists have found several new species of flatworms and tapeworms in three-toed amphiumas.

Conservation status: Three-toed amphiumas are not considered threatened or endangered. ■

FOR MORE INFORMATION

Books:

Bernhard, Emery. *Salamanders.* New York: Holiday House, 1995.

Duellman, William E., and Linda Trueb. *Biology of Amphibians.* Baltimore, MD: Johns Hopkins University Press, 1994.

Lawlor, Elizabeth P. *Discover Nature in Water and Wetlands.* Mechanicsburg, PA: Stackpole, 2000.

Llamas Ruiz, Andres. *Reptiles and Amphibians: Birth and Growth.* New York: Sterling, 1996.

Petranka, J. W. *Salamanders of the United States and Canada.* Washington, DC: Smithsonian Institution Press, 1998.

Web sites:

"Amphiumidae (Gray, 1825) Amphiuma/Congo Snakes." *Livingunderworld .org.* http://www.livingunderworld.org/caudata/database/amphiumidae (accessed on April 11, 2005).

Heying, H. "Amphiumidae." *Animal Diversity Web.* http://animaldiversity .ummz.umich.edu/site/accounts/information/Amphiumidae.html (accessed on April 11, 2005).

"Three-Toed Amphiuma." *Smithsonian National Zoological Park.* http:// nationalzoo.si.edu/Animals/ReptilesAmphibians/Facts/FacSheets/ Threetoedamphiuma.cfm (accessed on April 11, 2005).

order

CHAPTER

PHYSICAL CHARACTERISTICS

Caecilians (sih-SILL-yuhns) are long, legless amphibians with a dual-action jaw. Some have tails, but most do not. Amphibians (am-FIB-ee-uhns) are vertebrates (VER-teh-brehts), or animals with a backbone, that have moist, smooth skin; are cold-blooded, meaning their body temperature is the same as the temperature of their surroundings; and, in most instances, have a two-stage life cycle. Some species of caecilians are land dwellers, and some are water dwellers.

The most striking feature of caecilians is a series of rings that make these amphibians look like earthworms. The rings run the length of the body starting just behind the head. The rings are inside the body and attached to the vertebrae (VER-teh-bree), or the bones that make up the spinal column. Some caecilians have one ring per vertebra (VER-teh-bruh, the singular of vertebrae); some have two rings, especially toward the rear of the animal; and some have three. The skin is folded over the rings, making grooves between the rings. In some species the grooves go all the way around the body, and in some they only go part of the way around. The second and third sets of rings make shallower grooves than the main set. The species with three rings per vertebra have a short tail, and the tail also has rings. Some species of caecilians have scales just under their skin.

Between the nostrils and the eyes on each side of the head, caecilians have a tentacle that is pumped out and in as needed. The tentacles are sense organs that respond to chemicals and touch. Inside each tentacle is a fluid-filled channel that runs

phylum

class

subclass

● **order**

monotypic order

suborder

family

IT'S ALL IN THE JAW

All vertebrates except caecilians have a single pair of muscles used for closing their jaws. These muscles pull up on the lower jaws. Caecilians have this mechanism of jaw closure, but they also have a second mechanism in which another pair of muscles assists in closing the jaws. The second muscle pulls down on part of the lower jaw, causing the forward, toothed portion of the lower jaw to close by rotating upward. The action is much like that of a seesaw.

from the tip of the tentacle to a chamber that opens into the part of the brain that controls the sense of smell. There is a hole in the skull through which the tentacle pumps out and in. This hole can be anywhere between the eyes and the nostrils. Scientists use the location of the hole to tell different species of caecilians apart.

The eyes of caecilians are small and covered by skin or, in some species, bone. The eyes of many species have lost some or all of their muscles, and some have lost the lens and have only a small retina and optic nerve. Even with the lack of eye parts, most caecilians can distinguish light and dark.

Caecilians have a somewhat flat head with nostrils at the tip of the snout and a large mouth. In some caecilian species the lower jaw is the same length as the upper jaw, and the mouth opens at the front of the animal's head. In other species, the lower jaw is shorter than the upper jaw, a feature that improves burrowing ability. The mouths of these species open on the bottom of the animal's head. Caecilians have two rows of teeth on the upper jaw and one or two rows on the lower jaw. The tops of the teeth have different shapes among species, but all teeth are hinged and usually curve backward, apparently to prevent the loss of prey the animals have caught.

The skin of caecilians has glands that release a substance that is poisonous to many predators. Most caecilians are dark gray to grayish brown to deep purple, often with a lighter head and belly. Some caecilians, however, are brightly colored. For example, a species on the African island of São Tomé is bright yellow. A South American species is deep bluish purple with bright white grooves between its rings. Some species are dark gray to grayish brown to brownish black with bright yellow side stripes. Most adult caecilians are 12 to 24 inches (30 to 60 centimeters) long, but some species are much smaller or larger. The smallest adult caecilians are about 4.5 inches (11 centimeters) long. The largest are more than 63 inches (160 centimeters) long.

GEOGRAPHIC RANGE

In the Western Hemisphere, caecilians live in an area that extends from central Mexico through Peru, Bolivia, Paraguay, and northern Argentina. The water-dwelling or partially water-dwelling species live mainly in the regions of the Orinoco and Amazon rivers, but some live in an area that extends from Colombia to northern Argentina and Uruguay. In the Eastern Hemisphere caecilians live in eastern and western Africa except the Sahara, in the Seychelles, India, Sri Lanka, Southern China, Cambodia, Laos, Vietnam, and much of Malaysia to the southern Philippines. Caecilians do not live in Madagascar, much of central Africa, or Australia.

LOOKS AREN'T EVERYTHING

Caecilians look like giant earthworms with a big mouth, but unlike earthworms, caecilians are vertebrates, which means they have backbones. In addition, caecilians don't just look like earthworms; they eat them!

HABITAT

Some caecilians live in moist soil that is rich in decayed plant matter. They also live in leaf litter and sometimes even in the lower parts of plants. Other caecilians live in water all or most of the time.

DIET

Caecilians are meat eaters. Land-dwelling species prey on animals that they can reach on the ground, including earthworms; termites; insects, such as crickets, that have shed their outer layer; and many other invertebrates (in-VER-teh-brehts), or animals without backbones. Large caecilians have been known to eat lizards and baby rodents. The water-dwelling species nose about at the water's bottom to find food, or they scrape food from logs and rocks. They eat water insects, shrimp, and small fish.

BEHAVIOR AND REPRODUCTION

Caecilians are excellent burrowers in the ground or in leaves. They pump their tentacles in and out while they are moving in order to investigate their surroundings. Caecilians sometimes twist their bodies rapidly when subduing prey that they have grasped with their mouths. Scientists do not know how water-dwelling and partially water-dwelling caecilians behave because these animals live in dark, cloudy water and are hard to observe.

Some caecilians lay eggs that hatch into free-living larvae that have small gills and tail fins. Larvae (LAR-vee) are animals in an early stage that change body form in a process called metamorphosis (MEH-tuh-MORE-feh-sis) before becoming adults. Gills are organs for obtaining oxygen from water. Scientists believe the eggs are laid in burrows or under grass or leaf litter on land. The female guards the eggs until the newly hatched larvae wriggle into nearby streams, where they live until metamorphosis. After metamorphosis the caecilians again become land dwellers. Other caecilians go through metamorphosis while inside the eggs, so they hatch with the body form of adults.

While inside the female, some species of caecilians have fetal (FEE-tehl) teeth that are different from adult teeth. The developing young use the teeth to chew a nutrient liquid made by the inner lining of the egg tubes inside the mother and to stimulate production of this liquid. The fetal teeth are shed at or near birth.

CAECILIANS AND PEOPLE

Caecilians eat insects that are harmful to people. The burrowing movements of land-dwelling caecilians turn soil and thus keep it in good condition.

CONSERVATION STATUS

The World Conservation Union (IUCN) lists one species of caecilians as Endangered and three species as Vulnerable. Endangered means facing very high risk of extinction in the wild. Vulnerable means facing high risk of extinction in the wild.

FOR MORE INFORMATION

Books:

Duellman, William E., and Linda Trueb. *Biology of Amphibians.* Baltimore, MD: Johns Hopkins University Press, 1994.

Lamar, William W. *The World's Most Spectacular Reptiles and Amphibians.* Tampa, FL: World, 1997.

Lawlor, Elizabeth P. *Discover Nature in Water and Wetlands.* Mechanicsburg, PA: Stackpole, 2000.

Llamas Ruiz, Andres. *Reptiles and Amphibians: Birth and Growth.* New York: Sterling, 1996.

Petranka, J. W. *Salamanders of the United States and Canada.* Washington, DC: Smithsonian Institution Press, 1998.

Web sites:

"Caecilian." *Animal Bytes.* http://www.sandiegozoo.org/animalbytes/t-caecilian.html (accessed on April 11, 2005).

Hawes, Alex. "On Waterdogs, Mudpuppies, and the Occasional Hellbender." *Zoogoer.* http://nationalzoo.si.edu/Publications/ZooGoer/2000/2/waterdogsmudpuppieshellbender.cfm (accessed on April 11, 2005).

Summers, Adam. "Squeeze Play." *Natural History.* http://biomechanics.bio.uci.edu/_html/nh_biomech/caecilian/caecilian.htm (accessed on April 11, 2005).

AMERICAN TAILED CAECILIANS
Rhinatrematidae

Class: Amphibia
Order: Gymnophiona
Family: Rhinatrematidae
Number of species: 9 species

phylum

class

subclass

order

monotypic order

suborder

▲ family

PHYSICAL CHARACTERISTICS

American tailed caecilians (sih-SILL-yuhns) are medium-sized caecilians with a true, but short, tail. There are a few vertebrae (VER-teh-bree), or the bones that make up the spinal column, behind the cloaca, and these are considered a true tail. The cloaca (kloh-AY-kuh) is the chamber in some animals that holds waste from the kidneys and intestines, holds eggs or sperm about to be released to the outside, holds sperm entering a female's body, and is the passage through which young are born.

Caecilians look like earthworms. A series of rings runs the length of the body starting just behind the head. The rings are inside the body and attached to the vertebrae. American tailed caecilians have three rings per vertebra (VER-teh-bruh, the singular of vertebrae). The skin is folded over the rings, making grooves between the rings. The second and third sets of rings make shallower grooves than the main set.

The mouth of American tailed caecilians opens at the front of the head, and the upper and lower jaws are the same length. The jaws have a dual-action mechanism, like a seesaw. The tentacle openings in these caecilians are next to their eyes. American tailed caecilians are either purplish gray or gray with yellowish stripes along the sides of the body. Adult American tailed caecilians are 8 to 13 inches (20 to 33 centimeters) long.

GEOGRAPHIC RANGE

American tailed caecilians live in northern South America, including parts of Brazil, Colombia, Ecuador, French Guiana, Guyana, Peru, Surinam, and Venezuela.

HABITAT

American tailed caecilians live in tropical rainforests in moist spots full of leaf litter, rotten logs, and burrows in the soil. The larvae live mainly in streams. Larvae (LAR-vee) are animals in an early stage that change body form in a process called metamorphosis (MEH-tuh-MORE-feh-sis) before becoming adults.

DIET

Scientists are not sure what American tailed caecilians eat. They have found large amounts of soil in the intestines of these animals, which is evidence that they eat earthworms. Undigested earthworms and the remains of insects also have been found inside caecilians.

BEHAVIOR AND REPRODUCTION

American tailed caecilians burrow in soil and leaf litter. They sometimes twist their bodies rapidly when subduing prey they have grasped in their mouths. Scientists do not know how American tailed caecilians reproduce. They believe that most species lay eggs and that the females coil around the eggs to protect them. Larvae of one species have been found.

AMERICAN TAILED CAECILIANS AND PEOPLE

American tailed caecilians have no known importance to people.

CONSERVATION STATUS

American tailed caecilians are not considered threatened or endangered. Although not threatened according to the World Conservation Union (IUCN), caecilians are rarely found. Scientists are not sure whether this is because these animals are rare or because they are highly secretive and difficult to find.

Marbled caecilian (*Epicrionops marmoratus*)

MARBLED CAECILIAN
Epicrionops marmoratus

Physical characteristics: Marbled caecilians reach a length of about 12 inches (30 centimeters). They have a stocky build, and the tail is about 1 inch (2.5 centimeters) long. The back is dark purple with scattered yellowish blotches. The sides and belly are yellow with scattered dark purple spots.

Geographic range: Marbled caecilians live on the Pacific slope of Ecuador.

Habitat: Marbled caecilians live in rainforests. They also live along streams in areas that have been cleared of trees.

Diet: Marbled caecilians probably eat earthworms and small insects and crustaceans. Crustaceans (krus-TAY-shuns), such as crayfish, are water-dwelling animals that have jointed legs and a hard shell but no backbone.

Behavior and reproduction: In captivity marbled caecilians dig their own burrows in moist soil. They find earthworms and crickets by scent and lunge forward to grasp them in their jaws. To eat larger earthworms, which struggle when caught, marbled caecilians grasp the worm in their mouth and then rapidly spin around to break the worm in half. The caecilian then swallows the grasped part of the worm. Crocodiles and alligators use the same method to subdue and rip apart their prey.

Scientists are not sure how marbled caecilians reproduce. Larvae of this species have been found in leaf litter and stone rubble on the bottoms of small streams. This finding is evidence that marbled caecilians are an egg-laying species.

Marbled caecilians and people: Marbled caecilians have no known importance to people.

Conservation status: Marbled caecilians are not considered threatened or endangered. ■

FOR MORE INFORMATION

Books:

Lamar, William W. *The World's Most Spectacular Reptiles and Amphibians.* Tampa, FL: World, 1997.

Lawlor, Elizabeth P. *Discover Nature in Water and Wetlands.* Mechanicsburg, PA: Stackpole, 2000.

Llamas Ruiz, Andres. *Reptiles and Amphibians: Birth and Growth.* New York: Sterling, 1996.

Petranka, J. W. *Salamanders of the United States and Canada.* Washington, DC: Smithsonian Institution Press, 1998.

Web sites:

"Caecilian." *Animal Bytes.* http://www.sandiegozoo.org/animalbytes/t-caecilian.html (accessed on April 11, 2005).

Hawes, Alex. "On Waterdogs, Mudpuppies, and the Occasional Hellbender." *Zoogoer.* http://nationalzoo.si.edu/Publications/ZooGoer/2000/2/waterdogsmudpuppieshellbender.cfm (accessed on April 11, 2005).

Summers, Adam. "Squeeze Play." *Natural History.* http://biomechanics.bio.uci.edu/_html/nh_biomech/caecilian/caecilian.htm (accessed on April 11, 2005).

Class: Amphibia

Order: Gymnophiona

Family: Ichthyophiidae

Number of species: 39 species

family
CHAPTER

PHYSICAL CHARACTERISTICS

Asian tailed caecilians (sih-SILL-yuhns) are medium-sized to large caecilians that have a true tail. The mouth opens at the bottom of the head because the upper jaw is longer than the lower jaw. The jaw has a dual-action mechanism like a seesaw. The tentacle openings in Asian tailed caecilians are in front of the eyes, usually no more than halfway to the nostrils.

Caecilians look like earthworms. A series of rings runs the length of the body starting just behind the head. The rings are inside the body and attached to the vertebrae (VER-teh-bree), or the bones that make up the spinal column. Asian tailed caecilians have three rings per vertebra (VER-teh-bruh, the singular of vertebrae). Some species have as many as 420 rings. The skin is folded over the rings, making grooves between the rings. In Asian tailed caecilians the grooves go all the way around the body. The second and third sets of rings make shallower grooves than the main set. Asian tailed caecilians have a large number of scales under the skin in all the ring grooves.

Asian tailed caecilians are either solid purplish gray or purplish gray with paler stripes of the same color. Adult Asian tailed caecilians are 7 to 22 inches (18 to 56 centimeters) long from tip of snout to tip of tail.

GEOGRAPHIC RANGE

Asian tailed caecilians live in India, Sri Lanka, the Philippines, southern China, Thailand, Myanmar, Laos, Vietnam, Indonesia, and the Malay Archipelago west of Wallace's line.

phylum

class

subclass

order

monotypic order

suborder

▲ **family**

HABITAT

Asian tailed caecilians live in leaf litter and soil in tropical rainforests. Many species do well, however, in areas that have been cleared of trees for farming.

DIET

Little is known about the feeding habits of Asian tailed caecilians. Scientists have opened up these animals and found large amounts of soil, which is evidence that an animal eats earthworms. The scientists also have found partially digested earthworms and pieces of insects inside caecilians. In captivity Asian tailed caecilians are fed earthworms, crickets, and even strips of beef, fish, and chicken.

BEHAVIOR AND REPRODUCTION

Asian tailed caecilians are burrowers. Newly hatched larvae are attracted to light. Larvae (LAR-vee) are animals in an early stage that change body form in a process called metamorphosis (MEH-tuh-MORE-feh-sis) before becoming adults. In captivity adults leave their burrows at night and crawl on the surface. In their natural habitats Asian tailed caecilians have been found on the surface at night during heavy rains.

At mating time, male Asian tailed caecilians place sperm directly inside a female's cloaca. The cloaca (kloh-AY-kuh) is the chamber in some animals that holds waste from the kidneys and intestines, holds eggs or sperm about to be released to the outside, holds sperm entering a female's body, and is the passage through which young are born. Fertilization (FUR-teh-lih-ZAY-shun), or the joining of egg and sperm to start development, takes place inside the female's body. The female then lays large white eggs strung together by jelly strands. The female takes care of the eggs in hidden nests until hatching.

Upon hatching, the larvae of Asian tailed caecilians leave the nest and wriggle to a stream, where they spend an unknown amount of time feeding on small water animals until they transform into young that look like small adults but are not yet able to reproduce. At this point, Asian tailed caecilians leave the stream and take up a land-based, burrowing lifestyle.

ASIAN TAILED CAECILIANS AND PEOPLE

Asian tailed caecilians have no known importance to people.

CONSERVATION STATUS

The World Conservation Union (IUCN) lists two species of Asian tailed caecilians as Vulnerable, or facing high risk of extinction in the wild.

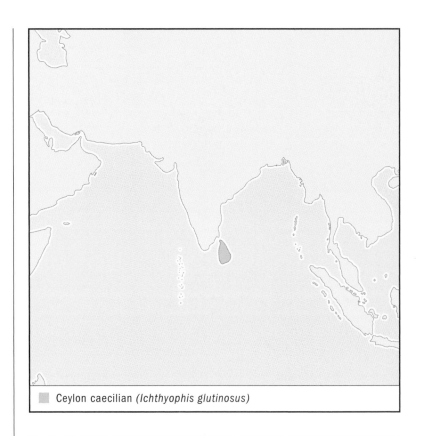

Ceylon caecilian (*Ichthyophis glutinosus*)

CEYLON CAECILIAN
Ichthyophis glutinosus

Physical characteristics: Ceylon caecilians are medium-sized to large caecilians that reach a length of 9 to 16 inches (23 to 41 centimeters). Adults have 342 to 392 rings along the body. The tentacle openings are closer to the eyes than to the nostrils and are close to the sides of the mouth. These caecilians are purplish gray with yellowish cream stripes on the sides.

Geographic range: Ceylon caecilians live in Sri Lanka.

Habitat: Most Ceylon caecilians have been found in areas that were once rainforests but have been converted to farmland. These animals were found in piles of rotting plant matter and manure and in loose, wet soil. One caecilian was dug up from the soil of a moist meadow.

Diet: Newly transformed and adult Ceylon caecilians mainly eat earthworms but also eat other small invertebrates (in-VER-teh-brehts), or animals without backbones, that they find in the leaf litter and soil. Scientists do not know what the larvae eat in the wild, but in captivity they eat small bloodworms and earthworms.

Behavior and reproduction: When it grasps its earthworm prey, a Ceylon caecilian moves backward into its burrow while vigorously twisting its head and neck to subdue the worm. Sometimes the caecilian spins its body to break the earthworm into smaller, more manageable pieces.

Scientists know little about how Ceylon caecilians mate. The females lay twenty-five to thirty-eight large white eggs in jelly strings then place them in hidden nests in the soil. They then coil around the eggs until they hatch. The newly hatched larvae are 3 to 4.5 inches (8 to 11 centimeters) long. The larvae go through metamorphosis after about 280 days.

Ceylon caecilians and people: Ceylon caecilians have no known importance to people.

Conservation status: Ceylon caecilians are not considered threatened or endangered. ■

FOR MORE INFORMATION

Books:

Duellman, William E., and Linda Trueb. *Biology of Amphibians.* Baltimore, MD: Johns Hopkins University Press, 1994.

Lamar, William W. *The World's Most Spectacular Reptiles and Amphibians.* Tampa, FL: World, 1997.

Lawlor, Elizabeth P. *Discover Nature in Water and Wetlands.* Mechanicsburg, PA: Stackpole, 2000.

Llamas Ruiz, Andres. *Reptiles and Amphibians: Birth and Growth.* New York: Sterling, 1996.

Petranka, J. W. *Salamanders of the United States and Canada.* Washington, DC: Smithsonian Institution Press, 1998.

Web sites:

"Caecilian." *Animal Bytes.* http://www.sandiegozoo.org/animalbytes/ t-caecilian.html (accessed on April 11, 2005).

Hawes, Alex. "On Waterdogs, Mudpuppies, and the Occasional Hellbender." *Zoogoer.* http://nationalzoo.si.edu/Publications/ZooGoer/2000/2/ waterdogsmudpuppieshellbender.cfm (accessed on April 11, 2005).

Summers, Adam. "Squeeze Play." *Natural History.* http://biomechanics .bio.uci.edu/_html/nh_biomech/caecilian/caecilian.htm (accessed on April 11, 2005).

KERALA CAECILIANS
Uraeotyphylidae

Class: Amphibia

Order: Gymnophiona

Family: Uraeotyphylidae

Number of species: 5 species

phylum

class

subclass

order

monotypic order

suborder

▲ **family**

PHYSICAL CHARACTERISTICS

Kerala caecilians (sih-SILL-yuhns) are small to medium-sized caecilians. Their upper jaw is much longer than the lower jaw, so the mouth opens on the bottom of the head. This type of jaw makes the animals good burrowers. Red caecilians have a short tail and small eyes. The tentacle openings are far forward of the eye, below the nostrils.

Caecilians look like earthworms. A series of rings runs the length of the body starting just behind the head. The rings are inside the body and attached to the vertebrae (VER-teh-bree), or the bones that make up the spinal column. Kerala caecilians have two rings per vertebra (VER-teh-bruh, the singular of vertebrae). The skin is folded over the rings, making grooves between the rings. The grooves of Kerala caecilians do not go all the way around the body. The second set of rings makes shallower grooves than the main set. Kerala caecilians have a large number of scales under the skin of the grooves.

Kerala caecilians are either nearly solid dark gray or dark gray with a whitish to yellowish cream belly. Newly transformed young Kerala caecilians and adults are 6 to 12 inches (14.5 to 30 centimeters) long.

GEOGRAPHIC RANGE

Kerala caecilians live in the Western Ghats, which are mountains in Kerala State, which is in southern India.

HABITAT

Kerala caecilians live in moist soil and leaf litter in rainforests and areas that have been cleared of trees within the rainforest region. These animals usually are found in moist soil near streams, marshes, and other bodies of water.

DIET

Kerala caecilians eat earthworms and insects.

BEHAVIOR AND REPRODUCTION

Kerala caecilians dig burrows. Other than that, scientists do not know how Kerala caecilians behave or reproduce. They believe these caecilians are egg layers and that they hatch looking like small adults rather than as larvae. Larvae (LAR-vee) are animals in an early stage that change body form in a process called metamorphosis (MEH-tuh-MORE-feh-sis) before becoming adults. However, larvae of at least one species, red caecilians, have been found, which suggests that the other species also may have larvae.

KERALA CAECILIANS AND PEOPLE

Kerala caecilians have no known importance to people.

CONSERVATION STATUS

Kerala caecilians are not considered threatened or endangered.

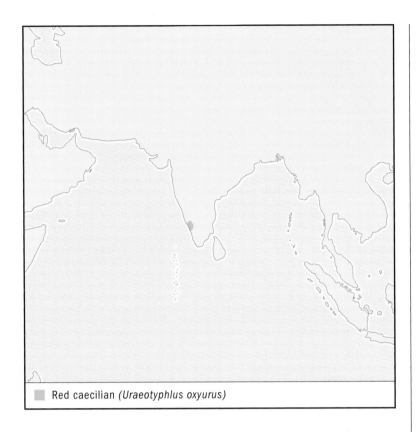

Red caecilian (*Uraeotyphlus oxyurus*)

RED CAECILIAN
Uraeotyphlus oxyurus

Physical characteristics: Red caecilians have a somewhat thick body and are 7 to 12 inches (18 to 30 centimeters) long. They are solid dark bluish gray and slightly paler on the belly. Red caecilians have 98 to 107 rings in the main set and 89 to 104 rings in the second set. They have a large number of scales in the ring folds.

Geographic range: Red caecilians live in Kerala, India.

Habitat: Red caecilians live in moist soil and forest floor litter in and near rainforests.

Diet: Scientists believe red caecilians eat earthworms and insects.

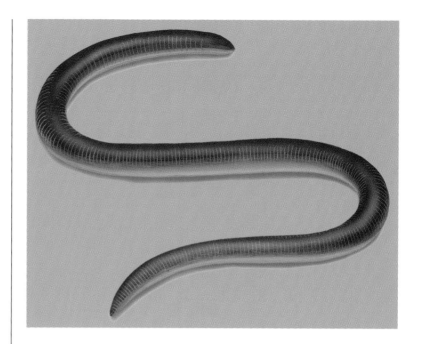

Kerala caecilians live in moist soil and leaf litter in rainforests and areas that have been cleared of trees within the rainforest region. (Illustration by John Megahan. Reproduced by permission.)

Behavior and reproduction: Scientists believe red caecilians are burrowers. They are not sure how these caecilians mate. The larvae go through metamorphosis when they are about 3.5 inches (9 centimeters) long.

Red caecilians and people: Red caecilians have no known importance to people.

Conservation status: Red caecilians are not considered threatened or endangered. ■

FOR MORE INFORMATION

Books:

Duellman, William E., and Linda Trueb. *Biology of Amphibians.* Baltimore, MD: Johns Hopkins University Press, 1994.

Lamar, William W. *The World's Most Spectacular Reptiles and Amphibians.* Tampa, FL: World, 1997.

Lawlor, Elizabeth P. *Discover Nature in Water and Wetlands.* Mechanicsburg, PA: Stackpole, 2000.

Llamas Ruiz, Andres. *Reptiles and Amphibians: Birth and Growth.* New York: Sterling, 1996.

Petranka, J. W. *Salamanders of the United States and Canada.* Washington, DC: Smithsonian Institution Press, 1998.

Web sites:

"Caecilian." *Animal Bytes.* http://www.sandiegozoo.org/animalbytes/t-caecilian.html (accessed on April 11, 2005).

Hawes, Alex. "On Waterdogs, Mudpuppies, and the Occasional Hellbender." *Zoogoer.* http://nationalzoo.si.edu/Publications/ZooGoer/2000/2/waterdogsmudpuppieshellbender.cfm (accessed on April 11, 2005).

Summers, Adam. "Squeeze Play." *Natural History.* http://biomechanics.bio.uci.edu/_html/nh_biomech/caecilian/caecilian.htm (accessed on April 11, 2005).

Class: Amphibia

Order: Gymnophiona

Family: Scolecomorphidae

Number of species: 6 species

family

phylum

class

subclass

order

monotypic order

suborder

▲ family

PHYSICAL CHARACTERISTICS

Buried-eyed caecilians (sih-SILL-yuhns) are small to medium-sized caecilians. The mouth opens on the bottom of the head because the upper jaw is longer than the lower jaw. The holes for the tentacles are on the bottom of the snout toward the sides, below the nostrils and even with, or slightly in front of, the front edge of the mouth. Buried-eyed caecilians are usually dark purplish gray on the back and sides and cream colored on the belly. Adult buried-eyed caecilians are 6 to 18 inches (15 to 46 centimeters) long.

Buried-eyed caecilians have characteristics that set them apart from other caecilians: The eyes, which are undeveloped and can only distinguish light from dark, are attached to and move with the tentacles and may be exposed when the tentacles are extended. Otherwise, they are covered with, or buried under, bone. Another distinguishing characteristic is that buried-eyed caecilians have no sound-conducting bones in their middle ears.

Caecilians look like earthworms. A series of rings runs the length of the body starting just behind the head. The rings are inside the body and attached to the vertebrae (VER-teh-bree), or the bones that make up the spinal column. Some species of buried-eyed caecilians have one ring, and some have two rings per vertebra (VER-teh-bruh, the singular of vertebrae). The skin is folded over the rings, making grooves between the rings. Some species of buried-eyed caecilians have a small number of scales, and some have no scales, under their skin folds.

Buried-eyed caecilians have no tail. Instead, they have a thick shield of skin at the end of their body. This shield is bluntly rounded and flattened on the bottom side. The opening of the cloaca lies in a shallow, oval space. The cloaca (kloh-AY-kuh) is the chamber in some animals that holds waste from the kidneys and intestines, holds eggs or sperm about to be released to the outside, holds sperm entering a female's body, and is the passage through which young are born. The males of some species have hard spines on the penis.

In some species of buried-eyed caecilians the females are longer than the males because they have many more vertebrae and rings than the males. This characteristic may help the females because the body provides more space for developing young. Male buried-eyed caecilians have larger heads than females. Scientists believe this feature may help males fight one another for mates and territory.

GEOGRAPHIC RANGE

Buried-eyed caecilians live in Cameroon in the west of Africa and Malawi and Tanzania in the east of Africa. No caecilians of any kind have been found in central Africa. This distribution pattern is odd, because the vast region of the upper Congo seems ideally suited for caecilians. Caecilians probably live in central Africa but just have not been found.

HABITAT

Buried-eyed caecilians live in tropical rainforests and areas that have been cleared of trees, usually in hilly or mountainous regions. These animals usually are found in moist areas under logs and in leaf litter on the forest floor. They sometimes are dug up from moist soil. In Tanzania and Malawi, buried-eyed caecilians have been found in turned soil and in piles of old plant matter on farms.

DIET

Scientists believe buried-eyed caecilians eat earthworms and insects. In captivity they eat earthworms and small crickets.

BEHAVIOR AND REPRODUCTION

Buried-eyed caecilians are excellent burrowers. They pump their tentacles in and out when they are moving and otherwise investigating their surroundings. Their tentacles are thought to be sense organs for "tasting" their immediate surroundings. Because they have found bite marks on male caecilians in captivity and in nature, scientists believe the males fight one another for mates and for territory.

Some buried-eyed caecilians give birth to live young. After mating, the female keeps the fertilized (FUR-teh-lyzed) eggs, or those that have joined with sperm, inside her in egg tubes. Scientists believe the egg tubes make a nutritious liquid that the developing young eat with special teeth that are lost after they are born. These teeth are comblike, and they also may be used to stimulate the egg tube to secrete the "milk" near the mouth of the feeding young. Scientists believe the species of buried-eyed caecilians that do not give birth to fully developed young are egg layers. The young develop inside the eggs but have the adult body form when they hatch. Scientists believe the female takes care of the eggs until they hatch.

BURIED-EYED CAECILIANS AND PEOPLE

Buried-eyed caecilians have no known importance to people.

CONSERVATION STATUS

Buried-eyed caecilians are not considered threatened or endangered.

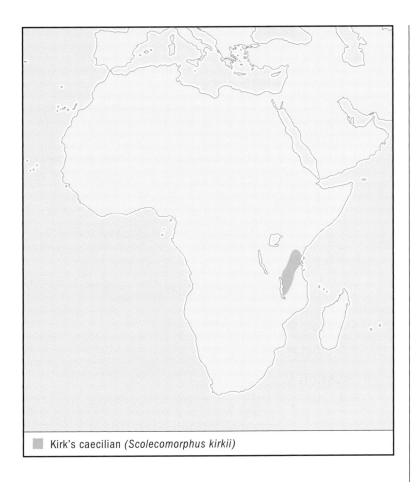

Kirk's caecilian (*Scolecomorphus kirkii*)

KIRK'S CAECILIAN
Scolecomorphus kirkii

Physical characteristics: Kirk's caecilians reach a length of 8.5 to 18 inches (22 to 46 centimeters). They have 130 to 152 rings. The purplish gray color on the back extends down the sides of the animal almost to the center of the belly. The rest of the belly is cream colored. The top and sides of the head are dark like the rest of the upper part of the body, but there is a lighter area along the tentacle. The black retina of the eye at the base of the tentacle is visible through the skin and skull bones.

Geographic range: Kirk's caecilians live in Malawi and Tanzania.

Habitat: Kirk's caecilians live in tropical rainforests and farming areas, usually in mountainous regions. They live under and in surface leaf litter and in the soil.

Diet: Kirk's caecilians probably eat earthworms and insects.

Behavior and reproduction: Kirk's caecilians are efficient burrowers. They stick out their tentacles to investigate their surroundings. They also can make their eyes stick out beyond their skull bones. Scientists do not know how Kirk's caecilians mate. They do know that these caecilians give birth to young that have the body form of adults.

Kirk's caecilians and people: Kirk's caecilians have no known importance to people.

Conservation status: Kirk's caecilians are not considered threatened or endangered.   ◼

FOR MORE INFORMATION

Books:

Duellman, William E., and Linda Trueb. *Biology of Amphibians.* Baltimore, MD: Johns Hopkins University Press, 1994.

Lamar, William W. *The World's Most Spectacular Reptiles and Amphibians.* Tampa, FL: World, 1997.

Lawlor, Elizabeth P. *Discover Nature in Water and Wetlands.* Mechanicsburg, PA: Stackpole, 2000.

Llamas Ruiz, Andres. *Reptiles and Amphibians: Birth and Growth.* New York: Sterling, 1996.

Petranka, J. W. *Salamanders of the United States and Canada.* Washington, DC: Smithsonian Institution Press, 1998.

Web sites:

"Caecilian." *Animal Bytes.* http://www.sandiegozoo.org/animalbytes/t-caecilian.html (accessed on April 11, 2005).

Hawes, Alex. "On Waterdogs, Mudpuppies, and the Occasional Hellbender." *Zoogoer.* http://nationalzoo.si.edu/Publications/ZooGoer/2000/2/waterdogsmudpuppieshellbender.cfm (accessed on April 11, 2005).

Summers, Adam. "Squeeze Play." *Natural History.* http://biomechanics.bio.uci.edu/_html/nh_biomech/caecilian/caecilian.htm (accessed on April 11, 2005).

Class: Amphibia

Order: Gymnophiona

Family: Caeciliidae

Number of species: 107 species

family
CHAPTER

PHYSICAL CHARACTERISTICS

Tailless caecilians (sih-SILL-yuhns) are small to very large caecilians that have a very short tail or no true tail. These caecilians are 4 to 63 inches (10 to 160 centimeters) long. Some tailless caecilians live on land, and some live only in water. Tailless caecilians have a flat head. The mouth opens on the bottom of the head because the upper jaw is longer than the lower jaw. The eyes are covered by skin or, in some species, by both skin and bone. The tentacles lie between the eyes and the nostrils.

Caecilians look like earthworms. A series of rings runs the length of the body starting just behind the head. The rings are inside the body and attached to the vertebrae (VER-teh-bree), or the bones that make up the spinal column. Tailless caecilians have one ring per vertebra (VER-teh-bruh, the singular of vertebrae). The skin is folded over the rings, making grooves between the rings.

GEOGRAPHIC RANGE

Tailless caecilians live in Central and South America; the eastern and western parts of Africa, but not the Sahara; the Seychelles; India; Sri Lanka; the Philippines; and the region that extends from southern China through the Malay Peninsula.

HABITAT

Tailless caecilians live in tropical forests and grasslands and on stream banks. Land-dwelling tailless caecilians live in loose, moist, soil rich in decayed plant matter and leaf litter. They are

phylum

class

subclass

order

monotypic order

suborder

▲ **family**

often found under rocks, logs, and waste material, such as piles of coffee hulls. Many of these caecilians are found near streams. Some tailless caecilians live in grassland, and scientists find them by rolling the grass layer away from the soil. Tailless caecilians that live in water for part or all of their life cycle live on the banks of streams and rivers and sometimes travel onto nearby land or farther out into slow-moving water. Water-dwelling tailless caecilians hide under hanging branches, logs, and other floating objects.

DIET

Tailless caecilians are sit-and-wait predators, staying in their burrows or on the ground and then grabbing prey animals that wander near them. These caecilians eat earthworms, termites, other small invertebrates, and even small lizards and rodents. Invertebrates (in-VER-teh-brehts) are animals without backbones. Tailless caecilians lunge at their prey, grabbing it with their strong jaws and powerful jaw muscles. They force prey animals into their mouths and gradually swallow them. Some tailless caecilians move backward into their burrows, turning rapidly on their body in a corkscrew motion in order to break the prey into bite-sized morsels. Water-dwelling tailless caecilians hunt for their prey by poking around with their snout at the bottom of the stream.

BEHAVIOR AND REPRODUCTION

Little is known about the behavior of land-dwelling tailless caecilians because of their secretive, soil-dwelling nature. Some of these animals emerge from deep in the soil or leaf litter to look for food at dusk or dawn, often during light rain. Tailless caecilians are expert burrowers, digging head-first through moist soil that is rich in decayed plant matter. Species may differ in their ability to burrow efficiently in different kinds of soils. Tailless caecilians appear to spend most of their time in their burrows, but they also can travel quite far from their burrows. Scientists know little about the behavior of the water-dwelling and partially water-dwelling tailless caecilians because these animals typically live in slow-moving streams and rivers that have a lot of plant material that obstructs the view of the animals.

At mating time a male tailless caecilian inserts sperm directly into the female's reproductive tract. Scientists have observed tailless caecilians in aquariums coiling around each other before the male places the sperm in the female. The eggs are fertilized (FUR-teh-lyzed), or joined with sperm, inside the female's body.

Tailless caecilians use several methods of reproduction. Some species lay eggs that hatch into free-living larvae. Larvae (LAR-vee) are animals in an early stage that change body form in a process called metamorphosis (MEH-tuh-MORE-feh-sis) before becoming adults. Some species lay eggs on land, and the larvae develop and go through metamorphosis before hatching, so that when they hatch they have the body form of adults. In some species the young develop in the egg ducts of the female, eating nutrient liquid made by the egg ducts. These young also are born with the body form of small adults. The females of some species of tailless caecilians take care of their eggs by coiling their bodies around the cluster of eggs. They also take care of newly hatched young.

TAILLESS CAECILIANS AND PEOPLE

Tailless caecilians help to control damaging insects, such as termites. Because they actively burrow, rather than following root channels or other ready-made holes in the ground, tailless caecilians aid in turning the soil and maintaining good soil condition. In some parts of the world, people think caecilians are nasty, dangerous animals. In other places, however, people eat them. Some people keep tailless caecilians as pets in aquariums.

CONSERVATION STATUS

The World Conservation Union (IUCN) lists one species of tailless caecilians as Endangered and one species as Vulnerable. Endangered means facing very high risk of extinction in the wild. Vulnerable means facing high risk of extinction in the wild. Changes in land use are restricting the geographic ranges of tailless caecilians, and some populations get a fungus disease.

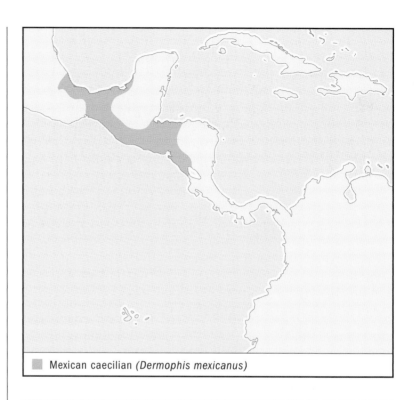

Mexican caecilian (*Dermophis mexicanus*)

MEXICAN CAECILIAN
Dermophis mexicanus

Physical characteristics: Mexican caecilians are 12 to 20 inches (30 to 50 centimeters) long and have a thick body. They are dark gray with paler markings on the belly, jaw, and tentacles. The grooves between the rings are darker than the main body color.

Geographic range: Mexican caecilians live in an area that extends from the lowlands and mountains of central Mexico south to northern Panama.

Habitat: Mexican caecilians live in moist soil that breaks up easily and in leaf litter.

Diet: Mexican caecilians are sit-and-wait predators. They eat invertebrates and vertebrates (VER-teh-brehts), or animals with a backbone, that live or travel in soil or leaf litter, including earthworms,

termites, insects such as crickets that have shed their outer layer, and even small lizards and baby mice.

Behavior and reproduction: Mexican caecilians spend most of their time in burrows in loose, moist soil. They often come out at dusk in a light rain to look for food on the surface. These caecilians make their own burrows in many kinds of soil rather than using the burrows of other animals. Mexican caecilians move with an accordion-like motion and with side-to-side, wavy movements.

Mexican caecilians give birth to fully developed young. They are ready to reproduce when they are two to three years old. The male places the rear part of his cloaca into the cloaca of the female and transfers sperm directly to her reproductive tract. The cloaca (kloh-AY-kuh) is the chamber in some animals that holds waste from the kidneys and intestines, holds eggs or sperm about to be released to the outside, holds sperm entering a female's body, and is the passage through which young are born. Fertilization (FUR-teh-lih-ZAY-shun), or the joining of egg and sperm to start development, takes place inside the female.

Male Mexican caecilians make sperm eleven months of the year, but all females give birth at about the same time, in May and June when the rainy season begins. The young take eleven months to develop. Inside the female the developing young use up the yolk supply of their eggs about three months into the development period. The mother then releases a nutrient liquid from glands lining her egg ducts. The developing young move around in the egg ducts, eating the liquid. They have special teeth that they use to stimulate release of the nutrient liquid and to help take it into their mouths. These teeth are shed at birth, and the adult teeth, which are very different from those of the young inside the mother, grow out within a few days. The developing young have gills that have three branches, and each of the three branches has many more branches. The developing young use the gills and their skin to breathe while in the egg ducts. Gills are organs for obtaining oxygen from water.

Female Mexican caecilians give birth to three to sixteen young, which are 4 to 6 inches (10 to 15 centimeters) long at birth. These young are quite large considering the mother is only 12 to 18 inches (30 to 45 centimeters) long.

Mexican caecilians and people: Mexican caecilians are valuable to humans. They turn soil as they make their burrows, and they eat insects, such as termites, that can be harmful to people or their property.

Conservation status: Mexican caecilians are not considered threatened or endangered. Their numbers are high in some areas, but their habitat is being changed as trees are cut down to make way for farming. Mexican caecilians seem to adapt to some kinds of farm use. For example, there are large numbers of tailless caecilians on coffee farms, where the coffee hulls are thrown in piles to decay, thus forming the moist organic soil that is best for Mexican caecilians and their earthworm prey. ■

Cayenne caecilian (*Typhlonectes compressicauda*)

CAYENNE CAECILIAN
Typhlonectes compressicauda

Physical characteristics: Cayenne (kye-EHN) caecilians are water dwellers. They have a fin on the back that runs the length of the body. The body is flat from side to side, making the caecilians look more like eels than earthworms. These caecilians have large passages inside the head between the nose and the roof of the mouth, and they have well-developed lungs. Cayenne caecilians have one ring per vertebra, and the grooves between the rings are deep. These caecilians are gray to dark blue or black. Adults are 12 to 22 inches (30 to 55 centimeters) long. The cloaca region is flat, forming a disk that is paler in color than the rest of the body.

Geographic range: Cayenne caecilians live throughout the Guianas and the Amazon region of South America.

Habitat: Cayenne caecilians live in slow-moving, warm tropical rivers and streams.

Diet: Cayenne caecilians root around in the mud of the sides and bottoms of the waterways in which they live. They eat shrimp, insect larvae, and small fish. These caecilians have a strong bite mechanism. In captivity cayenne caecilians feed on pieces of earthworms and liver. Cayenne caecilians seem to sense the presence of prey by touch or motion.

Behavior and reproduction: Cayenne caecilians share burrows with one another and leave the burrows at sunset to look for food. These animals have mucus glands all over their bodies. The mucus is poisonous and tastes bad to fish. Predators of cayenne caecilians include large fish, snakes, and birds.

Cayenne caecilians mate by nudging and coiling around each other. The male places sperm in the female, and fertilization takes place inside her body. Cayenne caecilians give birth to fully developed young, which are born seven to nine months after fertilization. A female can give birth to six to fourteen young at a time. The developing young have gills that are shed soon after birth. The developing young have teeth they use to eat a nutrient liquid made by the female's egg ducts. These teeth also are shed soon after birth, and then the adult teeth grow in.

Cayenne caecilians and people: Cayenne caecilians are sold in aquarium stores as rubber eels or black eels. Only rarely do store owners identify them as amphibians (am-FIB-ee-uhns), which are vertebrates (VER-teh-brehts), or animals with a backbone, that have moist, smooth skin; are cold-blooded, meaning their body temperature is the same as the temperature of their surroundings; and, in many instances, but not in the case of cayenne caecilians, have a two-stage life cycle.

Conservation status: Cayenne caecilians are not considered threatened or endangered. They have been collected extensively by fishermen, scientists, and pet dealers. ■

FOR MORE INFORMATION

Books:

Duellman, William E., and Linda Trueb. *Biology of Amphibians.* Baltimore, MD: Johns Hopkins University Press, 1994.

Lamar, William W. *The World's Most Spectacular Reptiles and Amphibians.* Tampa, FL: World, 1997.

Lawlor, Elizabeth P. *Discover Nature in Water and Wetlands.* Mechanicsburg, PA: Stackpole, 2000.

Llamas Ruiz, Andres. *Reptiles and Amphibians: Birth and Growth.* New York: Sterling, 1996.

Petranka, J. W. *Salamanders of the United States and Canada.* Washington, DC: Smithsonian Institution Press, 1998.

Web sites:

"Caecilian." *Animal Bytes.* http://www.sandiegozoo.org/animalbytes/t-caecilian.html (accessed on April 11, 2005).

Hawes, Alex. "On Waterdogs, Mudpuppies, and the Occasional Hellbender." *Zoogoer.* http://nationalzoo.si.edu/Publications/ZooGoer/2000/2/waterdogsmudpuppieshellbender.cfm (accessed on April 11, 2005).

Summers, Adam. "Squeeze Play." *Natural History.* http://biomechanics.bio.uci.edu/_html/nh_biomech/caecilian/caecilian.htm (accessed on April 11, 2005).

Species List by Biome

CONIFEROUS FOREST
Ailao moustache toad
Annam broad-headed toad
Bana leaf litter frog
Brown frog
Cascade torrent salamander
Coastal giant salamander
Eastern narrow-mouthed toad
European fire salamander
Fire-bellied toad
Great crested newt
Mandarin salamander
Oriental fire-bellied toad
Schmidt's lazy toad
Smooth newt
Two-lined salamander
Yellow-bellied toad

DECIDUOUS FOREST
Arboreal salamander
Asian horned frog
Bell's salamander
Brown frog
Cascade torrent salamander
Common squeaker
Darwin's frog
Eastern narrow-mouthed toad
European fire salamander
Fire-bellied toad

Golden-striped salamander
Goliath frog
Great crested newt
Green treefrog
Hairy frog
Hamilton's frog
Harlequin frog
Kinugasa flying frog
Lynch's Cochran frog
Mandarin salamander
Marine toad
Maud Island frog
Mesoamerican burrowing toad
Mexican caecilian
Micro frog
Mocquard's rain frog
Natal ghost frog
Nilgiri tropical frog
Oriental fire-bellied toad
Pacific giant glass frog
Painted frog
Painted Indonesian treefrog
Painted reed frog
Paradox frog
Parsley frog
Phantasmal poison frog
Pumpkin toadlet
Rock River frog
Rocky Mountain tailed frog
Ruthven's frog

South American bullfrog
Smooth newt
Sumaco horned treefrog
Talamancan web-footed
  salamander
Tusked frog
Two-lined salamander
Yellow-bellied toad
Yucatecan shovel-headed
  treefrog

DESERT
Sandhill frog
Water-holding frog

GRASSLAND
Asian horned frog
Banded rubber frog
Brown frog
Bubbling kassina
Budgett's frog
Darwin's frog
Fire-bellied toad
Gray four-eyed frog
Great crested newt
Mandarin salamander
Marbled snout-burrower
Marine toad
Mesoamerican burrowing toad

Mocquard's rain frog
Natal ghost frog
Northern spadefoot toad
Oriental fire-bellied toad
Painted frog
Painted reed frog
Paradox frog
Parsley frog
Patagonia frog
Plains spadefoot toad
Pointed-tongue floating frog
Riobamba marsupial frog
Smooth newt
Tiger salamander
Tusked frog
Yellow-bellied toad
Yucatecan shovel-headed
  treefrog
Water-holding frog

LAKE AND POND
Amazonian skittering frog
Brown frog
Bubbling kassina
Bullfrog
Common plantanna (African
  clawed frog)
Eastern narrow-mouthed toad
Fire-bellied toad
Golden-striped salamander
Gray four-eyed frog
Great crested newt
Hokkaido salamander
Hourglass treefrog
Japanese fire-bellied newt
Lesser siren
Mandarin salamander
Marine toad
Midwife toad
Mudpuppy
Olm
Oriental fire-bellied toad
Painted frog
Painted reed frog
Paradox frog
Patagonia frog

Perez's snouted frog
Phantasmal poison frog
Philippine barbourula
Pointed-tongue floating frog
Pyburn's pancake frog
Riobamba marsupial frog
Smooth newt
South American bullfrog
Surinam horned frog
Surinam toad
Three-toed amphiuma
Tropical clawed frog
Two-lined salamander
Yellow-bellied toad

RAINFOREST
African wart frog
Amazonian skittering frog
Blue-toed rocket frog
Eungella torrent frog
Free Madagascar frog
Golden dart-poison frog
Golden toad
Gold-striped frog
Hip pocket frog
Hourglass treefrog
Kirk's caecilian
La Palma glass frog
Long-fingered slender toad
Marbled caecilian
Perez's snouted frog
Philippine barbourula
Pyburn's pancake frog
Red caecilian
Ruthven's frog
Seychelles frog
South American bullfrog
Surinam horned frog
Tusked frog
Wilhelm rainforest frog

RIVER AND STREAM
Ailao moustache toad
Annam broad-headed toad
Asian horned frog

Brown frog
Bullfrog
Cascade torrent salamander
Cayenne caecilian
Ceylon caecilian
Coastal giant salamander
Common plantanna (African
  clawed frog)
Darwin's frog
Dusky salamander
Eungella torrent frog
Fire-bellied toad
Goliath frog
Green treefrog
Hairy frog
Harlequin frog
Hellbender
Hokkaido salamander
Japanese clawed salamander
La Palma glass frog
Lesser siren
Long-fingered slender toad
Lynch's Cochran frog
Marbled caecilian
Midwife toad
Mudpuppy
Natal ghost frog
Nilgiri tropical frog
Olm
Oriental fire-bellied toad
Pacific giant glass frog
Painted frog
Painted reed frog
Paradox frog
Phantasmal poison frog
Philippine barbourula
Pyburn's pancake frog
Rock River frog
Rocky Mountain tailed frog
Ruthven's frog
Schmidt's lazy toad
Semirechensk salamander
South American bullfrog
Surinam toad
Texas blind salamander
Three-toed amphiuma

Tropical clawed frog
Two-lined salamander
Yellow-bellied toad

WETLAND
Banded rubber frog
Bubbling kassina
Budgett's frog
Brown frog
Bullfrog
Ceylon caecilian
Common plantanna (African
  clawed frog)
Darwin's frog

Eastern narrow-mouthed toad
Fire-bellied toad
Free Madagascar frog
Green treefrog
Kinugasa flying frog
Kirk's caecilian
Lesser siren
Malaysian painted frog
Marbled snout-burrower
Marine toad
Micro frog
Mocquard's rain frog
Northern spadefoot toad
Oriental fire-bellied toad
Painted frog

Painted reed frog
Paradox frog
Perez's snouted frog
Pointed-tongue floating frog
Riobamba marsupial frog
Ruthven's frog
Schmidt's lazy toad
Semirechensk salamander
Surinam horned frog
Surinam toad
Three-toed amphiuma
Yellow-bellied toad
Yucatecan shovel-headed
  treefrog
Water-holding frog

Species List by Geographic Range

ALBANIA
Brown frog
European fire salamander
Great crested newt
Smooth newt

ALGERIA
Painted frog

ANDORRA
European fire salamander
Great crested newt
Smooth newt

ANGOLA
Bubbling kassina
Common plantanna (African
  clawed frog)
Hairy frog
Marbled snout-burrower
Painted reed frog
Tropical clawed frog

ARGENTINA
Budgett's frog
Darwin's frog
Gray four-eyed frog
Marine toad
Patagonia frog

ARMENIA
Brown frog

AUSTRALIA
Eungella torrent frog
Green treefrog
Hip pocket frog
Marine toad
Northern spadefoot toad
Painted frog
Sandhill frog
Tusked frog
Water-holding frog

AUSTRIA
Brown frog
European fire salamander
Fire-bellied toad
Great crested newt
Smooth newt
Yellow-bellied toad

BAHAMAS
Eastern narrow-mouthed toad

BELARUS
European fire salamander
Great crested newt
Smooth newt

BELGIUM
Brown frog
European fire salamander
Great crested newt
Midwife toad
Parsley frog
Smooth newt

BELIZE
Marine toad
Mesoamerican burrowing toad
Mexican caecilian
Yucatecan shovel-headed
  treefrog

BENIN
Bubbling Kassina
Goliath frog
Painted reed frog

BOLIVIA
Amazonian skittering frog
Budgett's frog

Hourglass treefrog
Marine toad
Perez's snouted frog
Surinam toad

BOSNIA AND HERZEGOVINA
European fire salamander
Great crested newt
Olm
Smooth newt

BOTSWANA
Bubbling kassina
Common plantanna (African clawed frog)
Painted reed frog

BRAZIL
Amazonian skittering frog
Blue-toed rocket frog
Cayenne caecilian
Gold-striped frog
Hourglass treefrog
Marine toad
Paradox frog
Perez's snouted frog
Pumpkin toadlet
Rock River frog
Ruthven's frog
South American bullfrog
Surinam horned frog
Surinam toad

BULGARIA
European fire salamander
Great crested newt
Smooth newt

BURKINA FASO
Bubbling kassina
Painted reed frog

BURUNDI
Bubbling kassina
Common plantanna (African clawed frog)
Painted reed frog

CAMBODIA
Pointed-tongue floating frog

CAMEROON
African wart frog
Bubbling kassina
Common plantanna (African clawed frog)
Goliath frog
Hairy frog
Marbled snout-burrower
Painted reed frog
Tropical clawed frog

CANADA
Bullfrog
Coastal giant salamander
Coastal tailed frog
Dusky salamander
Mudpuppy
Plains spadefoot toad
Rocky Mountain tailed frog
Tiger salamander
Two-lined salamander

CHAD
Bubbling kassina
Painted reed frog

CHILE
Common plantanna (African clawed frog)
Darwin's frog
Gray four-eyed frog
Marine toad

CHINA
Ailao moustache toad

Malaysian painted frog
Mandarin salamander
Oriental fire-bellied toad
Pointed-tongue floating frog
Schmidt's lazy toad
Semirechensk salamander

COLOMBIA
Amazonian skittering frog
Cayenne caecilian
Golden dart-poison frog
Gold-striped frog
Hourglass treefrog
La Palma glass frog
Lynch's Cochran frog
Marine toad
Pacific giant glass frog
Perez's snouted frog
Pyburn's pancake frog
South American bullfrog
Sumaco horned treefrog
Surinam horned frog
Surinam toad

COSTA RICA
Golden toad
Harlequin frog
La Palma glass frog
Marine toad
Mesoamerican burrowing toad
Mexican caecilian
South American bullfrog
Talamancan web-footed salamander

CROATIA
European fire salamander
Great crested newt
Olm
Smooth newt

CYPRUS
Brown frog

CZECH REPUBLIC
Brown frog
European fire salamander
Great crested newt
Smooth newt

DEMOCRATIC REPUBLIC OF THE CONGO
Common plantanna (African
  clawed frog)
Common squeaker
Hairy frog
Marbled snout-burrower

DENMARK
Brown frog
European fire salamander
Fire-bellied toad
Great crested newt
Smooth newt

ECUADOR
Hourglass treefrog
La Palma glass frog
Marbled caecilian
Marine toad
Pacific giant glass frog
Phantasmal poison frog
Riobamba marsupial frog
South American bullfrog
Sumaco horned treefrog
Surinam toad

EL SALVADOR
Marine toad
Mesoamerican burrowing toad
Mexican caecilian

EQUATORIAL GUINEA
Common plantanna (African
  clawed frog)
Hairy frog

Marbled snout-burrower

ESTONIA
Brown frog
European fire salamander
Great crested newt
Smooth newt

ETHIOPIA
Bubbling kassina
Ethiopian snout-burrower
  (Lake Zwai snout-burrower)
Painted reed frog

FINLAND
Brown frog
European fire salamander
Great crested newt
Smooth newt

FRANCE
Brown frog
European fire salamander
Great crested newt
Midwife toad
Painted frog
Parsley frog
Smooth newt

FRENCH GUIANA
Cayenne caecilian
Gold-striped frog
Hourglass treefrog
Marine toad
Paradox frog
Pyburn's pancake frog
Ruthven's frog
South American bullfrog
Surinam toad
Surinam horned frog

GABON
African wart frog

Bubbling kassina
Common plantanna (African
  clawed frog)
Hairy frog
Marbled snout-burrower
Painted reed frog
Tropical clawed frog

GERMANY
Brown frog
Common plantanna (African
  clawed frog)
European fire salamander
Fire-bellied toad
Great crested newt
Midwife toad
Smooth newt

GHANA
Bubbling kassina
Goliath frog
Painted reed frog

GREECE
Brown frog
European fire salamander
Fire-bellied toad
Great crested newt
Smooth newt
Yellow-bellied toad

GUATEMALA
Marine toad
Mesoamerican burrowing toad
Mexican caecilian
Yucatecan shovel-headed
  treefrog

GUINEA
Bubbling kassina
Goliath frog
Painted reed frog

GUINEA-BISSAU
Bubbling kassina
Painted reed frog

GUYANA
Cayenne caecilian
Gold-striped frog
Hourglass treefrog
Marine toad
Paradox frog
Pyburn's pancake frog
Ruthven's frog
South American bullfrog
Surinam horned frog
Surinam toad

HONDURAS
Marine toad
Mesoamerican burrowing toad
Mexican caecilian
South American bullfrog
Yucatecan shovel-headed
  treefrog

HUNGARY
Brown frog
European fire salamander
Great crested newt
Smooth newt
Yellow-bellied toad

INDIA
Mandarin salamander
Nilgiri tropical frog
Pointed-tongue floating frog
Red caecilian

INDONESIA
Asian horned frog
Long-fingered slender toad
Malaysian painted frog
Painted Indonesian treefrog
Pointed-tongue floating frog

IRELAND
European fire salamander
Great crested newt
Smooth newt

ITALY
Brown frog
European fire salamander
Great crested newt
Olm
Painted frog
Parsley frog
Smooth newt
Yellow-bellied toad

IVORY COAST
Bubbling kassina
Goliath frog
Painted reed frog

JAPAN
Hokkaido salamander
Japanese clawed salamander
Japanese fire-bellied newt
Kinugasa flying frog
Marine toad
Oriental fire-bellied toad

KAZAKHSTAN
Semirechensk salamander

KENYA
Banded rubber frog
Bubbling kassina
Common plantanna (African
  clawed frog)
Common squeaker
Marbled snout-burrower
Painted reed frog

KOREA
(NORTH AND SOUTH)
Oriental fire-bellied toad

LAOS
Bana leaf litter frog

LATVIA
European fire salamander
Great crested newt
Smooth newt

LESOTHO
Bubbling kassina
Common plantanna (African
  clawed frog)
Natal ghost frog
Painted reed frog
Tropical clawed frog

LIBERIA
Bubbling kassina
Goliath frog
Painted reed frog

LIECHTENSTEIN
European fire salamander
Great crested newt
Smooth newt

LITHUANIA
European fire salamander
Great crested newt
Smooth newt

LUXEMBOURG
Brown frog
European fire salamander
Great crested newt
Midwife toad
Parsley frog
Smooth newt

MACEDONIA
European fire salamander
Great crested newt
Smooth newt

MADAGASCAR
Free Madagascar frog
Mocquard's rain frog

MALAWI
Bubbling kassina
Common plantanna (African
  clawed frog)
Kirk's caecilian
Painted reed frog

MALAYSIA
Asian horned frog
Malaysian painted frog
Painted Indonesian treefrog
Pointed-tongue floating frog

MALI
Bubbling kassina
Painted reed frog

MALTA
Brown frog
European fire salamander
Great crested newt
Painted frog
Smooth newt

MEXICO
Arboreal salamander
Bell's salamander
Bullfrog
Lesser siren
Marine toad
Mesoamerican burrowing toad
Mexican caecilian
Plains spadefoot toad
Tiger salamander
Yucatecan shovel-headed
  treefrog

MOLDOVA
European fire salamander

Great crested newt
Smooth newt

MONACO
European fire salamander
Great crested newt
Smooth newt

MOROCCO
Painted frog

MOZAMBIQUE
Banded rubber frog
Bubbling kassina
Common plantanna (African
  clawed frog)
Common squeaker
Marbled snout-burrower
Painted reed frog

NAMIBIA
Bubbling kassina
Common plantanna (African
  clawed frog)
Painted reed frog
Tropical clawed frog

NEPAL
Mandarin salamander

NETHERLANDS
Brown frog
European fire salamander
Great crested newt
Midwife toad
Smooth newt

NEW ZEALAND
Green treefrog
Hamilton's frog
Maud Island frog

NICARAGUA
Marine toad
Mesoamerican burrowing toad
Mexican caecilian
South American bullfrog

NIGER
Bubbling kassina
Painted reed frog

NIGERIA
Bubbling kassina
Goliath frog
Hairy frog
Marbled snout-burrower
Painted reed frog

NORWAY
Brown frog
European fire salamander
Great crested newt
Smooth newt

PANAMA
Harlequin frog
La Palma glass frog
Marine toad
Mexican caecilian
South American bullfrog

PAPUA NEW GUINEA
Wilhelm rainforest frog

PARAGUAY
Budgett's frog
Marine toad

PERU
Amazonian skittering frog
Cayenne caecilian
Gold-striped frog
Hourglass treefrog

Marine toad
Perez's snouted frog
Phantasmal poison frog
Ruthven's frog
South American bullfrog
Sumaco horned treefrog
Surinam toad
Surinam horned frog

PHILIPPINES
Asian horned frog
Marine toad
Painted Indonesian treefrog
Philippine barbourula

POLAND
European fire salamander
Fire-bellied toad
Great crested newt
Smooth newt

PORTUGAL
Brown frog
European fire salamander
Golden-striped salamander
Great crested newt
Midwife toad
Parsley frog
Smooth newt

REPUBLIC OF THE CONGO
African wart frog
Common plantanna (African clawed frog)
Tropical clawed frog

ROMANIA
European fire salamander
Great crested newt
Smooth newt

RUSSIA

European fire salamander
Great crested newt
Oriental fire-bellied toad
Smooth newt

RWANDA
Bubbling kassina
Common plantanna (African clawed frog)
Painted reed frog

SAN MARINO
European fire salamander
Great crested newt
Smooth newt

SÃO TOMÉ AND PRÍNCIPE
Common plantanna (African clawed frog)

SENEGAL
Bubbling kassina
Painted reed frog

SERBIA-MONTENEGRO
European fire salamander
Great crested newt
Olm
Smooth newt

SEYCHELLES
Seychelles frog

SIERRA LEONE
Bubbling kassina
Goliath frog
Painted reed frog

SINGAPORE
Painted Indonesian treefrog

SLOVAKIA
European fire salamander
Great crested newt
Smooth newt

SLOVENIA
European fire salamander
Great crested newt
Olm
Smooth newt

SOMALIA
Banded rubber frog

SOUTH AFRICA
Banded rubber frog
Bubbling kassina
Common plantanna (African clawed frog)
Common squeaker
Marbled snout-burrower
Micro frog
Natal ghost frog
Painted reed frog
Tropical clawed frog

SPAIN
Brown frog
European fire salamander
Golden-striped salamander
Great crested newt
Midwife toad
Painted frog
Parsley frog
Smooth newt

SRI LANKA
Ceylon caecilian

SUDAN
Bubbling kassina
Painted reed frog

SURINAME
Cayenne caecilian
Gold-striped frog
Hourglass treefrog
Marine toad
Paradox frog
Pyburn's pancake frog
Ruthven's frog
South American bullfrog
Surinam horned frog
Surinam toad

SWAZILAND
Bubbling kassina
Common plantanna (African clawed frog)
Natal ghost frog
Painted reed frog

SWEDEN
Brown frog
European fire salamander
Fire-bellied toad
Great crested newt
Smooth newt

SWITZERLAND
Brown frog
European fire salamander
Great crested newt
Midwife toad
Smooth newt
Yellow-bellied toad

TAIWAN
Malaysian painted frog
Painted Indonesian treefrog

TANZANIA
Banded rubber frog
Bubbling kassina
Common plantanna (African clawed frog)
Kirk's caecilian

Painted reed frog

THAILAND
Asian horned frog
Mandarin salamander

TOGO
Bubbling kassina
Goliath frog
Painted reed frog

TRINIDAD AND TOBAGO
Surinam toad

TUNISIA
Painted frog

TURKEY
Brown frog
European fire salamander
Fire-bellied toad
Great crested newt
Smooth newt

UGANDA
Bubbling kassina
Common plantanna (African clawed frog)
Painted reed frog

UKRAINE
European fire salamander
Great crested newt
Smooth newt

UNITED KINGDOM
Common plantanna (African clawed frog)
European fire salamander
Fire-bellied toad
Great crested newt
Smooth newt

Yellow-bellied toad

UNITED STATES
Arboreal salamander
Bullfrog
Cascade torrent salamander
Coastal giant salamander
Coastal tailed frog
Common plantanna (African clawed frog)
Dusky salamander
Eastern narrow-mouthed toad
Hellbender
Lesser siren
Marine toad
Mesoamerican burrowing toad
Mudpuppy
Plains spadefoot toad
Rocky Mountain tailed frog
Texas blind salamander
Three-toed amphiuma
Tiger salamander
Two-lined salamander

URUGUAY
Marine toad
Paradox frog

VENEZUELA
Marine toad
Paradox frog
Pyburn's pancake frog
Ruthven's frog
Surinam toad

VIETNAM
Ailao moustache toad
Annam broad-headed toad
Bana leaf litter frog
Mandarin salamander
Pointed-tongue floating frog

ZAMBIA
Bubbling kassina

Common plantanna (African clawed frog)
Painted reed frog

Bubbling kassina
Common plantanna (African clawed frog)

Common squeaker
Marbled snout-burrower
Painted reed frog

Index

Italic type indicates volume number; **boldface** type indicates entries and their pages; (ill.) indicates illustrations.

X

Xenopus laevis. See Common plantannas

Y

Yellow-bellied toads, *1:* 37–40, 37 (ill.), 38 (ill.)

Z